THE CENTRAL AMERICA FACT BOOK

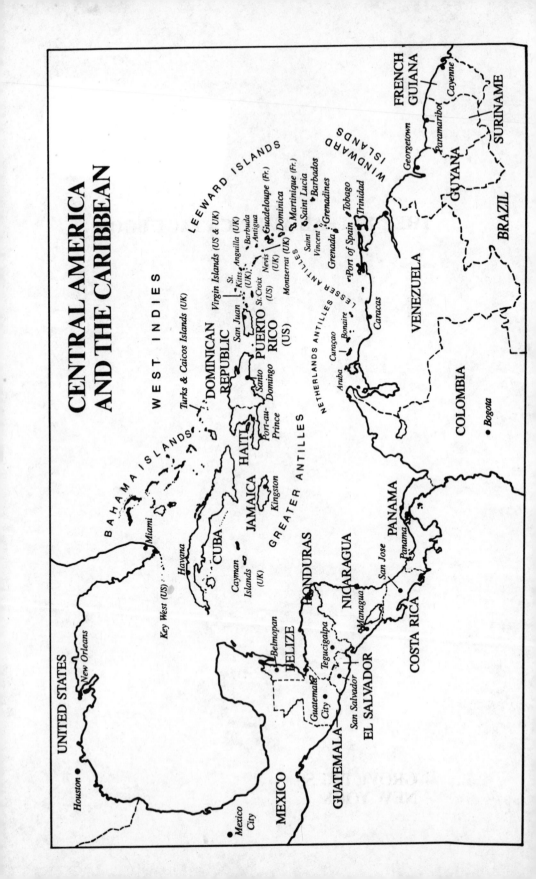

THE CENTRAL AMERICA FACT BOOK

by TOM BARRY and DEB PREUSCH

GROVE PRESS
NEW YORK

The Inter-Hemispheric Education Resource Center is a non-profit organization that produces reports, books, and slide/tape shows on Mexico, Central America, and the Caribbean. For more information:

The Resource Center
P.O. Box 4506
Albuquerque, New Mexico 87196

Published by Grove Press
a division of Wheatland Corporation
841 Broadway
New York, N.Y. 10003

Library of Congress Cataloging-in-Publication Data

Barry, Tom, 1950-
    The Central America fact book.

    Includes index.
    1. Central America—Politics and government—
1979-   . 2. Central America—Economic conditions—
1979-   . 3. Central America—Foreign relations—
United States. 4. United States—Foreign relations—
Central America. I. Preusch, Deb. II. Title.
F1439.5.B37   1986   972.8′053   85-17179
ISBN 0-394-55011-0
ISBN 0-8021-3038-0 (pbk.)

Printed in the United States of America

This book is printed on acid-free paper.

10 9 8 7 6 5

Contents

List of Tables

CENTRAL AMERICA STATISTICS

	Belize	Costa Rica	El Salvador	Guatemala	Honduras	Nicaragua	Panama	U.S.
Population (millions) (1985)	0.16	2.6	5.0	8.0	4.4	3.0	2.0	239
Population Density (persons/sq. mile)	20	130	610	190	100	50	70	65
Rural Population (percent of total popn)	51	55	57	59	61	45	44	23
Average Household Size (# of persons)	4.9	5.0	5.0	4.7	5.4	6.9	4.0	2.8
# Years for Population to Double	25	28	26	22	20	20	33	96
Labor Force (thousands of persons)	38	715	1785	2465	850	940	1160	110,000
Unemployment/ Underemployment (percent of labor force)	15+	25	40+	65+	70+	25	45	8–10
Dependency Ratio (number of children and elderly dependent upon every 100 members of the labor force)	116	68	93	87	101	100	76	52
Per Capita GDP in 1984 ($U.S.)	1140	1570	710	1190	750	870	2020	14,100
Rural Poverty (percent of rural population in absolute poverty)	-	40	74	70	77	57	-	
Terms of Trade, 1984 (1970 = 100)	-	70	83	62	85	57	53	70
Foreign Debt (million $US)	-	4050	2300	1910	2250	3900	3550	
Energy Consumption (kg/ per capita)	-	580	210	220	240	280	730	11,630
Infant Mortality (deaths/1,000 live births)	21	19	53	70	87	43	22	12
Life Expectancy (years at birth)	70	74	65	61	60	62	71	75
Death Rate from Enteritis, Diarrheal Diseases (deaths/100,000 persons)	-	<26	105	166	49	74	31	<13

SOURCES: *Statistical Yearbook for Latin America*, ECLA/UN 1983; *Statistical Abstract of Latin America*, Vol 23, 1984; *Economic and Social Progress in Latin America*, IDB 1985; *World Development Report*, IBRD, 1984; "1985 World Population Data Sheet of the Population Reference Bureau, Inc.," 1982; *Handbook of International Trade and Development Statistics*, UNCTAD, 1984 Supplement; *World Factbook 1985*, CIA; "Annual Report to the Director," PAHO, 1984; *Yearbook of Labor Statistics*, ILO, 1983; *Worldmark Encyclopedia of the Nations: Americas*, 1984

ACKNOWLEDGMENTS

The Central America Fact Book is the direct result of the success of *Dollars and Dictators: A Guide to Central America*, which was published by Grove Press in 1983. The authors of *The Central America Fact Book* are grateful to all those who have assisted the Resource Center's continuing research on Central American issues.

Special thanks go to Beth Wood for her excellent editing, Mary Ann Fiske for the compilation of the TNC list, and Chuck Hosking for research. We would also like to thank the part-time workers and volunteers at the Resource Center: Barbara Bush-Stuart, Camille Jones, Phil Brinkman, and Bill Blomstrom.

We are grateful to those who contributed their expertise by commenting on the manuscript: Bob Armstrong, Marc Edleman, Fred Goff, Eva Gold, Nora Hamilton, Steve Hellinger, Marc Herold, Milton Jamail, David Kaimowitz, Peter Kornbluh, Cheryl Morden, Fred Morris, Reggie Norton, Roxanna Pastor, Bob Stix, Daniel Suman, and Jean Walsh. We particularly want to thank Joy Hackel of Policy Alternatives on the Caribbean and Central America (PACCA), who provided invaluable research assistance as well as commenting on portions of the manuscrip'.

We relied on many sources of written information. Several periodicals stand out as providing timely news and analysis about Central America: *Central America Bulletin*, *NACLA* (North American Congress on Latin America) *Report on the Americas*, and *Washington Report on the Hemisphere*. We made regular use of two clipping services managed by the Data Center in Oakland: Information Services on Latin America (ISLA) and the Central America Monitor. We also depended on *Mesoamerica* (Costa Rica), *Central America Report* (Guatemala), and the Latin America Weekly Newsletters (London).

Without the financial support from Kit Tremaine, Michael Kelley, and the Sunflower Foundation, the *Central America Fact Book* would not have been possible. Finally, we would like to thank Lisa Rosset and others at Grove Press for their concern that information about the escalating crisis in Central America reach a broad group of readers.

Introduction

> "When I use a word," Humpty Dumpty said, in a rather scornful tone, "it means just what I choose it to mean—neither more nor less."
> "The question is," said Alice, "whether you *can* make words mean so many different things."
> — Lewis Carroll, *Through the Looking Glass*

CONVULSED BY revolution and counterrevolution, Central America is, according to Jeane Kirkpatrick, "the most important place in the world today for the United States." This string of tiny nations that joins the Americas has suddenly been thrust onto center stage. Regarded until recently as a sorry collection of banana republics, Central America has become "the main challenge to U.S. interests." Many worry that this tumultuous region may become the next Vietnam.

For all the attention given Central America, widespread confusion surrounds basic issues and definitions. Like Alice, many trying to understand this unfamiliar region are confronted by a topsy-turvy world where words and their meanings have become quite jumbled. Press accounts and White House statements frequently cloud rather than clarify the issues. Terms like *terrorists, democrats, dictators, rebels,* and *human rights violators* are used to refer to totally different political actors in different countries. Guerrillas are terrorists in one country but freedom fighters in another. People once called dictators are later labeled democrats. Because they have been used to mean so many different things, the words used to describe the crisis—*freedom, national security, democracy, intervention, elections, aid*—do little but confuse.

The *Central America Fact Book* was written to dispel some of the confusion about the issues in Central America. We call it a fact book because it presents the background and the facts about the major economic sectors, leading political actors, military conflicts, extent of foreign involvement, and domestic issues of each of the seven Central American nations.

Facts, like words, are subject to interpretation. While the emphasis is on a presentation of all the relevant facts, we do not shy away from interpretation and analysis. Throughout the book, we question the validity of many assumptions that guide U.S. economic and political policy in Central America. We argue, for example, that the facts do not support Washington's contention that U.S. national security is threatened in Central America.

In our view, two distinct sets of hypotheses are being tested in Central America. On the one side, Washington and its allies contend that the priority for Central America should be political and economic stabilization. The key elements of their view are short-term stability, an export-oriented economy, private-sector dominance, and reliance on the United States. On the other side are the advocates of structural changes, who propose new economic priorities that stress production for the internal market, widespread participation in the political process, and the satisfaction of the basic needs of all classes in society. The proponents of reform opt for national self-determination and reduced U.S. control.

The themes of stabilization and reform weave through this book. At the outset, then, it may be useful to delineate the main differences between these opposing camps as a framework for understanding the Central American crisis.

TWO VIEWS OF THE CRISIS

Stabilization	Reform
Outside interference by Soviets and Cubans is at the root of the region's political crisis.	The roots of the crisis arise from inequities in land and income distribution and repression of popular discontent and attempts at reform.
Stability is the key to economic and political progress.	For the vast numbers at the bottom of society, stability means the continuation of the status quo that keeps them poor.
Economic growth will benefit the entire society.	The extreme disparity in levels of wealth because of concentration of land in the hands of a few, the maintenance of low wages, and repression of labor organizing prevent benefits of economic growth from even trickling down.
Increased emphasis on agricultural exports and export manufacturing will strengthen the economy.	Emphasis on export production keeps economies weak and dependent. Governments need to achieve a better balance between export production and production to meet domestic needs. Production for export should include more processing and should stress labor-intensive industries
Governments should reduce dependency on traditional export crops by promoting nontraditional export crops.	Governments should address the need to increase local food production to cut down on food imports. More land should be used to achieve food self-sufficiency.

The public sector is a drain on the economy and should be reduced. The private sector should be encouraged with government incentives. A thriving private sector will solve a nation's economic and social problems.

Only the public sector can solve many underdevelopment problems like lack of infrastructure, education, transportation, and marketing systems. The private sector has proven the main obstacle to needed tax, labor, and land tenure reforms.

New foreign investment will boost economic development by increasing employment, available capital, and technology.

Foreign investment has not provided the key to economic progress in the past. Cost of attracting foreign capital would be better spent developing labor-intensive local industry.

It is in the best interests of Central American nations to be closely aligned with the United States.

It is in the best interests of Central American nations to be nonaligned so that they can diversify trade and sources of foreign capital.

Emphasis should be on bilateral trading arrangements between individual nations and the United States.

Emphasis should be on trade and cooperation among the Central American nations.

U.S. economic aid will spur development. Aid to the private sector and for export-led development will mean progress for the entire society.

In the last 25 years, U.S. economic aid has done little to set Central America on the path to economic development. Most aid now goes to stabilize unpopular governments and subsidize the private sector.

U.S. military aid is essential to protect democratic governments against external and internal threats.

U.S. military aid strengthens repressive military and economic elites, thereby blocking needed reforms.

Because revolutionary movements and societies present a security threat to the United States, they must be stopped.

No Central American nation has ever represented a threat to the national security of the world's number one superpower.

Peace can be achieved only by military defeat of leftist guerrillas.

Peace and long-term stability can be achieved only by integrating representatives of disenfranchised and dissident groups into the political process.

Because revolutions can be exported, they should be crushed.

Revolutions are internal processes that cannot be exported.

There is no room for socialist and revolutionary governments in Central America.

Pluralism should prosper in the region, allowing room for societies that experiment with new solutions to Central America's serious economic and political problems.

PART ONE

CHAPTER 1

The United States in Central America

If Central America were to fall, what would be the consequences for our position in Asia and Europe and for our alliances such as NATO? . . . The national security of all the Americas is at stake in Central America. If we cannot defend ourselves there, we cannot expect to prevail elsewhere. Our credibility would collapse, our alliances would crumble.
—President Ronald Reagan, from speech to Joint Session of Congress, April 27, 1983

AS A PRESIDENTIAL candidate in 1980, Ronald Reagan already had begun to revive the cold war. About Central America, Reagan said flatly: "The Soviet Union underlies all the unrest that is going on."[1] His party's platform deplored "the Marxist Sandinista takeover of Nicaragua and Marxist attempt to destabilize El Salvador, Guatemala, and Honduras." Warning of possible future counter-revolutionary action against Nicaragua, the platform stated: "We will support the efforts of the Nicaraguan people to establish a free and independent government. . . . We will return to the fundamental principle of treating a friend as a friend, and self-proclaimed enemies as enemies." With the ascendancy of Ronald Reagan to the presidency, the days of Gunboat Diplomacy returned to Central America.

The United States began meddling in Central American affairs soon after the Mexican-American War in the mid–1800s when politicians and investors looked to the region as the next U.S. frontier. Private U.S. adventurers called *filibusteros* led mercenary armies that swaggered their way through Central America looking for fortune and power. By the 1900s U.S. gunboats were dashing in and out of Central American ports to enforce political order and "protect U.S. property." In 1927, explaining the reason why the United States had committed Marines to fight against the guerrilla forces of Augusto Cesar Sandino in Nicaragua, Undersecretary of State Robert Olds put U.S. policy on Central America in perspective:

The Central American area constitutes a legitimate sphere of influence for the United States, if we are to have due regard for our own safety and protection. . . . Our ministers accredited to the five little republics . . . have been advisers whose advice has been accepted virtually as law . . . we do control the destinies of Central America and we do so for the simple reason that the national interest dictates such a course. . . . There is no room for any outside influence other than ours in this region. We could not tolerate such a thing without incurring grave risks. At this moment a deliberate attempt to undermine our position and set aside our special relationship in Central America is being made . . . the Nicaraguan crisis is a direct challenge to the United States. . . . Until now Central America has always understood that governments which we recognize and support stay in power, while those which we do not recognize and support fall. Nicaragua has become a test case. It is difficult to see how we can afford to be defeated.[2]

A crucial part of the "national interests" to which Olds referred is economic. In 1954, for example, Washington helped topple the government of Guatemala which had infringed upon the domain of the U.S.-based United Fruit Company. The first chapter in this section outlines the chief economic interests in Central America today. These interests—investment, trade, aid, and finance—dominate the small economies of Central America. Businesses owned by U.S. corporations stand among the largest enterprises in each country. The United States is the region's major trading partner and the source of most of its financing.

While U.S. trade and financing are of major importance to the Central American countries, the economic significance of the region to the United States is minimal. The source of no important raw materials, Central America represents only 1 percent of all U.S. trade and investment.

Yet in considering U.S. aggression against Nicaragua, the economic argument cannot be dismissed. The United States sees Central America as part of Latin America—an area which provides the second largest market for U.S. products after Western Europe and accounts for nearly 80 percent of U.S. direct and financial investment in the third world. Any threat to U.S. interests in one country—be it Nicaragua, Chile, or El Salvador—is viewed as a threat to the totality of U.S. economic control. Washington fears that a rash of imitative nationalist or revolutionary governments could threaten its considerable economic interests in Latin America. As economist Arthur MacEwan, writing in 1972 about U.S. involvement in Vietnam, observed: "I think it is essential to bear in mind the distinction between protecting a particular interest and protecting the rules which define the system and protect all such particular interests . . ."[3]

Another major area of U.S. involvement in the region has been its economic aid program. The first large doses were sent in 1954 to Guatemala after U.S.-backed military leaders overthrew the reformist administration that challenged United Fruit. The Cuban Revolution of 1959 caused Washington to develop an entirely new approach to military and economic aid for Latin America. Accompanying its new focus on counterinsurgency training for Central America's armed forces was an economic aid strategy that aimed to counter Cuba's revolutionary influence by bettering living conditions and encouraging top-down reforms throughout Latin America. President Kennedy warned that if a "peaceful revolution" of economic and political reforms were postponed, violent revolutions would be "inevitable." The Alliance for Progress was based on the belief that U.S. aid could promote reform as a remedy for revolution if it were accompanied by military counterinsurgency programs.

The Alliance for Progress poured generous sums of economic aid into the Central American nations. Soon the oligarchies and military found that they could get the aid even if they refused to make the social and economic changes prescribed by the alliance. Because the funds were channeled through the military dictatorships and economic elites, aid served only to reinforce existing power structures. The Alliance for Progress quickly degenerated into an alliance for the status quo. Emphasis of the aid programs switched from social progress to economic growth—on the theory that the rising tide of a growing economy "lifts all," as President Kennedy put it.

The first of the inevitable revolutions came in 1979 when the Sandinistas of Nicaragua overthrew the Somoza dictatorship, which had stuffed its pockets with U.S. economic aid. In reaction to the Sandinista revolution, the U.S. government released a new flood of economic aid to the Central American nations, except for Nicaragua. Under President Reagan, gone are all but the most token references about the need for reforms. With his Caribbean Basin Initiative (CBI), President Reagan offered funding for government stability and for private-sector support. He told the nations of Central America "to make use of the magic of the marketplace, the market of the Americas."

The recommendations of the National Bipartisan Commission on Central America (Kissinger Commission) in 1984 offered a more comprehensive plan for the region. Those recommendations were incorporated into President Reagan's Central America Democracy, Peace, and Development Initiative Act, which called for over $8 billion in economic assistance to the region by the end of the decade. Although the act never was passed as a unit, most of its main features were approved as part of foreign assistance appropriations for Central America.

While the Kissinger Report acknowledged the need for development to alleviate the poverty of the region, it also underlined the necessity for military aid to confront the perceived "Soviet–Cuban" threat. In line with this view of reality, the United States is injecting vast sums of economic aid in hopes of strengthening shaky governments and fostering private-sector growth. To receive this largesse, governments have had to adopt conditions that increase U.S. economic and political control over the region.

Hand in hand with the aid program has been the massive militarization of Central America. This military build-up is based on two tenets of U.S. foreign policy: the domino theory and the supposed Soviet-Cuban threat in the Caribbean

Basin. President Reagan expressed his domino theory shortly after he became president. "What we are doing," said the president, "is going to the aid of a government that asked for help against guerrillas and terrorists . . . who aren't just aiming at El Salvador but who are aiming at the whole of Central and South America . . . [and] eventually, North America."[4]

Refusing to recognize internal roots of the unrest, President Reagan insists that the Soviets, the Cubans, and now the Nicaraguans direct all political turmoil in the region. Dismissing negotiations as a solution to head off a regional war, President Reagan has instead adopted a strategy of confrontation, saying that there can be no peace in Central America until the guerrillas are militarily defeated and the Sandinistas ousted. Left unchallenged, this commitment to a military solution may lead the United States back to the days when U.S. gunboats were bombarding tropical ports and U.S. Marines were fighting a losing battle against a peasant army in the hills of Nicaragua.

---

1 *New York Times*, October 20, 1980.
2 Confidential Memorandum, Robert Olds, January 2, 1927, National Archives, quoted in Richard Millett, *The Guardians of the Dynasty: A History of the US-Created Guardia Nacional de Nicaragua and the Somoza Family* (Maryknoll: Orbis, 1977).
3 *Review of Radical Political Economy*, Spring 1972, pp.50–52.
4 Statement by President Reagan, March 6, 1981.

CHAPTER 2

A Capital Idea?:
Foreign Economic Presence

*Citicorp has 350 to 400 subsidiaries. I wish I did have a list of
all of them. It took me three days just to find out what companies
we had in Ohio—let alone trying to track the ones in Central
America. This kind of business here, that kind of business there . . .*
—Citicorp information specialist in New York

FOREIGN ECONOMIC interests in Central America can be separated into three
major categories: 1) direct corporate investment, 2) trade, and 3) private, bilateral, and multilateral financing which result in external debt. All three categories
are currently dominated, to varying degrees, by the United States and U.S.-
based corporations.

TABLE 2A

FOREIGN ECONOMIC INTERESTS IN CENTRAL AMERICA

Investment

U.S. Direct Investment	$5.3 billion
Number of U.S. Businesses	2055

Trade

U.S.-Central American Trade (exports plus imports)	$4.1 billion

Financing

Central America's External Debt	$18 billion

SOURCES: U.S. Department of Commerce, *Survey of Current Business*, August 1985; "The Resource Center Compilation
of Corporations, 1986"; IDB, *Social and Economic Progress in Latin America* 1985.

A Tradition of Foreign Economic Control

The first foreign nation with economic interests in Central America, Spain exploited the region's resources and labor and completely controlled its trade for three centuries. When Spain's colonial grasp of Central America loosened in the eighteenth century, British merchants and bankers stepped in to take hold of the region's trade and finances. Great Britain was the first foreign power to extend its economic interests beyond trade to include investment in the region.

In the 1800s, British financiers lent the tenderfoot nations the money they needed to build the region's modern infrastructure. Loans were contracted by the burgeoning coffee oligarchy to build the ports, roads, and railways they needed to ship their commodity to the expanding market of coffee lovers in Europe. In Guatemala and Costa Rica, British as well as German capital stood behind the coffee export houses. The British had established themselves in Belize and the Caribbean coastal areas of Nicaragua and Honduras, and dominated trade with all the nations of Central America.

The British Foreign Office, not the U.S. State Department, was the original practitioner of Gunboat Diplomacy in Central America. In 1844 and again in 1850 the British blockaded the Salvadoran port of La Union to press its debt claims.[1] The British Foreign Secretary at the time declared that England reserved the right to use its naval forces to collect debts owed to British financiers.[2]

The United States did not look beyond its ever-expanding borders to Central America until around 1850. Its signing of the Clayton-Bulwer Treaty with England in 1850 gave the United States equal rights to any future trans-isthmus waterway. The treaty also decreed that both nations would refrain from territorial acquisition in Central America. At this time, the United States had only slight commercial interest in the region. In the 1860s, the United States supplied El Salvador with only 3 percent of its imports.[3]

By the 1870s, U.S. trade with the region had begun to pick up. Steamships from New Orleans began hauling bananas and tropical woods back to the United States, and several U.S.-owned silver and gold mines opened. But it was U.S. finance capital rather than direct investment that was dominant in this period. By the turn of the century, U.S. financiers had made inroads into the British domination of finance in the region through loans for railroads and utilities.

A common method used by U.S. bankers to maneuver their way into the region was to offer to pay a nation's entire European debt with one large U.S. loan. As a guarantee of repayment, the U.S. government would place the country under a customs receivership, which resulted in U.S. control of a country's trade revenues. Such a situation occurred in Nicaragua after the United States backed a coup in 1909 against the Liberal Party government of José Zelaya Santos. Zelaya had angered the United States by negotiating a hefty loan with London banks. In 1911, the United States installed a Collector General of Nicaraguan customs to insure that a new $1.5 million loan from U.S. bankers Brown Brothers and J.W. Seligman Company would be paid back. Nicaragua remained under a customs receivership until 1949.

U.S. bankers not only serviced the debts of Central American nations but also provided the capital for new roads, electric plants, and communications systems—infrastructure projects that facilitated mineral exploitation and export-crop production. Through the early 1900s, private banks managed all U.S. international loans through bond sales and short-term lending. The U.S. banks had become an exporter of private capital, with the muscle of Gunboat Diplomacy backing them up. The depression of the 1930s, however, put a crimp in U.S. international lending. Though U.S. bankers were not suffering, they were concerned that the U.S. government no longer had the power or inclination to take up the Big Stick against delinquent debtors.

The New Corporate Investors

Following on the heels of the U.S. banks, investors discovered Central America between 1900 and 1930 when U.S. banana companies established their economic enclaves along the Caribbean coasts of Guatemala, Honduras, Nicaragua, and Costa Rica. During the lulls preceding each world war, direct investment increased: the $12 million in U.S. direct investment in 1887 grew to $77 million by 1914 and zoomed to $206 million in 1929.

TABLE 2B

U.S. DIRECT INVESTMENT IN CENTRAL AMERICA
(excluding Belize and Panama)
($ million)

	1887	1914	1929	1940	1950	1959	1967	1977	1983
Central America	12	77	206	149	254	389	501	677	784

SOURCES: CEPAL; *Survey of Current Business*, November 84.

The first large investments were by the banana companies, but after World War I there was a spate of investment in utilities, aviation, trade and insurance. Between 1929 and World War II, direct investment actually declined, first because of the Great Depression and later because of the war. The years after World War II brought a new surge of U.S. investment. Major U.S. banks financed the cotton boom of the 1950s, and industrial corporations set up food-processing operations and factories to produce consumer goods. The founding of the Central American Common Market (CACM) in 1961 attracted U.S. corporations eager to produce for the expanded regional market. Direct investment in the region doubled between 1950 and 1970.

Global Reach of TNC Investment

The expansion of U.S. investment in Central America during these two decades corresponded with the rise of the transnational corporation (TNC). During World War II, most of the old colonial trade barriers came crashing down, and opened a world of opportunities resources, and markets for aggressive corporations. It was in this postwar era that many corporations became truly global operations. Although maintaining headquarters in their home countries, many TNCs count on foreign subsidiaries to provide for the majority of their incomes.

Three different kinds of TNCs control the major economic activity in Central America. Agribusiness TNCs like United Brands and Hershey produce cash crops like bananas and cocoa for export, either on their own plantations or by contracting with local growers. Industrial TNCs like Colgate-Palmolive and Exxon produce goods for both the domestic and export markets. The third category of TNCs is in the service sector which includes banks, commercial enterprises, and trading companies. Banking TNCs like BankAmerica and Citicorp provide loans to private and public borrowers either from branch banks or from their international headquarters. TNCs like McDonalds and Price Waterhouse are also categorized as part of the service sector. Trading companies buy and sell the commodities produced in Central America.

The global reach of TNCs extends into the most remote corners of Central America, enticing *campesinos* (peasants) with ads for snack foods, selling pesticides, and promoting the production of cash crops. TNCs have established manufacturing plants within the region that put the finishing touches on imports and then market these products as *"Hecho en Centroamerica"* (Made in Central America). One such factory in El Salvador cuts and packages imported paper into consumer-size rolls of toilet paper to be sold by Kimberly-Clark.

Direct foreign investment by TNCs is no longer on the upswing in Central America or in any other part of the third world. In recent years a new group of U.S. investors (mostly small firms) have set up contract production and processing operations for nontraditional exports like vegetables and flowers. TNCs have moved away from direct production to concentrate more on control over the trading and processing of commodities produced for them by private contractors or state corporations. Having gained control of the regional market for manufactured goods in the 1960s and 1970s, TNCs are no longer expanding in Central America, although there have been some efforts to attract labor-intensive export-manufacturing plants to industrial parks in the region.

Strength in Numbers

In Central America, TNCs from the United States are ubiquitous. Over 2000 firms with U.S. investment are doing business in Central America. This figure includes only those companies that have offices and actual operations—not the

TABLE 2C

SELECTED U. S. CORPORATIONS IN CENTRAL AMERICA
(Corporations with more than six subsidiaries in Central America)

Corporation	Number of Subsidiaries	Number of Central American Countries
American International	12	4
Beatrice	12	5
Borden	8	3
Bristol-Myers	10	6
Castle & Cooke	19	2
Chevron	8	5
Citicorp	9	6
Coca-Cola	7	5
Colgate-Palmolive	11	6
Cummins Engine	7	7
Exxon	15	7
GTE	7	6
General Mills	11	4
H.B. Fuller	28	6
IU International	7	3
ITT	8	5
McKessen	8	5
Monsanto	8	6
Murphy Oil	11	1
Nabisco	8	4
R.J. Reynolds	17	4
SCM	17	5
Shell Oil	10	5
Texaco	14	7
Transway	18	6
United Brands	18	5

SOURCE: *The Resource Center, "Compilation of Corporations," 1985.*

uncounted thousands that distribute their consumer and capital goods in the region. In many cases, a TNC has investment in more than one company. United Brands, for example, has 18 different Central American companies under its

TABLE 2D

LARGEST U.S. CORPORATIONS IN CENTRAL AMERICA
(Listed by Industry, Rank within their Industry
and Number of Central American Countries with Subsidiaries)

Rank	#	Rank	#	Rank	#
Chemical		**Petroleum**		**Food & Beverage**	
1. Du Pont (EI) de Nemours	4	1. Exxon	7	1. Dart & Kraft	1
2. Dow Chemical	3	2. Mobile	3	2. Beatrice	5
3. Allied	4	3. Texaco	7	3. General Foods	-
4. Union Carbide	3	4. Standard Oil (Indiana)	1	4. Pepsico	4
5. Grace (W.R.)	1	5. Chevron	5	5. Coca-Cola	5
6. Monsanto	6	6. Atlantic Richfield	1	6. Consolidated Foods	1
7. American Cyanamid	2	7. Shell Oil	6	7. Anheuser-Busch	-
8. FMC	3	8. U.S. Steel	2	8. Nabisco	4
9. Celanese	1	9. Phillips Petroleum	2	9. General Mills	4
10. Hercules	2	10. Tenneco	-	10. Ralston	2
				11. Archer Daniels Midland	-
Pharmaceutical		**Grain**		12. Borden	3
1. Johnson & Johnson	3	1. Cargill	3	13. CPC International	2
2. American Home Products	3	2. Continental Grain	-	14. IC Industries	2
3. Bristol-Myers	6	3. Ralston Purina	2	15. Pillsbury	1
4. Pfizer	3	4. General Mills	4	16. H.J. Heinz	1
5. Merck	3	5. CPC International	2	17. Campbells	-
6. Warner Lambert	3	6. Bunge	-	18. United Brands	5
7. Lilly (Eli)	2	7. Pillsbury	1	19. Quaker Oats	5
8. Abbott Laboratories	3	8. Quaker Oats	5	20. Con Agra	1
9. Smith Kline Beckman	1	9. Kellogg	1		
10. Upjohn	2	10. Grain Terminal Association	-	**Accounting**	
				1. Price Waterhouse	6
Soap		**Office Machines**		2. Arthur Anderson	3
1. Procter & Gamble	2	1. IBM	6	3. Coopers & Lybrand	4
2. Colgate-Palmolive	6	2. Xerox	6	4. Peat, Marwick & Mitchell	5
3. Avon Products	2	3. Honeywell	1	5. Deloitte, Haskins & Sells	4
4. Revlon	2	4. Hewlett-Packard	3	6. Ernst & Whinney	1
5. Chesebrough-Pond's	4	5. Digital	1	7. Touche Ross	1
				8. Anderson Young	4

= Number of Central American nations within which the corporation has subsidiary operations.

SOURCES: Fortune, April 29, 1985; Who Audits America, 12th ed., June, 1984; and 1984 World's Directory of 51,000 Largest U.S. Corporations (Petaluma, CA: Baldwin H. Ward Publications), Vol. 1; The Resource Center, "Compilation of Corporations," 1985.

wing, ranging from a telecommunications firm to a cattle-ranching subsidiary. H.B. Fuller has 28 firms, including chemical-, paint-, and carpet-manufacturing subsidiaries. Transway has 18 different subsidiaries ranging from Coordinated Caribbean Transport to Tropigas, the region's main natural gas distributor. Eighteen of the TNCs have operations in five or more countries.

Most of the large U.S. TNCs have a presence in Central America. One-third of the top 500 U.S. industrial corporations direct business ventures in the region, including 67 of the top 100 U.S. corporations. (See Appendix II.) These TNC giants dominate most sectors of the regional economy. Of the top 20 food and beverage corporations in the United States, 16 are found in Central America. All the leading chemical, pharmaceutical, accounting, office machine, and soap-manufacturing companies have business in the region. Nine of the top ten petroleum companies have business activity there.

U.S.-based TNCs are concentrated most heavily in the manufacturing sector, which accounts for a third of all U.S. firms (partially or totally owned) doing business in Central America. Companies in sales and service sectors each account for a quarter of the U.S. businesses while agribusiness companies account for only 5 percent of total U.S.-owned firms in the region. (See Table 2G.) While this numerical breakdown of U.S. corporate presence does indicate the nature of U.S. economic involvement in the region, it does not account for the widely varying impact of different corporations. The presence in Honduras of United Brands' banana operations, for example, has a greater impact on employment and national income than the retail sales activity of Sears Roebuck.

Value of Investment by U.S. TNCs

There is over $5.3 billion of U.S. direct investment in the seven nations of Central America, according to figures supplied by the U.S. Department of Commerce. About 85 percent of this capital is found in Panama. Panama dominates the investment picture in Central America primarily because of the $2 billion found in that country's International Finance Center. But even without the financial investment, Panama still has a commanding lead in the amount of U.S. direct foreign investment. The location of the trans-isthmus oil pipeline, the expansive Colon Free Zone, and several oil refineries represent most of the remaining U.S. investment in Panama.

Investment figures from the U.S. Department of Commerce do not accurately portray the full extent of U.S. investment in the region because they: 1) report only the book value or historical costs of U.S. investment, not the resale value of the business; 2) identify only direct investment as 10 percent or more of voting securities; 3) have set a $500,000 minimum investment standard which eliminates from the figures the many hundreds of small-business operations or ventures like hotels and ranches owned by U.S. citizens in the region; 4) exclude the value of management, licensing, and technology contracts; and 5) include only direct investment, not the assets of foreign affiliates.[4]

The book value of U.S. investment falls far short of the actual value of U.S. plant and equipment in Central America. The U.S. Embassy in Costa Rica estimates U.S. investment in Costa Rica to be worth $550 million while the Department of Commerce figures show only $227 million for the same investment. The same holds true in Guatemala, where U.S. Embassy estimates of U.S. investment are double those of the U.S. Department of Commerce.

TABLE 2E

U.S. DIRECT INVESTMENT IN CENTRAL AMERICA, BY COUNTRY
($ million)

	1977	1980	1983	% Change 1977–1983
Belize	21	24	30	43
Costa Rica	178	303	227	28
El Salvador	79	105	113	43
Guatemala	155	229	198	28
Honduras	157	288	251	60
Nicaragua	108	89	−5	−105
Panama	2442	3170	4519	85
Total CA	3140	4208	5333	70
CA w/o Panama	698	1038	814	17

*Negative number due to: 1) intracompany account deficits by U.S. parents to Nicaraguan affiliates and 2) nationalization of Standard Fruit.

SOURCE: Department of Commerce, *Survey of Current Business*, November 84

Non-U.S. TNC Presence

TNCs based in the United States clearly dominate foreign investment in Central America, but many of the world's largest non-U.S. TNCs also have operations in the isthmus. Ten of the top 25 TNCs listed in *Fortune* magazine's ranking of the world's leading corporations have operations in the region.[5] Royal Dutch Shell does business in each of the seven Central American countries as does Swiss-owned Nestle. The Japanese giant Matsushita has battery-manufacturing plants in Costa Rica and El Salvador. West German-based Bayer manufactures chemicals and pharmaceuticals in Costa Rica, El Salvador, Nicaragua, and Guatemala. At least 65 other non-U.S. TNCs are active in the region. About a quarter of them hail from Great Britain, followed by those from Canada, West Germany, Switzerland, and Japan.

TABLE 2F

NON-U.S. TNCs IN CENTRAL AMERICA
(with subsidiaries in three or more countries)

Corporation	Business	B	C	E	G	H	N	P
Nestle	Food production & pharmaceutical sales	X	X	X	X	X	X	X
Shell	Petroleum exploration, refining & sales	X	X	X	X	X	X	X
Siemens	Electrical equipment		X	X	X	X		X
Lloyds Bank	Banking			X	X	X	X	X
BAT Industries	Tobacco products manufacturing	X	X			X	X	X
Babcock Int'l	Computer & swimming-pool sales					X	X	X
Bayer AG	Chemicals, pharmaceutical, & medical products manufacturing	X	X	X			X	

SOURCE: The Resource Center, "Compilation of Corporations," 1985.

Down on the Farm

Until the 1960s, when TNCs began to set up manufacturing plants, the banana companies dominated U.S. investment in Central America. The three banana giants—United Brands, Castle & Cooke, and R.J. Reynolds—still rank among the largest foreign investors in the region, but they have cut back their role in direct production. This is in keeping with a worldwide trend: agribusiness corporations are selling off their plantations and mills to reduce their risks. Two recent examples of this trend are the sale of Tate & Lyle's sugar-production facilities to the government of Belize, and the sale of United Brands' plantations on Costa Rica's Pacific coast to the government. Banana companies also contract production from "associate producers" who sell all their bananas to the TNCs at a specified price.

The decreased ownership of production by TNCs has not significantly reduced their control. The foreign corporations retain hold of the industry by controlling the technology, transportation, trading, and marketing of the commodities they once produced. There is little TNC investment in the production of cash crops like coffee and cotton. Instead, TNC control is exercised by the trading TNCs like Cargill and Volkart Brothers. These multicommodity traders can set the prices of the commodities produced in Central America because there is no effective cartel of producers to bargain for an increased share of their value. (See Chapter 6.)

Another dimension of TNC domination of agribusiness in Central America is the control of the pesticide and fertilizer market by corporations like Bayer,

Shell, and Chevron. The marketing of seeds is also under TNC control. Central American farmers now buy their seeds from such unlikely sources as Shell, Monsanto, and Occidental Petroleum.

On the International Assembly Line

In the 1960s, scores of TNCs came to Central America to establish manufacturing plants to produce for the regional market that CACM created. Originally conceived to spur industrialization in the region, CACM resulted in a rush of TNC investment. The big foreign companies either bought out or pushed out most independent industrialists. This investment surge by TNCs leveled off in the 1970s as the regional market became saturated.

Looking for new investment that would offer jobs to the urban unemployed and increase their foreign exchange, the Central American nations then tried to attract assembly plants. Government funds were used to build industrial parks and free zones for labor-intensive manufacturing plants that would assemble electronics and clothing for export. El Salvador was the first to embark on this development strategy of the 1970s. Corporations like Texas Instruments and Maidenform opened assembly plants to use cheap Central American labor. Salvadoran workers, laboring for $4 a day on sewing machines, piece together imported straps and bra cups for export back to the United States.

Rather than set up their own assembly plants, some TNCs contract with local firms to assemble products to their specifications. Like the TNC-owned export-manufacturing plants, these subcontracting companies employ mostly female labor for the tedious assembly and stitching tasks. The promotion of Central America as an export platform for TNCs looking for cheap labor continues to be the main industrial-development strategy of the region. (See Chapter 7.)

TNCs at Your Service

Over 500 U.S. firms provide an array of services to Central American consumers and businesses. While these firms account for only a small share of direct investment in the region, they financially drain the region with their steep charges for shipping, advertising, consulting, accounting, and communications services. Often, the shipping of commodities costs more than the Central American producers receive for them. The banana corporations have their own shipping companies while other TNCs, like Transway (Coordinated Caribbean Transport), handle additional regional exports.

TNCs like Sheraton and Holiday Inn own the largest hotels in Central America, and travelers in the region are served by all the major U.S. car rental companies. ITT and GTE provide communications services, and the eight leading U.S. accounting firms keep the books for other TNCs and government agencies.

TNC food processors like Philip Morris and Nabisco pay advertising TNCs to create new desires for largely non-nutritional snack foods. Tobacco companies

have increased their advertising in third-world countries to compensate for reduced rates of cigarette consumption in developed countries. A UN study said
that advertising and media TNCs are using telecommunication satellites "to
project corporate images and ideology worldwide" that are based largely on "a
western elitist ideology and on a complex of values antithetical to cultural pluralism."[6]

TABLE 2G

U.S. COMPANIES IN CENTRAL AMERICA
(Number of all U.S. branch companies, subsidiaries, and affiliates)

	Manufacturing					Agric	Natural Resources			Financial		Services				Sales	Total
	Pharm. Chem.	Food	Indus. Goods	Cloth Text.	Other Consumer	Prod.	Mining	Petro.	Timber	Banks	Insur.	Trans.	Rest. Hotel	Consult-ing	Other		
Belize	1	3	2	1	0	13	2	4	5	1	0	2	19	3	1	14	71
Costa Rica	14	26	58	9	40	43	5	3	2	9	4	18	5	26	12	89	363
El Salvador	3	12	22	3	12	4	1	2	0	1	5	7	4	21	10	37	144
Guatemala	15	41	61	4	43	22	3	14	3	14	19	17	16	48	33	130	483
Honduras	2	29	41	16	34	19	7	16	9	11	4	19	14	26	21	77	345
Nicaragua	8	9	22	1	11	3	2	1	0	2	3	6	1	9	8	32	118
Panama	11	30	41	18	40	9	1	22	1	29	22	57	11	74	41	124	531
REGIONAL TOTAL	54	150	247	52	180	113	21	62	20	67	57	126	70	207	126	503	2055
% of Total	3	7	12	3	9	5	1	3	1	3	3	6	3	10	6	24	

SOURCE: The Resource Center, "Compilation of Corporations," 1985.

Banking TNCs Take an Interest

For many Central Americans, their hometown bank is really a TNC. Lloyds
of London has domestic banking branches in the region, as do the top three U.S.
banks. In Honduras, Chase Manhattan has a controlling interest in the country's
major bank, Banco Atlantida, whose slogan is *Amigo a Amigo* (Friend to Friend).
Hondurans who do not seek the friendship of Chase Manhattan can walk across
the plaza to Banco de Honduras, owned by Citicorp.

Their on-the-spot presence in the Central American countries enables these
TNC banks to influence national economic and political decisions. They are
often the major source for loans provided to industries and agribusinesses. They
frequently become owners of businesses in the countries where they have branches.
In Central America, U.S. banks have owned breweries, country clubs, sugar
mills, textile mills, poultry farms, and other banks.[7]

Another dimension of foreign banking interests in Central America is the region's business elites' common practice of placing their income in U.S. banks, particularly those in Miami. Florida banks have become the cache for the region's money makers. The amount of deposits in U.S. banks from Central Americans surpasses the amount deposited in banks within the region.

What the TNCS Say

While TNCs generally applaud President Reagan's conservative, business-oriented politics, many do not totally support his confrontational stand in Central America. One extensive 1981 survey of U.S. corporations in the region revealed that TNCs do not think Reagan's approach is the best for business.[8] In contrast to Reagan, virtually all the TNC managers who responded to the survey placed the origins of the political and economic crisis in the region's internal problems, rather than in Cuban or Soviet influence. They also agreed that the Central American nations face a choice between major reforms and revolutionary change that would be far more sweeping than that in Nicaragua. John Purcell, author of a report based on this survey, observed that some corporate officials "fear that Reagan's policy would polarize Central American society and make lasting stability impossible."

Concerning Nicaragua, the survey revealed that most of them objected to the U.S. cutoff of aid to the country. They talked of the need to moderate the policies of the Sandinistas rather than eliminate them. The experience of TNCs in Nicaragua was, except during the peak war period, that they could profitably conduct business there.

The TNCs have generally resisted moderate reforms, such as better labor laws, that would assuage the social tension in the region, but at the same time they also recognize that repression has its limits. "Repression works in the short run," noted a BankAmerica official, "but it doesn't work in the long run. Our interests and concerns are matters of the long run. What we want is long-term stability."[9]

U.S. economic aid programs that have subsidized new corporate investment in agribusiness and promoted increased U.S. trade in the region have served some businesses well. But on the whole, TNCs in Central America are suffering some of the consequences of their own past activities. While TNCs reaped the profits of economic growth from 1960 to 1979, the social tensions intensified because of low wage rates and economic development patterns that did not improve the circumstances of most Central Americans. The resulting political crisis along with the militarization of the region has not benefited business.

TNC-Directed Development

Given the right circumstances, foreign investment could contribute to economic development. Those circumstances, however, have rarely been present in Central America, where TNCs are virtually unregulated. When governments have tried to regulate the TNCs, the corporations have retaliated from their superior position. Because many of the TNCs doing business in the Central American countries have annual revenues greater than the entire Gross Domestic Product (GDP) of their host nations, they can afford to cut back production while they wait for governments to comply with their demands. They can break contracts knowing that Central American governments do not have the power to enforce most of their statutes. If push comes to shove, the TNCs know they can shove harder, especially when they have the U.S. Embassy standing behind them as they invariably do.

The Reagan administration proposes increased foreign investment as the primary solution to the economic woes of Central America. Yet, evidence shows that expanded TNC involvement in underdeveloped capitalist countries does little but increase economic underdevelopment. TNCs create patterns of economic development that meet their own global needs for resources, labor, and markets but only rarely correspond with the actual development needs of their host countries. Given the sad results of past uncontrolled TNC investment in the region—from the early days of United Fruit to the more recent experience with runaway factories and finishing-touch industries—economic development based on U.S. foreign investment will lead only to continued instability.

Trading Interests

The United States conducts over $4 billion in trade with Central America. For the United States, this is a paltry sum, amounting to less than 1 percent of U.S. trade each year. For the Central American nations, the sum has a much greater significance. It amounts to over half of all their extra-regional trade

These nations depend on their giant neighbor to the north as their major market for all agricultural and industrial exports. In the case of some exports like bananas, sugar, and meat, the dependence is almost complete. This reliance on U.S. trade creates the possibility that Washington could make economic life even more difficult for Central American nations, like Nicaragua, that do not fall in line with U.S. policies.

Central America depends more on the United States as a trading partner, but the United States receives more of the advantages in trading with the region. Each year U.S. exports to Central America exceed its imports by several million dollars. As the overall U.S. trade deficit widens and competition picks up from its industrial rivals, the United States will be ever more concerned about maintaining its areas of trade superiority even in small markets like Central America.

Commerce with Central America, however, is not strategically important to the United States. There is little mineral or petroleum production in the region, and the earlier forecasts of major oil reserves in Guatemala appear unjustified. (Table 2H lists the Central American exports that account for 10 percent or more of U.S. imports.) Only with bananas does Central America supply the majority of U.S. imports. While items like men's pajamas and women's brassieres imported from Central America are statistically important, the United States hardly relies on the region for these manufactured products.

TABLE 2H

U.S. IMPORTS FROM CENTRAL AMERICAN COMMON MARKET

Product*	Percent Supplied by CACM Countries
Bananas	63
Cigars	22
Brassieres	21
Oil Seed	20
Cotton	18
Coffee	16
Variable Resistors	14
Beef	13
Shrimp	13
Sugar & Molasses	11
Men's Pajamas	11
Lead	10

*Only items for which CACM provides 10 percent or more of U.S. imports are included.

SOURCE: U.S. Dept. of Commerce, *U.S. General Import Schedule A Commodity Groupings by World Area*, April 1981.

Foreign Financing

Before the days of TNCs and corporate subsidiaries, the bankers and bond agents were drawing profits out of Central America in the form of loan payments. They established a debtor-creditor relationship with the fledgling nations of the isthmus. When the debtor nations did not pay, their ports were invaded and their treasuries seized.

Today, foreign financial flows to Central America come from three main sources: 1) multilateral loans and grants from International Financial Institutions (IFI), 2) bilateral loans and grants from foreign governments, and 3) private loans from TNC banks. The United States exercises control in all three types of financial channels to Central America. Control of the financial flow to Central America allows creditors to determine the structure of economic development. As creditors, the financial institutions can also force governments to adopt economic policies that run contrary to national interests.

The accumulated debt from multilateral, bilateral, and TNC bank loans has reached colossal proportions. To meet their debt-serving payments, the Central American governments are squeezing the money out of social programs and out of the wages of workers. Their combined $18 billion external debt blocks further development in Central America and represents the single largest manifestation of foreign economic presence and influence in Central America.

Multilateral Lending

The IFIs were established at the end of World War II to foster the expansion of trade and development in the international capitalist market. The World Bank and the International Monetary Fund (IMF) were the two original IFIs. The IMF was designed to provide emergency loans when a country experienced a temporary balance-of-payments crisis due to sudden downturns in trade. The World Bank, in contrast, provides loans for development projects. The three components of the World Bank are the International Bank for Reconstruction and Development (IBRD), the International Development Association (IDA), and the International Finance Corporation (IFC). In Latin America, the World Bank was accompanied in 1959 by the Inter-American Development Bank (IDB). In the last four decades, combined lending from these IFIs amounted to $7.4 billion.

TABLE 21

FOREIGN FINANCIAL INTERESTS IN CENTRAL AMERICA

Outstanding Loans to TNC Banks (1983)	$ 4.3 billion
Multilateral Financing 1946–1984	$ 7.4 billion
Bilateral Financing (U.S.) 1946–1984	$ 4.5 billion

SOURCES: AID, *U.S. Overseas Loans and Grants, 1945–1984; Book of International Settlements.*

Most loans from the IDB and the World Bank have been used to fund large infrastructure projects like dams and power plants designed to promote economic growth. Other loans have been used to increase agricultural and industrial production, and some funds have been used to improve health, housing, education, and sanitation. Both development banks have special divisions that attempt to encourage private-sector investment. The World Bank's private-sector department is known as the International Finance Corporation while the IDB's Inter-american Investment Corporation provides capital to new or expanding business ventures in Central America.

The loans from the IFIs are referred to as multilateral loans because the IFIs are international institutions that manage funds from all participating governments (nonsocialist nations) as well as substantial private capital. Unlike the United Nations General Assembly, voting power in these institutions is not equal. Instead of one vote being assigned to each nation, voting power is determined by the level of financial commitment.

Because of its high percentage of contributions to the IFIs, the United States is in a superior position to influence or veto lending decisions. The voting power of the U.S. representative in IFIs ranges from 20 to 35 percent, while the combined voting power of the Central American nations is generally less than 1 percent.

TABLE 2J

MULTILATERAL VOTING POWER
(percent share of votes)

Organization	U.S.	Central America
IMF	19.3	0.8
IBRD	19.2	0.5
IDA	19.5	1.1
IFC	25.6	0.6
IDB	34.5	3.0

SOURCES: 1984 Annual Reports: World Bank, IMF, IFC, and IDB.

The United States has a "very practical commercial reason for participation" in the multilateral institutions, noted Treasury Secretary Donald Regan. The Department of the Treasury estimates that for every dollar the United States puts into the World Bank, at least two dollars are returned to the United States through export sales. In 1980, U.S. firms received over $960 million in export sales generated by multilateral lending.[10] In a 1982 report on U.S. participation in IFIs, the Department of the Treasury concluded that the multilateral development banks "have been most effective in contributing to the achievement of our global economic and financial objectives and thereby also helping us in our long-term political/strategic interests."[11]

President Reagan has encouraged the IFIs to put more funds directly into private sector investments. Reagan also has demanded more strict conditions for multilateral loans. Beryl Sprinkel, a Treasury Department official, explained that "the United States will not vote for loans" unless the recipient country has provided incentives for production, a guarantee of free and open markets, and minimized government interference in the economy.[12]

While the IFIs provide the Central American nations with a relatively cheap source of development capital, they usually do not address the basic development problems of the region. Multilateral banks loan money for irrigation projects that do not improve the circumstances of the landless. Huge hydroelectric dams make electricity available to industries and affluent sections of Central American cities, but make little difference to the rural population who cannot afford electricity even if it were available. Because the IFIs are banks and not charitable institutions, they are interested in recovering their loans. They tend, therefore, to lend to agricultural and industrial endeavors that will increase exports and earn the debtor nations the foreign exchange needed to repay the loans.

Multilateral loans have funded development projects that attempt to increase economic growth and improve social conditions without tackling unequal power structures, income levels, and distorted land tenure systems. The loans in fact are channeled through the governments and business institutions that have benefitted from the skewed land and income distribution patterns in Central America. As a result, multilateral loans have reinforced the very entities responsible for the region's slow and uneven growth.

It is not that the IFIs are reluctant to demand structural change in Central America. Like the financiers of the turn of the century, the World Bank and the IMF have been quick to intervene when their debtor nations cannot meet their repayment schedules. Since 1979, an ever-increasing number of IFI loans are tied to "structural adjustment" and "austerity" programs that force Central American governments to pay the overdue debt. These programs generally hit the lower classes much harder than the economic elite. Careful not to disturb the local oligarchies, these "structural adjustment" and austerity programs put no pressure on the Central American governments to implement agrarian programs or enact tax laws that will better distribute social income.

Although the IFI charters specify that loans should be considered only on their economic merit, the United States has let its politics guide its voting patterns for multilateral loans. Since 1981, the United States has consistently voted against loans for Nicaragua while advocating loans for U.S. allies in Central America. Washington said its negative votes on Nicaraguan loans were due to Nicaragua's "inappropriate macro-economic policies." In a January 1985 letter to the IDB president, Secretary of State George Shultz objected to Nicaragua's economic policies but also said he opposed all lending to Nicaragua because the loans would probably be used "to help consolidate the Marxist regime and finance Nicaragua's aggression against its neighbors." Shultz warned that IDB approval of loans to Nicaragua would jeopardize continued U.S. funding of the IDB.

That kind of pressure combined with negative U.S. votes caused multilateral lending to Nicaragua to fall off drastically after 1981. In 1984, Nicaragua received no new multilateral loans. In contrast, U.S. efforts to stabilize Central America have been abetted by generous multilateral loans to other Central American nations. An examination of IDB loans since 1980 illustrates the U.S. influence in this regional multilateral institution:

- $25 million loan for rural road construction in Guatemala from 1977–1984. Rural roads have also been AID's priority in Guatemala.
- Two loans totalling $36 million for rural development in Costa Rica's "strategic" Northern Zone.
- Two loans totalling $61 million for El Salvador's agrarian reform in 1980–1981.
- $400 million loan in 1985 for El Salvador's National Plan of social and economic development.
- $18 million loan in 1983 for repair of El Salvador's bridge across Rio Lempa, which had been damaged by guerrilla sabotage.
- $18 million in 1983 for community centers and municipal development in the Guatemalan Highlands.

Bilateral Aid from United States

The other form of official financial flow to Central America is bilateral lending, most of which comes from the U.S. government. Other governments also sponsor economic assistance programs but they are insignificant when compared with the $4.5 billion that the United States has pumped into the region since World War II. Like multilateral development lending, U.S. aid programs seldom fund projects that confront the basic economic inequities in the region. Even more than IFIs, the U.S. Agency for International Development (AID) stresses projects that advance private enterprise. More than ever before, AID is using its funds as leverage to demand changes in the economic policies of recipient governments. If a government fails to meet its demands, AID withholds further payments until the desperate government complies. (See Chapter 3.)

TNC Bank Lending

The third form of foreign financing comes from TNC banks. During the 1970s there was an explosion of lending by TNC banks to the Central American nations. As the debt crisis worsened, Central American governments appealed to the TNC banks for commercial loans to keep their budgets balanced.

This private lending went to pay debts rather than to development or infrastructure projects. These loans provided short-term relief for the region's seven countries but complicated the long-term debt picture. Bank loan interest rates were as much as double the multilateral and bilateral rates, and commercial bank loans were often one-year or medium-term agreements. During the 1970s, Central

TABLE 2K

CUMULATIVE MULTILATERAL AND BILATERAL ECONOMIC LOANS TO CENTRAL AMERICA, 1946–1984
($ million)

	IBRD	IDA	Multilateral IFC	IDB	IMF	Total Multi.	DA ESF	PL 480	Exim	Bilateral Other	Total Bilat.	Total
Belize	5.3	0	0	0	4.9	10.2	21.6	3.0	0	11.3	35.9	46.1
Costa Rica	406.4	4.6	6.7	615.0	240.7	1273.4	536.7	91.1	70.4	99.1	797.3	2070.7
El Salvador	215.1	25.6	1.0	607.7	196.1	1045.5	760.5	204.0	23.4	61.2	1049.1	2094.6
Guatemala	346.0	0	18.2	738.3	187.1	1289.6	333.7	94.3	46.2	112.8	587.0	1876.6
Honduras	503.3	82.6	10.4	611.4	181.3	1389.0	503.0	82.5	36.0	51.1	672.6	2061.6
Nicaragua	231.1	60.0	9.5	403.7	88.8	793.1	291.3	45.0	48.7	59.4	444.4	1237.5
Panama	544.8	0	8.3	584.9	328.0	1466.0	328.3	27.6	136.1	114.0	606.0	2072.0
ROCAP	0	0	0	170.9	0	170.9	340.8	0	0	15.8	356.6	527.5
Regional Total	2252.0	172.8	54.1	3731.9	1226.9	7437.7	3115.9	547.5	360.8	524.7	4548.9	11986.6

ROCAP—Regional Office for Central America and Panama: IBRD—International Bank for Reconstruction and Development; IDA—International Development Association; IFC—International Finance Corporation; IDB—Inter-American Development Bank; IMF—International Monetary Fund; DA—Development Assistance; ESF—Economic Support Funds; PL480—Food for Peace; Exim—Export Import Bank.

SOURCES: AID, *U.S. Overseas Loans and Grants July 1, 1945–September 30, 1984*; Center for International Policy.

America's debt to TNC banks increased 20 times to over $4 billion. TNC banks based in the United States accounted for about half of this commercial debt. Reflecting this dramatic increase in international lending in the 1970s, the portion of the profits of the nine leading U.S. banks that came from international sources increased from 22 to 55 percent.

In the 1980s, the TNC banks have become more reluctant to supply the private sector in Central America with credit because of the region's political and economic turmoil. With U.S. banks shying away from financing the private sector in Central America, the economic downturn has worsened and Central American governments have gone begging to multilateral and bilateral sources for substitute financing.

Behind the spree of private international lending in the 1970s was the assumption that if things got rough the U.S. government would bail out its TNC banks. A leading European banking specialist, Pierre Latour, told a congressional hearing in 1975, "Though it was never articulated in so many words, many bankers must . . . have assumed that loans to (third-world) governments would be underwritten by the official aid programs of the developed world."[13] Part of this bailout has occurred in the form of Economic Support Fund (ESF) assistance from the U.S. Agency for International Development (AID). The TNC banks have also pressured the IFIs and the U.S. government to clamp down harder on Central American nations by imposing more strict austerity programs.

Dominant Special Interests

In 1914, President Woodrow Wilson lambasted U.S. bankers and investors for exploiting the region and continually hollering for the Marines. "[The] foreign interests must go," said Wilson. "Not that foreign capital must leave Central America, but that it shall cease to be a dominant special interest. . . . Material interests are to be set aside entirely. . . ." Continuing, he asked, "Who commonly seeks the intervention of the United States in Latin American troubles? . . . Always the foreign interests, bondholders, or concessionaries. They are the germs of revolution and the cause of instability."[14]

---

1 Philip L. Russell, *El Salvador in Crisis* (Austin: Colorado River, 1984), p.22.
2 Ibid.
3 Ibid.
4 In 1977, the assets of US affiliates in Central America (not including Panama or Belize) amounted to $1.8 billion while US direct investment was only $698 million.
5 Among the top 25 international TNCs are the following 10 corporations that have business operations in Central America:

Rank	Corporation
1	Royal Dutch/Shell Group of Companies
5	Unilever
8	Societe Nationale Elf Aquitaine
9	Matsushita Electric Industrial Co. Ltd.
11	Philip Gloeilampenfabriken
14	Siemens AG
15	Nissan Motor Co., Ltd.
18	Bayer AG
19	Hoechst
22	Nestle

SOURCE: The Resource Center, "Compilation of Corporations," 1985.

6 Fredrick F. Clairmonte and John H. Cavanagh, "Transnational Corporations and Services: The Final Frontier," in UNCTAD, *Trade and Development*, No. 5, 1984.
7 Committee on Banking Currency and Housing, House of Representatives, "International Banking," May 1976, pp.231–270.
8 John Purcell, "Perceptions and Interests of US Business in Relation to the Political Crisis in Central America," in Richard E. Feinber (ed.), *Central America: nte national Dimensions of the Crisis* (New York: Holmes & Meier, 1982).

9 Robert Henriques Girling, "Economic Value of Central American Trade and Investments to the US Economy," (manuscript), February 1982, p.7.

10 Hearings before the Subcommittee on International Finance, Committee on Banking, Housing and Urban Affairs, Senate, *International Monetary Fund and Related Information*, 1980, p.119.

11 Treasury Department, *United States Participation in the Multilateral Development Banks in the 1980s*, 1982, p.4.

12 *The Banker*, July 1981, p.37.

13 *Multinational Monitor*, April 1980, p.13.

14 Walter LaFeber, *Inevitable Revolutions: The United States in Central America* (New York: Norton, 1983), p.51.

CHAPTER 3

AID Rushes In

AID wants to be an octopus. They already manage the economy and the war. Now they want to control humanitarian work as well.
    —Eugenia Marin, San Salvador representative for Catholic
    Relief Services, 1985

AID HAS FLOODED into Central America since President Reagan took office. In 1985, the region received 7 times its 1980 share. Currently, four-fifths of total U.S. assistance to Central America is economic aid in the form of development projects, food shipments, and Economic Support Funds. Reagan touts this assistance as the positive side of U.S. involvement. In 1984, he said that he was proud that U.S. aid to Central America was "primarily economic and humanitarian." Congress has been asked to approve increased economic aid budgets on grounds that "more" will eliminate the root causes of social unrest.

Evidence suggests that very little of the economic aid flowing into Central America either furthers development or helps to reduce poverty and hunger. The overwhelming amount of U.S. economic aid is used to shore up privileged elites (stabilization), block true reform movements (pacification), and strengthen U.S. ties in the region (private-sector support).

- Stabilization: Propping up friendly governments with generous trade credits insurance, balance-of-payments assistance, and budget deficit relief.
- Pacification: Supporting civic-action and rural development programs, often coordinated with counterinsurgency campaigns.
- Private Sector Support: Funding national and foreign private enterprise.

The Agency for International Development (AID), which is part of the State Department, disburses the major portion of U.S. economic assistance in the form of Economic Support Funds (ESF), Development Assistance, and Food for Peace (PL480). Other economic aid (not funded by AID) programs that affect Central America are the United States Information Agency (USIA), Overseas Private Investment Corporation (OPIC), Export-Import Bank (Eximbank), Commodity Credit Corporation (CCC), and Office of Disaster Assistance. (Table 3C.)

TABLE 3A
U.S. ECONOMIC AND MILITARY AID TO CENTRAL AMERICA

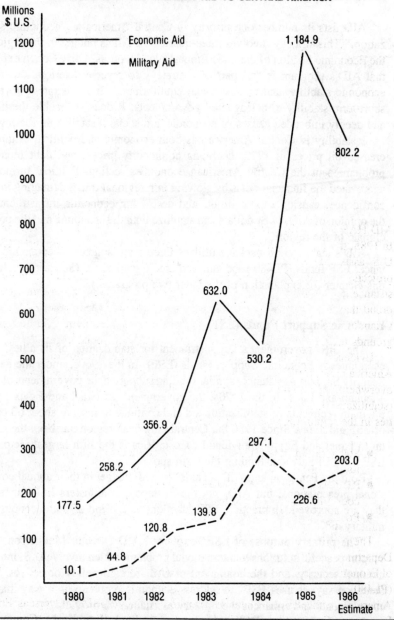

Millions $ U.S.

—————— Economic Aid

– – – – – Military Aid

1,184.9

802.2

632.0

530.2

356.9

258.2

297.1

203.0

177.5

226.6

139.8

120.8

44.8

10.1

1980 1981 1982 1983 1984 1985 1986 Estimate

SOURCES: AID, *U.S. Overseas Loans and Grants July 1, 1945–Sept. 30, 1984; AID Congressional Presentation: FY 86*, Main Volume, pp. 668 and 675; Elizabeth Hunt, AID, October 24, 1985; Jim Seville, State Department, October 3, 1985.

Stabilization: Crisis Management

AID lists its number one priority in Central America as "economic stabilization." This strategy involves three-quarters of AID's budget in the region. At the Economic Section of the U.S. Embassy in Honduras, Larry Cohen explained that AID's program is "all part of a strategy to reverse deterioration, restore economic stability, and restore social equilibrium."[1] It is a strategy to restore short-term stability to beleaguered governments. It does not tackle the historic and deeply imbedded causes of economic and social instability in the region.

Instability in Central America has both economic and political origins. Increased oil prices in 1979, declining commodity prices, and debt repayment problems sent the Central American economies reeling. Political turmoil has aggravated the financial crisis by slowing intraregional trade, damaging investor confidence, causing capital flight, and destroying economic infrastructure. In the opinion of AID, U.S. dollars can stabilize both the economic and the political climate of the region.

AID's stabilization package utilizes three main sources of economic assistance: ESF funds, PL480 food aid, and credit guarantees. (See sections later in this chapter for explanation of the latter two programs.)

Economic Support Funds (ESF)

The U.S. government's key instrument for stabilization of its allies' shaky economies is Economic Support Funds (ESF). In the 1960s, under the name of Security Support Assistance, similar funding supported the governments of South Vietnam and Laos. In the 1970s, the governments of Israel and Egypt became the main recipients of stabilization aid and continue to receive about 60 percent of ESF aid today. Since 1980 the Central American region has been the runner-up to Israel and Egypt. Individually, Costa Rica is the fifth largest recipient of ESF, with El Salvador holding the sixth spot.[2]

Both the Pentagon and AID include the ESF budget in their annual congressional presentations; but AID, not the Pentagon, administers ESF funds once they are approved. In practice, ESF functions as a blend of both economic and military aid.

"The primary purpose of ESF," explained AID Director McPherson, "is to support peaceful solutions to international problems which involve U.S. interests, national security, and the attainment of U.S. foreign policy objectives."[3] The Pentagon says it uses ESF "to address economic problems in a way that both complements and enhances the military assistance we provide."[4]

In Central America, ESF assistance usually takes the form of "cash transfers" to the national treasuries and central banks of each nation. The funds are mainly used to cover balance-of-payments deficits. They allow governments to pay their external debts.

ESF money that is transferred to the government's central bank is also sold at lower-than-market exchange rates to the private sector to encourage businesses to import U.S. goods. Peter Bielack, AID's public information officer in San Salvador, explained that these transfers do not fund the kind of development that many people associate with economic aid. He said: "You cannot see almost one half of our aid because it goes to the private sector."

Despite repeated predictions by the AID mission, increased ESF financing has not resulted in substantial new private investment. Huge sums of cash transfers have simply disappeared in El Salvador. A study by AID's Inspector General in 1983 found that Salvadoran business owners deliberately falsified invoices to show that imported fertilizer and other U.S. goods they were buying cost more than they actually did. Large portions of these transactions were then deposited into private bank accounts in Miami and Switzerland.[5]

Support for Militarization

Stabilization funding is closely connected with the militarization of the region and the continuation of the war in El Salvador. A congressional study found that the usual distinction between military and economic aid was "artificial" in the case of El Salvador. It said that money used to reconstruct infrastructure could not be considered economic aid because it responds to "military attacks and is an attempt to restore the status quo prior to the attacks rather than to reform and develop the economy to improve the quality of life." Ninety million dollars of ESF assistance to El Salvador has been used to replace infrastructure damaged in the civil war.[6] "When the guerrillas bomb a bridge or knock down a power line, we move in new bridges and power lines with helicopters," said Peter Bielack of the U.S. Embassy.

ESF funds, which totaled $705 million from 1981–1985 in the case of El Salvador, also bear a relation to the war. Like infrastructure repair, these funds do little to actually develop the economy. Instead, cash transfers are used simply to keep governments financially solvent without addressing the economic conditions that caused the civil war. Furthermore, as pointed out by the congressional study, "the Salvadoran government could never have tripled its spending on the Armed Forces without cash transfers."[7]

In Costa Rica and Honduras, the flood of ESF funds enables both those countries to divert government revenues into the build-up of their military and police forces. Hundreds of millions of ESF dollars also make these nations more willing to yield to U.S. foreign policy dictates. Both countries allow their territories to be used as *contra* bases despite building domestic controversy. The authorization of ESF assistance to Guatemala enabled that country to maintain its high degree of militarization. One U.S. congressional representative complained about the ultimate use of ESF funds. "You know," he said, "that economic support assistance is simply a device to say to a country: Look, take your money and buy weapons, and we will cover your foreign exchange problems with it."[8]

Changing Policy

In its regional strategy statement for 1984, AID stated that it "will use the whole [stabilization] program as leverage to seek policy changes more aggressively than ever before." To qualify for ESF funds, recipient governments must sign economic assistance agreements with AID in which they promise to make certain policy modifications, maintain an ongoing "policy dialogue" with AID, and share such economic information as AID may require.

Rather than requiring the countries take measures to meet the basic needs of their people, end human rights violations, or implement long overdue tax and land reforms, AID commonly pressures Central American governments to do the following:

- Encourage U.S. investment.
- Remove financial and investment constraints.
- Devalue currencies.
- Increase credit and reduce taxes for export businesses.
- Remove tariff protections for local industries.
- Eliminate food subsidies and reduce social services.
- Liberalize economies by removing restrictions on flows of foreign exchange.
- Revoke labor laws that keep manufacturing wages higher than agricultural wages.
- Improve opportunities of private sector.

AID's Economic Recovery Program for Honduras acknowledged that Honduras "will have to accept an even lower standard of living in order to place the economy on a sound footing." AID even told the Honduran government to adopt more user fees for health, family planning, and education as a measure to "stabilize" the economy. These suggestions do not sit well with Hondurans who see dollars pouring into newly created private-sector organizations. ESF cash transfers provide large business owners with dollars at reduced exchange rates, while programs benefiting the poor are being cut.

The democratic ambitions of Central Americans are undercut when their governments have to follow the wishes of Washington in addition to those of the traditional powerbrokers in the military and oligarchy. The AID Mission in Tegucigalpa encouraged the formation of a Honduras-U.S. Joint Economic Working Group to advise the government on economic planning, particularly as regards foreign investment.

In Panama, the United States has funded an Investment Council to advise the government on economic policy. The AID Mission presented the Panamanian government with a list of tasks to implement. These included the elimination of rent control and lowered standards on housing construction, measures which would "reduce costs and encourage private investment." In Costa Rica, AID created a private-sector organization called CINDE to lobby for policy changes beneficial to business.

A U.S. Embassy official in Costa Rica noted that ESF helped the country get "back on its feet" after a serious debt crisis in 1981. Washington "strongarmed them" to accept the IMF's austerity program. Costa Rica was also pressured to reduce the power of its Central Bank while strengthening commercial banks. On two occasions, AID stalled the delivery of promised economic aid until Costa Rica complied with economic reforms. A Costa Rican legislator assessed this kind of leverage as "economic blackmail."

The Strains on Stabilization

When AID announced the stabilization strategy for Central America in 1981, it told Congress that ESF funds would begin diminishing in 1985. That was a short-lived promise. By 1984, the administration had introduced a five-year stabilization program for the region that would provide over $8.4 billion in economic assistance through the end of the decade.

The stabilization strategy has many weaknesses, but the major one is its reliance on short-term solutions. No matter how much money is injected into the private sectors and central banks of the region, the problems of unjust land tenure, lack of reliable markets, falling commodity prices, and distorted income distribution will remain.

The stabilization strategy also increases the dependency and debt burden of Central America. As Honduran peasant leader Esteban Enriquez noted: "The government is accepting endless quantities of U.S. aid that it will never be able to pay back. This is very bad politics for a small country like ours. The aid program doesn't do anything to solve the deep problems of Honduras. Instead of being defenders of the poor, the United States is the defender of a system that brings misery to the poor. The aid goes to the few that benefit from that system."[9]

Ironically, U.S. stabilization efforts threaten to destabilize countries like Honduras and Costa Rica, where aid is given on the condition that the governments follow austerity programs that target the poor. The politicians of Honduras, Costa Rica, and the United States are counting on the continued passivity of these nations' populations in the face of wage freezes, social service cuts, and higher utility bills.

Overall, the stabilization strategy worked well as a short-term fix. In El Salvador, it propped up a government that would have collapsed without massive quantities of aid. Immense transfers of aid to Honduras and Costa Rica kept those nations within the anti-Nicaragua alliance. Increasing economic aid to Guatemala is now crucial to a nation rocked by the same debt and balance-of-payments burdens experienced earlier by its neighbors. With Nicaragua, Washington has pursued the opposing strategy of destabilization, denying access to U.S. trade, credit, and financial support.

Pacification: Techos, Trabajo, y Tortillas

Conflict in Vietnam was seen to occur at two distinct levels—military and pacification. Too often we find ourselves today repeating the mistakes of history by trying to differentiate between those measures which lend themselves to internal defense and those which are key to internal development. They cannot be separated. They must be viewed as a totality and prosecuted as such.

—David L. Caldon, U.S. Southern Command

This analysis of SOUTHCOM (U.S. Southern Command in Panama) by Lieutenant Caldon is being adopted by the Central American military and AID in Central America. The tools of pacification, according to Lieutenant Caldon, are "humanitarian aid, development assistance, and economic support." All these programs must occur simultaneously with military assistance to fight the war against subversion in Central America, said Caldon, adding that this is an "unconventional" war in which exist no clear "battle lines."[10]

The 1980s are not the first time AID has joined in counterinsurgency campaigns in Central America. In the late 1950s, AID rushed in to shore up Guatemala's military government of Colonel Castillo Armas. Then, in the 1960s, AID funded pacification projects in the areas of Guatemala where the guerrilla resistance was the strongest. Agricultural credit and access roads funded by AID were combined with military/civic action programs run by the U.S.-directed Guatemalan army in the departments of Izabal and Zacapa. As one U.S. government official told Congress: "Guerrilla activity tends to generate a need for increased U.S. development assistance."[11]

In the 1970s in Nicaragua, AID targeted the regions where the Sandinistas were gaining support. Jaime Wheelock described the INBIERNO agricultural project as a "program of counterinsurgency created by AID."[12] The project, which created a data bank of information on residents of the region, was coordinated with the National Guard's civic-action program.

In Central America, AID funds pacification in the following ways:

- Limited land reform programs to reduce rural tensions.
- Rural development programs, which include education, housing projects, and health services to place the disenfranchised rural population under government jurisdiction.

- Colonization and resettlement projects to place people in areas advantageous to military strategy.
- Material aid for military-controlled model villages in the form of electricity infrastructure, housing materials, clinics, social services, schools, and technical assistance.
- Food-for-work projects to employ and keep track of displaced persons.
- Road building ventures to employ potentially rebellious population groups and increase military access to isolated areas.
- Expansion of the Peace Corps, Voice of America, and other groups that promote U.S. values to Central Americans.
- Exchange programs which bring thousands of Central American professionals, union leaders, students, and government bureaucrats to the United States.
- The "fostering of democratic institutions" like private-sector organizations, U.S.-trained labor unions, and center-right political parties.
- Support for elections that give regimes more domestic and international credibility.

Guatemala: Pacification of the Highlands

In the late 1970s, rebel forces launched a guerrilla war against the military regime in Guatemala. Different from earlier guerrilla organizations, the new rebel armies had developed widespread support among the Indian (majority) population of the *Altiplano* (Highlands)—the poorest area of Guatemala. When the military suffered substantial losses, it responded with a campaign of indiscriminate terror against Indians aimed at wiping out the guerrillas' base of popular support.

This first phase of the counterinsurgency campaign included massacres and the burning of villages, while the second stage was termed *"Frijoles y Fusiles"* (Beans and Rifles) and later *"Techos, Trabajo, y Tortillas"* (Housing, Work, and Tortillas). The official name for Guatemala's pacification program is the Plan of Assistance to the Areas of Conflict (PAAC).

The military organized Indian boys and men into civil defense patrols, feeding them with donated food from the United Nations and the United States. Assisted by these newly established patrols, the military began rounding up the Indians who had fled from its scorched-earth tactics. These displaced persons were given food-for-work jobs constructing roads and building *pueblos modelos* (model villages) in which they were to live. The military directed this pacification work through its own Civil Affairs divisions and through the Committee for National Reconstruction (CRN). The CRN is directed by the military, but a staff of civilian employees from an array of government ministries carry out the work. Overseeing all "development" work in the areas of conflict is the new Inter-Institutional

Coordination System, which brings all government ministries involved in development under army supervision.

Both the army and the CRN conceived of these model villages later on as *"polos de desarrollo"* (development poles). Through these development poles and model villages, the military could maintain better control of the Indian population and at the same time address the causes of the Indian rebellion through rural development programs. The civil patrol members are required to report all suspicious activity of their fellow villagers to the local military commander. A classic pacification plan, the Guatemalan program was based on the experiences of the Israelis in the occupied territories and of the U.S. military in Vietnam.[13]

AID Provides the Funding

Both AID and the Guatemalan government have selected the *Altiplano* as their priority for development projects. In 1984, nine out of ten AID projects were in the Highlands. That same year, President Mejía Víctores designated the Highlands as the focus for his government's development programs. In July 1984, the government decreed that the Guatemalan army would assume control over all civilian ministries in the Highlands.

In his 1984 budget presentation, AID Administrator McPherson hinted at the pacification objectives of U.S. economic aid for Guatemala. He said that the entire AID program "is directed at the rural poor, especially the Indians. The program facilitates economic stabilization and rural development, and addresses the underlying social/economic conditions that fan insurgency."[14]

Asked why AID now channels all its funds to the Highlands, Robert Queener, the agency's Central America desk officer, said:

> We have always had an interest in the Highlands, but this really increased three to four years ago. The region became the single-minded focus in the 1980s because the population there has been left out of development for so long. We want to see the government meet their needs. We persuaded the government of Guatemala to develop the Highlands, which was a policy change for them. It was also for social and political stability. That is the area where the insurgency has been the strongest.[15]

As with pacification programs in other Central American countries, AID's activities in the Guatemalan Highlands include training and support for colonization projects, road construction, bilingual education, food-for-work, health clinics, technical and credit assistance for agricultural projects, rural electrification and housing, and the funding of PVOs like the Salvation Army and Project Hope.

Since the Guatemalan military controls all development and humanitarian assistance to the Highlands, as well as all civilian ministries, AID funds to that region contribute to the army's pacification program. "We depend on AID for our programs in the Highlands," acknowledged CRN's director Colonel Germán Grotewald Cerezo.[16]

In 1985, Congress approved higher levels of economic and non-lethal military aid for Guatemala, specifying that the aid not be used for "rural resettlement." AID has promised not to target its aid for the development poles but acknowledges that population within those areas do benefit from its programs.

Lack of Development

By 1984, the military's pacification program for the Guatemalan Highlands was showing signs of success. Although guerrillas continued to operate in the region, their population base was considerably diminished. Army terror combined with a multi-dimension campaign quieted Indian support for the guerrillas.

The development phase of Guatemala's pacification program may prove more difficult for AID and the Guatemalan army. Many model villages have been constructed. But they will not become "development centers" unless Washington and the Guatemalan generals can also create an economy that is able to sustain the Highlands population. Once the roads are built, the model cities erected, and the food-for-work projects end, the pacified population will be left without work and without food.

Encouraged by agricultural technicians and economists from AID and from Israel and Taiwan, the Guatemalan army hopes to solve this problem by establishing nontraditional cash-crop farms. These will be complemented by agro-industries to process the vegetables.

To effect this plan, AID is funding the construction of food-processing facilities. It is also paying for hundreds of agricultural technicians to teach Indian *campesinos* how to grow winter vegetables that will be processed in Guatemala and then shipped to the United States. This scheme may prove to be little more than a paper dream of AID planners. The total absence of a domestic market and the inability of AID to attract U.S. markets for large quantities of vegetables make nontraditional crop production an improbable development alternative.

El Salvador: Pacification as the "Key Battlefield"

There are three parts to the pacification strategy in El Salvador: 1) agrarian reform, 2) elections and support for the Christian Democrats, and 3) civic action, relief, and development programs that are part of the counterinsurgency war.

Washington designed the agrarian reform plan to reduce support among the *campesino* population for the revolutionary forces. AID funded the land distribution program, and the American Institute for Free Labor Development (AIFLD) organized the conservative rural unions that generated *campesino* support for the program. The AID consultant that authored Phase III of the agrarian reform, Roy Prosterman, designed a similar AID-implemented program during the Vietnam War.

The second part of AID's pacification strategy for El Salvador was the creation of a base of support for a center-right government run by the Christian Democrats. From 1982–1984, AID spent over $10 million to promote a series of elections that it predicted would place the Christian Democrats in political power.[17] AID funds were used to publish comic books that proclaimed: Your vote will end the violence because it will strengthen the democratic government while the loyal national army eliminates the communist threat. U.S. Ambassador Thomas Pickering insisted that the comic book guerrillas be depicted as wearing red berets— for "communists"—even though no Salvadoran guerrillas have been sighted wearing them.[18]

During the 1984 presidential campaign, two-thirds of the 600 organizers of the AID-funded and AIFLD-trained Salvadoran Communal Union (UCS) worked full time on Duarte's campaign.[19] AID also paid for the election process itself, including the computerized vote-counting system ($3.4 million), and covered the expenses of international observers ($0.8 million). Because of the degree of U.S. involvement in the Salvadoran elections, authors Edward Herman and Frank Brodhead termed them "demonstration elections," stating that the efforts were made for show more than for actual democratic change.[20]

While AID was coordinating the elections (in which only center and right politicians participated), the CIA channeled money to the Christian Democrats. The CIA's involvement recalled its similar support for the Christian Democrats in Chile when they defeated Salvador Allende in 1964. Similarly, during the Vietnam War, the CIA poured millions of dollars into the campaign treasury of Nguyen Van Thieu, who was in a political position similar to that of Napoleon Duarte.

The third part of AID's pacification strategy relates directly to the military war against the FMLN. In 1983, at the urging of the U.S. Embassy, the Salvadoran military announced its initiation of the National Plan for Defense and Internal Development. The National Plan, which relies almost exclusively on AID funding, bears a striking resemblance to the pacification campaign launched by the United States during the Vietnam War.

U.S. officials in San Salvador acknowledged that the National Plan was modeled after AID's Civil Operations and Rural Support (CORDS) pacification program implemented in Vietnam.[21] In El Salvador, three government entities manage the pacification program: the National Commission for the Restoration of Areas (CONARA), the National Commission for Assistance to the Displaced (CONADES), and the army's Military/Civic Action unit.

According to the director of the AID-funded pacification program in Vietnam, the objective of CORDS was to "help neutralize the active insurgent forces" by generating "rural support for the Saigon regime" through community development programs.[22] Among the official functions of CORDS were refugee resettlement, rural development, social welfare, public safety, land reform, and technical support.[23]

Operation Well-Being

El Salvador's National Plan was kicked off in the Department of San Vicente under the name of "Operation Well-Being." The first phase of Operation Well-Being involved brutal sweeps by the military through San Vicente to remove the guerrillas. As a result of the military terrorism, over 1500 Salvadoran *campesinos* fled to Honduras. Refugees in Honduran camps recall that the military flew over their villages in light planes, playing music and talking about the peace and amnesty offered by Operation Well-Being. Later, larger planes, A-37s, returned with bombs that forced them to flee.[24]

The second phase of the San Vicente operation was the use of CONARA, CONADES, and Military/Civic Action to supervise a community development program that involved food-for-work projects, rebuilding of town halls, the formation of civil-defense patrols, and resettlement of displaced people into army-controlled model villages. U.S. military advisers were involved in the first phase of the pacification, with AID supervising the second phase called "rural development." CONARA manages the infrastructure repair, housing, and the organization of the model villages.

Unlike those of Guatemala, the model villages in El Salvador were constructed from abandoned towns and repopulated with displaced people. CONADES has primary responsibility for the food-for-work and other programs that assist displaced people who have not been resettled. As with Guatemala's Committee for National Reconstruction (CRN), CONADES is coordinated by national and local committees. Representatives of most government ministries, such as health, education, and housing, make up the committees, which are directed by military officers. Neither CONADES nor CRN could exist without AID funding.

Former Undersecretary of State Thomas Enders called the pacification program in San Vicente "the key battlefield" of the war.[25] Other State Department officials said the war would be won or lost with Operation Well-Being. But even with plenty of AID money and technical assistance, Operation Well-Being foundered. The main problem was that the U.S.-trained "hunter battalions" had failed to "secure" the area. Their scorched-earth tactics drove thousands of refugees into Honduras and into the larger cities, but they did not dislodge the guerrillas.

Outside the major cities, the *"muchachos"* (young ones) still controlled large portions of the countryside. *Campesinos* refused to form civil defense patrols because they did not want to have anything to do with the military. While AID construction projects were repairing the "model villages," these villages were often in the hands of the *muchachos*.

The mayor of Santa Clara told a reporter that "to keep our schools open and our AID work projects functional, we have to accept terms the guerrillas set."[26] Operation Well-Being brought increased violence and Salvadoran military presence but was not able to build a social structure which the government could control—even counting on tens of millions of dollars in AID food, housing materials, and construction funds.

Framework of Counterinsurgency

The continuing military stalemate led the armed forces to adopt an escalated counterinsurgency strategy in 1984 that involved increased aerial bombardment and strafing of guerrilla-controlled zones. Since they did not succeed in driving the guerrillas out, the military intended to force the civilians to leave. Twelve areas were declared free-fire zones, meaning the armed forces would destroy anything that moved. Army commanders said they were draining the sea to deny the fish (guerrillas) their sustenance (civilian population).

In 1984, AID revamped its pacification program to deal with the flood of refugees driven from guerrilla-controlled zones by the air war. Deciding that the Salvadoran pacification agencies were too inefficient, AID enlisted the assistance of U.S. organizations like Project Hope and CARE to feed, house, provide medical care, and assist in the resettlement of hundreds of thousands of displaced.

Involvement of U.S. humanitarian agencies in El Salvador duplicated the role of these agencies in the CORDS program in Vietnam. One difference between the two wars is the number of internal refugees. In the more populous South Vietnam, an estimated 8 percent of the population was displaced by the war. By early 1985, at least 25 percent of Salvadorans had fled their homes.[27]

Many Salvadoran and U.S. humanitarian organizations have refused to participate in AID's work with displaced persons. A senior U.S. Catholic relief official called it "a highly political pacification program." Reverend Octavio Cruz, director of the San Salvadoran archbishop's relief efforts, said, "U.S. aid always comes with the framework of their counterinsurgency policy."[28]

Because of the increased numbers of displaced people, AID slowed down other portions of the pacification campaign that involve community development and increased its attention to the care and resettlement of the refugees. Many are being resettled on abandoned Phase I (of the agrarian reform) farms with the help of CONADES, CONARA, and several U.S. organizations. The Salvadoran government and AID jointly drew up a plan called Project 1000 which would resettle the displaced in a thousand different sites including the Phase I lands. The government nicknamed this proposed resettlement project "*Techos, Trabajo, y Tortillas*"—the very name adopted by the Guatemalan military for their pacification campaign.

In 1980, AID initiated its pacification program in El Salvador in hopes of stifling rebellion. With these hopes dashed, AID programs are now more directly linked to the counterinsurgency war. "The U.S. government is not a neutral party here," said one troubled international relief worker. "There is a military strategy, including bombing, to displace people from areas the government cannot control and a linked strategy to then feed, care for and pacify those refugees."[29]

TABLE 3B

U.S. AID TO EL SALVADOR, 1980–1985

Purpose	Amount ($ million)	Percent	Project	Project Amount ($ million)
Reform & Development	267	15	Agrarian Reform (P)	137
			Judicial/Government Reforms	19
			Quality of Life Improvement (P)	104
			USIA Scholarships	8
Direct War Related	523	30	Arms & Ammunition	162
			Maintenance/General Supplies	120
			Aircraft	99
			U.S. Training Personnel	94
			Ground Transport and Communications	47
Indirect War Related	767	44	Cash Transfers (S)	585
			Aid to Displaced Persons (P)	92
			Infrastructure Rebuilding (S)	90
Commercial Food Aid	182	11	Pacification Projects (P)(S)	91
			Displaced Persons (P)(S)	46
			Miscellaneous	46
	$1739	100		

(P) Component of Salvadoran pacification program.
(S) Component of Salvadoran stabilization program.

SOURCE: Arms Control and Foreign Policy Caucus, U.S. Aid to El Salvador: An Evaluation of the Past, A Proposal for the Future, February 1985. [Numbers may not total due to rounding-off.]

Costa Rica and Honduras: Securing the Perimeter

The pacification target in Costa Rica is its Northern Zone—the underdeveloped area that stretches along the Nicaraguan border. It is sparsely populated land used as a base for the Nicaraguan counterrevolution. Tensions have been building in the Northern Zone as a result of friction between the *contras* and the local population. The isolation and poverty of the area have also created discontent.

In 1983, AID initiated its $20 million Northern Zone Infrastructure Development Project. This area was chosen for the extensive development project because the Costa Rican government had expressed "concern about the feelings of isolation and frustration expressed by the population and its proximity to and the constant destabilizing influence of Nicaragua." The Northern Zone area is characterized by "a low level of satisfaction of basic needs." The large proportion of residents (about 25 percent) with Nicaraguan heritage also concerns Costa Rican political leaders.

With road and school construction, as well as attention to the area's agricultural problems, project designers hope to better integrate the border population into the Costa Rican economy. In addition, a colonization scheme will settle landless Costa Ricans into isolated border areas. The Inter-American Development Bank has complementary development activity in the area, and the Peace Corps, CARE, and the World Food Program are also working in the Northern Zone. AID's project description acknowledges that the Northern Zone was given priority funding for "geopolitical reasons."[30]

The U.S. government is interested in using this strategic area to train U.S. troops as it does in the Honduran-Nicaraguan border region. In the event of U.S. or Costa Rican hostilities with Nicaragua, Washington would like to count on the support of the border population. The Pentagon also wants U.S. troops to know the lay of the land and have a good infrastructure of roads to depend upon.

Since neither Honduras nor Costa Rica faces significant internal armed opposition, Washington's pacification programs are mostly preventive. In Honduras, AID works with the U.S. Army's Medical Civilian Action Projects (Medcaps) to provide medical and dental services to poor Hondurans. Medcaps frequently visit the Honduran-Salvadoran border area. A U.S. military official said the Medcap visits are designed to "win hearts and minds" and preempt possible support for future guerrillas.

AID has funded so many projects in Honduras that about every Honduran government agency is involved. By funding housing, health, education, and agricultural programs, AID hopes to project a positive image of the United States. The build-up of the Peace Corps delegation in Honduras—one of the largest in the world—is also part of this public relations strategy. Captain Robert S. Perry of the U.S. Southern Command wrote: "Civic actions build an important people-to-people reservoir of trust and confidence in their government and the U.S.," and "cast the military in the role of a positive social agent."[31]

But AID projects also directly relate to the regional war. On the Salvadoran border in Honduras, AID has earmarked funds for a refugee camp and a program to relocate refugees into government-controlled areas. Along the Nicaragua border, AID's programs assume a different dimension. Economic assistance in the region called La Mosquitia is closely related to the U.S.-directed *contra* war against Nicaragua.

In 1981, Washington pushed the United Nations High Commission on Refugees (UNCHR) to set up refugee camps for Miskito Indians. The decision to establish refugee camps along the border was resisted by many members of UNCHR, who felt that the Miskitos should be encouraged to return to Nicaragua. They argued that refugee camps that provided food and shelter would only encourage more cross-border migration and provide a base for the *contras*. Political and economic pressure from the United States prevailed, and the camps were established and used by the Steadman Fagoth and other *contra* leaders to shelter the families of their recruits.

Working alongside the United Nations in La Mosquitia are several U.S.-funded PVOs, including CARE and World Relief, and a team of Peace Corps volunteers. In 1984, AID became directly involved in the border area through a $7.5 million "humanitarian assistance" project in the area of Rus Rus, near a major *contra* base. The project provides direct economic assistance to 3000 Miskito refugees as well as building roads and bridges in the strategic region. AID allocated $500,000 of the project budget to rebuild the bridge connecting the main road to the site of the main *contra* encampment. The funds are used not only for infrastructure for the *contras* but also to help attract Miskito refugees to the area while providing food and medical care to families of Indian *contras*.[32]

The AID project for the Rus Rus area was proposed to Congress by Senator Jeremiah Denton (R-Alabama) and Representative Bob Livingston (R-Louisiana). Livingston requested that AID fund the project after hearing of the plight of the Miskitos from Louisiana state representative Louis "Woody" Jenkins. Jenkins is the principal figure in a right-wing organization called Friends of the Americas, which provides aid to the Miskitos in the Rus Rus area. Jenkins said he established Friends of the Americas "to aid the victims of communist aggression."[33] (See Chapter 4.)

The AID "humanitarian assistance" project for the Miskitos of Rus Rus highlighted the growing coordination between the aid projects of private anti-Sandinista groups in the United States and those of AID and the CIA. In mid-1985, Congress approved $27 million in "humanitarian assistance" to the *contras* in Honduras. The aid is distributed to the *contras* through a special agency set up within the State Department.

Such assistance violates the Geneva Convention and Protocols which establish clear guidelines for humanitarian assistance in war zones. These guidelines state that organizations distributing the aid should be independent of parties to the conflict and that aid should be distributed on the basis of need to noncombatants. Neither AID, the CIA, nor the array of right-wing private groups sending aid (on U.S. military transports) meet those specifications.

Private-Sector Support: The Magic of the Subsidized Marketplace

Immediately after becoming president, Ronald Reagan directed AID to let loose "the magic of the marketplace" in Central America. AID was commissioned to design projects that would encourage private-sector development and U.S. investment. In his 1981 speech to the National Association of Manufacturers, President Reagan declared: "Free people build free markets that ignite dynamic development for everyone."

In response to President Reagan's mandate, AID has created a flurry of programs that do the following:

- Create and strengthen private-sector organizations.
- Promote nontraditional agricultural exports and light manufacturing.
- Provide low-interest credit to the local private sectors.
- Support the establishment of free trade zones and industrial parks to attract U.S. investors.
- Inject dollars into the bankrupt economies for use by private businesses.
- Provide insurance and loans for U.S. corporations to invest in Central America, mainly through the Overseas Private Investment Corporation (OPIC).
- Facilitate U.S. trade with the region through programs like Eximbank.
- Assist the private sector with training and technical assistance by the Peace Corps and private voluntary organizations (PVOs).
- Establish new AID-funded financial institutions that provide capital to businesses.
- Persuade Central American governments to change their investment and financial policies to benefit private enterprise.
- Use economic aid to force governments to sign investment treaties and other agreements that favor U.S. investment.

Bureau of Private Enterprise

While the entire AID bureaucracy follows the private-sector approach to development, the newly created Bureau of Private Enterprise (PRE) is the cutting edge of Reagan's "magic-of-the-marketplace" philosophy. Chosen as PRE's first director was Elise Du Pont, wife of Delaware's governor and member of the corporate family by the same name. PRE counts on a Reagan-appointed advisory council of corporate executives to direct its operations.

During its first few years, PRE has concentrated on agribusiness and has attempted to involve the U.S. business community in Central America's agro-export system. PRE spent a quarter of a million dollars to fund an agribusiness workshop to "address how American capitalism can be mobilized to work in partnership" with the local private sector.[34]

Another purpose of PRE, which has raised questions about the extent of U.S. intervention in the internal affairs of Central American countries, is to assist the "privatization" of government corporations by financing their divestiture. As AID puts it, the agency is "committing funds to set privatization in motion." For example, PRE is offering funds to set up a "for-profit health sector" based on health councils in the United States.

While it tries to reduce Central American governments' role in the economy, in line with the "magic of the marketplace" philosophy, PRE—in an apparent contradiction of its own philosophy—uses U.S. government funds to set up private businesses in the region. The government agency sponsors feasibility studies for prospective U.S. investors. PRE both loans money and actually invests in new businesses, particularly those that involve U.S. interests in the production of nontraditional exports. These investments range from snow-pea cultivation in Guatemala to a fashion-apparel factory in Costa Rica. PRE also funds feasibility studies for prospective U.S. investors. As AID Director Peter McPherson explained: "Our new emphasis seeks a partnership of government and the private sector in the total development—not just involvement at the implementation stage."[35]

PRE's Office of Policy and Program Review studies "the investment climate" of the Central American countries. It has hired Business International and Coopers & Lybrand to review the policies of Central American governments and suggest what should be changed to create a better "investment environment." PRE's recommendations are often integrated into AID's grant contracts with recipient countries. To receive AID money, the countries have to agree to change certain policies, like lowering taxes on export businesses and decreasing the control of Central Banks over foreign exchange

In its 1985 *Development Strategy Statement*, AID stated: "The most beneficial impact on the private sector can be achieved through reforms in the public sector. Since procedures which allocate credit, import licenses, and foreign exchange have the most pervasive impact on the economy, these are the areas where primary attention will be concentrated."[36] PRE Director Du Pont said these efforts will create "strong, sophisticated markets for U.S. products and services, providing hospitable locations for investments and joint ventures by U.S. companies seeking stable risk taking environments."[37]

"The strengthening of the private sector," AID asserted, "is central to our long-term objectives."[38] While private business may play an important role in economic development, questions arise when government aid places such an emphasis on private enterprise. For all the millions being spent on private-sector promotion, there have been only a handful of new business investments directly related to PRE.

Magic Not Working

In testimony to the Congressional Committee on Foreign Affairs, political scientist Lars Schoultz criticized the role of PRE in developing countries. He advocated a congressional prohibition on AID's use of foreign aid to "meddle in the internal affairs" of foreign countries by pressuring them to change their domestic policies. Schoultz pointed out, "There is no magic in a government foreign aid institution, however well-intentioned and well-staffed by committed capitalists."[39] He also noted that a "significant portion" of AID funds for the private sector are ending up in the "cash drawers of U.S. corporations."[40]

The concept of private-led growth in Central America ignores the region's history. For almost a century, a small private sector along with U.S. investors have dominated the economy and concentrated its wealth. The experience of the 1960s and 1970s when the region enjoyed sustained economic growth revealed the myth of "trickle-down" economics. Economic growth is not necessarily accompanied by a proportional reduction in absolute poverty. Given the history of the region, government support for the private sector hardly seems the best way to economically develop Central America or to improve conditions for its multitude of *campesinos* and workers.[41]

TABLE 3C

USES OF U.S. ECONOMIC AID

Type of Aid	Purpose			How It Works
	Stabilization	Pacification	Private-sector support	
Economic Support Funds (ESF)	✔		✔	ESF assistance is the primary form of stabilization aid. These funds are usually transferred directly to the central banks of the recipient countries to solve balance of payments difficulties and budget deficits. For governments like Guatemala and El Salvador, where large portions of the budget pay for military expenses, the infusions of ESF funds allow the governments to increase the military budget without endangering the nation's financial

Type of Aid	Purpose			How It Works
	Stabilization	Pacification	Private-sector support	

stability. ESF assistance also supports the private sector because AID specifies that the dollars be used to cover U.S. imports desired by businesses. The government sells the dollars at the official rate to the private sector and then uses the local currency from the dollar sales to cover its budget expenses.

Type of Aid	Purpose			How It Works
Development Assistance		✔	✔	Development assistance loans and grants are for specific AID projects. The agrarian reform project in El Salvador and roadbuilding and rural development projects in Guatemala are examples of pacification programs. Development assistance projects often provide jobs, housing, health care, and community development facilities to population groups the Central American governments are trying to pacify. Many development assistance projects also directly promote the domestic private sector and U.S. investors by funding nontraditional agribusiness, industrial parks, private-sector organizations, and infrastructure projects.
Food for Peace (PL480)	✔	✔		Food aid is an important component of both stabilization and pacification strategies. Title I food aid stabilizes governments with balance-of-payments difficulties by providing shipments of U.S. food to governments. Title I food is then sold on the local

Type of Aid	Purpose			How It Works
	Stabilization	Pacification	Private-sector support	

market and the local currency from those sales is used to support pacification programs in Guatemala and El Salvador. Title II food is directly distributed through displaced-persons and food-for-work projects that are often part of government pacification programs.

Bureau of Private Enterprise (PRE) — *(Private-sector support)* ✔ — Directs development assistance money for projects that will benefit the private sector.

Overseas Private Investment Council (OPIC) — *(Private-sector support)* ✔ — Finances and insures U.S. private investment. Withdrawal of OPIC insurance, as in the case of Nicaragua, can contribute to destabilization.

Eximbank and Commodity Credit Corporation — *(Stabilization)* ✔ / *(Private-sector support)* ✔ — By insuring the payment by foreign importers of U.S. manufactured and agricultural products, Eximbank and Commodity Credit Corporation promote U.S. trade with Central American nations. They help to stabilize countries by keeping imports flowing into the country even though national foreign exchange reserves are low.

Private Voluntary Organizations (PVOs) — *(Pacification)* ✔ / *(Private-sector support)* ✔ — PVOs often assist pacification efforts by managing food-distribution, health-care, rural-development, and displaced-persons projects that are coordinated with military counterinsurgency campaigns. The Reagan administration has increased the involvement of PVOs

Type of Aid	Purpose			How It Works
	Stabilization	Pacification	Private-sector support	
			in private-sector support programs, like the International Executive Service Corps's consulting work on behalf of businesses in Central America.
American Institute for Free Labor Development (AIFLD)	✔	✔		The task of AIFLD is to keep the Central American work force from becoming politically active. It attempts to divide the union movement by keeping its affiliated unions out of coalitions with more militant unions. Its funds pay for ideological training, union organizing, and community development projects for its members. It is closely tied to U.S. corporate interests and promotes cooperative labor-management relations with the philosophy that "what's good for business is good for the workers."
Peace Corps		✔	✔	During the Reagan administration, the Peace Corps has become increasingly tied to the U.S. strategy of pacifying Central America and aiding the domestic private sector.
United States Information Agency (USIA)		✔		The USIA promotes the "American way of life" and "anticommunism." Through radio and television programs, regular contact with national newspapers, and publications, the USIA propagates U.S. foreign policy and the official U.S. view of current events. It tries to tie national political and

Type of Aid	Purpose			How It Works
	Stabilization	Pacification	Private-sector support	
				business leadership to the United States through scholarship and travel programs. A primary focus of USIA in Central America is a propaganda campaign against Nicaragua.
Office of Disaster Assistance (ODA)		✔		In Central America, ODA funds from the State Department are primarily used not to aid victims of natural disaster but to relocate and care for internal refugees who were displaced because of government counterinsurgency campaigns.

OPIC: Insurance for TNCs

The Overseas Private Investment Corporation (OPIC) is the U.S. government insurance company for TNCs. Congress created OPIC in 1969 to foster the "participation of U.S. private capital and skills in the economic and social progress of developing countries through programs of political risk insurance."[42] The U.S. Treasury backs up the insurance policies issued by OPIC.

Since 1971, OPIC has been insuring and guaranteeing U.S. investors against loss on their overseas investments due to expropriation, inconvertibility of currency, wars, revolution, or insurrection. In 1981, Congress approved new legislation that expanded the coverage to include "civil strife," which insures more limited forms of violence against U.S. business property. This increased coverage was "expected to involve lower-value claims, windows broken rather than whole factories blown up."[43]

In addition to insuring U.S. investments, OPIC also provides direct loans and underwrites investment surveys. As of 1985, OPIC insurance covered $460 million worth of U.S. investment in Central America. It also had $30 million in direct financial arrangements with U.S. investors in the region.[44]

The largest insured projects in recent years were in oil and mining, including silver mining by Amax in Honduras ($16 million), the oil pipeline in Panama constructed by Northville Terminal ($33 million), and oil exploration in Belize by the U.S.-owned Petro Belize ($50 million). Large TNCs insured by OPIC in Central America include Castle and Cooke, BankAmerica, Phelps Dodge, U.S. Tobacco, Citibank, and Cargill.

OPIC insurance and financing in Central America increasingly goes to firms involved in small agribusiness ventures. Since 1982 OPIC has insured or loaned money to five citrus ventures, several ornamental plant farms, as well as coffee, jojoba, cardamom, and tobacco plantations owned by U.S. investors.

Instrument of Foreign Policy

"OPIC is unquestionably a valuable development and export promotion tool," said Henry Geylin, the president of the Council of the Americas, "but not to be overlooked is its important value as a tangible and flexible instrument of foreign policy." OPIC is one of the many instruments of foreign policy that Reagan has used to fashion his Caribbean Basin program. OPIC President Craig A. Nalen said, "The administration has placed a high priority on strengthening U.S. ties with this area whose economic and political development objectives are so closely allied with our own."[45]

Kimberly-Clark made the news when it dropped sponsorship of the "Lou Grant" television series in reaction to actor Ed Asner's public opposition to U.S. policy in El Salvador. In 1979, the company had received $4 million in OPIC insurance for a new factory in San Salvador. "The project will increase the amount of hygienic paper products available to local distributors," OPIC explained. "Professional and technical training will be provided by the project which will employ 304 workers."[46]

OPIC insurance increases the U.S. government's vested interest in upholding "friendly" Central American governments, no matter how repressive they may be. Conversely the United States has a stake in toppling governments that threaten U.S. interests. The claims on OPIC by companies nationalized by the Allende government in Chile almost drained OPIC reserves before a U.S.-backed coup ousted the progressive Chilean government. In Nicaragua, after the 1979 overthrow of the U.S.-backed dictator, U.S. corporations that made claims against OPIC for losses included American Standard, General Mills, Citizens Standard Life Insurance, Sears Roebuck, and Ralston Purina.

In Guatemala, OPIC does not insure toilet-paper manufacture, but it does insure the manufacture of bathroom fixtures by American Standard. In its 1984 human rights report on Guatemala, Americas Watch pointed out that Section 502B of the Foreign Assistance Act prohibits economic assistance, including insurance (except that which directly benefits the needy), to governments engaged in gross violations of internationally recognized human rights.[47] Despite this prohibition, which Americas Watch said should apply to Guatemala, OPIC increased American Standard's insurance in 1984. In a country where less than 15 percent of the population has sewage facilities in their homes, it would be hard to justify American Standard's bathroom fixture manufacturing plant in terms of fundamental needs.

Eximbank: Financing U.S. Exports

Eximbank provides U.S. commodities with a competitive edge by using U.S. government funds to finance and insure payment for U.S. exports. It will pay U.S. exporters if the purchaser defaults.

Because of the unsettled economic conditions in Central America, Eximbank has been leery about financing exports to that region. Since 1945, Eximbank provided about $4 billion in exports to the region, but after 1979 its financing began to decline. In 1984, the Reagan administration created a new financing facility under Eximbank specifically to be able to finance exports to Central America. Called the Trade Credit Insurance Program, it uses AID funds to guarantee exports to the region. Eximbank Director William Draper said that the new program, which will finance up to $300 million in U.S. exports to Central America, is one of several initiatives called for by President Reagan to foster "Central American democratic self-determination."[48]

Eximbank has a history of mixing political motives in its export-promotion operations. In Chile, Eximbank cut off all loan guarantees to the Allende government, making it extremely difficult for Chilean businesses to obtain needed products such as machinery and spare parts from the United States. A similar fate befell Nicaragua. After the Sandinistas took power in 1979, Eximbank's program of loans, grants, and insurance ground to a halt. Such policies also have the indirect effect of making it difficult for the country to obtain other external financing. Eximbank President Henry Kearns said that if a borrower "is in trouble with us, there's literally no private institution in the U.S. that will lend to him."[49]

Funds for Agriculture, but Not for Food

Although AID sends a large amount of assistance to Central America under the category called Agriculture, Rural Development, and Nutrition, malnutrition has not been alleviated and production of basic foods remains low in Central America. Virtually none of U.S. agricultural-related projects have anything to do with producing and distributing more food for the Central American people. The projects build roads, extend electrification for those who can afford it, subsidize the processing and export of winter vegetables, and provide credit for pesticide purchases. A 1984 Congressional Research Report found that "AID's new agricultural projects seem to be aimed less at food production or directly helping the rural poor than at expanding the output of commercial crops and promoting agricultural exports."[50]

German Catalan, a regional director of the Guatemalan Ministry of Agriculture's extension service, said that, because of AID funding, most of his agency's work has been the promotion of nontraditional crops. He said: "Diversification may work if there is a market. We have shown that a small grower can increase his income with diversification. But the opportunities are so limited. It depends on the U.S. market, and now there seems to be so much competition to send winter vegetables to the United States. The only market we have is the United States, because here in San Marcos people don't eat and cannot afford broccoli and snow peas. Diversification is a solution for very few small farmers. It is almost impossible for small growers who live in the isolated areas of the *Altiplano* to diversify their production. Right now, they don't even have enough land to produce the corn to feed themselves."[51]

Roads for Barefoot Farmers

In Guatemala, where over half of the rural population are seriously malnourished, none of the four main agricultural programs address the lack of sufficient local food production and distribution. The Highlands Agricultural Development Project involves nontraditional crop production and the maintenance of rural-access roads. The Small Farmer Development Project is mainly a roadbuilding project. In 1985, the Farm-to-Market Roads Project stressed the importance of rural-road maintenance. And the Small Farmer Diversification Project finances "research on diversified crop technologies to shift production from basic grains to higher value fruits and vegetables."

Over $9 million of the $16 million Small Farmer Development Project has been used to build rural roads in the Highlands, which AID says will enable small farmers to get nontraditional crops to the market. But as a government agronomist pointed out: "You'll see that there is a military outpost at the end of all the new roads. The roads are for the security of the country. The government has never been concerned about the welfare of the Indians in the *Altiplano*. The Indians say, 'We have our backs, we have our mules, and we have our paths. We don't need roads because we don't have cars.'"

The agronomist went on to describe one case with which he was familiar. The government told an Indian community in the El Quiché department that it wanted to build a new road. "But the people said they didn't want a road. They were afraid it would bring more military. They wanted the government to build a health center. But they got a road because AID and the military wanted to build one."[52]

Gary Smith, a U.S. Department of Agriculture (USDA) consultant for AID in Guatemala, said, "The first thing that these roads do is to get the military out to where the action is. Secondarily, they may help the small *campesinos* get some services. But it is an illusion that these roads will mean that farmers will diversify. It is hard for those that live near the main highway to Guatemala City to market their vegetables let alone the Indian peasants in northern El Quiché."[53]

Land Titling

Instead of true land redistribution, AID tends to fund programs that give limited legal rights to farmers without clear title to the land they farm and colonization programs that resettle landless *campesinos* on government land in remote areas.

Commenting on AID's activities in Honduras, Esteban Enriquez of the National Campesino Union (UNC) said, "The land titling program is a conservative project that aims to protect private property and to promote the interests of the bourgeoisie. What the *campesino* needs is more land and technical help, but most foreign aid supports the land titling program which mostly benefits the medium-sized coffee growers. It is not agrarian reform that they are doing. It is something more conventional."

The Politics of Food Aid

In the typical U.S. city, the flag waves in front of the post office, school, and fire station. An occasional patriotic gas station or car dealer will also display 10-foot flags as an advertising gimmick. But in Central America, the U.S. red, white, and blue brightens the packages, cans, and bags of food that millions eat every day.

You can see them everywhere—the market place of San Vicente, El Salvador, the model villages of the Guatemalan Highlands, and the Miskito refugee camps in Honduras. Under the flag come the words "Donated by the People of the United States of America. Not to be sold or exchanged." Central American families are constantly reminded of the "goodwill" of the "people" of the United States—whether it is emblazoned on a can of cooking oil or on an old grain bag that now holds most of their possessions.

A major element in U.S foreign policy in Central America, food aid props up governments that Washington favors and helps them win the support of the hungry population. The Marshall Plan in post-war Europe sparked the food aid program. "Food," said Secretary of State George Marshall, "is a vital factor in our foreign policy."[54] In the 1950s, food aid also became an essential factor in U.S. domestic policy. Congress expanded the food aid program when it passed Public Law 480 (PL480) or the Food for Peace program in 1954, which was designed "to increase consumption of U.S. agricultural commodities, improve the foreign relations of the United States, and for other purposes." Washington and U.S. agribusiness discovered that food aid was an ideal way to unload the country's agricultural surplus while simultaneously developing future commercial markets for U.S. food products.

The United States may be the biggest, but it is not the only food benefactor to the region. The United Nations also distributes food up and down the isthmus. Most UN food goes to refugees and displaced people and comes primarily from U.S. donations (bearing the U.S. emblem) to the UN's World Food Program.

Stabilization Tool

There are two main types of food aid under PL480: Titles I and II. Title I food is sold to allied governments on concessionary terms, usually with 2 to 5 percent interest over a 20- to 40-year repayment period. Recipient governments resell Title I food at market prices and use the income to finance public expenditures. The aid also helps financially strapped governments by enabling them to import food without spending scarce foreign exchange. In its regional strategy plan for Latin America, AID explains that Title I is necessary "to preserve political stability and prevent severe decline in employment and living standards during periods of adjustments."

AID points out that PL480 plays "an important role in providing balance-of-payments support [and] makes it a valuable supplement to direct AID resources. It is similar to ESF in many respects. It increases, sometimes substantially, the magnitude of the total assistance package we are able to offer governments, and this increases our ability to influence their decisions."[55] Tom King, an AID official in El Salvador, put it this way: "PL480 is very important for the foreign exchange crunch. . . . It also keeps wheat in the country—there's plenty of pasta, spaghetti, bread, etc."[56]

Before 1980, AID targeted very little Title I food to Central America. In the case of El Salvador, less than $1 million in Title I shipments went to the country from 1946–1979, but close to $140 million was delivered from 1980–1984. Title I food aid as a component of total food aid to El Salvador rose from 55 percent in 1980 to 90 percent in 1984.

No Title I food was allotted for Costa Rica until 1982, but in 1983 the country was already receiving nearly $28 million. "Without this food aid, Costa Rica would be in real trouble," commented a U.S. Embassy official.[57] One country without the benefit of Title I shipments is Nicaragua, which since 1980 has been cut off from this assistance.

Besides stabilizing Central American governments, Title I agreements enable the United States to direct local currency earned by governments from Title I sales to domestic pacification programs. In Guatemala, the AID Mission specified that the income earned from Title I sales be used in the Highlands for road-building, food-for-work programs, and other projects that are part of the Guatemalan government's pacification plan. In El Salvador, Title I income is used by the government under a plan devised by AID for refugee resettlement and for its National Plan of pacification.

Title I food agreements are officially categorized as concessionary sales. A recent study by the U.S. Government Accounting Office (GAO) found that these payments are not being collected. The study revealed that El Salvador made no payments on its food aid debt from 1981–1983.[58]

Food for Pacification

The other main type of the PL480 program, Title II, refers to the channeling of basic food commodities like corn and vegetable oil through the UN's World Food Program (WFP) and international humanitarian organizations like Catholic Relief Services for distribution to the hungry and malnourished.[59] Worldwide, the United States supplies about 25 percent of the commodities distributed by the World Food Program. In Central America, as much as 95 percent of UN food in countries like El Salvador comes from the United States.[60] In recent years, UN food distribution has increased tremendously. From 1980 to 1984, the WFP deliveries increased almost 20 times in Guatemala and over 3 times in El Salvador.[61]

In both El Salvador and Guatemala, the local military commanders play a major role in the distribution of WFP food. In Guatemala, WFP and other Title II food is distributed mainly in the Highlands, the major location of the government's pacification program. The military entices refugees into its model villages with promises of food, and it uses food-for-work programs to maintain control. Explaining the strategic value of food aid, an official of the army's civil-affairs division said, "If the subversives had invited these people to go with them, but had given them a means of subsistence . . . these people maybe would be winning."[62]

Title II food deliveries play a similar role in the pacification program in El Salvador. The food is given to displaced persons living under government control, but not to the displaced and needy in zones of guerrilla influence. With food-for-work projects, the military can keep refugees under its supervision while they carry out development programs like roadbuilding and housing construction. Food recipients must carry an identification card issued by the Salvadoran government, making it possible for the military to closely monitor a large population group.

Press reports have revealed that PL480 food finds its way into the barracks of El Salvador.[63] Some of the PL480 food also winds up in the marketplaces of El Salvador, even though the containers all say "Not to be sold or exchanged." The use of food aid in Central America is reminiscent of similar programs during the Vietnam War, when food aid was also an integral part of U.S. presence. During the Vietnam War years, one half of all PL480 deliveries went to Vietnam and Cambodia. The food was sold to pay the South Vietnamese army. PL480 also fed the Vietnamese who were moved into "strategic hamlets" as part of the counterinsurgency program. As in Vietnam, the Central American Food for Peace program is really food to pacify.

TABLE 3D

FOOD AID (PL480) TO CENTRAL AMERICA
FY 1946-1985, BY COUNTRY
($ million)

Country	1946-1979	1980-1984	1985
Belize	3.0	0	0
Costa Rica	19.1	72.0	21.4
El Salvador	34.3	169.7	52.7
Guatemala	59.3	35.0	25.4
Honduras	23.3	59.2	18.4
Nicaragua	25.4	19.6	0
Panama	21.0	6.6	0
REGION	182.4	362.1	117.7

SOURCES: AID, *U.S. Overseas Loans and Grants, July 1, 1945–September 30, 1984*; Elizabeth Hunt, AID, October 24, 1985.

White Bread vs. Corn Tortillas

While PL480 often adversely affects local markets and food-production systems, it has been a boon for the U.S. trade balance. The U.S. Department of Agriculture declares that "PL480 is one of the U.S.'s most successful market development tools."[64] Seven of the top ten nations that purchase U.S. agricultural products were formerly recipients of U.S. food aid.

The PL480 program changes the dietary patterns in recipient countries. In countries like Nicaragua, people became accustomed to wheat as their staple food from PL480 shipments. When the food shipments ceased in the early 1980s, consumers still wanted bread at their dinner tables instead of corn-based tortillas. At the U.S. Embassies in Central America, the U.S. Foreign Agriculture Service sponsors food fairs that exhibit U.S. food products and has even introduced programs in schools to show students how to bake with wheat.

PL480 primarily benefits the grain trading and milling companies. Over the last three decades, almost $35 billion worth of U.S. agricultural commodities have been exported to foreign countries under PL480. The major grain companies like Cargill and Continental Grain handle all this trade. Nearly 40 percent of all U.S. grain exports are shipped under PL480.[65] And when the grain arrives in the ports of Central American nations, U.S. corporations like Pillsbury, Cargill, and Ralston Purina are there to mill the grain into flour for local bakeries or produce feed for cattle companies (10 percent of Title I food to Central America is really cattle and chicken feed).

Both Title I and Title II of PL480 enable recipient governments to postpone necessary reforms like land redistribution and programs to assist small farmers, while they create economic and political dependency. Because Title I food is sold on the market to those who can afford it, it fails to reach those most in need. PL480 acts as a disincentive to local producers by increasing the supply of food in the market. Despite these serious drawbacks, President Reagan called the PL480 program "one of the greatest humanitarian acts ever performed by one nation for the needy of other nations."[66]

Commodity Credits for Cooperating Countries

The Commodity Credit Corporation (CCC) is another U.S. food program employed in Central America. CCC guarantees U.S. agricultural exporters payment for their commodities purchased by foreign buyers. CCC covers 98 percent of the value of their goods and 8 percent of the interest. Like the guarantees offered by Eximbank, CCC credits make it easier for Central American nations to purchase U.S. food.

Studies by the Comptroller General's office concluded that the CCC programs mean "substantial economic benefits in the form of domestic budget and balance-of-payments support" for recipient governments.[67] The credits allow governments to buy food commodities at lower than average prices and then resell those products on their domestic markets for a substantial profit.

In the past, CCC officials made credit allocation decisions themselves. Since 1980, however, the State Department has participated in decision making about the CCC program in Central America. Despite the precarious state of the region's economy, CCC credits have soared. Before 1980, only $16 million in CCC credits were offered to Central America. In contrast, from 1980 to 1984 close to $300 million in CCC credits were granted to the region. The two largest beneficiaries were El Salvador and Guatemala. In 1984, Guatemala alone received $72 million in CCC credits—which covered most of Guatemala's food purchases from the United States that year.

Latin America Commodities Report, a respected business newsletter published in London, observed that "commercial agricultural credits offer a more discreet way for the Reagan administration to assist controversial military regimes such as Guatemala and Chile because they do not require Congressional approval."[68]

PVOs: Funding for Loyalty

Another face of the U.S. government's presence in Central America is the increasing activity of private voluntary organizations (PVOs), which are nonprofit, private organizations, many of which receive AID funds for their humanitarian and development projects. In some cases, government money covers almost the entire budget of a PVO. The American Institute for Free Labor Development (AIFLD) receives 96 percent of its funding from AID, while other PVOs like CARE and Project Hope depend on U.S. government grants for about 50 percent of their funding.

Washington's new geopolitical interest in Central America has attracted an upsurge of PVO activity in the region. PVO projects range from population control and food distribution to business consulting. Some PVOs came to the region for humanitarian reasons and try to avoid any association with the foreign-policy strategies of the United States, while others like AIFLD are clearly instruments of U.S. policy.

Assisting the Private Sector with Public Funds

A growing number of PVOs working in Central America promote a private-business approach to economic development. The International Executive Service Corps (IESC), founded by David Rockefeller, encourages retired business executives to volunteer their time helping business in foreign countries. Derogatorily referred to as the "Paunch Corps," IESC assists such Central American businesses as Coca-Cola, TACA Airlines, the right-wing *El Diario de Hoy* in San Salvador, and world-class Honduras Maya Hotel. In Costa Rica, an IESC consultant prepared a master plan for a modern, perpetual-care cemetery. Also in Costa Rica, IESC gave assistance to a Colgate-Palmolive subsidiary that produces cookies and crackers for the Central American market.

Numerous PVOs profess to use AID funds to help small farmers. But most often the aid does not end up in the hands of the really small farmers but goes to medium-size farmers that already have experience in commercial marketing. PVOs like Technoserve and Agricultural Cooperative Development International (ACDI) encourage farmers to grow nontraditional cash crops that are sold to U.S. brokers. Another PVO, the Pan American Development Foundation (PADF), sets up national "development foundations" throughout Central America to channel bilateral and multilateral aid into the region's private sector.

In Belize, PADF assisted the Peace Corps on a project to expand cocoa production by small farmers who contract with Hershey Foods. Other PVOs that focus on private-sector development are Winrock International, Partnership for Productivity, and Project Sustain.

Volunteering for Pacification

The use of PVOs by the U.S. government to further pacification plans in El Salvador and Guatemala and to assist Nicaraguan refugees has caused much controversy in the U.S. PVO community. Since 1983, AID has been petitioning

PVOs to manage pacification-related programs. The American Council of Voluntary Agencies for Foreign Service (now merged into a group called InterAction) reported an almost desperate search by AID for PVOs willing to work with the governments of El Salvador and Guatemala. Many PVOs have repeatedly refused to work with AID in El Salvador or Guatemala, but others are playing an essential role in the pacification plans of those countries.

The controversy dates back to the Vietnam War when PVOs like the Salvation Army, CARE, Catholic Relief Services (CRS), World Vision, Save the Children, and Project Hope received AID funding for their work in the CORDS pacification program. John Rigby, former director of International Voluntary Service, said the agency was "burned" in Vietnam. "We finally realized you can't be working where there's a shooting war, take funds from one of the combatants, and still be true to your neutrality."[69]

As they did in Vietnam, PVOs in El Salvador are managing programs in community development, food distribution, and refugee resettlement that are part of the government's pacification plans. Dave Kornfield, World Relief's Latin American director, observed that AID was going from PVO to PVO "looking for ways to use their funds, covered by humanitarian agencies, so that they can carry out their objectives under cover." He said, "That makes the humanitarian agencies a simple extension of their foreign policy."[70]

In both Guatemala and El Salvador, the pacification plans include the relocation of displaced and terrorized populations into army zones of control. To assist in this effort, the U.S. government has provided food and medical supplies to displaced persons and has funded work and economic development programs for "model villages" set up by the governments.

In El Salvador, Project Hope embarked on a major health care project for displaced persons. Project Hope officials told a nurse interviewing for the program that "they were definitely going in with the U.S. line, very much on the side of the U.S. government" and that "we'd be going around in government helicopters for our safety."[71]

AID funded Project Hope to work with the Salvadoran government agency CONADES on a survey of the displaced. Many refugees have refused to register with CONADES because they fear its close connections with the Salvadoran military. A military officer sits on the board of CONADES in each community. Project Hope also received AID funds to work with a low-cost housing program that would resettle displaced persons on abandoned Phase 1 agrarian cooperative lands. In El Salvador and Guatemala, Project Hope distributed supplies collected by the Knights of Malta, an elite right-wing Catholic organization.

Other PVOs in El Salvador include Save the Children, AIFLD, and Technoserve, all of which receive AID funds to work on rural development programs as part of the country's agrarian reform. The IESC has received a special grant to work with small businesses and farmers. Catholic Relief Services distributes U.S. food, and the Overseas Education Fund assists community development in government zones.

An official of a relief program in El Salvador said, "There is a strategy of depopulation of guerrilla-controlled zones, much of it by bombing. There exists an organizational link between this military strategy—which creates refugees— and the humanitarian strategy to feed, care for, and pacify those refugees. It is politics disguised as humanitarian assistance."[72] Gary Cozette, a Presbyterian observer from the Ecumenical Food Program, which distributes food to over 20,000 displaced persons, said that working with AID programs means "working with a government which gives bombs on the one hand and food on the other."[73]

Father Octavio Cruz of the Catholic Church's Caritas program agreed with this view: "We have not and will not take AID money because we consider that the United States is not a neutral government. Its humanitarian aid comes within a counterinsurgency package."

In 1984, AID tried to maneuver around the objections of Caritas by asking Catholic Relief Services (CRS) to deliver AID food to Caritas. Regional Caritas director Monsignor Roland Bordelon stated in 1984: "No matter how much U.S. AID denies this, the plan is a highly political 'pacification program.'"[74]

In Guatemala, many PVOs abandoned their projects in the Highlands when government repression worsened in 1979. But since 1983, the AID Mission has encouraged PVOs to return to the Highlands. The main PVOs that have yielded to U.S. pressure are CARE, Project Hope, and the Salvation Army. The Penny Foundation, a Guatemalan PVO, is using AID funds to finance the voluntary sale of agricultural land by large landowners. This land-marketing program is Guatemala's version of agrarian reform. The Penny Foundation is also working with the Guatemalan government in sponsoring land sales within the model villages.

The Salvation Army and Project Hope along with a Guatemalan PVO called PAVA (Program of Assistance to the Inhabitants of the Highlands) received funds from AID's Displaced Persons Resettlement Project. This organization works with the military and the Committee for National Reconstruction (CRN) to resettle refugees in the *Altiplano*. Many of these refugees have been placed in "model villages" created by the Guatemalan military government. A principal figure in PAVA is Harris Whitbeck, who was public-relations adviser to former president Ríos Montt.

CARE has projects in Guatemala's Northern Transverse Strip, where it is working on an AID-funded colonization program that is part of the military's pacification plans for the critical area along the Mexican border. CARE distributes food rations to resettle refugees and sponsors a cardamom cultivation and export project.

An official of the Salvation Army acknowledged that AID told the PVO that it would have a better chance of being funded if it agreed to work in the Highlands. AID approached the Salvation Army repeatedly but with no success. Finally, the AID request was approved by the Guatemala office of the Salvation Army but then turned down on a regional level. The request then went to the national board, which overrode the regional veto. According to the same Salvation Army official, the national directors agreed to the AID request based on the argument that the Salvation Army is a nonpolitical organization so it cannot refuse aid for political reasons. "But they don't see the other side. They don't understand that it's just as political to be giving aid."

In Honduras, PVOs receive U.S. aid to work with Nicaraguan refugees. World Relief coordinates refugee work in the area of Mocoron where most Miskitos live. Save the Children, CARE, and the Peace Corps also work with Miskito refugees.

In its 1983 budget presentation to Congress, AID said that PVOs perform a critical role in "achieving development goals in many situations." It said that "PVOs are often able to work in circumstances impossible for the U.S. government and reflect very directly the goodwill of the American people themselves."[75] In testimony to Congress, Douglas Hellinger of the Development Group for Alternative Policies warned that many PVOs are increasingly willing to compromise their own independence for additional AID funding. He called this "funding for loyalty." "It is clear," said Hellinger, "that AID is intent to utilize PVOs to its own advantage."[76]

Addressing the issue of private relief agencies, a coalition of PVO officials, including Oxfam America, Moravian Church, and Church World Service, published a statement in mid-1985 that advised the U.S. government "to take special care not to compromise the impartiality of private agencies. . . . We should also point out that just because an organization calls itself 'private' and is channelling contributions from American citizens to people in other countries, its work does not thereby necessarily qualify as humanitarian."

TABLE 3E

PVOs THAT RECEIVE FUNDS FROM AID
FOR PROGRAMS IN CENTRAL AMERICA
(partial list, grouped by category of program)

Name of PVO	Percent of Funds from U.S. Gov't.
Business	
Credit Union National Assn	82
Technical assistance for credit union development	
International Executive Service Corps	54
Management and technical assistance consulting	
National Association of the Partners of the Alliance	67
Supports technical assistance exchange program	
New TransCentury Foundation	100
Management consulting service to private agencies	

Name of PVO	Percent of Funds from U.S. Gov't.
Pan American Development Foundation	55
Finances private sector development activities	
Technoserve	44
Technical Assistance to self-help enterprises	
Winrock Int'l Livestock Research & Training Center	33
Research/training in animal agriculture	

Development

CARE	45
Relief and development programs	
National Rural Electric Cooperative Association	45
Technical assistance for electrification projects	
Private Agencies Collaborating Together	98
International consortium of private development agencies	
Save the Children Federation	51
Child sponsorship and self-help organization	
Volunteers in Technical Assistance	86
Technology design and problem solving for development	

Population

Pathfinder Fund	90
Family planning program development	
Planned Parenthood Federation of America	77
Family planning services	

Religious

Catholic Relief Services—USCC	66
Overseas aid and development	
Church World Service	34
Disaster relief and development programs	
Salvation Army World Service	47
Community services	
World Relief Corporation	29
Promotes emergency relief activities	
World Vision Relief Organization	58
Provides food/medical relief supplies	

Services

American Institute for Free Labor Development	98
People to People Health Foundation (Project HOPE)	44
Education in health services	

SOURCE: AID, Bureau for Food for Peace and Voluntary Assistance, *Voluntary Foreign Aid Programs 1983–1984.*

AIFLD: Training for Moderation and Anticommunism

The American Institute for Free Labor Development (AIFLD) was founded in 1962 to promote anticommunist, pro-U.S. unions in Latin America. It was formed as a coalition of government, corporate, and labor interests that were concerned about the growth of what they saw as militant anti-imperialist unions of workers and peasants. AIFLD set out to train union members in the principles of "free trade unions" and instill in them the ideals of capitalist democracy. Although sponsored by the AFL-CIO and backed by many corporate leaders, AIFLD since its formation has received the vast majority of its funding from the U.S. government.

Like the Alliance for Progress, AIFLD was established largely as a reaction to the Cuban Revolution. AIFLD's first chairperson was J. Peter Grace of W.R. Grace & Company. Grace was a good friend of President Kennedy, who appointed him to head the influential Department of Commerce Committee of the Alliance for Progress. The committee's task was to evaluate the Alliance for Progress and to recommend ways the Alliance could further the interests of private enterprise in Latin America. Because of his simultaneous involvement in AIFLD, Grace also helped to direct the course of labor organizing in the hemisphere.

"We must bear in mind," said Grace, "that we cannot allow communist propaganda to divide us between liberals and conservatives, or between business and labor, or between the American people and their government."[77] The Grace Foundation of W.R. Grace & Company was a financial contributor to AIFLD. The foundation also gave to such groups as the American Council for the International Promotion of Democracy Under God, and Citizens for a Free Cuba.[78] Other corporations that offered financial support to AIFLD were United Fruit, Anaconda, Merck, and Pan American World Airways.

Training the American Way

Since 1962, AIFLD has trained over 100,000 union members through in-country seminars. Honduras leads the list of AIFLD in-country trainees with 2205 union members receiving AIFLD instruction in 1983 alone.[79] Besides the in-country sessions, AIFLD has trained hundreds of Central American labor leaders in the United States at its Front Royal Institute and the George Meany Center. Carefully selected unionists then continue education in labor economics at Georgetown or Loyola Universities.[80]

Regardless of location, AIFLD training emphasizes ideological instruction. Its course on "Political Theories in Central and South America" offers "intensive and comprehensive training for trade union leaders in the complex field of ideologies."[81] For Central Americans, AIFLD sponsors a special course about trade union work in the banana industry.

At the George Meany Center in Maryland, AIFLD runs a seven-week program that covers economics, trade unions, the political aspects of development, and democracy. Upon concluding their studies in the United States, the trade unionists begin a nine-month "salaried internship program" financed by AIFLD.[82] Graduates of the course return home to organize free trade unions and to spread their newly acquired political knowledge. Through international secretariats, AIFLD operates a program that since 1976 has brought the enlistment of "128,000 new union members and the formation or re-establishment of more than 1000 unions in Latin America and the Caribbean."[83]

Extolling the virtues of the American Institute for Free Labor Development to his corporate colleagues, J. Peter Grace said, "Through AIFLD, business, labor, and the government have come together to work toward a common goal in Latin America, namely supporting the democratic form of government, the capitalistic system and general well-being of the individual. It is an outstanding example of national consensus. . . ."[84]

This unity among labor, business, and government is now less official since J. Peter Grace stepped down from his position with AIFLD, and all present board members are union representatives. Grace assured the board, however, that he and other corporate leaders would maintain "close and friendly" ties with AIFLD and its membership. This close relationship continues in another organization called the Friends of the Democratic Center in Central America (PRO-DEMCA), which formed in 1981 as the Citizens' Committee for Pro-Democratic Forces in Central America. Both J. Peter Grace and AIFLD's current director William Doherty are directors of PRODEMCA.

A new unit of AIFLD is its Agrarian Union Development Department (AUDD). AUDD encourages small to medium farmers to form associations that would facilitate access to credit and markets. Its most extensive work has been in El Salvador, but AUDD is also active in Guatemala, Costa Rica, and Honduras. AUDD *campesino* associations oppose land takeovers and militant demonstrations against lopsided land distribution patterns in the region.

Staying Away from Politics

In discussing his organization, AIFLD's information director John J. Heberle said, "We try to stay out of politics, but the people we're involved with are involved."[85] At least in Central America, AIFLD's efforts to stay out of politics are not discernible. AIFLD organized a coalition of peasants and workers to support the Christian Democratic Party in El Salvador, has an influential role in the anti-Sandinista Democratic Coordinating Committee in Nicaragua, and gave money to the campaign of a favored presidential candidate in Panama.

Then there is the covert side of AIFLD, which has frequently been accused of having close connections with the CIA. On one occasion, *Business Week* called the AFL-CIO's involvement in foreign unions "labor's own version of the CIA." In 1968, the *Washington Post* mentioned that William C. Doherty Jr., the executive director of AIFLD, was involved in CIA operations. But it was Philip Agee, former CIA operative and author of *Inside the Company: CIA Diary*, who detailed the alliance of the CIA and AIFLD in Latin America. Agee described AIFLD as a "CIA-controlled labor center financed through AID [with] programs in adult education and social projects used as a front for covering trade-union organizing activity." Philip Agee labeled Doherty a "CIA agent in labor operations."[86]

Corporations with Latin American investments have good reason to back AIFLD, considering the organization's advocacy of capitalism. AIFLD's bills since 1962, however, have not been paid by private business but by the U.S. government. Grants from AID cover 96 percent of AIFLD's annual budget. When presenting AID's budget request to Congress, AID Administrator Peter McPherson said: "We need to have a free-labor movement in these countries and there needs to be some recognition of the role they can play in the private enterprise environment."[87] Congress has been generous to AIFLD. In 1984, AIFLD had over $50 million in contracts with AID.

AIFLD has operations in all seven Central American countries. Following is a brief description of its activity in each country.

AIFLD in Central America

Belize: Since the nation's independence from Britain in 1981, AIFLD has worked with the Trade Union Congress in an effort to build a U.S.-affiliated union movement.

Costa Rica: In Costa Rica, AIFLD has counted on the firm support of President Monge, who was a founder of the AIFLD-affiliated Costa Rican Confederation of Labor and formerly served as general secretary of ORIT. With a special grant from AID, AIFLD operates a Campesino Union Strengthening project that aims to fortify the "democratic agrarian union movement" in Costa Rica. It is trying to build up the small rural component of the Costa Rican Confederation of Democratic Workers (CCTD) to oppose the growing militancy in the Costa Rican countryside. Asked if any of the AIFLD unions in Costa Rica supported the 1984 banana strikes, Roberto Cazares, AIFLD's regional director, replied: "We don't strike, we're democratic. Those are communist unions." Expressing a common AIFLD philosophy toward strikes, Cazares said that they "cause unrest in the country" and "may mean that the company will go broke."[88]

El Salvador: AIFLD has proved to be a critical part of Washington's pacification strategy in El Salvador. AIFLD has trained leaders of the General Confederation of Unions (CGS), the union with connections to the governing party of the military. Its anticommunist line and close association with government bureaucrats made the CGS an ideal instrument for AIFLD in El Salvador. Because of its support for the military dictatorship, CGS was expelled from the International Confederation of Free Trade Unions in 1979.

AIFLD signed an agreement in 1962 with AID and the Salvadoran Ministry of Agriculture to train *campesino* leaders as part of the Alliance for Progress. AIFLD's current executive director, William Doherty Jr., joined AIFLD's program in El Salvador in 1966 and organized a series of seminars with *campesino* leaders and the Christian Democratic Party. The Christian Democrats and AIFLD wanted to organize the peasant population as a base of support for the political party. They also saw the need for a *campesino* organization that would take support away from the more militant federations that were gaining strong support in the countryside. In mid-1968, AIFLD brought together 20 local groupings of *campesinos* to form the Salvadoran Communal Union (UCS). While other associations were targeted by death squads and military repression in the 1970s, UCS was comparatively free to continue its work.

During the 1970s, AIFLD groomed UCS to play a crucial role in an agrarian reform program. Its chance came in 1980 when Washington backed a civilian/military government that announced a land distribution program. AIFLD technicians entered the country in droves that year, setting up their office in the top two floors of the Hotel Sheraton.

AIFLD consultants played a larger role in the design of the Salvadoran agrarian reform than did the government's own Institute for Agrarian Transformation. The beneficiaries of the land distribution were organized by UCS and two new AIFLD peasant groups known as ACOPAI and ANIS. Besides its involvement in the agrarian reform program, AIFLD rallied its associated unions in El Salvador to support the U.S.-sponsored elections from 1982–1985. In 1984, AIFLD created the Popular Democratic Unity (UPD) as an umbrella organization to campaign for the Christian Democrats.

AIFLD's role in El Salvador is to stabilize the political system by stabilizing the Christian Democratic government. It has served as an apologist for President Duarte even though he let the agrarian reform program wither away and did not protest the military's repression of the labor movement. In 1985, AIFLD took its support away from the UPD coalition, which had grown more belligerent as Duarte failed to deliver on his promises to help workers. It formed a new, more conservative organization called the Democratic Workers' Central (CTD), which it hoped would undermine the increasingly militant UPD.[89]

Guatemala: The AFL-CIO joined the anticommunist campaign against the progressive Arbenz government in 1954 when it sent a letter to President Arbenz demanding that he purge all communists from the government. The federation's *CIO News* regularly published virulent attacks against the leftward drift in Guatemala. After the CIA-directed coup that brought President Castillo Armas to power in 1954, unions that had formed and flourished during the previous 10-year period of progressive national politics were disbanded. At the urging of

Washington, Castillo Armas then invited AFL-CIO officials and the former Cuban Federation of Labor (under Batista) to "reorganize" the country's unions. In 1955, the Trade Union Council of Guatemala was formed as an affiliate of ORIT.

In 1983, AIFLD with the cooperation of President Ríos Montt began to reorganize the rural and urban workforce with the formation of the Confederation of Trade Union Unity (CUSG). A primary reason for the formation of the CUSG was so Guatemala could meet the "labor rights" requirements of the CBI program. AIFLD backs the National Campesino Confederation (CNC), an association of mostly small farmers. Because of their conservative politics, both unions experience less repression than other unions, although the CUSG has become increasingly progressive.

Honduras: After a prolonged strike in 1954, banana workers forced the companies to recognize their right to collective bargaining. Critical to the peaceful settlement of the strike was the mediation of ORIT advisers, who convinced the TNCs to negotiate an agreement with the workers. Working with the company, ORIT then proceeded to replace the most militant union leadership with ORIT-trained union leaders. This formed the basis of the conservative, anticommunist union movement in Honduras.

Albert Ruiz, a Honduran labor leader at the time, noted that before the 1954 strike, neither the AFL nor the CIO would offer Honduran workers the time of day:

> After the strike, the AFL-CIO, the U.S. Embassy, and ORIT have fallen on us like the plague, offering us scholarships to "study in Puerto Rico," and getting us all kinds of favors from our employers. . . . The U.S. consuls overwhelm us with visas. . . . The greatest interest in these scholarship students is to be found on the north coast, land of the Banana Companies. . . . Not only do these companies easily grant their permission for their workers to spend months on leave, but they are favored with the choicest jobs, and are placed, very "democratically" as union leaders, when they return . . .[90]

Receiving the cooperation of the military, ORIT sponsored the formation of 15 additional unions in Honduras within a year after the banana strike was settled. AIFLD continued ORIT's role of managing a passive union movement in Honduras. Today, AIFLD maintains close ties with the National Association of Campesinos and the Honduran Workers Federation. Besides keeping a lid on labor unrest, the AIFLD unions have backed the Honduran government's close alignment with U.S. foreign policy in the region.

At a 1983 conference at which AIFLD's Bernard Packer presided, the AIFLD-linked SITRATERCO banana union passed resolutions supporting the buildup of "our defense forces" because of the "warlike attitude of our neighbors."[91]

Nicaragua: The Confederation for Trade Union Unity (CUS) presented only minimal opposition to the Somoza dictatorship. Unlike the other unions, CUS had the privilege to organize openly during the Somoza regime. For that reason as well as its ties to the United States through AIFLD, CUS had little support among the country's workers. After 1979, AIFLD financial backing to CUS increased over fourfold within two years. In 1982, however, the Nicaraguan government effectively ended AIFLD's direct presence by asking two AIFLD officials to leave after one of them was identified as a U.S. intelligence agent.

AIFLD keeps its connection to CUS by funding U.S. speaking tours of CUS leaders. CUS (affiliated with ORIT) along with the Christian Democratic CTN (affiliated with CLAT) are members of the anti-Sandinista Democratic Coordinating Committee. In 1984, CUS members occupied the union's offices protesting the leadership's decision to remain part of the Democratic Coordinating Committee. Many CUS members disagree with Sandinista policies but do not want to be associated with the counterrevolution. Workers also objected to the alliance forged by CUS leadership with the conservative association of large business owners known as COSEP. Victoria Garcia de Castillo, the CUS representative in 1984 to the Council of State, said she wanted CUS to withdraw from the anti-Sandinista coalition which was "defending the interests of the business men of COSEP."[92] The split between leadership and rank and file on this important political question weakened the AIFLD union.

CUS has a relatively small membership of several thousand workers. Sebastian Castro, a representative of the government's Sandinista Workers Union (CST), said: "I've been participating in unions for a long time in Nicaragua, and never have I felt like they [CUS] do any work. All I ever see them doing is defending U.S. policy here in Nicaragua, which means being against the people of Nicaragua."[93]

Panama: AIFLD's contention that it does not get involved in politics contrasted with revelations in 1984 that it funneled money from PRODEMCA (see section on USIA) through an AIFLD labor organization in Panama to support the presidential candidacy of Ardito Barletta. Panama is well-connected with AIFLD through the Confederation of Panamanian Workers, whose secretary-general sits on AIFLD's international board.

While it has succeeded in dividing the labor movement and giving credibility to antilabor governments, AIFLD has failed to create a dynamic union movement that has wide popular support. Marcial Caballero, the president of the National Campesino Union in Honduras, said that AIFLD unions are weak because of their overly compromising philosophy about labor/management relations. "AIFLD promotes a strategy that says there can be cooperation between the worker and the boss," explained Caballero. "However, we believe and have found it to be true that only by pressure and through struggle does the boss give concessions to the workers."[94]

As the political conflict builds in Central America, unionists in the United States have become more aware of the repression suffered by Central American workers and of AIFLD's strategic role in supporting U.S. foreign policy. Progressive rank and file unionists have demanded that the AFL-CIO separate itself from AIFLD for the following reasons:

- Weak unions in Central America mean that U.S. TNCs are more likely to transfer operations from the United States to the region.
- Increased repression causes migration of Central Americans to the United States looking for jobs.
- Governments backed by AIFLD in El Salvador, Honduras, and Guatemala undermine independent trade unions' activities.
- Strong unions in both the United States and Central America are necessary to reduce poverty and increase expendable income.

Peace Corps: A Changing Role

Peace Corps volunteers these days might never go near a mud hut or talk to a *campesino*. Some work directly out of the chambers of commerce trying to drum up U.S. investment, while others provide technical assistance like bookkeeping to small businesses. In Costa Rica, Guatemala, Belize, and Honduras, Peace Corps volunteers produce investment-feasibility studies and develop plans for promising agribusiness operations that will involve U.S. businesses. Other volunteers draw up investment profiles of their host countries or distribute technical information from the U.S. Department of Commerce that promotes the purchase of U.S. products.

Gone is the philosophy that the Peace Corps should help the most needy. Today the Peace Corps is the "Peace Corporation" where the emphasis is on private enterprise. Directing this new thrust is the Private Sector Office of the Peace Corps. An increasing number of Peace Corps projects assist in nontraditional cash-crop production to help commercial farmers take advantage of the Caribbean Basin Initiative provisions. "We are excited about what input we can have into CBI," exclaimed Peace Corps Director Loret Miller Ruppe.[95]

In 1980, there were only 354 Peace Corps volunteers in all Central America. Although the Peace Corps withdrew its contingent from El Salvador and Nicaragua in 1980, the total number of volunteers in Central America grew to 643 in 1984 in the remaining countries. In line with the recommendations of the Kissinger Commission, the Peace Corps plans to send an additional 1500 volunteers to the region between 1985 and 1989.

Philosophical Green Berets

The Peace Corps expansion campaign is known as the Peace Corps' Initiative for Central America. It has been proposed that the expanded Peace Corps include a "literacy corps" in Guatemala to "teach Spanish to Mayan Indian dialect speakers."[96] This will complement the Guatemalan army's own plans to incorporate the Indian population into "the national identity." A similar plan is now in effect in Honduras. The Kissinger Commission recommended the literacy corps as an apparent response to the highly successful "literacy brigades" that produced spectacular increases in Nicaraguan literacy rates (in native languages) after the revolution. Director Ruppe kicked off the organization's drive to find new Spanish-speaking volunteers with a speech at the Miami Chamber of Commerce. Miami was selected, she said, because of its large bilingual population (mostly Cuban Americans).

New Peace Corps volunteers are given lectures on ideology to prepare them for their experience in Central America. Among other topics, the trainees receive instruction on the "philosophy, tactics, and menace of Communism."[97] Former Peace Corps director Sargent Shriver said that ideological instruction has grown more intense since he left the agency. "We didn't think we ought to make them into philosophical Green Berets," commented Shriver.[98]

The Returned Peace Corps Volunteers Committee on Central America opposes the Peace Corps expansion in Central America. Francine Dionne, a spokesperson for the group, said, "They have declared the Peace Corps an instrument of U.S. foreign policy and a tool of the Reagan administration."[99]

USIA: Information for Central America

The United States Information Agency (USIA), the official U.S. propaganda organization, promotes U.S. policies and way of life. The USIA sponsors speaking tours in Central America on U.S. policy and funds an International Visitors Program that brings thousands of Central Americans to the United States for tours and education. USIA's Voice of America (VOA) "tells America's story" on its radio waves throughout the world. The VOA's latest thrust is Project Truth, which counters Soviet statements about U.S. foreign policy and disseminates information about the positive aspects of U.S. life. VOA has grown dramatically since President Reagan took office, increasing its budget by 70 percent from 1981 to 1984.

Amplifying America's Voice

Voice of America designated Central America as one of its priority areas in the world. In 1984, VOA signed agreements to expand operations in Belize and Costa Rica. The two new stations are part of a greater plan for 11 new VOA transmitters in the Caribbean Basin.

In Guatemala, Voice of America started broadcasting its program "Buenos Dias, America" for the first time in 1983. According to VOA, the program informs "Latin America about the true reality of Guatemala."[100]

Inaugurated in 1985, Radio Costa Rica programs originate from a station located near Costa Rica's northern border with Nicaragua and is expected to reach Managua. U.S. Ambassador Curtin Winsor said the radio station offers an alternative to "the vile propaganda and hate spewed forth by the regime in Managua and the Cubans." Nicaragua's foreign minister retorted that by supporting the installation of the VOA transmitter the Costa Rican government "appears to be supporting the policy of aggression against Nicaragua, thereby casting doubt on Costa Rica's proclamation of neutrality."[101]

Because Costa Rican law prohibits foreign interests from broadcasting in the country, VOA funded the local Association for Information and Culture to establish Radio Costa Rica. Thirteen Costa Rican business owners formed the association specifically to contract with the VOA for Radio Costa Rica. Although the broadcasting of a medium-wave radio system into another country is a violation of Costa Rica's constitution, a diplomat at the U.S. Embassy in Costa Rica said "radio transmitters don't function according to borders."[102]

A number of smaller short-wave stations not directly associated with VOA have also been broadcasting into Nicaragua. The Honduran-based *contras* set up Radio 15 of September (independence day from Spain in 1821) in 1981. Another CIA-funded station in Honduras is Radio Miscut, which broadcasts in the languages of the Miskito Indians. From Costa Rica comes the Voice of Free Nicaragua, which was set up by the ARDE *contras*. The station claimed to be transmitting from "somewhere in the high mountains of Nicaragua," but was later discovered to be broadcasting from northern Costa Rica.[103]

The U.S. government is also financing yet another dimension of this "air war" against Nicaragua. Two Costa Rican television stations are installing three television transmitters in northern Costa Rica, which will broadcast television signals into Nicaragua stronger than that of the Sandinista government's own television programming. According to an engineer working on the new television transmitters, "They're going to have a tremendous signal, the most powerful in Central America. It's going to just blast across the border."[104]

To Further Understanding

USIA's leadership training program brings Central American students to the United States to "familiarize them with the American system and the principles of democracy." Together with AID, USIA coordinates Central America Peace Scholarships which plans to bring 10,000 Central Americans to the United States for training in the next five years. The U.S. government also trains Central American students within the region at the USIA-funded Binational Centers in Costa Rica and Honduras.

Through its office in the U.S. Embassy in each country, USIA maintains contact with the local press. It distributes news releases to the daily newspapers and places films and news programs with local television and radio stations. In El Salvador, all the major radio stations receive VOA programs. USIA news and cultural programs receive prime time showing on two Salvadoran television networks. A USIA book translation service based in the U.S. Embassy in San Salvador places 150 translated books each year as textbooks in some 20 Central American universities. USIA's priority in El Salvador is "to work with U.S. and third-country journalists to further their understanding of U.S. policy in El Salvador and Central America."[105]

War of Ideas

Not only does USIA propagate the U.S. government's views, but it also is concerned that friends in the third world get their information out to the U.S. public. The USIA has funded a U.S. right-wing public-relations agency called the Mid-America Committee for International Business and Government Operation to instruct third-world governments on ways to achieve better relations with the U.S. press. In 1983, USIA paid the agency $170,000 to conduct a series of seminars for third-world politicians and military officers. "The purpose of these seminars," said the USIA contract, "is to provide media-training assistance to [foreign] government officials and their armed forces . . . [and] to strengthen their effectiveness in the 'War of Ideas.'"

The owner of the agency contracted to perform these services is Ian MacKenzie, formerly the registered agent and publicity man for the late Anastasio Somoza. After his contract with the Nicaraguan dictator was suddenly terminated by the 1979 Sandinista revolution, MacKenzie found lucrative work as the public-relations agent for Haiti's Jean-Claude "Baby Doc" Duvalier.

The first of MacKenzie's seminars concerned the "War of Ideas" in Latin America. Among the officials who attended the information workshop were representatives from the right-wing regimes in Guatemala and Chile and four officials from El Salvador, including representatives from the armed forces, the Defense Ministry, and the extreme right-wing ARENA party.[106]

A behind-the-scenes force in the war of ideas in El Salvador is the shadowy Venezuelan Institute for Popular Education (IVEPO), the public-relations organization in San Salvador that manages the government's propaganda campaign. Depending on the CIA and other U.S. agencies for its funds, this organization of 72 employees manages the "communications policies" of the Salvadoran government.[107]

National Endowment for Democracy

In a speech before the British Parliament in 1982, President Reagan announced his support for a study to determine how the United States could more effectively contribute to the development of democratic values and institutions abroad. A subsequent $400,000 study by the American Political Foundation recommended the appropriation of $18 million to the USIA for a new organization called the National Endowment for Democracy (NED). Its executive director is Carl Gershman, the former senior counselor to Jeane Kirkpatrick. In the authorizing legislation, two organizations were singled out for funding by NED: the AFL-CIO's Free Trade Union Institute and the U.S. Chamber of Commerce's National Chamber Foundation.

In its first year, NED's $18 million was used as follows: $11 million to the Free Trade Union Institute, $1.7 million to the Center for International Private Enterprise of the National Chamber Foundation, $1.5 million to the National Democratic Institute for International Affairs, $1.5 million to the National Republican Institute for International Affairs (two organizations associated with Republican and Democratic parties), and $2.3 million for NED's administration and discretionary grants. In 1984, NED's budget for democracy promotion was increased to $31 million. Although 100 percent of NED's funding comes from U.S. tax dollars, it is exempt from public requests under the Freedom of Information Act.

In 1985, NED granted Caribbean Central American Action (CCAA) over $200,000 to organize a get-out-the-vote campaign for Guatemala's national assembly elections, which excluded left-of-center parties. The National Republican Institute for International Affairs (a unit of the U.S. Republican Party) worked alongside CCAA in Guatemala during the election campaign. In Panama, NED funded the YMCA International Division to "train young people in political leadership."

Democracy Building

NED has been used to establish another "democracy-building" organization called the Citizens' Committee for the Pro-Democratic Forces in Central America (PRODEMCA). Among those sitting on PRODEMCA's board of directors are: J. Peter Grace, chairperson of W.R. Grace; William C. Doherty, Jr., executive director of AIFLD; Orville Freeman, chairperson of Business International; Michael Novak of the American Enterprise Institute; William Simon, former Secretary of the Treasury; and Albert Shanker, president of the American Federation of Teachers. Its executive director is Mary Temple, who was formerly executive director of an organization called Land Council for Rural Progress in Developing Countries. The Land Council paid the salary of Roy Prosterman, while both he and Temple were designing land-reform programs in El Salvador.

PRODEMCA was formed primarily to coordinate an anti-Sandinista campaign in the United States and to lend support to the *contras*. Its first activity was to host a press conference featuring Arturo Cruz of the Democratic Coordinating Committee, an opposition party in Nicaragua that boycotted the 1984 elections and is allied with the *contras*.

According to PRODEMCA's principles of purpose, it will mount mail campaigns, distribute media resources, sponsor speaking tours to Central America and the United States, and maintain an information bank and clearinghouse to help the "friends of democracy" in Central America. In its first year, PRODEMCA gave $100,000 to *La Prensa*, the anti-Sandinista newspaper in Nicaragua. A PRODEMCA grant of $200,000 went to the Nicaraguan Center for Democratic Studies, which was established by the Democratic Coordinating Committee. The center trains Nicaraguans "in the skills needed to sustain an independent democratic presence in Nicaraguan life."

Building Friendly Unions

A major thrust of NED is to counter antigovernment movements through the promotion of conservative trade unions closely tied to the United States. According to the AFL-CIO's Lane Kirkland, the union confederation reactivated its Free Trade Union Institute (FTUI, founded in 1978 as an arm of AFL-CIO's International Affairs Department) to implement the goals of the Kissinger Commission. Kirkland, William Doherty, and Albert Shanker as well as two other AFL-CIO officials serve on the board of the Free Trade Union Institute, which also has operations in Chile, the Philippines, Poland and South Africa.

In Guatemala, FTUI announced that it would support the Guatemalan Confederation of Trade Union Unity (CUSG). The FTUI says that "the labor movement was reborn, after a nightmare of years of persecution, with the formation of the [CUSG]." This group, added FTUI, "has raised the hopes of Guatemalan workers for an authentic democratic solution." FTUI failed to mention that then-President General Efraín Ríos Montt allowed the formation of the CUSG in 1983 to gain working-class support for his military regime and to weaken the popular appeal of the eight-year-old National Committee of Trade Union Unity (CNUS). The CUSG, which groups together unions tied to AIFLD and the Christian-Democratic-oriented Latin American Confederation of Workers (CLAT), has scant rank-and-file support in Guatemala.

Other unions receiving FTUI support are the Confederation of Honduran Workers, a conservative AIFLD-linked trade union associated with the Liberal Party government. In Nicaragua, FTUI funds go to the Confederation of Labor Unity (CUS), which represents less than 2 percent of Nicaraguan trade union members. CUS, which is closely linked to the Democratic Coordinating Committee, has called for renewed aid to the anti-Sandinista *contras*.[108]

In the Name of Development

In Vietnam, Washington called it the "other war." Along with massive military aid, the United States injected vast sums of economic aid into South Vietnam. The "other war" drew on the entire arsenal of U.S. foreign economic aid programs to shore up the shaky South Vietnamese government. In the midst of the fighting, AID tried to "win the hearts and minds" of the peasants with food-distribution and rural-development programs.

The "other war" has re-emerged in Central America. In the name of development and democracy, President Reagan is pouring economic assistance into the troubled region. Washington's economic commitment to the region has been staggering. The economic assistance for 1980–1984 was double the assistance given from World War II through 1979. Washington plans to double again the levels of aid by the end of the decade.

The president has told U.S. citizens that this huge expenditure will fund programs to eliminate the root causes of subversion. But a close look at these programs exposes another reality. The build-up of economic aid programs in Central America is little more than a second front of a larger counterinsurgency campaign. Like military aid, economic aid programs are being used to beat back encroaching pressures for change—not to deal with the roots of the crisis.[109]

If the United States were truly interested in promoting development in Central

TABLE 3F

**U.S. MILITARY AND ECONOMIC AID, FY 1946–1986,
BY COUNTRY AND PROGRAM**
($ million)

Country program	1946–1984	1980–1984	1984	1985	1986 estimate
Belize					
MAP	0.5	0.5	0.5	0.5	0.5
FMS	-	-	-	-	-
IMET	0.1	0.1	-	0.1	0.1
DA	11.6	10.6	3.9	7.6	5.0
PL480	3.0	-	-	-	-
ESF	10.0	10.0	-	14.0	1.9
Total	25.2	21.2	4.4	22.2	7.5
% Military	2%	3%	11%	3%	8%

Country program	1946–1984	1980–1984	1984	1985	1986 estimate
Costa Rica					
MAP	16.4	15.5	9.0	11.0	2.4
FMS	5.0	-	-	-	-
IMET	1.3	0.3	0.1	0.2	0.2
DA	229.7	79.3	15.5	20.5	10.9
PL480	91.1	72.0	22.5	21.4	23.0
ESF	307.0	307.0	136.0	160.0	120.5
Total	650.5	474.1	183.1	213.1	190.1
% Military	3%	3%	5%	5%	2%
El Salvador					
MAP	303.7	298.8	176.8	124.8	125.4
FMS	100.6	97.2	18.5	10.0	-
IMET	11.2	5.3	1.3	1.5	1.4
DA	331.3	216.2	41.2	87.8	70.1
PL480	204.0	169.7	54.5	52.7	50.8
ESF	429.2	429.2	120.2	285.0	177.0
Total	1380.0	1216.4	412.5	561.8	424.7
% Military	30%	33%	48%	24%	30%
Guatemala					
MAP	16.3	-	-		4.8
FMS	10.7	-	-	-	-
IMET	7.5	-	-	0.5	0.3
DA	290.2	41.9	4.5	58.5	33.0
PL480	94.3	35.0	13.2	25.4	18.4
ESF	43.5	10.0	-	12.5	47.9
Total	462.5	86.9	17.7	96.9	104.4
% Military	7%	0%	0%	1%	5%
Honduras					
MAP	131.6	126.0	76.5	66.3	58.7
FMS	52.4	39.9	-	-	-
IMET	12.4	3.9	0.9	1.1	1.0
DA	368.6	164.9	31.0	44.3	40.6
PL480	82.5	59.2	20.2	18.4	18.3
ESF	134.4	132.8	40.0	147.5	61.2
Total	781.9	526.7	168.6	277.6	179.8
% Military	25%	32%	46%	24%	38%

Country program	1946–1984	1980–1984	1984	1985	1986** estimate
Nicaragua					
MAP	7.7	-	-	-	-
FMS	8.0	-	-	-	-
IMET	11.5	-	-	-	-
DA	228.5	20.8	-	-	-
PL480	45.0	19.6	-	-	-
ESF	62.8	62.8	-	-	-
Total	363.5	103.2	-	-	-
% Military	7%	0%	0%	0%	0%
Panama					
MAP	12.6	8.0	8.0	10.0	3.8
FMS	18.5	15.0	5.0	-	3.8
IMET	6.8	2.1	0.5	0.6	0.6
DA	301.3	38.4	10.7	18.8	17.1
PL480	27.6	6.6	1.3	-	-
ESF	27.0	-	-	50.0	5.7
Total	393.8	70.1	25.5	79.4	31.0
% Military	10%	36%	53%	13%	26%
ROCAP*					
DA	339.9	61.9	15.5	62.5	49.1
ESF	0.9	0.9	0	98.0	51.7
Total	340.8	62.8	15.5	160.5	100.8
% Military	0%	0%	0%	0%	0%
TOTAL CENTRAL AMERICA					
MAP	488.8	448.8	270.8	212.6	199.4
FMS	195.2	152.1	23.5	10.0	-
IMET	50.8	11.7	2.8	4.0	3.6
DA	2101.1	634.0	122.3	300.0	225.8
PL480	547.5	362.1	111.7	117.9	110.5
ESF	1014.8	952.7	296.2	767.0	465.9
Total	4398.2	2561.4	827.3	1411.5	1005.2
% Military	17%	24%	36%	16%	20%

MAP = Military Assistance Program; FMS = Foreign Military Sales; IMET = International Military and Education Training; DA = Development Assistance; PL480 = Food Aid; ESF = Economic Support Funds; ROCAP = Regional Office for Central America and Panama *In 1985 AID created yet another regional office named Central America Regional. This office is managed out of Washington (ROCAP is out of Guatemala) and basically deals with scholarship programs. ROCAP and Central America Regional figures for FY85 are included under ROCAP

SOURCES: AID, U.S. Overseas Loans and Grants July 1, 1945–Sept. 30, 1984; AID Congressional Presentation: FY 86, Main Volume, pp. 668 and 675; Elizabeth Hunt, AID, October 24, 1985; Jim Seville, State Department, October 3, 1985.
**Until the end of the fiscal year which is October 31, additional funds can be appropriated for each account.

America, such a program would have to include the following elements: 1) support for regional institutions completely controlled by Central American nations, 2) projects that narrow the wide income gaps between the poor and the wealthy, 3) support for grassroots organizing and community institutions that work on behalf of the poor, 4) liberalized U.S. trade regulations to encourage the export of processed agricultural products, 5) support for international commodity agreements that would guarantee stable and more equitable prices for cash crops, and 6) U.S. backing for a plan to reduce the region's debt obligations.

As it is, U.S. economic aid is not backing reforms. Instead, Washington is bolstering client governments. Rather than promoting internal economic development, aid programs foster U.S. economic interests as a way of keeping Central America tied to the United States. Unfortunately, U.S. economic assistance is doing little to further democracy or development but is doing a great deal to back U.S.-led counterrevolution in the region.

1 Interview by Deb Preusch with Larry Cohen, US Embassy, Honduras, September 1984.
2 ESF world ranking for 1984 as follows: 1) Israel 2) Egypt 3) Pakistan 4) Turkey 5) Costa Rica 6) El Salvador.
3 Hearings before the Committee on Foreign Affairs, House of Representatives, *Foreign Assistance Legislation FY84–85*, February 1983, p.622.
4 Ibid., Department of Defense Presentation.
5 AID Inspector General, "Private Sector Support Program, Audit Report," April 20, 1983.
6 Rep. Jim Leach, Rep. George Miller, Sen. Mark Hatfield, "US Aid to El Salvador: An Evaluation of the Past, A Proposal for the Future. A Report to the Arms Control and Foreign Policy Caucus," Washington, February 1985, p.20.
7 Ibid., p.18.
8 Hearings before the Subcommittee on Foreign Operations and Related Agencies, Committee on Appropriations, House of Representatives, *Supplemental Appropriations for FY82, Part II*, May 13, 19, 20, and 25, 1982, p.43.
9 Interview by Tom Barry with Esteban Enriquez, National Campesino Union (UNC), Honduras, August 1984.
10 David L. Caldon, "The Role of Security Assistance in the Irregular Conflict Ongoing in the Caribbean Basin Today: Prevention—Deterrence—Counteraction," *DISAM Journal*, Winter 1982-1983.
11 Hearings before the Subcommittee of the Committtee on Appropriations, House of Representatives, *Foreign Assistance and Related Agencies Appropriations for 1968, Part 2, Economic Assistance*, 1967, p.1516.
12 Jaime Wheelock and Luis Carrion, *Apuntes Sobre el Desarrollo Economico y Social de Nicaragua* (Managua: Centro de Publicaciones Silvio Mayorga, 1980). Cited in Donald Castillo Rivas, *Centroamerica—Más Allá de la Crisis* (Mexico: Sociedad Interamericana de Planificación, 1983), pp.203–204.
13 Nancy Peckenham, "Bullets and Beans," *Multinational Monitor*, April 1984.
14 Testimony of Peter McPherson before the Subcommittee of the Committee on Appropriations, House of Representatives, *Hearing on Foreign Assistance and Related Program Appropriations FY84*, April 19, 1983, p.86.
15 Interview by Deb Preusch with Robert Queener, AID Office of Central America Affairs Washington, December 1984.
16 Interview by Deb Preusch with Colonel Grotewald, CRN Guatewala, July 1984.
17 Philip L. Russell, *El Salvador in Crisis* (Austin: Colorado River, 1984), p.96.
18 *Pacific News Service*, March 21, 1983.
19 According to UCS's Secretary-General Samuel Maldonado, AIFLD provides 75 percent

of the operating budget of the union. *Washington Post*, May 4, 1984. Maldonado was subsequently defeated as union head, and now directs the new AIFLD-sponsored union Democratic Workers Central.

20 Edward Herman and Frank Brodhead, *Demonstration Elections* (Boston: South End, 1984).

21 Chris Hedges, "Operation Well-Being: Salvadoran 'Phoenix' Trapped in the Flames," *Christian Science Monitor*, September 30, 1983.

22 Robert W. Komer, "Impact of Pacification on Insurgency in South Vietnam," *Journal of International Affairs*, Vol. 25, No. 1, 1971, p.292.

23 Ibid., p.290.

24 National Action Research on the Military Industrial Complex (from now on referred to as NARMIC), "The US Pacification Program in El Salvador: A Report on the Central American War," March 1984.

25 Hearings before the Subcommittee on Western Hemisphere Affairs, Committee on Foreign Affairs, House of Representatives, March 1, 1983, p.84.

26 Chris Hedges, "Rebels Pull Strings of US Aid Program in El Salvador Province," *Christian Science Monitor*, December 9, 1983.

27 Americas Watch, "Freefire: Fifth Supplement to the Report on Human Rights in El Salvador," March 1984, p.2.

28 Sam Dillion, "US Triples Refugee Aid in El Salvador," *Miami Herald*, December 17, 1984.

29 *National Catholic Reporter*, January 18, 1985.

30 AID, "Northern Zone Infrastructure Development Project Paper #515-0191," 1983.

31 Robert S. Perry, "Civic Action and Regional Security," *DISAM Journal*, Spring 1983.

32 James LeMoyne, "US Program in Honduras Helps Families of Nicaraguan Guerrillas," *New York Times*, April 19, 1985.

33 Ibid.

34 Prepared statement of Elise R.W. DuPont before the Committee on Appropriations, Senate, *Foreign Assistance and Related Programs Appropriations FY84*, March 3, 1983, p.447.

35 *Business America*, November 30, 1982, p.2.

36 AID, "Regional Strategic Plan for Latin America and the Caribbean," March 1983, p.31.

37 *Business America*, November 30, 1982, p.3.

38 AID, "Regional Strategic Plan...," p.30.

39 Prepared statement of Lars Schoultz before the Committee on Foreign Affairs, *Foreign Assistance Legislation for FY84–85 (Part 6)*, March 9, 1983, p.79.

40 Ibid.

41 See prepared statement of Richard S. Newfarmer before the Committee on Foreign Affairs, *Foreign Assistance Legislation for FY84-85*, March 9, 1983, pp. 56–75.

42 US Department of Commerce, "Description of US Aid Programs," December 1980.

43 Hearings before the Subcommittee on International Economic Policy and Trade, Committee on Foreign Affairs, House of Representatives, *Review of Activities of the Overseas Private Investment Corporation*, July 17, 1979, and February 7, 1980.

44 Interview by Deb Preusch with Robert Jordan, OPIC, November 27, 1985.

	Finance ($)	+	Insurance ($ million)	=	Total ($ million)
Belize	470,000		56.9		57.4
Costa Rica	19,495,500		23.7		43.2
El Salvador	3,635,000		4.5		8.1
Guatemala	1,000,000		1.7		2.7
Honduras	1,745,000		44.8		46.5
Nicaragua	2,119,294		3.2		5.3
Panama	1,657,000		24.1		25.8
Central America	30,121,794		158.9		189.0

45 *Topics*, June/July 1981, p.1.
46 Hearings before the Subcommittee on International Economic Policy and Trade, Committee on Foreign Affairs, op.cit.
47 Americas Watch, "Little Hope: Human Rights in Guatemala, January 1984 to January 1985," February 1985.
48 *Business Latin America*, May 30, 1984; *New York Times*, December 20, 1984.
49 *U.S. News and World Report*, July 19, 1971, cited in *NACLA Report on the Americas*, August 1974.
50 Jonathan E. Sanford, "US Foreign Assistance to Central America," Congressional Research Service Report No. 84–34F, March 2, 1984.
51 Interview by Tom Barry with German Catalan, Guatemala Ministry of Agriculture, August 1984.
52 Interview by Tom Barry with DIGESA agronomist, August 1984.
53 Interview by Tom Barry with Gary Smith, USDA Consultant Guatemala, August 1984.
54 Jonathan Fryer, *Food for Thought: The Use and Abuse of Food Aid in the Fight Against World Hunger* (Geneva: World Council of Churches, 1981), p.18.
55 AID Latin American Bureau, "Regional Strategic Plan for Latin America and the Caribbean," December 1983, p.25.
56 Interview by Deb Preusch with Tom King, AID El Salvador, August 1984.
57 Interview by Deb Preusch with Max Bowser, Agricultural Attaché Costa Rica, September 1984.
58 Government Accounting Office (from now on referred to as GAO), "Foreign Currency Purchases Can Be Reduced Through Greater Use of Currency Use Payments and Public Law 480 Commodity Sales Agreements," April 10, 1984.
59 A provision of the Title II program allows delivery of Title II commodities to governments that agree to use local currency from food sales to develop agricultural programs and to expand food production. In fact, Washington fails to monitor these agreements and permits governments to use the currency in the ways they see fit.
60 Interview by Deb Preusch with Ms. Segura, WFP El Salvador, July 1984.
61 Interview by Deb Preusch with Art Mead, FAO Washington, October 1984. Deliveries of WFP in 1984: Costa Rica, 700 metric tons (MT); El Salvador, 6100 MT; Guatemala, 11,200 MT; Honduras, 3900 MT; and Panama, 300 MT.
62 Nancy Peckenham, AFSC, "Guatemala 1983" (Philadelphia), December 1983.
63 *New York Times*, August 8, 1984; *Christian Science Monitor*, January 31, 1984.
64 *Foreign Agriculture*, July 1982, p.6.
65 Ibid., pp.8–9.
66 AID, *Front Lines*, August 1984.
67 Frances M. Lappe, Joseph Collins, David Kinley, *Aid as Obstacle* (San Francisco: Institute for Food and Development Policy, 1981), pp.129–130.
68 *Latin America Commodities Report*, January 1, 1984.
69 *National Catholic Reporter*, January 23, 1982.
70 Sam Dillion, *Miami Herald*, December 17, 1984, op.cit.
71 Ibid.
72 Inter-Religious Task Force on Central America, "Update Central America," March 1984, p.3.
73 *Pacific News Service*, December 18, 1984.
74 Sam Dillion, op.cit.
75 Testimony by David L. Guyer before the Committee on Foreign Affairs, House of Representatives, *Foreign Assistance Legislation for FY84–85*, February/March 1983, p.519.
76 Hearing before the Subcommittee on Foreign Operations and Related Agencies, Appropriations Committee, House of Representatives, *Foreign Assistance and Related Programs Appropriations for 1982, Part 3*, 1981, p.403.
77 American Institute for Free Labor Development (from now on referred to as AIFLD), "AIFLD: A Union to Union Program for the Americas," p.7.
78 North American Congress on Latin America (from now on referred to as NACLA), *NACLA Report on the Americas*, March 1976, p.13.
79 AIFLD, "Annual Progress Report 1962–1982, 21 Years of Partnership for Progress Erratum." In-country students trained by AIFLD, 1962 to 1983: Costa Rica, 14,213; El Salvador, 7903; Guatemala, 11,586; Guatemala (Central America Union Education In-

stitute—IESCA), 2464; Honduras, 32,456; Nicaragua, 13,889; Panama, 14,728; Central America total: 97,239.

80 AIFLD, "Annual Progress Report 1962–1982."

81 Ibid.

82 Jack Scott, *Yankee Unions, Go Home* (Vancouver: New Star, 1978), p.174.

83 AIFLD, "Annual Progress Report 1962–1982," op.cit.

84 J. Peter Grace, "Labor Boosts Living Standards," *Journal of Commerce*, April 14, 1966.

85 Interview by Deb Preusch with Jack Herberle, AIFLD Washington, May 1984.

86 Philip Agee, *Inside the Company: CIA Diary* (New York: Stonehill, 1975). p.607.

87 Hearings before the Subcommittee on International Economic Policy and Trade, Committee on Foreign Affairs, House of Representatives, *Is Partnership Enough?*, 1981, p.37.

88 Interview by Deb Preusch with Roberto Cazares, AIFLD Costa Rica, August 1984.

89 *Washington Report on Latin America*, May 28, 1985.

90 Alberto Ruiz, "Agentes Patronales en el Moviemiento Obrero Hondureno," *Octubre* (Tegucigalpa), November 2, 1957, p.2.

91 *Inforpress*, September 22, 1983.

92 *El Nuevo Diario*, August 21, 1984.

93 Interview by Deb Preusch with Sebastian Castro, CST Nicaragua, August 1984.

94 Interview by Tom Barry with Marcial Caballero, UNC Honduras, August 1984.

95 Prepared statement of Loret Miller Ruppe before the Committee on Appropriations, House of Representatives, *Foreign Assistance and Related Appropriations for 1984*, September 2, 1983, pp.58–80.

96 Peace Corps Press Release, February 22, 1985.

97 Hearings before the Committee on Foreign Relations, Senate, *Security and Development Assistance*, February 25, 1983, p.178.

98 *New York Times*, September 24, 1984.

99 Ibid.

100 *Enfoprensa*, October 14, 1983.

101 *Latin America Regional Report*, February 15, 1985.

102 *In These Times*, October 31, 1984.

103 *Africasia*, October 1984.

104 *Miami Herald*, October 6, 1984.

105 Information on USIA country programs comes from profiles provided by USIA to The Resource Center, 1985.

106 Jack Anderson, "USIA Gives PR Aid to Right-Wing Regimes," United Feature Syndicate, February 23, 1983; Jack Anderson, "US Paid Foreign Agent for Media Handling Seminar," United Feature Syndicate, March 4, 1983.

107 *Miami Herald*, July 14, 1985.

108 *Washington Report on the Hemisphere*, April 2, 1985.

109 For an excellent overview of the US strategy of economic aid, see: David Landes with Patricia Flynn, "Dollars for Dictators," in Roger Burbach and Patricia Flynn (eds.), *The Politics of Intervention: The United States in Central America* (New York: Monthly Review, 1984), pp.134–161.

CHAPTER 4

Militarization
of Central America

*We do not seek a military defeat for our friends. We do not seek
a stalemate. We seek victory for the forces of democracy.*
—Undersecretary of Defense Fred C. Ikle

AFTER THE CUBAN Revolution, Washington was determined to prevent similar revolutionary explosions elsewhere in the hemisphere. The Kennedy administration adopted a strategy that combined economic and military aid programs to avert another Cuba. The economic aid was to alleviate the root causes of rebellion by promoting reform and development. The main focus of the military aid was to counter internal insurgencies—not to help defend countries from external attack. The three components of this military aid plan were: 1) counterinsurgency training for the region's police and military, 2) increased aid for armed forces, and 3) military/civic action programs coordinated with U.S. economic aid.

The foreign policy of preventive revolution worked for the 1960s and most of the 1970s. In Central America, military and police forces bolstered by U.S. aid clamped down on reformers and revolutionaries alike, keeping the nations firmly within the U.S. orbit. But, in 1979, the Sandinistas toppled the Somoza dictatorship, and Washington suddenly saw its hold on Central America slipping.

Rather than reevaluate its long-term emphasis on counterinsurgency and counterrevolution, Washington deepened its military commitment in Central America. While searching for ways to undermine the Sandinista revolution, the Carter administration moved quickly to head off revolution in El Salvador. The Reagan administration opted for an uncompromising military response to social upheaval in the region. "The national security of all Americans is at stake in Central America," said the president. "If we cannot defend ourselves there, we cannot expect to prevail elsewhere."[1]

Under Reagan, the three elements of counterinsurgency adopted in the early 1960s—training, aid, and military/civic action—have all been incorporated into a regionwide militarization plan aimed at crushing leftist guerrilla opposition and turning back the Nicaraguan revolution. But there have been no quick victories for the Reagan administration. Each year, the United States has taken another step closer to direct intervention by U.S. armed forces. By insisting on a military solution to a crisis caused by festering injustices, the United States is getting caught in a Vietnam-like quagmire. As in Vietnam, Washington cannot convincingly point to any light at the end of the tunnel.

The Cost of Militarization

The extent of militarization can best be seen by the increase of U.S. military aid to the region. The amount of aid going to this small region is staggering. From 1981 through 1985, the United States committed over $800 million in military aid to Central America—over four times as much as was provided in the previous four decades. El Salvador and Honduras now rank as the second and third highest per capita recipients of military assistance grants in the world. In 1984, these two countries received 76 percent of all military assistance to Latin America. (See Table 3F.)

Military Aid

Military aid comes in several different packages. The four main types are the following:

Foreign Military Sales (FMS) Financing Program: Furnishes direct credits at both Treasury and concessional interest rates to purchase U.S. defense articles, services, and training.

TABLE 4A

FOREIGN MILITARY SALES, BY COUNTRY, FY 1980–1985
($ million)

	1980	1981	1982	1983	1984	1985
Belize	-	-	-	-	-	-
Costa Rica	-	-	-	-	-	-
El Salvador	5.7	10.0	16.5	46.5	18.5	10.0
Guatemala	-	-	-	-	-	-
Honduras	3.5	8.4	19.0	9.0	-	-
Nicaragua	-	-	-	-	-	-
Panama	-	-	5.0	5.0	5.0	-
Central America	9.2	18.4	40.5	60.5	23.5	10.0

SOURCES: U.S. AID, U.S. Overseas Loans and Grants and Assistance from International Organizations: Obligations and Loan Authorizations, July 1, 1945–September 30, 1984; Jim Seville, State Department, October 3, 1985.

Military Assistance Program (MAP): Provides grant funding for the purchase of defense articles and services as well as for the training and technical assistance in the use of military equipment.

TABLE 4B

MILITARY ASSISTANCE PROGRAM, BY COUNTRY, FY 1980–1985
($ million)

	1980	1981	1982	1983	1984	1985
Belize	-	-	-	-	0.5	0.5
Costa Rica	-	-	2.0	4.5	9.0	11.0
El Salvador	-	25.0	63.5	33.5	176.8	124.8
Guatemala	-	-	-	-	-	-
Honduras	-	-	11.0	38.5	76.5	66.3
Nicaragua	-	-	-	-	-	-
Panama	-	-	-	-	8.0	10.0
Central America	-	25.0	76.5	76.5	270.8	212.6

SOURCE: U.S. AID, U.S. Overseas Loans and Grants and Assistance from International Organizations: Obligations and Loan Authorizations, July 1, 1945–September 30, 1984; Jim Seville, State Department, October 3, 1985.

International Military Education and Training (IMET): Provides professional military training on a grant basis for selected foreign military and related civilian personnel both in the United States and at overseas facilities. (Table 4D.)

Economic Support Fund (ESF): Provides balance-of-payments cash transfers on a grant or loan basis to countries selected for their special political and security interest to the United States. ESF is technically administered by AID but is rarely "developmental." It is basically a security/military program designed to prop up existing Central American regimes. (See Chapter 3.)[2]

Commercial Sales

Also part of U.S. military support are two categories of military sales: Commerce Department Sales and Direct Commercial Sales. Commerce Department Sales include items not on the U.S. Munitions list but which could have military application. Exported to Central America under this category are transport planes, trainer aircraft, helicopters, and computers. Crime-control equipment such as leg irons, shackles, handcuffs, and shields also can be purchased through the

Commerce Department. These sales are generally under $1 million a year for Central American countries, but El Salvador bought $6 million worth of military-related equipment through the Commerce Department in 1984.

Central American nations can also buy U.S.-made light arms and combat-support equipment directly from U.S. manufacturers without using U.S. military-aid programs. Among the materiel sold to Central American police and military under the category of Direct Commercial Sales are shotguns, rifles, submachine guns, and riot-control equipment. Commercial military sales to Central America were $5.3 million in 1984 and over $68 million from 1950 through 1984.

TABLE 4C

DIRECT COMMERCIAL SALE OF MILITARY EQUIPMENT, BY COUNTRY, 1950–1984
($ thousand)

	1981	1982	1983	1984	1950–1984
Belize	186	100	100	26	631
Costa Rica	57	150	150	77	1604
El Salvador	17	300	200	1115	3852
Guatemala	7	750	100	37	5984
Honduras	923	500	500	2712	9288
Nicaragua	5	50	50	1	4349
Panama	752	1000	1000	1405	42781
Central America	1947	2850	2100	5373	68489

SOURCE: U.S. DOD, Foreign Military Sales, Foreign Military Construction Sales and Military Assistance Facts as of September 30, 1984.

The Business of Arming Central America

Plenty of money can be made in the business of militarizing Central America. From supplying the Guatemalan military Huey helicopters to cleaning latrines in Honduras, U.S. military contractors have a stake in expanding U.S. intervention. More than 25 defense contractors supply weapons to Central American armies either through U.S. military aid or commercial sales. Cessna sends the A-37 Dragonfly attack jets to Honduras and El Salvador. General Electric supplies those countries with the Minigun that fires up to 6000 rounds a minute. Motorola provided El Salvador with a microwave communications system. Litton Industries managed the construction of the Regional Military Training Center (CREM) in Honduras. Other arms and aircraft manufacturers that supply Central American armies include: Bell Helicopter (Textron); Cessna; McDonnell Douglas Corporation; Eagle Bob Tail Tractors; General Electric; Maremont Corporation; Colt

Industries; Motorola, Inc; Sentinel Electronics; Magnavox Government and Industrial Electronics; and Bridge Electronics.[3]

Private enterprise is also involved in shipping arms to the region and training Central American personnel in the use of military equipment. Taca Airlines has a contract to ship military freight. Bell Helicopter and Motorola have both given technical training courses to soldiers in Guatemala and El Salvador. In Honduras, the Defense Department found a new role for private business. It contracted Herbert International of Birmingham for "base support" at the Palmerola Air Base. Herbert International caters meals, cuts grass, and collects trash under the contract, which Senator Jim Sasser (D-Tennessee) termed "most unusual." The senator said that the Pentagon may be contracting out jobs that soldiers ordinarily do "to artificially lower the number of U.S. military personnel in Honduras."[4]

Training the Troops

The Defense Security Agency (DSA) manages what the DOD describes as its most cost-effective military-aid program. This is the International Military Education and Training Program (IMET), which trains military officers from Central America and other third-world nations.

Before the military build-up which began in 1980, IMET training grants were the major form of U.S. military assistance to countries in the region. Between 1950 and 1985, the U.S. government trained over 25,000 Central American military officers through the IMET program. IMET training takes place either

TABLE 4D

NUMBER OF TRAINEES UNDER IMET, BY COUNTRY, 1950–1984

	1981	1982	1983	1984	1950–1984
Belize	0	16	19	23	58
Costa Rica	37	55	79	37	919
El Salvador	256	736*	1223	111	4439*
Guatemala	0	0	0	0	3360
Honduras	261	328	332	346	4876
Nicaragua	0	0	0	0	5740
Panama	293	219	301	270	6244
Central America	847	1354*	1954	787	25636*

*Does not include 1600 Salvadoran troops trained in the United States during 1982.

SOURCE: U.S. DOD, Foreign Military Sales, Foreign Military Construction Sales and Military Assistance Facts as of September 30, 1984.

within the countries themselves, at U.S. military schools in Panama, or in the United States at the counterinsurgency schools located at Fort Bragg and Fort Benning. Former Secretary of Defense Robert McNamara once said: "Probably the greatest return on our military assistance program investment comes from the training of selected officers and key specialists at our military schools— leaders, the men who will have the know-how and impart it to their forces. I need not dwell upon the value of having in positions of leadership men who have the first-hand knowledge of how Americans do things and how they think. It is beyond price to make friends of such men."[5]

The DOD can cite a long list of officers trained in IMET programs that went on to attain positions of leadership within their countries: Anastasio Somoza (former Nicaraguan dictator), General Benedicto Lucas García (former Army Chief of Staff in Guatemala), General Walter López (armed forces chief in Honduras), General Humberto Romero (former president of El Salvador), General Efraín Ríos Montt (former president of Guatemala), General Oscar Mejía Víctores (former president of Guatemala), General Manuel Antonio Noriega, (commander-in-chief in Panama), and General Juan Alberto Melgar Castro (former president of Honduras). Other well-known graduates from other Latin American countries include Leopoldo Galtiera of Argentina, Augusto Pinochet of Chile, and Alfredo Stroessner of Paraguay.

The three main areas of IMET training are armed counterinsurgency, ideological instruction, and military/civic action programs. Central American officers take courses such as Counterinsurgency Operations, Urban Counterinsurgency, and Military Intelligence Interrogation and receive training in psychological warfare and the use of propaganda. They learn how to manage civic action programs, which are part of pacification campaigns. IMET training also stresses the role of the military in "nation building," and gives the officers instruction in economics, engineering, and food distribution.

Overseeing the U.S. military build-up in Central America is the U.S. Southern Command (SOUTHCOM). From its headquarters 500 feet above the Panama Canal at Quarry Heights, SOUTHCOM manages 14 bases and about 9000 military personnel in Latin America and the Caribbean. Until the recent militarization of Central America, SOUTHCOM was a sleepy military division known mostly for its role in training thousands of Latin American military officers at its bases in the Canal Zone. Under the command of General Paul Gorman, SOUTHCOM became the driving force behind the rapidly expanding U.S. military effort in Central America. Gorman personally maintained close relations with the military leadership in the region and pushed hard for increased U.S. military intervention. In early 1985, Lieutenant General John Galvin replaced Gorman, a change advocated by the State Department, which resented Gorman's meddling in political issues.

School of the Americas

Since 1946, the main U.S. military training school for Central American military officers has been the U.S. Southern Command's School of the Americas, located for 40 years in the Panama Canal Zone.[6] By 1985, the school, known unofficially as "La Escuela de Golpes" (School of Military Coups), had trained close to 45,000 Latin American officers. Over one-third of all the graduates from the School of the Americas came from Central American nations. Of all the Latin American nations, Nicaragua has had the largest number of officers trained at the school. El Salvador, because of the recent influx of military students, ranks third.[7]

The number of students at the School of the Americas dropped to an all-time low in 1980, but under the Reagan administration enrollment increased sixfold. The great numbers of students from Honduras and El Salvador accounted for most of the increase. Of the almost 4000 Salvadoran officers trained at the School of the Americas since 1946, 80 percent of them received instruction since 1980.[8]

Under the terms of the 1977 Panama Canal Treaty, ownership of Fort Gulick, the U.S. army base which housed the school, was transferred to the Panamanian Defense Forces. In 1985, the School of the Americas moved temporarily to Fort Benning, Georgia. The U.S. Army has discussed the possibilities of moving the school from its temporary location at Fort Benning to Honduras, Belize, or Puerto Rico.

The school's credo states that it is "a monument to peace and understanding in the hemisphere,"[9] but many Panamanians have objected to its presence in their country. An editorial in a leading daily in Panama City stated that the school was "sadly renowned for counting almost all Latin American dictators among its students." Panamanian president Jorge Illueja in 1984 described the school as "the biggest base for destabilization in Latin America."[10]

In the last several years, the school has increased instruction in military/civic action programs. The courses in civic action explore the role of the military in national development. They also explain the ways that civic action programs like food distribution and roadbuilding can be integrated into pacification campaigns. More than half of the school's courses now fit under the category of civic action.[11]

When the School of the Americas was closing its doors at Fort Gulick, its director, Colonel Michael Sierra, said that its role as an organization for providing professional education and development to the armies of Latin America will continue."[12]

Two other military training schools for Latin Americans remain in Panama.

The U.S. Navy instructs Latin American naval officers at the Small Craft Instruction and Technical Training School.[13] In addition, the Interamerican Air Forces Academy (IAFFA), operated by the U.S. Air Force, trains Latin American pilots.[14] Ninety percent of the pilots of the Salvadoran Air Force have been trained at the flight school, including the country's air force chief.[15] Also in Panama is the U.S. Army's Jungle Operation Training Center for U.S. soldiers. According to its deputy commander, Major Fred Berger, the Center is "getting bigger and bigger," reflecting increasing emphasis on preparing U.S. troops for intervention in tropical third-world countries.[16]

The Pentagon provides in-country training to Central American troops through Mobile Training Teams (MTT). The MTTs are teams of U.S. advisers, usually members of the Army Special Forces attached to the 193rd Infantry Brigade stationed in Panama.

From mid-1983 to mid-1985, Central American soldiers were also trained at the Regional Military Training Center (CREM) near Puerto Castilla in Honduras. After Honduras objected to the priority given to the training of Salvadoran soldiers, the base was closed down. Both U.S. advisers and Salvadoran officers now train most Salvadoran soldiers at a training center established in 1984 at La Unión in El Salvador.

Small numbers of Central American troops come to the United States for training. The main training bases are Fort Bragg (North Carolina) and Fort Benning (Georgia). Salvadoran air crews have also been trained to operate AC-47 gunships by the Air Force's 16th Special Forces Squadron at Duke Field in Okaloosa County, Florida.

Once again, the United States has begun to train police forces in Central America. In 1974, Congress banned foreign police-training programs because they were found to lead to systematic torture and disappearances of dissidents. A new section added in 1985 to the Foreign Service Act allows the United States to train police forces in any country with no human-rights violations, no standing army, and "a long-standing democratic tradition." This clause provided the legal justification for the large-scale training of Costa Rica's national guard units.

Salvadoran police are also being trained by U.S. advisers. The FBI has trained a judicial police unit, and a special police counterterrorist unit has also been trained by U.S. experts. In 1985 a $22 million "regional counterterrorist program" was authorized for Central America that provides extensive police training throughout the region.

War Games Prepare for Intervention

In 1981, Operation Ocean Venture kicked off a series of Caribbean Basin war games, which the Pentagon says will continue at least through 1988. From 1981 to 1985, the U.S. military conducted over 40 war maneuvers in the Caribbean Basin. Before 1983, most of the maneuvers were held on islands off

Puerto Rico. The war games sponsored by SOUTHCOM in Central America were limited to annual exercises called Kindle Liberty held in Panama. Since 1983, there have been several massive war exercises conducted every year in Honduras.

During the Big Pine III "training exercise" in 1985, over 10,000 U.S. forces and 39 U.S. war ships simulated war campaigns in Honduras. The back-to-back Big Pine III and Universal Trek '85 exercises in Honduras represented the most intricate military maneuvers the United States has ever conducted in the Western Hemisphere.[17]

The maneuvers have stirred the resentment of Hondurans who claim that the games undermine national sovereignty and push the country toward a regional war. Demonstrations organized by that nation's trade unions have called for the United States to pull its troops out of the country. Even the Honduran military has expressed concern. "The United States," said one Honduran officer, "is converting the country into a kind of fixed aircraft carrier from which it sends out psychological war signals to Central America and the Caribbean."[18]

Most of those signals are directed at Nicaragua. During the war maneuvers, the Honduran and U.S. military accompanied by U.S. National Guard teams practice defending the country against a simulated Nicaraguan tank attack. They also launch their own mock attacks on simulated Nicaraguan ports.

While the U.S. military says the maneuvers are designed to train Honduran troops, the scale of the games and the involvement of thousands of U.S. soldiers and guardsmen indicate that the games provide an opportunity to train U.S. forces for eventual real fighting in the region. Colonel Charles Pearcy, who heads SOUTHCOM's task force in Honduras, said: "I can say with some confidence

TABLE 4E

U.S. MILITARY PERSONNEL IN CENTRAL AMERICA, BY COUNTRY, AS OF DECEMBER 31, 1984

	Total	Army	Navy	Marine Corps	Air Force
Belize	4	3	1	0	0
Costa Rica	16	6	0	10	0
El Salvador	119	93	0	23	3
Guatemala	18	6	0	11	1
Honduras	619*	553	2	56	8
Nicaragua	12	3	0	8	1
Panama	9412	6676	391	147	2198

*Does not include as many as 6,000 U.S. troops participating in occasional military maneuvers.

SOURCE: DOD, *Worldwide Manpower Distribution by Geographical Area, Dec. 31, 1984.*

that the exercises have provided us with a significantly improved capability to operate in the region."[19]

The games serve the following purposes: 1) build infrastructure of ports and airstrips for possible U.S. invasion of Nicaragua, 2) intimidate the Sandinistas, 3) prepare U.S. military for regional war in Central America, 4) provide indirect aid to the *contras* by way of equipment and infrastructure improvements, 5) prepare the Honduran military as a U.S. surrogate force.

In Panama, the U.S. military conducts separate war games with the Panamanian Defense Forces. In 1985, some 10,000 U.S. soldiers and national guardsmen participated in two war games—Blazing Trails and Kindle Liberty—that included an emphasis on civic action programs including roadbuilding by the U.S. Army. Originally, the exercises were labeled Minuteman I and Minuteman II to highlight the participation of the U.S. civilian-soldiers from the National Guards of Puerto Rico, Louisiana, and Florida.

Both the U.S. and Panamanian governments said the war maneuvers, which lasted five months, are justified by the 1977 Torrijos-Carter Canal Treaty under which the United States is committed to "protect and defend" the Panama Canal. The exercises, however, did not take place near the canal but in isolated jungle regions. Political parties, university organizations, and unions denounced the war games as an affront to Panamanian sovereignty.[20]

CIA: Intelligence and Terrorism

The "spooks," as they are commonly called in the U.S. foreign service community, are having a field day in Central America. The CIA's activities include mining harbors, publishing comic books with instructions on sabotage and "neutralization," manipulating elections, advising national armies, and forming their own guerrilla army. It was estimated that at least 150 agents are operating in El Salvador and several hundred in Honduras.[21] The number of agents working in Costa Rica has tripled in recent years.

For all its agents in Central America, the CIA's intelligence has failed to establish any credible evidence that the Soviet Union, Cuba, or Nicaragua have been directing the guerrilla movements in El Salvador and Guatemala. In one congressional briefing, the CIA said that "lots of ships have been traced" from the Soviet Union with arms shipments to Central America, but could only show a few examples upon questioning from the committee. Concerning the alleged Salvadoran guerrillas' relationship with Cuba and the Soviet Union, the CIA told Congress, "You don't plan an operation like what is being run in El Salvador if you haven't gone to somebody's command and general staff college." When the congressional committee asked for evidence that the guerrilla leaders had been trained by the Cubans or Soviets, the CIA replied that it meant the comment only as "a figure of speech."[22]

The main focus of CIA operations in Central America has been the destabilization and eventual overthrow of the Sandinista government. The CIA started
working with ex-National Guardsmen immediately after the Sandinista triumph.
But it was not until 1982 that they began to build the *contra* force into a guerrilla
army capable of causing serious military and political difficulties for the Sandinista government.

At first, the Reagan administration claimed that the CIA's "covert aid" to
the *contras* was used to pressure the Sandinistas to stop shipping arms to the
Salvadoran guerrillas. Later, Washington said the *contras* merely wanted to
influence the Sandinistas to adopt policies more acceptable to the United States.
By 1985, President Reagan acknowledged that the CIA-backed *contras* he called
"freedom fighters" wanted to push the Sandinistas to the point where they would
cry "uncle." Contrary to the messages given the U.S. public and the Congress,
the CIA and the *contras* had been working on a timetable drawn up in early
1982 that projected the counterrevolutionaries would be marching into Managua
at the end of 1983.

The nature of the CIA involvement with the *contras* became clear in 1984
when the U.S. media covered the "murder manual" produced by the CIA for
the *contras*. The 44-page booklet entitled "Psychological Operations in Guerrilla
Warfare" instructed the *contras* to hire professional criminals to use "selective
violence to neutralize" Nicaraguan public officials, provoke unrest at demonstrations, label those Nicaraguan civilians killed while attempting to flee as
"enemies of the people," and blackmail citizens into collaborating in terrorist
activities.

Parts of the booklet were a word-for-word translation of a manual developed
at Fort Bragg during the Vietnam War. A 16-page comic book supplement
includes instructions in techniques of petty sabotage, ranging from plugging
toilets and making false hotel reservations to pulling down power lines and
throwing Molotov cocktails at Nicaraguan police.

But the CIA did more than simply fund the *contras* (with an authorized $73
million through 1984) and distribute comic books. In 1983, when it realized that
the *contra* forces were incapable of seriously challenging the Nicaraguan government, it initiated its own series of terrorist acts aimed at disrupting the Nicaraguan economy and society. It contracted mercenaries to blow up bridges,
bomb the port of Corinto, set oil storage facilities afire, and mine the harbors
of Sandino, Corinto, and El Bluff. The mines used by the CIA had been manufactured for use in the Mekong Delta in Vietnam. President Reagan told Congress that the mining of Nicaragua's harbors constituted an act of "collective
self-defense."[23]

In Honduras, the CIA coordinated the supply and the attack plans of the
contras using the infrastructure set up by the U.S. military during its war maneuvers. The General Accounting Office in its 1984 study of the military build-
up in Honduras said the Aquacate Base was "substantially less than temporary"

.d indicated that it was now being used as a "forward-basing" facility for CIA-backed *contras*.[24] At the Palmerola Air Base, the CIA enjoys separate quarters, and it shares the Jamastran air strip, only 20 miles from the Nicaraguan border, with the *contras*.

In Nicaragua, the CIA has tried to make inroads through the Catholic Church. Four of Managua's archbishops, main financial supporters have been repeatedly linked with CIA operations and anticommunist church organizations in Latin America. These contributors are AID, W.R. Grace & Company, Misereor, and Adveniat.[25] The contributions flow through the church's Commission for Social Promotion (COPROSA). Misereor and Adveniat are West German organizations active in Latin America.[26] The chairman of W.R. Grace was a founder and the first chairman of the CIA-influenced American Institute for Free Labor Development (AIFLD). There have been charges, too, that the CIA backs the anti-Sandinista daily *La Prensa* and is orchestrating the news campaign against the leftist government. Similar charges were leveled against *El Mercurio* during the Allende government in Chile and the *Daily Gleaner* during the Manley government in Jamaica.

The CIA channeled $2 million into the 1984–1985 election campaign in El Salvador. The chief beneficiary was the Christian Democratic Party of Napoleon Duarte, which received close to $1 million and narrowly defeated Roberto D'Aubuisson in the presidential election. Senator Jesse Helms (R-North Carolina) charged that CIA funding "bought the election" for Duarte. The CIA portrayed its participation as a nonpartisan effort to help streamline election logistics, provide media advice and technical assistance, and ease the financial burden on interest groups such as trade unions and peasant cooperatives.[27]

The CIA has also been involved in funding right-wing paramilitary groups in El Salvador, Honduras, and Guatemala. A 1980 State Department document acknowledged that the U.S. government maintained links with the paramilitary assassination squads in those three countries. In its attempt to improve the "counterinsurgency capabilities of the armed forces," the document said, Washington was "seeking to bring under unified command the paramilitary units operating in the country (El Salvador), and establishing and/or improving communications and cooperation among armed forces and paramilitary organizations in Guatemala, El Salvador, and Honduras."[28]

In Guatemala, the CIA has been linked to the National Liberation Movement (MLN), which is known as the "party of organized violence," and a death squad closely associated to the MLN called *La Mano Blanca*.[29] Two highly placed members of the Salvadoran security forces were long-time paid informants of the CIA: General José Alberto Medrano, the founder of the paramilitary organization ORDEN, and Colonel Nicholas Carranza. While chief of the Treasury Police, Carranza received $90,000 a year from the CIA. Carranza is a close associate of Roberto D'Aubuisson.[30]

Two airlines connected with the CIA carry out missions in Central America.

One of the planes used by the *contras* to bomb the Managua airport in 1983 was owned by Investair Leasing Company, a CIA-controlled company.[31] In 1984, CBS News reported that Evergreen Airlines along with Southern Air and Summit Aviation were shipping weapons to the *contras* for the CIA. Evergreen, which is headquartered at an isolated airstrip in Arizona, has ties to two CIA-associated airlines, Intermountain Aviation and Air America. The mysterious airline began working on a contract in 1983 to restore infrastructure destroyed in El Salvador's civil war. It was reported that the man who negotiated the AID-Evergreen contract was Colonel Nicholas Carranza.[32]

Other U.S. intelligence agencies active in Central America are the Defense Intelligence Agency (DIA), the National Security Agency (NSA), and the State Department's Bureau of Intelligence and Research (INR). The Army's Intelligence Support Activity (ISA) unit, which was established in the wake of the abortive hostage rescue attempt in Iran in 1980, is involved in supporting CIA covert activities in Central America.[33]

Also included in the Pentagon's intelligence arsenal is the Joint Special Operations Command at Fort Bragg, which has provided both equipment and personnel for "special operations" in Central America. In addition, the Joint Special Operations Agency, headed by a lieutenant general from the Marine Corps, conducts all "special forces operations and war plans against terrorists."[34] The relationship between the CIA and the Special Forces of each branch of the military is not defined but it is commonly acknowledged that the CIA uses the Special Forces for its covert missions. This working relationship extends to former members of the Special Forces who form the core of the mercenary groups active in Central America.

Private Anticommunist Aid to Central America

Encouraged by the Reagan administration, an array of right-wing private organizations have created a new dimension to the Central American political crisis by providing mercenaries, combat instruction, and material aid to anti-communist operations. The origins of this practice date back to 1979, when Somoza's son and Nicaragua's former defense minister started drumming up private support in the United States for a counterrevolutionary campaign against the Sandinistas. Somoza worked through a private right-wing group called the Caribbean Commission.

The aid from the private groups has gone mainly to the *contras* and Nicaraguan refugees but a substantial amount has also been channeled to pacification efforts in Guatemala and El Salvador. While most of the private aid for the anticommunist troops arrives in the form of "humanitarian" assistance like clothing and medicine, the aid also includes combat instruction, weapons, aircraft, and salaries. These groups work closely with the CIA, AID, and the U.S. military in supporting U.S. strategy in Central America.

The Reagan administration has given its enthusiastic support to private-aid groups. When asked about the activities of these private groups, a Reagan aide said, "More power to them."[35] The Pentagon has assisted the efforts of right-wing groups by transporting their aid to Central America on U.S. planes and arranging contacts with military officers and *contra* leaders.[36] As a result of the Denton Amendment, passed in 1985, the Pentagon is allowed by law to ship "humanitarian" aid to Central America on a "space-available" basis. Andy Messing, director of the right-wing National Defense Council, briefed President Reagan on the importance of nonmilitary aid in counterinsurgency operations. "The thing that drives the commies nuts," said Messing, "is positive action, food, and medicine in those areas."[37]

The U.S. corporate community, particularly defense contractors, are a chief source of this anticommunist aid. Over 40 major pharmaceutical corporations— Parke-Davis, Eli Lilly, Upjohn, Squibb, and Searle, to name a few—have contributed to right-wing aid campaigns in El Salvador. In early 1985, Malcolm Forbes, the editor of *Forbes* business magazine, noted connections between the *contras*' war against Nicaragua and U.S. corporate interests. "For moral and strategic reasons, Congress had better vote a healthy flow of support for the *contras*," he editorialized. "Their fight is our fight, too."[38]

According to a report by the Arms Control and Foreign Policy Caucus (House of Representatives):

> These [private-aid] groups are largely operated by a small group of about half a dozen men, mostly with military or paramilitary background, whose close association often means that the groups work in tandem.
>
> Most of these groups are not traditional relief organizations or other established groups recognized as providing humanitarian aid, but rather are ultra-conservative or paramilitary groups on the fringes of American political opinion.[39]

Private aid to the contras is being backed by prominent religious leaders. Reverend Sun Myung Moon's Unification Church has ties with six private-aid groups: American Nicaragua Association, CAUSA USA, Council for Inter-American Security, Freedom Research Foundation, International Relief Friendship Foundation, and Nicaraguan Freedom Fund.

Two other prominent figures are retired generals, John K. Singlaub and Harry C. Aderholt, who have helped organize at least ten private-aid groups. Singlaub was recalled from his command in South Korea after publicly criticizing President Carter's foreign policy. In Korea, Singlaub also served in the CIA with Nestor Sanchez, the top Pentagon planner for Central America. As head of the Joint Unconventional Task Force in Vietnam, Singlaub pioneered new unconventional warfare techniques. Aderholt served in Vietnam as Singlaub's deputy. In 1984, Defense Undersecretary Fred Ikle asked Singlaub and Aderholt to participate in a government policy-making panel, which recommended increased emphasis on psychological warfare, military/civic action, and small-unit operations.[40] In line with those recommendations, the Pentagon in 1985 created a new office to coordinate humanitarian assistance.

Other military personnel, retired and active, also play prominent roles in private-aid groups: Robert K. Brown: served in the Phoenix program under Singlaub in Vietnam, founded *Soldier of Fortune* magazine; Lieutenant General Daniel Graham (ret.): former Chief of the Defense Intelligence Agency, officer of CAUSA USA; Mike Kelly: Air Force Deputy Assistant Secretary for Personnel, director of Freedom Research Foundation; General Edward Lansdale (ret.): played a key role in the creation of Special Forces and oversaw original pacification efforts in Vietnam, a member of Pentagon panel run by Singlaub, Lansdale sits on the board of the National Defense Council; M.S. McColl: served with Air Force Intelligence and CIA, director of Institute for Regional and International Studies; Colonel Mac McCoskrie (ret.): ran the Air Force Speial Operations training school before retiring, on the board of Air Commando Association; Andy Messing: major in Special Forces Reserve, director of National Defense Council Foundation and Conservative Caucus; Tom Posey: former Marine sergeant, founder of Civilian Military Assistance; M.G. "Pat" Robertson: former Marine combat officer, TV evangelist for the Christian Broadcasting Network; Phillip Sanchez: former Chief of the Defense Intelligence Agency and former ambassador to Honduras, officer of CAUSA USA; General Richard G. Stilwell (ret.): on Advisory Committee of Americares; Lieutenant General Gordon Sumner (ret.): chair of Council for Inter-American Security; General David Woellner (ret.): former Air Force special operations officer in Korea and Vietnam, president of CAUSA USA.

Below is a listing of the right-wing private aid groups active in Central America. Included in the listing are business connections of the organizations. Some firms have contributed to the organizations while others are connected through company officials on the boards of the organizations.

■

Right-Wing Groups Providing Aid to Central America

Air Commando Association (ACA): Fort Walton Beach, Florida. Principals: General Aderholt, Colonel Mac McCoskrie (ret.). Business Connections: Northrop Corp, Curt Messex. Former Air Force, Army, Navy and Marine Corps Special-Operations personnel can join this 1500-member group, which transports material aid from other private-aid groups to the contras and to the Salvadoran and Guatemalan military. Air Commando was the original name for military Special Operations. As part of Guatemala's pacification program, ACA opened a clinic in Nebaj, partially equipped clinics at Playa Grande and Chimaltenango, and has two more planned for Chisec and Santa Elena.

Americares Foundation: New Canaan, Connecticut. Principals: Robert Macauley (president), Prescott Bush (brother of Vice-President Bush), William Simon (Citicorp, Nixon's Treasury Secretary), J. Peter Grace (W. R. Grace), Zbigniew Brzezinski. Business Connections: W.R. Grace, Citicorp, GD Searle & Company, Sterling Drug, Merck & Co, Richardson Vicks, Ciba-Geigy. In 1984, "Mercylifts" by Americares brought $14 million in medicine and food to El Salvador, Guatemala, and Honduras. Local Knights of Malta members are in charge of distributing Americares' aid. The tax-exempt foundation promised to send $20 million in humanitarian aid to Central America in 1985. Founded in 1982, Americares was one of 19 recipients of the President's Volunteer Action Award in 1984.

Bay of Pigs (2506 Brigade) Veterans Association: Miami, Florida. This anti-Castro group contributes food and clothing to the contras as well as sponsoring mercenaries. It has sent U.S. mercenaries to Costa Rica, using the ranch of Bay of Pigs veteran John Hull as a base for raids inside Honduras. Other Cuban exile groups that support the *contras* include Freedom Fighters, and Alpha-66. Huber Matos, commander of the Movement for an Independent and Democratic Cuba, accompanied *contras* on combat missions inside Nicaragua along with other Cuban exiles.

Caribbean Commission (CC): New Orleans, Louisiana. Business Connections: Robinson Lumber. Principals: Dr. Arnold Ochsner, Archbishop Hannan of New Orleans, LA State Representative Woody Jenkins, Samuel Robinson. Formed in 1979 with help of pro-Somoza Nicaraguans, CC aims to "maintain, promote and strengthen the free enterprise system in the western hemisphere to prevent totalitarian infiltration." Aside from anticommunist education, CC distributes aid to *contras* in Honduras. Dr. Ochsner's father wrote the white-supremacist book *Disposessed Minority*. David Duke, a former KKK leader and founder of the National Association of White People, works closely with CC.

Christian Broadcasting Network (CBN): Virginia Beach, Virginia. Principals: M.G. "Pat" Robertson. CBN's religious television programming is broadcast throughout the United States and in 25 countries, including those in Central America. Through "Operation Blessing" CBN provides aid to Nicaraguan refugees. During the Ríos Montt regime, CBN sent agricultural and medical technicians to help plan "model villages" for the Guatemalan military. Robertson, a former W.R. Grace official in Central America, directs the right-wing political lobby called National Planning Committee.

Civilian Military Assistance (CMA): Memphis, Tennessee. Principals: Tom Posey. Founder Tom Posey, a former Marine sergeant, candidly described the 1000-member CMA: "We like to think of ourselves as missionary-mercenaries. We do it for the cause." Almost all CMA members are Vietnam veterans living in the south-eastern United States. They work closely with *SOF* to train Salvadoran troops. CMA received national attention when two members were killed as their helicopter was shot down inside Nicaragua in September 1984. Its associate group is Civilian Refugee Military Assistance (CRMA), also based in Memphis. Fifty CMA members in Honduras train *contras* "in demolition, weapons, tactics . . ." In an application to the Treasury Department to become a firearms dealer, Posey said, "I plan to buy weapons and ammo to send them to El Salvador."

Confederation of the Associations for the Unification of the Societies of the Americas (CAUSA): New York, New York. As the political arm of Reverend Sun Myung Moon's Unification Church, CAUSA provides both cash and equipment to the *contras*. Headed by Air Force General David Woellner (ret.), its board includes former ambassador to Honduras Phillip Sanchez and the former chief of the Defense Intelligence Agency, Lieutenant General Daniel Graham (ret.). CAUSA brought *contra* leader Fernando Chamorro to the United States on an all-expense-paid trip to unite Nicaraguan exile groups. The International Relief Friendship Foundation, a CAUSA affiliate, sends aid to Miskito Indians in Honduras.

Conservative Caucus: Washington, DC. Principals: Andy Messing, Howard Phillips, Dr. Arnold Ochsner, Woody Jenkins. Directed by Howard Phillips and Andy Messing, the Caucus contributed to the "Shoeboxes for Liberty" campaign, which sent nonmilitary supplies to the *contras* in a Mississippi Air National Guard plane. A telling note was attached to the "shoeboxes": "We hope the small things in this box are useful in your struggle for freedom."

Council for the Defense of Freedom: The Council coordinates the work of anticommunist committees concerned with Nicaragua, Angola, El Salvador, Afghanistan, Kampuchea, and Vietnam. Members of the Nicaragua committee include: Father Enrique Rueda of the Free Congress Foundation, Dan Fefferman of the Freedom Leadership Foundation, Reed Irvine of Accuracy in Media, and Lynn Bouchey of the Council for Inter-American Security.

Council for Inter-American Security (CIS): Principals: Lieutenant General Gordon Sumner (consultant to the State Department's Bureau of Inter-American Affairs), Lynn Bouchey. In May 1985 the Council sponsored a "Nicaraguan Freedom Gala." Funds raised were used for a radio advertisement campaign in support of U.S. aid for the *contras*. CIS produced the film *Attack on the Americas*, promoted the "Shoeboxes for Liberty" campaign, and produces the newsletter *Westwatch*.

Council for National Policy: New Orleans, Louisiana. Principals: Joseph Coors, Herbert and Nelson Bunker Hunt, Pat Boone, Jerry Falwell, Senator Jesse Helms, Senator John East, General Singlaub, Dr. Ochsner, Pat Robertson, and Woody Jenkins. Business Connections: Adolph Coors, Viguerie Co, *Saturday Evening Post*, Hunt Energy, Amway, Mr. Steak, Columbia Pictures Communications, *Washington Times*.

An influential right-wing think tank, the Council regularly sponsors speaking tours for *contra* leaders. It coordinates its activity with U.S. military/civic action programs in Central America. Its advisory board is stacked with right-wing fundamentalists like Jerry Falwell of Moral Majority, James Robinson of the Robinson Evangelistic Crusade, and Jim Groen of Youth for Christ International.

Freedom Research Foundation (FRF): Principals: Jack Wheeler, Alex Alexier, Mike Kelly. FRF provides public relations services and networking help for third-world anticommunist groups. It is associated with and financed by the Reason Foundation of Santa Barbara and the Conservative Caucus. Jack Wheeler covers "anti-Soviet liberation movements" for the *Washington Times*. Also on FRF's board of directors are Alex Alexiev of the Rand Corporation and Mike Kelly, U.S. Air Force deputy assistant secretary for manpower and personnel.

Friends of the Americas (FOA): Baton Rouge, Louisiana. Principals: Diane and Woody Jenkins. FOA executive director Diane Jenkins and her husband, Louisiana State Representative Woody Jenkins, have opened outposts in Rus Rus and Danli in Honduras to distribute aid. FOA insists its donations go only to bonafide refugees, but Congressional staff members and Catholic Relief Service workers contend that FOA aid keeps refugees near the border and sustains contras. Steadman Fagoth of the *contras* acknowledged that his group received two shipments of food from FOA in one month in 1983. Its advertisements appeal for cash contributions for "a large airplane," for "boats and outboard motors," and for such war-oriented equipment as radios, walkie-talkies and a satellite dish. The "Shoe Boxes for Liberty" campaign is spearheaded by FOA. FOA uses an FDN contra safehouse in Tegucigalpa to store supplies and relies on Honduran Army trucks and a CIA-created airline called SETCO to transport supplies. FOA's liaison with the Honduran army, Captain Lionel Luque Jimenez, doubles as the army's liaison with the *contras*. In April 1985, President Reagan awarded Diane Jenkins the First Annual Ronald Reagan Humanitarian Award.

Institute for Regional and International Studies: Boulder, Colorado. Principals: General Singlaub, M.S. McColl. IRIS was formed by General Singlaub in 1984 to train the *contras* and Salvadoran police. M.S. McColl is the military affairs editor of *Soldier of Fortune*. Singlaub said this tax-exempt organization will "recruit people" with skills in intelligence gathering and psychological operations for use in Central America.

Knights of Malta: East Canton, Ohio. Principals: J. Peter Grace, William Simon, Prescott Bush Jr., William Casey (CIA director). This elite Catholic organization models itself after an order of soldier-monks that fought in the Crusades. Its formal name is the Sovereign Military Hospitaller Order of St. John, of Jerusalem, of Rhodes, and of Malta. The Knights, which have 10,000 members in 42 countries, are organized diplomatically as the world's only sovereign nation without its own territory. According to J. Peter Grace, the Knights of Malta can move its aid through diplomatic pouches without going through customs because it has ambassadors in 40 countries. They have aided Nicaragua's anti-Sandinista Archbishop Obando y Bravo. The Knights distribute Americare's donations. Its coordinator in Honduras is Roberto Alejos, the Guatemalan oligarch whose plantation was used by the CIA to train Cuban exiles for the Bay of Pigs invasion. Gerald Coughlan, the head of the Knights in El Salvador, is retired FBI and an executive of International Harvester in El Salvador where Americares shipments are warehoused.

National Defense Council Foundation (NDC): Washington, DC. Principals: Andy Messing, General Aderholt (ret.), General Edward Lansdale (ret.) The Council sent aid to the Guatemalan military for use in the "model villages" near the Mexican border. NDC has also sent supplies to El Salvador and Honduras. Messing has close ties with General Singlaub (ret.) and has advised the Pentagon on counterinsurgency warfare programs in Central America. Gabriel Gomez del Rio (an anti-Castro Cuban who formerly worked with the AID Mission in Guatemala) is the Council's Latin America director and General Aderholt serves as military adviser.

Nicaraguan Freedom Fund (NFF): Principals: Jeane Kirkpatrick, William Simon, Midge Decter (Committee for a Free World), Michael Novak (American Enterprise Institute). Funded by the *Washington Times* newspaper (associated with Unification Church), this nonprofit organization raises funds for the *contras*. Kirkpatrick asked Ralston Purina to send its $2,500 payment for photographing her Siamese cat, Arthur, to the NFF.

Nicaraguan Refugee Fund (NRF): The sponsors of NRF represent a "who's who" of prominent U.S. citizens aiding the *contras*, including J. Peter Grace, Woody Jenkins, Nelson Bunker Hunt, Pat Robertson, Joseph Coors, W. Clement Stone, Wayne Newton, and Roger Staubach. In April 1985, NRF sponsored a $250-plate dinner honoring President Reagan.

Refugee Relief International (RRI): RRI, a tax-exempt, nonprofit organization, sends medical supplies to the Salvadoran military. The organization's brochure explains the purpose of private-sector aid: "This type of aid will defray costs that the U.S. government would ordinarily incur, thereby freeing a portion of its financial allocations for additional military and other assistance." Headed by Thomas Reisinger, of *Soldier of Fortune*, RRI works closely with the Air Commando Association. RRI says: "We believe in President Reagan's challenge for the 'private sector' to parallel government efforts in supplying needed assistance to those suffering in the midst of armed conflicts."

Soldier of Fortune (SOF): Boulder, Colorado. Principals: General Singlaub (ret.), General Aderholt (ret.) (unconventional warfare editor), Robert K. Brown. *SOF* has sent over a dozen training teams to El Salvador to supplement efforts of the U.S. Military Group. The training ranges from first aid instruction to sniping and anti-guerrilla urban warfare. *SOF* sent *contras* anti-aircraft weaponry capable of downing Sandinista helicopters. *SOF* republished the controversial CIA *contra* manual. *SOF* has been repeatedly charged with implementing paramilitary operations of the CIA.

U.S. Council for World Freedom (USCWF): Phoenix, Arizona. Principals: General Singlaub (ret.), Joseph Coors, Bert Hurlbut, Mr. and Mrs. John Howell. Business Connections: Howell Instruments, Coors, First Texas Royalty and Exploration. The USCWF, which received federal tax-exemption status in 1982, is the U.S. branch for the World Anticommunist League. Singlaub said he used the League's national and international contacts to send Nicaraguan *contras* boats, clothing, and weapons.

World Anticommunist League (WACL): Principals: Genera. Singlaub (ret.) (president). WACL's branch, the Latin American anticommunist League, has organized death squads in El Salvador, Guatemala, and Honduras. The chief of the Guatemalan chapter is Mario Sandoval Alarcón, a founder of *La Mano Blanca* death squad and former Guatemalan vice-president. WACL coordinates fundraising for the *contras* from U.S. individuals and corporations and from foreign sources. In a 1981 report, the Anti-Defamation League of B'nai B'rith described the WACL as a "gathering place for extremists, racists, and anti-Semites" and that it was founded in 1966 with "heavy support from Taiwanese and South Korean leaders."

World Medical Relief (WMR): Detroit, Michigan. Principals: General Aderholt. Business Connections: Kresge, General America Life Insurance, Manufacturers Bank, Detroit Edison. WMR has sent aid to El Salvador but focuses now on aiding the *contras* and anti-Sandinista Miskito Indians. During 1960s and 1970s, WMR distributed $100 million in medical supplies to U.S. counterinsurgency projects in Laos in which General Aderholt participated. WMR conducted a program of "humanitarian relief" that distributed medical supplies to CIA-backed mercenary tribes known as the Meos.

Sources: Fred Clarkson, "Privatizing the War," *Covert Action Information Bulletin*, Winter 1983; *New York Times*, July 15, 1984; *National Catholic Reporter*, July 20, 1984, January 11, 1984, August 3, 1984, August 27, 1985; *Washington Post*, September 16 and 17, 1984, May 3, 1985; *New York Times*, July 15, 1984; *The Guardian*, March 13, 1985; *Boston Globe*, December 30, 1984; *The Nation*, October 6, 1984, March 9, 1985; *Pacific News Service*, May 24, 1984; *Washington Post*, December 27, 1984; Witness for Peace and Coalition for Nicaragua, *Private Funding of the Contra*, April 1985; *Congressional Record*, April 23, 1985; Peter Stone, "Who Says Old Soldiers Fade Away," *Boston Globe*, December 30, 1984; *Miami Herald*, May 5, 1985.

Israel: Arms Dealer and Military Adviser

Ranked as the seventh largest international arms trader, Israel's military-industrial complex dominates that country's economy and accounts for almost 15 percent of the workforce and 25–40 percent of the country's exports. About 150 military contractors do business in the country, but 90 percent of the production comes from four industries: Israeli Aircraft Industries, Israeli Military Industries, Tadiran, and Soltam. In 1983 arms sales accounted for 16 percent of Israel's foreign revenues—the highest rate of any arms-exporting nation.[41]

Israel's swift ascent as an international arms trader was made possible by over $30 billion in U.S. military and economic aid from 1962 through 1985. From 1981 through 1984, Israel received 32 percent of total U.S. military aid to the world. From 1950 to 1985, Washington has waived repayments of $15 billion in Foreign Military Sales. Each year, Israel is exempted from repayment of at least $500 million. For the balance of the sales agreements, Israel enjoys special repayment terms of 30 years with a 10-year grace period.[42] Repayment period for most countries is 12 years.

Pointing to the symbiotic nature of the U.S.-Israeli relationship, Yaakov Meridor, Israel's minister for economic coordination, said in 1981: "We shall say to the Americans: 'Don't compete with us in the Caribbean area or in any other country where you can't operate in the open. Let us do it.' I even use the expression, 'You sell the ammunition and equipment by proxy. Israel will be your proxy.'"[43]

In 1981, the Reagan administration proposed that the two countries sign a "strategic cooperation" agreement by which third-world nations can purchase Israeli military hardware with U.S. credit. A Tel Aviv newspaper reported that discussions over such an agreement were brought up again in 1984 but it was not known if an agreement was ever reached.[44]

There has also been discussion about the creation of a special fund to finance Israeli aid to El Salvador. Captured PLO weapons in Lebanon have gone to El Salvador, Guatemala, Honduras, and the *contras*. The weaponry going to Central America includes Arava planes, Galil assault rifles, and Uzi submachine guns, as well as bazookas, mortars, and grenade launchers.

In the last few years, Israel has gone beyond its role as a commercial arms supplier. El Salvador and Costa Rica demonstrated their appreciation by moving their embassies from Tel Aviv to Jerusalem, becoming the first two countries to officially recognize Israel's possession of the occupied city. In 1984, Israel reciprocated by reopening its embassy in San Salvador which had been closed since 1959.

According to Binyamin Beit Hallahmi, an Israeli professor who specializes in Israel's relationship with third-world nations, Israel is "actively involved in so-called trouble spots where the U.S. cannot be involved directly. Guatemala is the prime example."[45] Israeli military sales to Guatemala stepped up in the mid-1970s when Great Britain persuaded the United States to reduce sales because of Guatemala's hostility to the then British colony Belize. In the late 1970s, Israeli specialists joined Argentine and Chilean experts in interrogation and intelligence operations. Israel's involvement increased when Ríos Montt took power in 1982 and extended to training in counterinsurgency. Ríos Montt's chief of staff called Israel "Guatemala's number one friend."

The Guatemalan military borrowed some of their concepts for their strategic model-villages program from Israel's experience. The director of PAAC (Plan of Assistance to the Areas of Conflict) said, "Many of our technicians have been trained in Israel. The kibbutz and moshav models are very much part of our spirit."[46] When speaking of their plan for "integrated nationalism," Guatemalan generals called it the "Palestinization" of the Highlands' Indian population.

In 1984, Guatemala opened its first munitions factory in the province of Alta Verapaz. The plant, which produces ammunition for Israeli weapons, was set up with the assistance of the Israeli firm Eagle Military Gear. Guatemala announced that up to 30 percent of production would be sold to El Salvador and Honduras.

Israelis helped fund and staff the country's Army Transmissions and Electronics School, established in 1981 to train Guatemalan officers in the use of sophisticated counterinsurgency equipment. Tadiran Israel Electronic Industries (partly owned by the U.S. corporation GTE) has a small plant in Guatemala that assisted the military in the compilation of computerized information on 80 percent of the population. As many as 300 Israeli advisers have been in Guatemala since the early 1980s, including radar-system operators at the international airport, military advisers, and development experts. Appreciative of Israel's assistance, the Guatemalan government awarded Israel's ambassador its highest honor, the medal of the Order of Quetzal.

The Institute for Strategic Studies in London reported that a full 80 percent of El Salvador's military purchases between 1972 and 1980 came from Israel. After Washington became involved in 1980, Israel took on a secondary role. But in 1981, when Congress set a limit on military aid to El Salvador, Israel lent El Salvador $21 million from the aid it had received from the United States. In 1984, the Israeli newspaper *Ha'aretz* reported that Washington has proposed that Israel become a conduit for U.S. aid to anticommunist forces in Central America. The paper said that the United States would establish a fund independent of the government budget to finance projects in Central America. The State Department denied this report but acknowledged that Israel did have plans to increase its economic and military aid to El Salvador.[47]

The Democratic Revolutionary Front (FDR) has charged, however, that as many as 100 Israeli military advisers operate in El Salvador. FDR representative Arnoldo Ramos said that Central American governments respect the Israelis for their "ability to bend Washington's will for their ends."[48] The military chieftains of Central America admire Israel because it has resorted to military force in defiance of world opinion.

Israel was a principal supplier to Honduras in the 1970s, selling the country fighter planes, tanks, mortars, and light arms. In an agreement worked out with the CIA, Israel also supplies the *contras* with weapons captured from the PLO in Lebanon.

In the last several years, Israel has developed close ties with Costa Rica, where it has 100 development experts. Israel trained and reorganized the country's national police, and the two countries recently entered into an agreement whereby Costa Rica will receive 500 Galils.

Drawing on its experience in the settlement projects on the West Bank, Israel offered to coordinate a proposed border settlement project funded by AID on the Nicaraguan border.[49] The idea of this project is to settle the northern border with anticommunist Costa Rican farmers and supply them with infrastructure, credit, and technical services. They in turn would provide cover for a series of *contra* base camps in the region.

Meir Pa'il, an Israeli colonel and visiting scholar at Columbia University, said that Israel is an arms merchant in Central America "primarily because it needs to support the costly domestic arms production so crucial to its own defense, and to find sources of export strength for its very hard pressed economy. These economic realities provide compelling incentives for selling arms abroad."[50]

Profiles of Central American Armies

COSTA RICA

In 1949, Costa Rica took the unusual step of abolishing its army after a traumatic civil war. It was replaced with a Civil Guard under the minister of security, and later joined by the Rural Guard under the minister of the interior. The Rural Guard, created in 1969, has been used mainly to evict peasant squatters and to crack down on illegal liquor stills.

Although officially lacking an army, Costa Rica has embarked on a military build-up paid for and directed by Washington. The Reagan administration says that the country's Civil and Rural Guards need to be better trained and equipped to defend the country against neighboring Nicaragua. Washington initially skirted the 1974 congressional prohibition against the training of police forces by calling its military aid "security assistance." In 1985, President Reagan asked Congress to "allow U.S. military assistance to be furnished to the law enforcement agencies of countries such as Costa Rica, which rely on [the agencies] to provide for national defense and security."

Signs of this new militarization include creation of a U.S. trained Costa Rican Counterinsurgency Reaction battalion; establishment of a counterinsurgency training camp near the Nicaraguan border; the upgrading of three airstrips to accommodate huge C-130 transport planes; and the unprecedented in-country training by U.S. Special Forces advisers of 700 civil guardsmen in military skills in 1985. Costa Rica also counts on Israel and Taiwan to train guardsmen in counterinsurgency and "political warfare."

Washington renewed its military aid program to Costa Rica in 1982. Between 1950 and 1981, Costa Rica received less than $1 million in military aid (MAP). From 1982 through 1986, the country has received over $33 million in military aid.

General Paul Gorman, the former chief of SOUTHCOM, remarked that it would be easier, militarily, to take Managua from the south through Costa Rica than from north through Honduras.[51] The likely scenario for an invasion would be a border incident between Nicaragua and Costa Rica, with the United States coming to the aid of Costa Rica and taking on the Sandinista army. An adviser to Costa Rican President Monge told the *New York Times* in 1984 that "what

Reagan needs from Costa Rica is the moral support for an invasion of Nicaragua."[52]

Costa Ricans generally oppose the militarization of their country. Some members of the elite support increased training and aid to the guardsmen because of their fear that the current economic crisis might lead to popular militancy. The Costa Rican government is trying to cling to its position of neutrality but at the same time has felt forced to yield to U.S. pressure for increased militarization. Because the country is so dependent on U.S. economic aid, it is extremely vulnerable to U.S. pressure.

The main considerations of the military situation in Costa Rica are the following:

- Traditional neutralism and pacifism are being undermined by U.S.-sponsored militarization.
- Security forces have doubled from 1979 to 1984.
- Official and unofficial paramilitary forces have grown significantly.
- There has been a rapid evolution of Civil and Rural Guards from unskilled police forces into armed forces with counterinsurgency and defense capabilities.
- The Pentagon plans to build roads and repair bridges in the Northern Zone. Costa Rica has forestalled full implementation of this plan.
- *Contras* operate freely in the Northern Zone, where border incidents may provide a pretext for direct U.S. military involvement.

EL SALVADOR

On the main highways, billboards proclaim: "All for the Fatherland: People and Army United." Since 1982, El Salvador has had a civilian government, but the Salvadoran army remains the dominant institution. After more than five years of civil war, the Salvadoran army is better disciplined, better equipped, and over 4 times as large.

While the army is much stronger than it was in 1980 when the civil war broke out, it is still plagued by low morale. The reason for the lack of enthusiasm for the antiguerrilla war is that the ranks of the army are filled with peasants and poor urban workers. Unlike the guerrillas who are powerfully motivated, the government soldiers in this counterinsurgency war are more disposed to run than to fight. Explaining the army's recruitment methods, one colonel said, "In my district, people leave home and become soldiers so they can eat. To fill out the ranks, we go to a football stadium and round them up by force."[53]

The children of the upper classes are seldom found in the army. "I am sure," said Auxiliary Bishop Gregorio Rosa Chávez, "that well-off people who vehemently defend the military solution would think differently if their own sons, who now study, work, or simply idle away their youth in a frivolous or superficial life, had to go fight on the battlefields."[54]

Besides the lack of morale, the army is weakened by the absence of a strong officer corps. Historically, the army has produced only some 30 officers a year. The United States has tried to remedy this gap by training large numbers of noncommissioned officers. But most U.S. trained officers do not reenlist. Only 10 percent of the noncommissioned officers trained at Fort Benning have stayed in the army.[55]

The Salvadoran army expanded from 10,000 in 1978 to over 39,000 in 1984. Besides the other components of the armed forces—Air Force, National Guard, National Police, and Treasury Police—the army can count on the assistance of a civilian support network formed by the ORDEN members. A study by the Council on Hemispheric Affairs (COHA) said that "the training and equipment of ORDEN's personnel are probably as good as or better than those of the militias in Nicaragua."[56]

The nature of the civil war has sharply changed since 1980. Under the wing of the United States, the Salvadoran army has become an increasingly effective counterinsurgency force. With the ground war at a stalemate, the Pentagon introduced an air war to tiny El Salvador. By late 1984, its helicopter fleet had increased from less than 20 to between 50 and 60. Military operations also rely on six A-37 Dragonfly bombers that regularly drop U.S.-issue 500-pound and 750-pound bombs on the 25 percent of Salvadoran territory controlled by the guerrillas.[57]

Human-rights groups have condemned the indiscriminate killing caused by the air war. Targets for the Salvadoran pilots are set by U.S. surveillance planes that fly over the country every day. The intensified air war has forced civilians to flee guerrilla-controlled zones, thereby depriving the guerrillas of their base of support. The isolated guerrillas then become more vulnerable to military offensives and air attacks.

Pacification programs are another major feature of the army's strategy for victory. The chief components of the army's pacification campaign are the following:

- Formation of civil-defense patrols, but with far less success than a similar program in Guatemala.
- Psychological warfare, using films and military education programs to win over peasants in zones of conflict.
- Use of humanitarian aid and refugee programs run by AID-funded CONADES and CONARA to gain control over the populace (see Chapter 3).
- Reconstruction work in zones of conflict that give people temporary jobs and reduce support for the guerrillas.
- Forced resettlement projects that separate the population from the guerrillas, allowing the army to treat guerrilla strongholds as free-fire zones.

Long beholden to the country's oligarchy, the army has shifted its allegiance to Washington, which trains its troops and pays its bills. The ascendence of technological warfare—air surveillance, sophisticated communications, and the use of multimillion-dollar aircraft—has made the Salvadoran army more dependent than ever on U.S. military aid and training. In return for U.S. assistance, the army has agreed to refrain from military coups and to support the political process.

In early 1985, there were about 100 U.S. military personnel based in El Salvador. Two-thirds of them were serving as advisers to the Salvadoran army, often working at the regional military bases around the country. Their tasks include teaching mortar sighting and map reading, fixing helicopters, demonstrating prisoner interrogation, and giving instructions on amphibious attack tactics.[58] About 25 advisers work out of the U.S. defense attaché's office.

Military aid to El Salvador has steadily expanded since 1980. An increasing amount (90 percent in 1984) of U.S. military aid goes to El Salvador in the form of grants (MAP) rather than as foreign military sales (FMS). An estimated 20 percent of the arms shipped to El Salvador eventually ends up in the hands of the guerrilla organization FMLN.[59]

The main considerations of the military situation in El Salvador are the following:

- Increased discipline and professionalism of Salvadoran military but continued low morale.
- Adoption of more sophisticated counterinsurgency/pacification techniques along the lines of the Guatemalan military.
- New capacity to wage an air war, which has caused a wave of refugees to flee from guerrilla zones.
- Decreased human rights violations by armed forces but rising civilian deaths from indiscriminate bombing.
- Guerrilla opposition calls for negotiated settlement and government of "broad participation," while Washington and Salvadoran armed forces think that military victory is possible.
- Military tolerance of civilian government, knowing that a military coup would jeopardize continued high levels of U.S. aid.

GUATEMALA

In 1979, the army was caught unawares when a guerrilla offensive broke loose in the Highlands. President Lucas García struck back with a scorched-earth campaign that continued into 1983. In 1982, the Diocese of El Quiché had to close down because of constant repression and threats on the life of the Bishop. Rather than going directly after the guerrillas, the army targeted their popular base of support. Colonel Roberto Mata, the commander of an embattled section of El Quiché department, said the army aims "to separate the fish from the sea" by drying up the popular base of support.

For the last 30 years, the Guatemalan army has been developing its counterinsurgency techniques. The army summed up its role in the "Manual of Counterinsurgency," which states: "Counter-subversive war is total, permanent, and universal, and it requires the massive participation of the population like the subversive war it confronts ... our objective is the population."

During the 1960s and 1970s, most of its top military officials received U.S. counterinsurgency training. After the Carter administration's human-rights pronouncements against Guatemala in 1977, the Guatemalan government turned to Taiwan, Israel, and Argentina for military aid and guidance. Israel supplied most of the arms, while Taiwanese advisers have guided civic actions and economic development programs. In a 1984 agreement, the Taiwan government pledged to provide military training and to help the Guatemalan armed forces improve their image. "The Taiwan military are specialists in psychological warfare and their experience will be available for our use," explained General Rodolfo Lobos Zamora.[60]

Having succeeded in substantially weakening the guerrillas and reducing the links between the guerrillas and the population, the army introduced a pacification program as part of its counterinsurgency campaign. The Guerrilla Army of the Poor (EGP), one of the two main guerrilla groups, says the military is using this pacification program "to reconstruct the basis for the domination of political, ideological, and social resources on the tops of the ashes and death left by destruction and massacres."[61] According to the EGP, the basic purposes of the pacification campaign are to:

- Increase military control in isolated areas.
- Destroy community ties among the Indian population.
- Block popular support of revolutionary organizations.
- Break down the traditional Indian agrarian economy and replace it with nontraditional cash-crop production.
- Attract refugees living in Mexico and those hiding in the mountains with food-distribution and housing programs.

Army in Guatemalan Politics

Between 1871 and 1981, 18 out of 23 government heads in Guatemala have been military men or have borne military titles while in office. The country's pattern of military control was broken only by two reformist governments in power between 1944 and 1954.[62]

General Oscar Mejía Víctores serves as the commander-in-chief of the country's military. The center of power in Guatemala is the Council of Commanders, a secretive organization composed of base commanders and the military's high command. It is believed to function as a type of legislature where all the country's major political and economic decisions are made. Local authority throughout Guatemala is exercised by the zone commander, who rules with extensive autonomy within his military zone.[63]

In 1984, the military permitted elections for a constituent assembly and scheduled presidential elections for November, 1985. By ending direct military rule, the army hopes to attract more international aid and investment to boost its drooping economy. Indeed, the "democratization" of Guatemala was cited by the Reagan administration to justify increased economic and military aid to the country.

While the army promised to back out of the National Palace, it proceeded to extend its control by setting up an Inter-Institutional Coordination system. In each of the country's 22 departments, the system brings together representatives of private enterprise, the local government, and various ministries, as well as the military zone commander, into a council that coordinates all government programs for the department. The military commander presides over the council.

The Role of Washington

Despite the phasing out of new military loans and grants to Guatemala in 1978, the United States continued to be an important source of weapons. From 1978 through 1983, the U.S. Department of Defense, the U.S. Department of Commerce, and private U.S. companies sold at least $11.1 million in military equipment to Guatemala.[64] In addition, Guatemala purchased about $20 million in "civilian" helicopters that it currently uses for military purposes. Deliveries of U.S. military equipment from previous agreements also permitted U.S. government sales of $9 million in military equipment during this period. In addition, new cash sales by private companies were permitted.

In 1981, the Reagan administration allowed the Guatemalan military to buy $3.2 million in trucks and jeeps, which were sold through the Commerce Department. To make the sale possible, the Commerce Department shifted those items from the list of equipment withheld from gross human rights violators to a newly created list of items permitted under the heading "Control for Regional Stability." As such, the trucks and jeeps used by the military were not considered military equipment and subject to the law that does not permit military aid to be given to governments that consistently violate internationally recognized human rights.[65]

The Reagan administration has gradually renewed direct military aid to Guatemala. In 1984, it permitted the sale of military spare parts, saying that the aid "would serve our human rights and security objectives in Guatemala."[66] In 1985, Washington resumed a small military-training program "to expose key officer personnel to U.S. military doctrine and practice." Over $10 million in non-lethal military aid is scheduled annually for the rest of the decade.

Even during the Carter years, the United States maintained a military presence in Guatemala. In 1982, it was discovered that an army Green Beret captain had been teaching counterinsurgency tactics at a government military school, and an air force colonel had instructed 17 military pilots.[67] Presently, about 20 U.S. military personnel are stationed in the country, including a military assistance group at the U.S. Embassy which has provided advice and training to the Guatemalan armed forces.

Shortly after he arrived in the country, the U.S. Ambassador to Guatemala, Alberto Martinez Piedra, said that the renewal of U.S. military aid would allow "the incipient democracy" to defend itself and better protect its "democratic opening."[68] Also calling for renewed military aid was the right-wing Heritage Foundation, which in its 1984 report *Mandate for Leadership II* stated that the country has "strategic significance to regional and U.S. security" General Wallace H. Nutting, the head of SOUTHCOM in 1982, argued that the situation in Guatemala was potentially more serious than in El Salvador. "The population is larger, the economy is stronger, the geographical position is more critically located in a strategic sense," he said. "The implications of a Marxist takeover in Guatemala are a lot more serious than in El Salvador."[69]

The main considerations of the military situation in Guatemala are the following:

- Provision of counterinsurgency training and assistance in pacification programs by Taiwan and Israel.
- Integration of military officers into the nation's oligarchy.
- Military's resistance to involvement in U.S.-sponsored regional militarization plans.
- Inability to crush guerrilla opposition despite a disciplined army and sophisticated counterinsurgency and pacification campaigns.
- Use of international assistance by the military to operate an effective pacification program.
- An excellent intelligence network featuring computerized files and widespread monitoring of unions, universities, and church groups.
- Army control through departmental coordinators that oversee all government programs in each region.
- Military seeking economic stability without reforms and using elections to attract international aid.

HONDURAS

In 1981, Hondurans had a chance to choose the country's first democratically elected government in 20 years. Their choices were two political parties: the National Party, which was closely allied with the military, and the Liberal Party, which promised to give civilians the upper hand for the first time in Honduran history. Hondurans opted for the Liberal Party and the promise of a demilitarization of Honduran politics.

But the citizens of Honduras did not get what they were promised. After 1981, the military grew stronger as a result of a huge increase in U.S. training and aid. Between 1978 and 1984, the armed forces doubled in size to 23,000. In those same years, U.S. military aid increased almost twentyfold. The military, with confidence spawned by this aid, talked of war with Nicaragua. In 1983, the military's commander-in-chief General Gustavo Alvarez Martínez boasted that by his next birthday he would be marching into Managua.

From 1981 until his ouster in early 1984, Alvarez was the most powerful man inside Honduras with the exception of the U.S. ambassador. President Suazo Córdova gave him free rein to speed up the militarization of Honduras by collaborating with the *contras*, assisting the Salvadoran military in boxing in the FMLN guerrillas and ushering in the U.S. military. Suazo Córdova, in turn, benefited from increased U.S. economic aid and the support of the military for his government.

The country was turned into a military outpost for the United States, which began conducting massive war games on Honduran soil and building a country-wide military infrastructure of bases, airstrips, and radar stations. Honduras was also drawn into a regional war, as U.S.-supported *contras* freely operated on its southern border, Green Berets instructed Salvadoran troops at a U.S.-constructed training center, and the U.S. military used Honduras as a base for regular reconnaissance flights over Nicaragua and El Salvador. As one Honduran military officer said, "We now have four armies [Honduran, U.S., Salvadoran, and *contras*] within our national territory."[70]

Honduras, which had no pressing disputes in 1979, has turned into a fulcrum of U.S. power in Central America and a base for aggression against Nicaragua. In 1980, the country agreed to allow the United States to use the country for its own military purposes in return for greatly increased military and economic aid. A permanent U.S. military contingent is based in Honduras, and total U.S. troop count has been as high as 12,000 during war games. Naval exercises have been even more extensive. The Ocean Venture war games of 1984 involved 30,000 U.S. and Honduran troops.[71]

Expanded Military Infrastructure in Honduras

Not only did the war games heighten the war fever in the region, but they also served to build up the military infrastructure. During the exercises, roads were constructed, airstrips widened or new ones created, barracks built, and ocean ports deepened.

Before the war games began in 1982, Honduras had three airfields capable of landing the giant C-130 Hercules transport planes. By the end of 1984, the country counted on at least eleven C-130-capable airstrips. The Pentagon claimed that the infrastructure created during the exercises is temporary. U.S. Army engineers building the airstrips smirk when they hear the facilities referred to as "temporary." "Our runway will be here for years to come because of the way we built it to withstand heavy rains," said one engineer, while another pointed out the army had ordered that power cables be placed underground, indicating the permanent nature of the facilities [72]

The U.S. military has upgraded or constructed airstrips at Aguacate, La Ceiba, Cucuyagua, La Mesa, Mocoron, Palmerola, Puerto Castilla, Puerto Lempira, San Lorenzo, and Trujillo. Another feature of the U.S. military presence is a radar station operated by U.S. Air Force personnel, which regularly monitors Nicaragua's air space. Besides these facilities, the U.S. Navy has proposed the construction of a $150 million naval base at Puerto Castilla to replace the obsolete facilities at Guantanamo Bay in Cuba.

The Palmerola Air Base is the center of the U.S. military presence in Honduras. Its airstrip has the only lighted facilities in the country, and can accommodate any aircraft in the U.S. military arsenal. Daily reconnaissance flights leave Palmerola to provide information on Salvadoran guerrilla movements to the Salvadoran army and on Nicaraguan forces to the *contras* and the CIA. The National Security Agency conducts reconnaissance missions over Nicaragua from the La Ceiba Air Force Base.

The Pentagon says the military bases in Honduras are to protect the country from an invasion by Nicaragua. When questioned closely, though, neither U.S. nor Honduran military officials think a conventional attack by Nicaragua is possible or likely. The real threat is internal subversion, as Honduras' General Shalikashvili told a congressional hearing. He said that the threat to Honduras arises from Cuba and Nicaragua "taking advantage of economic and social conditions in the region that we and our friends are trying to correct, but that we cannot correct unless we provide a security shield under which those economic, social, and governmental reforms can go forward."[73]

López Takes Charge

General Alvarez's ambitions for war and his own personal ambitions were curbed not by the civilian government but by a rival faction in the military that forced Alvarez to flee the country in March 1984. Air Force General Walter López became the new military chief.

Honduran military chieftains see themselves as ultimately responsible for the welfare of the country. Decisions are made by the Honduran Joint Chiefs, known as the Superior Council of the Armed Forces (COSUFA). Alvarez had ignored COSUFA, consulting only with those generals and colonels who supported him. López reinstituted COSUFA, which is a 42-man group of military officers.

López did not halt the process of militarization, but he did insist on more control over the process. Aspiring to be more than a game room for the U.S. military, Honduras now began clamoring for more economic and military aid.

In the words of one State Department analyst, Honduras was "squeaking, in an effort to get some grease."[74] In early 1986, López resigned following an internal power struggle within the military, which has been wracked by disputes between younger, more progressive officers and older, more corrupt ones who control the military high commmand.

The main considerations of the military situation in Honduras are the following:

- Size and spending of the armed forces have doubled since 1980.
- It has the largest and strongest air force in Central America, although El Salvador's is closing the gap.
- Its soldiers are poorly motivated.
- The ten new airstrips built by the U.S. military make the country a possible launching pad for U.S. military intervention in other countries.
- A low-level guerrilla war involving bombings and kidnappings confronts the military, which on at least one occasion has coordinated counterinsurgency operations against the guerrillas.
- The Honduran military is concerned about increased militarization of its historic foe, El Salvador.
- Increasing divisions within the military, with many young officers opposing U.S. involvement.
- The presence of *contra* forces is the cause of border incidents with Nicaragua and may be a pretext for an expanded war against the Sandinistas.

NICARAGUA

A direct American military intervention in Nicaragua would not be fought on the classic terms of one army against another," said Nicaraguan Defense Minister Humberto Ortega Saavedra. "An invading force will meet a very mobile, very irregular form of resistance. We have distributed our men and supplies around the country. This will make it very difficult to deal decisive blows against us."[75]

Nicaraguan military officials readily admit that their forces are no match for a U.S. invading force. Resistance to invasion would be in the form of guerrilla warfare, and they predict that the war against the United States would extend throughout the hemisphere as "friends of the Nicaraguan people" join forces with the Sandinistas.

Possible intervention scenarios include the following:

- The United States comes to the rescue of either Honduras or Costa Rica in the event of a border incident allegedly involving Sandinista troops.
- The United States recognizes a provisional government composed of *contra* political leaders and intervenes to back that "democratic" government.
- The United States launches naval and air strikes attacking manifestations of a Soviet build-up in Nicaragua.

● The United States responds to a CONDECA request for intervention similar to the request issued by the Organization of Eastern Caribbean States for a U.S. invasion of Grenada in 1983.

President Reagan has cited the expansion of Nicaragua's armed forces as justification for its own military build up in Central America. "Since 1979, their trained forces have increased from 10,000 to over 100,000," stated the president in 1984. "Why does Nicaragua need all this power? Why did this country of only 2.8 million build this large military force?"[76] The president was correct in saying that Nicaragua has built a large military force since 1979, but his figure of 100,000 soldiers was wildly exaggerated. A better estimate of total armed forces in Nicaragua would be 60,000.[77] Concerning the U.S. claims of a Sandinista build-up, there has been gross exaggeration. In an independent report, Lieutenant Colonel Edward King reported upon visiting Nicaragua that what a U.S. report had described as a military barracks on an aerial photograph was actually a "run down guard hut," and that two so-called "auxiliary buildings" were actually disused sheds.[78]

The country also has a 30,000- to 60,000-person militia that incorporates men, women, and children—ranging from 13 to 70 years old. Nicaragua's *milicianos* are citizens who have been provided with rudimentary arms and training in the hope that they can protect the areas where they live and work from *contra* attacks. A limited supply of weapons is shared among the *milicianos*.

The Nicaraguan build-up is defense—not offense—oriented. Nicaragua is the only country in Central America that has been subject to external attack. The United States began aiding the ex-National Guardsmen shortly after the Sandinistas overthrew the Somoza regime. At first, the support was channeled through Argentina.

In November 1981, the United States officially joined the counterrevolutionary war when President Reagan approved a $19 million CIA plan to reorganize the counterrevolutionaries into a force eventually capable of toppling the Sandinistas.

Officially, the *contras* were being funded to interdict arms flows between Nicaragua and El Salvador. Yet, not one arms shipment has ever been found by the *contras*. According to David MacMichael, a former CIA analyst in Central America, there is no credible evidence of any arms deliveries after 1981.[79] The Sandinista government testified at the World Court that Nicaragua did supply arms to the Salvadoran guerrillas for their January 1981 offensive, but there have been no arms shipments since then.[80] The *contra* war is the largest CIA operation since the Vietnam War. Nicaraguan deaths resulting from the *contra* war have been 4 times the proportional number of deaths of U.S. citizens during the Vietnam War.

The one area in which Nicaragua has military superiority over its neighbors is its tank fleet. But the fleet of some 50 tanks—most of them Soviet surplus dating back to the 1950s—does not constitute a threat to other Central American nations. The region's hilly terrain is not suitable to tank warfare, which explains why none of the other nations are interested in acquiring sizable tanks or arsenals of antitank weapons. Nicaragua would probably use its tank fleet as a first line of defense in Managua against a U.S. invasion.

Nicaragua does not have a sophisticated air force. As of 1985, the country owned no bombers or modern fighters and only some two dozen fixed-wing aircraft, which were relics of the Somoza regime. In 1984, Nicaragua acquired two sophisticated Soviet Mi24 Hind helicopter gunships to add to its fleet of 10 less advanced helicopters. The Soviet Mi24s are the most potent part of Nicaragua's air force, though they are not first-line offensive weapons. They have, however, proved effective in the war with the *contras*.

TABLE 4F

MILITARY FORCES IN CENTRAL AMERICA, BY COUNTRY, 1983–1984

	Army	Air Force	Navy	National Police*	Civil/Rural Guard	Other
Belize	———————800———————					1,800 British troops
Costa Rica	no regular armed forces				9,800	10,000**
El Salvador	39,000	2,350	300	6,000		2,500 National Guard
Guatemala	38,000	1,000	1,000	11,600	500,000–800,000	
Honduras	15,500	1,200	500	4,500		
Nicaragua	56,000	1,500	300		40,000	4,000 Border Guards
Panama	1,500	200	300	7,500		

*National Police includes Treasury Police in El Salvador and Guatemala, Public Security Forces in Honduras, and National Guard in Panama. Civil/Rural Guard includes civilian militia in Nicaragua, rural civil defense in Guatemala, and civil and rural guard in Costa Rica.

**Costa Rica's Organization for National Emergencies is a volunteer civil organization begun in 1982 to assist in national emergencies and to back up regular security forces.

SOURCES: Caribbean Basin Information Project, *On a Short Fuse: Militarization in Central America;* International Institute for Strategic Studies, *Military Balance 1984–85.*

The main considerations of the military situation in Nicaragua are the following:

- The inability of the *contras* to gain control of Nicaraguan territory or seriously threaten the Sandinista government.
- A highly committed army and militia determined to repel any foreign invasion.
- Offers by Nicaragua to allow international supervision of its borders with Costa Rica and Honduras.
- Increasing dependence on Soviet-bloc military and economic support in the face of the *contra* war and the threat of U.S. invasion.
- Widespread support of the military, in marked contrast to other Central American nations.
- A U.S. invasion not likely to draw either Cuba or the Soviet Union into military conflict with the United States.

The Foreign "Communist Threat"

The main rationale for U.S. military intervention in Central America is the Soviet-Cuban threat. This takes the form, says the Reagan administration, of a Soviet-Cuban military build-up in Nicaragua and Soviet-Cuban-Nicaraguan military aid to guerrillas in El Salvador, Guatemala, and Honduras.

The factors concerning the Soviet-Cuban "threat" in Nicaragua are the following:

- Soviet arms shipments to Nicaragua, although they have risen significantly, have not been sufficient to insure Nicaragua adequate defense from U.S.-sponsored *contra* attacks let alone sufficient to enable a successful attack on its neighbors. (The Reagan administration estimates the dollar value of Soviet-bloc military equipment to be $350 million from 1980 through 1984.)
- A report commissioned by the State Department states, "Soviet military aid to Nicaragua is unobtrusive, and sometimes ephemeral," and notes two administration claims of large weapons deliveries in 1983 that "proved hollow."[81]
- Reports of Soviet shipments of MIG-21 fighter jets have repeatedly proved false.[82]
- Cuban political and military influence in Nicaragua is strong but the Sandinistas have shown no signs of shedding their independence.
- Soviets have sent Nicaragua about 50 tanks, armored personnel carriers, heavy artillery, some 15 rocket launchers, 8 transport aircraft, 30 anti-aircraft missiles, and anti-aircraft guns.

- Washington claims that there are no fewer than 2000 Cuban military advisers as well as several hundred Soviet, East European, Libyan, and Palestinian military advisers in Nicaragua. Nicaragua acknowledges the presence of about 2000 Cubans but claims that all but a couple hundred are teachers, medical personnel, and civilian technicians.
- Communist parties in Nicaragua have little popular support and are often critical of the Sandinistas.
- Soviet response to U.S. invasion will be one of moral solidarity, not active support.

State Department consultant C. G. Jacobsen concluded Soviet support of the Sandinistas is largely of a political nature:

[The Soviet Union] had striven to give Managua the means, but the bottom line was that the Sandinistas would indeed have to defend themselves. Finally, one must note that Moscow apparently expects to benefit whatever the course of events. She appears to calculate that the political-ideological PR harvest that would accrue from an all-out U.S. invasion would outweigh the loss of immediate advantage. . . . [83]

TABLE 4G

FOREIGN MILITARY PRESENCE IN CENTRAL AMERICA, 1984

	United States	Soviet Union & Cuba
Military Aid	1981–1985: $814 million. (Does not include military construction, excess defense articles, commercial sales, economic support funds, or support from allies.)	1980–1984: $350 million from the entire Soviet Bloc.
Military Personnel	10,200 with 93 percent stationed in Panama, where U.S. SOUTHCOM is headquartered (Does not include as many as 6000 troops participating in occasional regional military maneuvers.)	Fewer than 100 Soviet Bloc advisers and 2000 Cuban personnel (Nicaragua says there are only 200–250 Cubans.)
Military Bases	11 U.S. Army, Navy and Air Force bases in Panama; Honduras and El Salvador each have one U.S. training base.	No bases in central America. One Soviet airfield in Cuba.

	United States	Soviet Union & Cuba
Foreign Training	1981–1984: 4942 IMET trainees.	265 military trainees in Soviet Union and 70 pilots trained by Bulgaria.
War Games in Caribbean Basin 1981–1985	More than 40.	Several maneuvers off Cuban coast.
Number of Direct Military Interventions	More than 30 since 1850.	None.
Military Commitment	Inter-American Treaty of Reciprocal Assistance (1947) among all Latin american nations & bilateral mutual security pacts with individual Central American nations could be used to justify U.S. intervention.	No secruity treaties with Central American nations.
	"El Salvador is on the mainland of the U.S., and we do have a responsibility for the defense of the continental U.S., over and above all other priorities." —Caspar Weinberger, U.S. Secretary of Defense.	"We will support Nicaragua politically in every way" — Soviet Ambassador to Nicaragua, after ruling out an armed response by the Soviet Union to U.S. military intervention in Nicaragua.

SOURCES: AID, *Overseas Loans and Grants July 1, 1945–September 30, 1985*; AID *Congressional Presentation FY86*, Main Volume; DOD, *Worldwide Manpower Distribution by Geographical Area December 31, 1984*; C.G. Jacobsen for the Department of State, "Soviet Attitudes Towards and Contacts with Central American Revolutionaries," June 1984; Colin Danby, David MacMichael, and Franz Schneiderman, COHA, "The Military Balance in Latin America: An Analysis and Critical Evaluation of Administration Claims," March 1, 1985; Caribbean Basin Information Project, "On a Short Fuse," 1985; Center for Defense Information, "Fact Sheet–Soviet Bloc Military Involvement in Nicaragua," February 1985; "Defense Monitor," Vol. 13, No.3, 1984.

The factors concerning the Soviet-Cuban-Nicaraguan support for the Salvadoran guerrillas are the following:

● In March 1984, Undersecretary of Defense Fred Ikle stated that roughly half of the guerrillas' weapons were U.S. weapons captured from Salvadoran troops. The FMLN claimed in 1984 to have captured military equipment equivalent to 20 percent of U.S. military aid to El Salvador in 1983.

- Reagan administration officials have refused to provide evidence to support their claims that Nicaragua materially supports the FMLN.
- While there was evidence of Cuban and Nicaraguan support of the FMLN in the first years of civil war (1979–1980), there has been only scant support since then.[84]
- There has been no capture of arms shipments between Nicaragua and El Salvador since 1981.
- There has been no evidence of Soviet material support for the guerrillas.
- The FMLN is Marxist but has never been close to Moscow.

In Central America, there has been no history of Soviet or Cuban intervention. However, on more than 30 occasions, the United States has invaded and occupied parts of Central America. If the United States does invade Nicaragua, there is little that Cuba or the Soviet Union can do. Neither country has made any commitment to defend Nicaragua. In the event of an invasion, Cubans present in Nicaragua would probably join the Sandinista defense as they did in Grenada, but there will be no additional personnel committed. Writing about this issue, C.G. Jacobsen, director of Soviet studies at the University of Miami, said: "In revolutionary circles, Moscow wants to be seen to have done everything to ensure (Nicaragua's) ability to survive and defend itself, but the bottom line that the regime must ultimately defend itself, is explicit."[85]

While the Soviets are not wholly committed to Nicaragua, neither are the Sandinistas puppets of Moscow. "Nobody is running this thing except the Sandinistas," one Western diplomat told the *Wall Street Journal*. The Sandinistas, he said, are not letting their Cuban advisers control the ministries, and "they aren't mortgaging the revolution."[86]

A Program for Peace

The militarization of Central America forms part of the overall stabilization strategy of the United States. At best, military victory over the Guatemalan and Salvadoran guerrillas would result in short-term political stability. The root causes of political and economic instability cannot be resolved by military solutions. Washington says that it wants peace, but it has refused to support the peace proposals of the Contadora Group (Mexico, Panama, Colombia, and Venezuela). It has also refused to negotiate with Nicaragua.

Possible steps toward peace in Central America might include:[87]

Nicaragua: End U.S. support for the *contra* war. Provide support for regional peace talks, such as the Contadora efforts. Recognize Nicaragua's right to determine its own type of government. Simultaneous withdrawal of foreign military advisers throughout Central America.

El Salvador: Negotiated settlement that involves powersharing among contending forces. Elections that involve all political parties. Cut-off of military aid, and use of economic aid to pressure government to make necessary reforms.

Honduras: Dismantling of U.S. bases. End U.S. support of *contras*. Withdrawal of U.S. troops. Use of economic aid to pressure government to make necessary reforms.

Guatemala: No military aid for military-controlled government. Condemnation of gross human-rights violations. No economic aid for pacification programs.

Costa Rica: Stop militarization and support country's position of neutrality and pacifism.

1 Presidential Address to Joint Session of Congress, April 28, 1983.
2 Descriptions of military-aid programs taken from Caribbean Basin Information Project, "On A Short Fuse: Militarization in Central America" (Washington), 1984.
3 NARMIC, "Up in Arms: U.S. Military Shipments to Central America" (AFSC: Philadelphia, July 1984).
4 Fred Hiatt, "Firm Gets Contracts for Honduran Camp," *Washington Post*, November 9, 1984.
5 Hearings before the Subcommittee on Foreign Operations Appropriations, Committee on Appropriations, House of Representatives, *Foreign Operations Appropriations for 1963, Part 1*, 1962, p.359.
6 Graduates of the School of Americas between 1946–1984 from Central America were: El Salvador (3967); Honduras (2985), Costa Rica (2108), Belize (6), Guatemala (1574); and Nicaragua (4693). Nicaragua was not eligible for IMET after 1979, and Guatemala received no IMET grants between 1977 and 1983. William H. Ormsbee, "US Army School of Americas: Profile of a Training Institution," *DISAM Journal*, Winter 1984–1985.
7 Ibid.
8 Ibid.
9 Mary Day Kent and Eva Gold, American Friends Service Committee (NARMIC/AFSC), "The US Army School of the Americas," 1984.
10 Joao Quartim, "Panama Closes the School for Dictators," *Africasia*, January 1985.
11 Ormsbee, *DISAM Journal*, Winter 1984–1985.
12 Ibid.
13 In 1984, instruction was expanded to offensive tactics using larger craft.
14 Graduates from the Interamerican Air Force Academy, 1943–1985: Belize (4); Costa Rica (45); El Salvador (877); Guatemala (724); Honduras (1242); and Nicaragua (811). Department of Defense Computer Printout, April 24, 1985.
15 *Airman*, November 1984, p.36.
16 NARMIC, *Invasion: A Guide to the U.S. Military Presence in Central America* (Philadelphia: AFSC, 1985) p.7.
17 *Time*, April 22, 1985.
18 *Central America Report*, March 1, 1985.
19 *New York Times*, June 4, 1985.
20 *Latin America Regional Reports* (from now on referred to as *LARR*), February 15, 1985.
21 *Defense Monitor*, Vol. 13, No. 3, 1984.
22 Subcommittee on Oversight and Evaluation, Permanent Select Committee on Intelligence,

House of Representatives, *US Intelligence Performance on Central America: Achievement and Selected Instances of Concern*, September 22, 1982.

23 *Congressional Quarterly*, April 14, 1984, p.835.
24 GAO, *Funding of Joint Combined Military Exercises in Honduras*, June 22,1984.
25 *Catholic Reporter*, August 31, 1984.
26 Ibid.
27 *Washington Post*, May 11, 1984.
28 Cited in Phillip Agee, *White Paper Whitewash* (New York: Warner Poddam, 1981), p.73.
29 Jack Anderson, "Despite Administration Policy, CIA Still Funding Top Terrorist," *Albuquerque Journal*, January 1, 1984.
30 *Washington Post*, May 24, 1984.
31 *The Nation*, October 10, 1983.
32 Personal communication with Chuck Bell, Staff director of the Fellowship of Reconciliation in Portland, Oregon.
33 *Washington Post*, April 24, 1983.
34 *New York Times*, June 8, 1984.
35 *Time*, December 24, 1984.
36 Fred Hiatt, "Private Groups Press Contra Aid," *Washington Post*, December 12, 1984.
37 *Washington Post*, December 12, 1984.
38 M. Forbes, Jr., "Forbes Comment," *Forbes*, February 25, 1985.
39 *Congressional Record*, April 23, 1985.
40 *Wall Street Journal*, September 6, 1984.
41 Victor Perera, "Uzi Diplomacy," *Mother Jones*, July 1985.
42 GAO, *US Security and Military Assistance Programs and Related Activities*, 1982.
43 See "Israel's Part in Central America, Part One," in *Central America Report*, December 7, 1984.
44 Report from *Ha'aretz* cited in *Latin American Weekly Report*, May 4, 1984.
45 *In These Times*, July 13, 1983.
46 See "Israel's Part in Central America, Part Two," *Central America Report*, December 14, 1984.
47 *New York Times*, April 22, 1984.
48 *The Guardian*, October 19, 1983.
49 *In These Times*, February 2, 1985.
50 Meir Pa'il, "The Folly of Israeli Arms Deals," *Genesis 2*, July/August 1983.
51 Eva Gold and Mary Kay Kent, AFSC, *A View of the US Role in the Militarization of Central America*, 1984.
52 *New York Times*, May 11, 1984.
53 *NACLA Report on the Americas*, May/June 1984, p.46.
54 *Central America Report*, February 8, 1985.
55 Ibid.
56 Council on Hemispheric Affairs (from now on referred to as COHA), "The Military Balance in Central America: An Analysis and Critical Evaluation of Administration's Claims," March 1, 1985.
57 Washington Office on Latin America, *Update Latin America*, September/October 1984.
58 Ibid.
59 *NACLA Report on the Americas*, May/June 1984.
60 *Enfoprensa*, August 24, 1984.
61 *Mesoamerica*, December 1984.
62 Institute on Policy Studies, "Background Information on Guatemala," June 1981, p.3.
63 *Central America Bulletin*, April 1985.
64 *The Defense Monitor*, Vol. 13, No. 3, 1984.
65 Ibid.
66 Department of Defense, *Foreign Aid and Related Programs for 1985*, 1984, p.229.
67 Ibid.
68 *Enfoprensa*, February 2, 1985.
69 *New York Times*, August 22, 1982.

70 Edward King, Unitarian Universalist Service Committee, "Out of Step, Out of Line: US Military Policy in Central America," September 1984.
71 COHA, March 1, 1985, op.cit.
72 LARR, June 8, 1984.
73 Hearings on HR4931 before the Subcommittee for Military Installations, Committee on Armed Services, House of Representatives, March 1984.
74 *Washington Post*, February 24, 1985.
75 *New York Times*, June 7, 1985.
76 Address by President Ronald Reagan, May 9, 1984.
77 COHA, March 1, 1985, p.2, op.cit.; International Institute for Strategic Studies, *The Military Balance*, 1984–85, p.123.
78 Edward King.
79 *New York Times*, September 8, 1985.
80 Ibid.
81 C. G. Jacobsen, Department of State, "Soviet Attitudes Towards Aid to, and Contacts with Central American Revolutionaries," June 1984.
82 COHA, March 1, 1985, p.8, op.cit.
83 Jacobsen, op.cit.
84 *New York Times*, September 9, 1985.
85 Jacobsen, op.cit.
86 *Wall Street Journal*, April 3, 1985.
87 See report by Policy Alternatives for Caribbean and Central America (PACCA), Institute for Policy Studies, "Changing Course: Blueprint for Peace in Central America and the Caribbean" (Washington), 1984.

PART TWO

CHAPTER 5

Hard Times:
An Economic Overview

*Teachers don't earn a bad wage compared to workers, but I
have to work three shifts to support my children. I feel washed-
out at the age of 34 years. Life is hard—it's enough to make
you cry. I don't pay very much, relatively, for my house, but
food uses up close to 70 percent of my wage. My fellow teachers
at school just say: "This life is too expensive. How long is this
nightmare going to last? This is reality. They are strangling us."*
—Salvadoran teacher with three children

FOR ALMOST 30 years (1950–1978), Central America boasted of one of the
highest economic growth rates in the world. Gross domestic product (GDP) grew
at an average annual rate of over 5 percent. Most Central American economies
expanded at an even faster pace than those of industrial nations. According to
the statistics, Central America was taking off economically.

During this boom period, per capita income of Central Americans practically
doubled. Average individual income in Nicaragua increased from $215 in 1950
to $412 (constant 1970 dollars) in 1978. There were other encouraging signs,
such as incipient industrialization.

Agriculture also diversified during this period. Central American countries
added sugar, cotton, and beef to their mainstay exports of coffee and bananas.
This diversification provided the region with not two but five cash crops to earn
foreign exchange. Infrastructure construction also boomed during these 30 years:
the Pan American highway stretched from Mexico to Panama City, paving the
way for agro-export activity in previously unexploited areas.

Huge hydroelectric dams were built across the major rivers. Weathered banana docks were replaced by modern ocean ports. Major cities prided themselves
on *rascacielos* (literally, skyscrapers), divided highways, and modern airports
lighted for night landing. TNCs joined the development boom as Sheraton hotels,
twin movie theaters, and shopping malls proclaimed economic progress.

Three factors fueled the region's economic dynamism: 1) expanding world
and regional trade after World War II, 2) private capital formation, and 3) large

infusions of foreign loans. The expanding world economy meant larger markets for Central American exports. In the three decades, the value of the region's exports increased twelvefold.[1] Foreign investment from the United States jumped from $254 million to $723 million (exclusive of Panama and Belize), and foreign aid injected an intoxicating $5.5 billion of new capital.

Development Not Shared

The rosy statistics of economic growth did nothing to alter the inequitable distribution of income and resources. Rapidly increasing income flowed straight into the bank accounts of the upper class, with a bit trickling down to a new middle class. Development by-passed the *campesinos* who toiled on the coastal plantations or on their own hillside plots. The boom also excluded the thousands of poor Central Americans who crowded into shanty towns on the edge of the capitals. These Central Americans experienced little or nothing of the much-touted "economic progress."

Champions of the "golden age" in Central America conveniently ignored the hard facts of the region's socioeconomic structure. This structure concentrated wealth and repressed any movement to broaden economic participation. A triumvirate of interests form the basis of economic and political power in the region:

- An oligarchy based in the coffee economy since 1950 had expanded into industry and diversified its agricultural interests to include sugar and cotton.
- A repressive security apparatus—trained and equipped by the United States—enforced oligarchic interests and often managed the government.
- A network of foreign corporations and banks directed industrialization in the region while relying on national elites as junior partners.[2]

Between 1950 and 1978 Central American governments followed an economic model that was an overlay of two development strategies: 1) regional industrialization controlled by TNCs mainly from the United States and 2) renovation of the traditional agro-export model prevalent since Spanish settlers began exporting indigo in the 1600s. Neither part of this economic-growth plan substantially benefited the vast majority of Central Americans.

While the diversification of cash crops did provide the region with new sources of income, it also exacerbated social tensions. Cotton and sugar expansion across the coastal plains displaced tens of thousands of small farmers who had been growing basic grains. Uprooted *campesinos* were forced to seek work in the cities or to join the growing numbers of seasonal workers. During this period, export agriculture became more mechanized, which further contributed to rural unemployment. Because of the increased emphasis on cash-crop production, the region produced less staple food and had to import increasing quantities of corn and beans. (See Chapter 6.)

Industrialization failed to improve the circumstances of unemployed workers living on the outskirts of the capital cities. During these 30 years, the manufacturing sector's contribution to GDP grew twice as fast as its ability to provide manufacturing jobs.[3] Those who did find jobs in industry were paid only survival wages. The profits from industrialization that were not siphoned off by the TNC headquarters in New York fell into the hands of local elites. (See Chapter 7.)

Expanding Poverty

Income distribution figures for Central America are startling. The poorest 20 percent of the population receives only 2 to 5 percent of the national income. In El Salvador even though the average per capita income was about $430 in 1980, the poorest 20 percent received only $46 each year. Since 1980, per capita GDP in El Salvador has dropped over $90 to a low of $340 in 1984.[4] In contrast, the wealthiest 20 percent of the population collects 65 percent of El Salvador's income. Although the economy had steadily expanded, the gap between the rich

TABLE 5A

INCOME DISTRIBUTION AND PER CAPITA INCOME LEVELS,* BY COUNTRY, APPROXIMATELY 1980

	Costa Rica		El Salvador		Guatemala		Honduras		Nicaragua	
	%	Average income	%	Average income	%	Average income	%	Average income	%	Average income
Poorest 20%	4.0	176.7	2.0	46.5	5.3	111.0	4.3	80.7	3.0	61.9
30% below the mean	17.0	500.8	10.0	155.1	14.5	202.7	12.7	140.0	13.0	178.2
30% above the mean	30.0	883.8	22.0	341.2	26.1	364.3	23.7	254.6	26.0	350.2
Richest 20%	49.0	1165.2	66.0	1535.0	54.1	1133.6	59.3	796.3	58.0	1199.8

*Income figures are in constant 1970 U.S. dollars.

SOURCE: CEPAL Review, April 1984, based on official data from the countries.

and the poor actually widened. For instance, in Guatemala, the bottom 50 percent of the population saw their income decrease during the 1970s.

Figures from 1980 show that two-thirds of Central Americans now live in poverty, without income to purchase such basic needs as food, shelter, and clothing. Over 40 percent live in a condition of extreme poverty, unable to obtain even the basic foodstuffs needed to meet minimum nutritional requirements. In rural areas, where cash crops are being produced, poverty is substantially worse. In the Guatemalan countryside, four out of five people do not receive income to cover essential food, housing, and clothing needs.

During the 1950–1978 growth period, the best illustration of the concentration of wealth is that of the Somoza clan in Nicaragua. The family fortune grew from around $60 million in the mid-1950s to $400 to $500 million by the mid-1970s.[5] The Somoza empire encompassed agricultural estates, sugar mills, food-processing industries, manufacturing plants, banks, and communications.

Rather than weakening the elite's hold over the economy, agricultural diversification and industrialization actually strengthened oligarchic control. While this expansion granted the new middle-class managers, bank tellers, and bureaucrats a small share of the national income, it provided little for the poor. The few things that did trickle down were items discarded by the upper classes— the empty pesticide drums used to collect water, the plastic packing material used for raincoats, the scraps of tortilla and gristle left on restaurant tables.

Economy Stagnates after 1978

The growth sustained during the 1950–1978 era sputtered to a standstill by 1980, and soon most national economies were rolling backward toward per capita GDP levels of the 1960s. While population was increasing every year by 3 percent, the region's economies were steadily shrinking. In 1984, the UN's Economic Commission on Latin America declared that the region is experiencing

TABLE 5B

INDEX OF PER CAPITA GDP
CONSTANT 1970 $U.S. WITH 1950 = 100

	1950	1960	1970	1978	1984
Costa Rica	100	134	189	251	217
El Salvador	100	119	148	171	120
Guatemala	100	110	145	198	173
Honduras	100	109	126	126	127
Nicaragua	100	123	177	187	160
Panama	100	120	189	198	219

SOURCES: Derived from data in CEPAL, "Preliminary Overview of the Latin American Economy During 1984," January 1985, and *Statistical Abstract of Latin America*, Vol. 23, 1984.

"an economic breakdown unlike any seen in Central America since the 1930s "

Five factors contribute to this recent economic stagnation: 1) falling commodity prices, 2) absence of strong economic growth in the developed nations, 3) deepening debt and rising interest rates, 4) increasing political crisis, and 5) contraction of the regional market.

Economic Trends in Central America

- Inequities in income and land ownership worsen.
- Majority of work force becomes unemployed or underemployed.
- National income and average personal income sink to levels of 10 to 20 years ago.
- Elites block necessary reforms in land tenure, taxation, and labor laws.
- Continuing instability in commodity prices combines with shrinking markets to prevent economic recovery.
- Intraregional trade drops even further.
- Capital flight dries up domestic capital.
- Austerity programs imposed by IMF, World Bank, and Washington squeeze the poor and spark civil unrest in cities.
- Debt crisis escalates.
- Consensus builds that external debt is unpayable and related austerity programs are impossible to bear.
- United States pours in economic assistance in a desperate attempt to prevent governments and economies from collapsing.
- Foreign and elite interests cling to worn-out development strategies that make countries more dependent on foreign governments, corporations, and markets.

The Imbalance of Trade

In international trade, Central America buys more than it sells. This imbalance of trade means that each year the region falls further and further behind in its payments for imported goods. The drop in imported oil prices and the reduction of import purchases since 1980 somewhat eased the balance of payments crisis. Despite these ameliorative factors, Central America in 1984 still bought $1.5 billion more than it sold.

Foreign exchange pays for many imports that the region could do without. VCRs, Mercedes-Benz automobiles, and Cabbage Patch dolls are luxury items these underdeveloped countries do not need and cannot afford. But the squandering of export income on luxury imports by local elites is hardly the cause of the region's trade imbalance.

The real problem concerns the region's terms of trade—the prices countries receive for their commodities in relation to what they must pay for their imports. About 85 percent of the region's exports are unprocessed agricultural commodities, whereas most of its imports are capital goods (like machinery), fuel, and manufactured merchandise. On the world market, the value of manufactured goods constantly climbs, while the value of basic commodities fluctuates wildly but is generally in decline.

Terms of trade for Central America worsened in the early 1980s. In the four years from 1981 to 1984, the deterioration ranged from 20 to 35 percent. Central American nations had to produce more and more exports just to stay even. Nicaragua has chosen to cut imports drastically as one way to deal with this terms-of-trade trap. Yet many imports—like petroleum, medicine, and farm machinery—are extremely difficult to do without.

One revealing way to examine this problem is to measure the increasing amount of exports needed to buy the same quantity of imports. In 1960, a ton of coffee could buy about 40 tons of fertilizer. By 1982, a ton of coffee could buy less than 2 tons of fertilizer.[6] While many obstacles to progress in Central America may be internal, the region has no control over external factors like the terms of trade.

TABLE 5C

INDEX OF TERMS OF TRADE
(1970 = 100)

	1970	1980	1984	Cumulative Rate of Change 1981–1984
Costa Rica	100	94	70	−25.3
El Salvador	100	103	83	−19.1
Guatemala	100	92	62	−33.3
Honduras	100	105	85	−18.9
Nicaragua	100	78	57	−26.6
Panama	100	72	53	−26.7
Non-oil-exporting Latin America	100	76	66	−14.3
Latin America	100	121	95	−21.7

SOURCES: Derived from data in *Statistical Abstract of Latin America*, Vol. 23, 1984; *CEPAL Review*, January 1985.

Debtor Nations

Economic growth from 1950 to 1978 came with a high price. By the late 1970s, the debts from an era of international borrowing began piling up faster than the Central American governments could pay them. The external debt—incurred to build infrastructure and to offset budget and trade deficits—swelled to unmanageable proportions. Between 1960 and 1980, Central America's external debt increased (in nominal dollars) over 40 times. By 1984, the debt climbed almost 70 percent more, to a grand total just under $18 billion. So immense is the current debt burden in Central America that each child born in the region starts life with a debt of almost $800 hanging over its head. The per capita debt is twice as much as most Central American *campesino* families earn in one year.

TABLE 5D

EXTERNAL PUBLIC DEBT, 1960–1984
($ million)

	1960	1970	1978	1980	1984
Costa Rica	55	230	1870	2520	4050
El Salvador	33	130	990	930	2300
Guatemala	51	180	820	1050	1910
Honduras	23	144	970	1720	2250
Nicaragua	41	220	960	2150	3900
Panama	59	290	1770	2850	3550
Central America	260	1190	7380	11220	17960

SOURCES: Derived from data in *Statistical Abstract of Latin America*, Vol. 23, 1984; *CEPAL Review*, January 1985.

In 1979, when the Sandinistas came to power in Nicaragua, they faced enormous debt accumulated by Somoza's squandering of loans that had been granted for road rebuilding, low-income housing, and other projects that never came to fruition. In Costa Rica, the debt is over four times the value of all exports from the country in 1984. Costa Rica has to hand over one-third of its exports earnings each year just to cover the interest payments on its external debt. The region's debt is so awesome and the national treasuries so depleted that many consider the debts uncollectable. The debt burden represents the single largest obstacle to economic development in the region.

It was not until 1980 that the severity of the debt crisis became a matter of common public concern. Heavily indebted countries like Costa Rica and Panama found themselves frantically turning over 80 percent of their new loans to pay their debt service payments. Costa Rican planners did not even know how much the country owed because no government agency had maintained a centralized record of the many development loans that it had received over the previous two decades. In 1981, Costa Rica shocked creditors with its announcement that it could pay neither the interest nor the principal of its external debt.

Since 1980 all the Central American nations have had to embark on austerity programs to try to squeeze the debt payments out of their economies. The International Monetary Fund (IMF) specified the austerity measures for all the countries, except Nicaragua (which imposed its own style of austerity program in 1984). These austerity programs routinely require wage freezes, increased utility bills, an end to food subsidies, devaluation, fewer imports, and reduced social services. Austerity programs tend to heighten social tensions because they demand that the poor make sacrifices to pay off loans that never benefited them.

External debt is not necessarily an obstacle to development. The debt crisis evolved because the borrowed funds were not used to establish a firm base for regional development. Responsibility for the debt crisis lies with 1) the governments themselves, 2) international financial institutions (IFIs) like the World Bank, 3) foreign-aid agencies (mainly the U.S. Agency for International Development [AID]), and 4) TNC banks.

Multilateral loans from IFIs and bilateral loans from AID in the 1960s set the Central American nations on the road toward greater debt. The IFIs and AID encouraged governments to borrow this money at low interest rates to build the dams, power plants, and ports they needed. Since most of the money was used to buy U.S. products like steel or machinery and to pay U.S. contractors, the developed nations, and particularly the United States, were the real beneficiaries of loans to Central American governments.

Concentration of Land

The agro-export system still dominates the Central American economy. It produces an overwhelming proportion of the region's export income and employs more workers than any other sector. Most of Central America's social, economic, and political problems are rooted in the history and structure of the agro-export system.

In his classic study *El Salvador: Landscape and Society*, David Browning wrote: "The Spaniard discovered, through conquest, possibilities for personal gain offered by fertile land and its existing inhabitants, and viewed these two in terms of their exploitation."[7] Such has been the history of agricultural development in Central America. When the Spanish left, the creole elite saw the possibilities for personal gain through the exploitation of Indian labor and their land. First, they exported indigo and cocoa, then coffee and bananas, and later cotton, sugar, and beef. Large landholdings (called *latifundios*) are used to produce cash crops, while the small farms (*minifundios*) grow most of the basic grains for domestic consumption.

The agro-export system in Central America was and still is the essence of an outward-directed role of economic development. It depends on the purchasing power and the tastes of foreigners. The commodities produced in the region are mostly diet supplements for consumers in industrial countries. The booms and busts of those commodities determine the financial condition of government treasuries. Because the national elites are the almost exclusive recipients of the income generated by cash crops, it does little to contribute to economic development. The expansion of this system of cash-crop production—without sufficient attention paid to building agro-industries and meeting local food needs—deepens underdevelopment in Central America. Indeed, the very concept of underdevelopment concerns the ever-worsening circumstances of an agrarian society selling to and buying from industrial ones.

Another basic problem with the agro-export system is the lack of ties with other sectors of each country's economy. The expansion of cash crops has done nothing to improve this situation since the agro-export crops are produced with imported machinery, fertilizers, and pesticides; and are then exported unprocessed.

Not only does the agro-export system keep Central America underdeveloped, but it is also responsible for the lopsided distribution of land and income in the region. Land distribution in Central America is among the worst in the world. Less than 1 percent of the farms occupy almost 40 percent of the farmland, while almost 25 percent of farmers squeeze onto less than 1 percent of total farmland.[8] Adding to this injustice, large land owners possess virtually all the best land, while the small farmers have to make do on eroded slopes. In Honduras, two-thirds of the fertile land is in the hands of about 5 percent of the farm owners. About 65 percent of this rich farmland is used to graze cattle for beef exports.[9]

Except for the banana lands, most of the cash-crop land is held by a small elite. In El Salvador this oligarchy is known as "*Los Catorce*" (the 14 families). Panamanians call them "*Rabiblancos*" (white-tailed birds). They own the land,

TABLE 5E

REGIONAL LAND CONCENTRATION
(by average farm size)

	Micro 1 acre	Sub-Family 5 acres	Medium/ Family 15 acres	Large 75 acres	Very large 800 acres
% of Farms	23	55	14	6	Less than 1
% of Acreage	Less than 1	10	16	35	38

SOURCE: SIECA, *VIII Compendio Estadistico para Centroamerico,* 1978.

the mills, the export houses, and into their hands flows the income from cash-crop production. As a UN study on Central America noted: "Sharp contrasts in land distribution lead naturally to a very unequal distribution of agricultural income."[10] Because most Central Americans lack income to cover their basic necessities, new industries cannot find a large enough local market for their goods.

Agrarian reform is both an issue of social justice in Central America and a matter of economic necessity. Without agrarian reform, countries will have to pay for more and more imported food. In the absence of agrarian reform, there is no consumer sector large enough to support the industrial sector the region needs to break its almost complete dependence on the agro-export system. The other compelling reason for agrarian reform is a political one. An expanding number of landless and near landless will eventually threaten the political stability of any agricultural country.

Domestic Problems

During the boom years, foreign loans (from IFIs, AID, and TNC banks) to a large degree substituted for domestic sources of capital. Governments borrowed foreign capital rather than increasing the taxes on property, income, and exports. Not wanting to anger the oligarchy, the Central American governments did not take the appropriate measures to restrict the flow of capital out of their countries. Large landowners and industrialists spirited their profits out of the country to Miami banks while relying on the state to supply credit for their plantings and investments.

Negligible property taxes have permitted landholders to leave their land idle

TABLE 5F

DIRECT TAXES AS PERCENT OF CURRENT REVENUES
(Direct taxes are primarily property and income taxes)

	1970	1975	1980	1984
Costa Rica	23.7	22.1	20.3	20.3
El Salvador	22.2	25.1	28.3	21.4
Guatemala	15.0	19.1	13.5	13.1
Honduras	25.0	25.5	31.1	25.5
Nicaragua	20.9	22.1	17.6	18.5
Panama	38.8	38.5	32.6	39.4

SOURCE: IDB, *Economic and Social Progress in Latin America*, 1985.

or to use their land inefficiently. As a percentage of the GDP, taxes on property, trade and income have declined since 1970. Several governments, like Guatemala, have yielded to pressure from big growers and export houses to reduce export taxes despite budgetary woes.

TABLE 5G

INTERNATIONAL TRADE TAXES AS PERCENT OF CURRENT REVENUES

	1970	1975	1980	1984
Costa Rica	29.8	30.3	26.3	32.2
El Salvador	40.5	36.1	37.0	24.0
Guatemala	28.0	27.7	34.7	16.8
Honduras	28.6	27.7	36.6	36.3
Nicaragua	28.1	20.2	22.7	15.9
Panama	23.5	19.6	11.6	12.7

SOURCE: IDB, *Economic and Social Progress in Latin America*, 1985.

Each year during the 1980s, the region has suffered a shortfall in its balance of payments of more than $1.5 billion. The flight of private capital from Central America after 1979 further debilitated the already unstable regional economy. An estimated $4 billion left the region for foreign banks between 1979 and 1982 alone. Only immense quantities of U.S. economic aid have kept the economies of U.S. allies in the region from collapsing. (See Chapter 3.)

After 1979, both private domestic investment and domestic savings plummeted in Central America. Between 1978 and 1983, private investment declined by nearly $1 billion in the region, with the most severe decreases felt in El Salvador and Panama. Despite massive injections of multilateral and U.S. bilateral assistance designed to promote the business, private investment has failed to perk up. Domestic savings have also fallen, signifying a continued lack of confidence in the stability of the region.

A Few Dollars a Day

The going rate for a day's labor in agriculture is around $3 in Central America. Wages in the cities range from $3 to $7 a day. In El Salvador, workers in clothing-assembly plants like Levi Strauss or Maidenform earn about $100 a month—a sum that barely covers the cost of a house rental. The governments of Central America do have minimum-wage laws but do not enforce them. The $3.20

minimum wage in Guatemala for rural workers is routinely ignored by growers, who sometimes pay downtrodden Indian farmworkers as little as $1 a day.

For rural workers, work is available only during the harvest season. Counted as employed in the official statistics are those who often work only four to five months as seasonal laborers during the summer harvests. William Durham, author of *Scarcity and Survival in Central America*, said that even the comparatively high estimates by AID of 40 to 60 percent unemployment in El Salvador, in his opinion, are underestimated. "The only thing more scarce than land in El Salvador," said Durham, "is a job. But you can find pieces of jobs. You can find temporary employment."[11] Recorded unemployment in the region ranges from 15 percent in Belize to 47 percent in Guatemala.

The Population Question

As the statistics of experience in developed nations show, birth rates are more a symptom of underdevelopment than a cause. This is certainly the case in Central America.

As family security and incomes increase, birth rates decline. Population density varies greatly, from 17 per square mile in Belize and 53 in Nicaragua to 610 per square mile in tiny El Salvador. Population growth rates have slowed in all Central American countries, but the region still has one of the fastest

TABLE 5H

TOTAL POPULATION, CENTRAL AMERICAN COUNTRIES, 1950–2000
(Millions of persons)

	1950	1960	1970	1980	1984	2000
Belize		.09	.12	.15	.16	.26
Costa Rica	.80	1.25	1.73	2.24	2.59	3.35
El Salvador	1.86	2.45	3.44	4.81	4.93	8.72
Guatemala	2.81	3.86	4.24	5.01	8.08	12.64
Honduras	1.43	1.85	2.51	3.69	4.25	6.92
Nicaragua	1.06	1.41	1.83	2.47	2.70	5.17
Panama	.80	1.06	1.43	1.94	2.00	2.86
Central America	8.9	12.0	15.3	20.3	24.7	39.9

SOURCES: *Statistical Abstract of Latin America*, Vol. 23, 1984 (1950–1980); USAID *Congressional Presentation FY86* (1984 estimates); *Caribbean Basin to the Year 2000* (2000 projections); IBRD, *World Tables* (Belize 1960–1980).

growing populations in the world. Central America remains less densely populated than many other places in the world. Nicaragua is less densely populated than the United States. El Salvador is no more densely populated than Massachusetts or the Netherlands. In terms of population density in agricultural areas, El Salvador is 40 percent less densely populated than China—a country that has managed to provide the basic food requirements for its entire population.

A major reason for high birth rates among the *campesino* population is that children represent an economic resource and a family's only social security system. In William Durham's examination of land scarcity and population in El Salvador, he found that the less land a family had, the more children they had. In El Salvador, children earn more than they cost their families.

Surveys by Durham in the village of Tenancingo (which was totally depopulated later, following a military bombardment) showed that families with little or no land were generally poorer than other families. The women of these land-poor families experienced the highest number of child mortality cases in the village.

To compensate for the higher child mortality and instability due to lack of land, *campesinos* average a higher number of births than those with bigger plots of land. Based on his land-population studies in the country, Durham said: "I see El Salvador's rapid population increase as related to the simultaneous concentration of land in the hands of a few large landowners."[12]

Population rates need to be addressed in Central America, but the overriding problem is the maldistribution and misuse of land. Most small farmers do not have enough land to provide for their families. The number of landless is multiplying. Yet one-fourth of the arable land is left idle by the large landholders, and one-fifth of all land in Central America is used for pasture.[13]

The State of the Population

Central America's turmoil cannot be separated from the miserable living conditions of its population. Dr. Nevin Scrimshaw of the MIT-Harvard International Food and Nutrition Program helped establish the Central American Institute of Nutrition in 1949. Thirty-five years later, in 1984, he told the Kissinger Commission on Central America: "The problems of Central America are not due to Marxist intervention or East-West Conflict. They are rooted in landlessness, poverty, and injustice." He said the crisis has been caused by "governments that protect the already privileged and tolerate a lack of education, health care, food, housing, water, and sanitation for most of the people."[14]

The life of the poor in El Salvador illustrates the common circumstances of the region's disenfranchised majority:

- Nineteen out of twenty small farmers do not have sufficient land for their own families.
- Six out of ten rural residents are landless.
- Eight of every ten Salvadorans begin their work history between the ages of six and ten.
- Three out of four people do not have access to drinking water.
- Four out of five do not have latrines.
- Cost of living between 1975 and 1984 jumped almost 250 percent, while wages increased less than 50 percent.
- Roughly four out of ten rural Salvadorans do not have enough money to pay for a basic diet of corn and beans, let alone a more varied diet and other living expenses.
- Over 200,000 children are in danger of going blind because of severe vitamin A deficiencies.
- There are only 375 doctors in rural areas, or about one for every 8000 rural Salvadorans.
- A majority of the population lives without electricity.
- Six out of ten Salvadorans living in the capital city make their homes in "informal" housing of shacks and illegal shelters.
- Eight of ten rural Salvadorans live in homes with dirt floors.
- Only one out of twenty rural Salvadorans has running water in the home.
- In the countryside, there is only one hospital bed for every 100,000 people.

Hunger and malnutrition are the fate for an increasing number of Central Americans. At least three out of four children in Honduras, Guatemala, and El Salvador are malnourished. Malnutrition causes mental deficiencies in four out of every five children born in rural Honduras.[15] Malnutrition is not limited to the young: at least 50 percent of Central Americans do not eat enough food to meet the minimal nutritional requirements. In 1984, 75 percent of the population in Guatemala could not satisfy their minimum needs, and 40 percent could not even afford a minimum diet. These figures compare to 63 percent and 32 percent, respectively, in 1980. Thus, the percentage of people who could not afford even the minimum food requirements increased by 25 percent in just four years. In those same four years, unemployment rose from 31 percent to 43 percent.[16]

Old Solutions Not Working

The economic reality Central America confronts today is not a passing thing. Falling commodity prices, shrinking markets, protectionism of industrial nations, deteriorating terms of trade, and impossible debt burdens are expressions of global economic forces. Within the region, efforts at economic planning must contend with a dwindling regional market, the drop in demand for consumer goods, flight of domestic capital, and continued concentration of land and income at the same time that a growing population is more and more likely to be landless, jobless, and hungry.

The United States offers a solution: more U.S. investment, more promotion of the private sector, more cash crops, and more austere living conditions for Central America's 24 million inhabitants. The mainstays of this exhausted and bankrupt development model—agricultural-exports and TNC-led industrializa-ton—have done more to create than to alleviate the economic conditions that prevail on the isthmus today. Repackaging, even with a dignified name like the Caribbean Basin Initiative, is unlikely to make for a more liveable future, as long as basics continue to be ignored or, worse, denied.

Other economic development models are imaginable, which proceed from quite different assumptions, set different priorities, and strive for distinct goals. For example, a model of economic development might seek to reduce the region's vulnerability to outside economic and political forces and intervention. It might emphasize the importance of meeting the most basic survival needs of the majority of the population as a prerequisite to demands for political stability. It might strive for coordination with other third-world efforts to adapt to, and influence, global economic forces. Such a model might regard the following as priorities for economic planning and authentic development:

- Emphasis on local production of food staples to reduce food imports and guarantee national and regional food security.
- Reform of land tenure, tax, and labor laws, combined with equitable enforcement.
- Both public- and private-sector initiatives to provide stable and productive employment.
- Emphasis on developing agro-processing and labor-intensive productive sectors.
- Acceptance by the public sector of responsibility to make investment in programs needed for economic and social progress.
- Development of expanded domestic markets once incomes and land distribution are more equitable.
- Elimination or high taxation of luxury imports.
- Emphasis on use of locally available resources to produce goods and services to meet domestic demand.
- Encouragement of regional trade and cooperation.
- Coordination with global efforts to relieve third-world debt obligations and secure more favorable and equitable terms of international trade.

Central America in Relative Terms

The average U.S. cat eats more beef than the average Central American person.

El Salvador's national budget is less than half the annual revenues of either the *New York Times* or the *Washington Post*.

The United States spends as much on digestive aids and shaving products as the total annual income of the country of Nicaragua.

If U.S. aid to El Salvador from 1982–1985 were instead divided among the poorest 20 percent of the Salvadoran population, it would have doubled their total income for the entire four-year period.

Sales for the Du Pont corporation are more than the combined GDPs of all seven Central American countries.

The amount a typical North American spends on alcoholic beverages in one year could cover the total living expenses for one Honduran for six months.

Colgate-Palmolive's annual sales are about the same as El Salvador's GDP. Beatrice Foods' annual sales are about the same as Guatemala's GDP.

The cost of one Sears VCR ($540) would cover the total living expenses for a Salvadoran for over ten months (per capita GDP—$630).

The people of Mesa, Arizona, have 5 times as many telephones as the entire country of Honduras.

If U.S. military aid to El Salvador in 1984 were instead divided among the poorest 20 percent of the Salvadoran people, their average annual income would quadruple.

The United States spends as much on cosmetics, hair care, and disposable diapers as the combined GDPs of Costa Rica, El Salvador, Nicaragua, and Honduras.

Nabisco earns more in sales each year than the combined GDPs of Belize, Costa Rica, El Salvador, Honduras, Nicaragua, and Panama.

TABLE 51

PER CAPITA INCOME, 1983
(in 1982 U.S. dollars)

United States	$14100	████████████████████
Panama	$ 2020	███
Costa Rica	$ 1570	██
Guatemala	$ 1190	██
Belize	$ 1140	██
Nicaragua	$ 870	██
Honduras	$ 750	█
El Salvador	$ 710	█

SOURCES: IDB, *Economic and Social Progress in Latin America, 1985 Report*; *World Population Data Sheet, 1985.*

1 Value of exports of goods and services increased from $250 million in 1950 to $3.2 billion in 1978. *CEPAL Review*, April 1984.
2 Triumvirate concept from James F. Petras and Morris H. Morley, "Economic Expansion, Political Crisis, and US Policy in Central America," in Marlene Dixon and Susanne Jonas (eds.), *Revolution and Intervention in Central America* (San Francisco: Synthesis, 1981), pp.69–88.
3 While manufacturing's portion of the labor force grew from 10.5 perent to 13.9 percent, its share of the GDP grew more than 50 percent, from 10.6 percent to 16.7 percent.
4 These per capita GDP figures are in constant 1970 $US. *CEPAL*, "Preliminary Overview of the Latin American Economy During 1984," January 1985.
5 *Latin American Economic Report*, January 27, 1978.
6 Fidel Castro, *The World Economic and Social Crisis* (Havana: Council of State, 1983), p.62.
7 David Browning, *El Salvador: Landscape and Society* (Oxford: Clarendon, 1971), p.33.
8 SIECA, *VIII Compendio Estadistico Centroamerico* (Guatemala: SIECA, 1978).
9 Jacobo Schatan, *La Agroindustria y el Sistema Centroamericano* (Mexico: CEPAL, 1983), p.46.
10 Ibid., p.37.
11 See interview with William Durham in *The Stanford Magazine*, Summer 1984.
12 William H. Durham, *Scarcity and Survival in Central America* (Stanford: Stanford University, 1979).
13 IDB, "Economic and Social Progress in Latin America," (Washington), 1984.
14 See statement of Dr. Nevin S. Scrimshaw in National Bipartisan Commission on Central America, "Report of the National Bipartisan Commission on Central America" (Washington), January 1984, p.794.
15 Study by National Infant Care Institute, cited in *Boletin Informativo Honduras (CEDOH)*, October 1984.
16 *Central America Bulletin*, August 1985.

CHAPTER 6

Agriculture:
The New Plantation

Now there is nothing but coffee. In the great hacienda named
California that covers the flanks of the volcano Alegría, . . . there
were formerly a hundred or more properties planted in maize,
rice, beans, and fruit. Now there is nothing but coffee in the
highlands and pasture in the lowlands.
— *La Patria* newspaper, San Salvador, 1928

FROM THEIR MISSIONS in Guatemala Spanish friars of the 1600s could see indigo and cocoa plantations worked by Mayan farm laborers. Most regarded the Mayan farm laborers as heathens who were more animal than human. A few friars did protest the brutal exploitation by the Spanish colonists. In their journals, they described how Indians would often drop dead from exhaustion amid piles of fermenting indigo. The forced labor on *latifundios* (plantations) meant that the Indian *campesinos* (peasants)* were often not able to maintain their own farms. Pulled away from their corn harvests, thousands died from hunger and destitution.

The history of Central America is closely linked to the evolution of the region's agricultural system. The rise of the infamous oligarchies, the loss of communal Indian lands, the military's repression of land-hungry *campesinos*, and the region's economic underdevelopment are results of an agro-export system that began so cruelly with the Spanish.

Coffee was the first of the modern cash crops to spread over the isthmus. Today, the rich soil of the volcanic highlands, river valleys, and coastal plains produces five main agro-exports: coffee, bananas, cotton, sugar, and beef. Because they are cultivated to earn foreign currency (mostly dollars), these exports are called cash crops. These agricultural commodities earn about three-fourths of Central America's foreign exchange. Not only do producers of the major agro-

---

*Campesino and peasant are used interchangeably to designate those Central Americans whose lives are tied to the land either as owners of small parcels of land or as hired agricultural laborers.

exports occupy the best land, but they also receive most of the region's agricultural credit.

In striking contrast, peasants cultivate small plots of corn and beans for domestic consumption on the worst land. They desperately try to scrape life out of eroded mountain slopes, but each year the *campesinos'* digging sticks find the soil more barren and lifeless. Less than 5 percent of the agricultural credit in countries like El Salvador and Guatemala goes to farmers producing staple foods on *minifundios*. Because these tiny parcels of land cannot provide a year-round subsistence living, *campesinos* must also labor as seasonal field hands on cash-crop plantations.

Direct foreign investment in Central American agribusiness is limited to bananas and production of nontraditional crops like vegetables and flowers. The actual production of coffee, cotton, sugar, and beef is in the hands of local oligarchies of large landholders, mill owners, and exporters. True control of these commodities, however, rests with the network of TNCs that ship, trade, process, and distribute them in the world market.

TABLE 6A

TOP AGRICULTURAL EXPORTS

	1st	2nd	3rd	4th	5th
Belize*	sugar	citrus	wood		
Costa Rica	coffee	bananas	meat	sugar	rice
El Salvador	coffee	cotton	shrimp		
Guatemala	coffee	cotton	sugar	bananas	
Honduras	bananas	coffee	meat	sugar	shrimp
Nicaragua	coffee	cotton	sugar	bananas	meat
Panama	bananas	sugar	shrimp	coffee	

* Marijuana, probably the leading agro-export of Belize, is not included in official trade figures.
SOURCE: UNCTAD, *Handbook of International Trade and Development Statistics*, 1984 Supplement.

Coffee: Harvest of Oligarchs

In the 1800s, indigo and cocoa gave way to a new export crop that spread across the volcanic highlands. When European tastes turned to coffee, the Central American elites were quick to meet the new demand. They found the fertile volcanic soils of the higher elevations of the isthmus to be ideal for coffee cultivation. On what were once communal Indian lands, crews of Indian laborers were forced to pick basket after basket of red coffee cherries. By the end of the century, coffee exports accounted for over 90 percent of the region's agro-exports.

Still reigning king of Central America's agro-export sector, the coffee industry ranks as the region's number one exporter and employer. Over 15 percent of the world's coffee comes from Central America, whose main purchasers are the United States and West Germany. Coffee is the leading export of Guatemala, El Salvador, Nicaragua, and Costa Rica.

Central America's coffee business involves three stages: 1) cultivation, 2) hulling the coffee cherries at *beneficios*, and 3) export of the beans by export houses and state marketing agencies. Although there are many small landowners that grow coffee, a handful of coffee magnates dominate all three stages. In Guatemala, 1 percent of the coffee growers control 70 percent of the cultivation; just 36 families own the vast amount of El Salvador's coffee lands.[1]

These large coffee producers form the traditional landed oligarchy and bear responsibility for the long history of repression and exploitation of the region's *campesino* population. The unjust wages and miserable conditions on the coffee *fincas* in El Salvador led to the 1932 peasant rebellion in El Salvador, which resulted in as many as 30,000 deaths, mostly of Indian *campesinos*.

Memories of the massacre, or *matanza*, halted rural organizing in El Salvador for more than 40 years. At a 1980 convention of coffee producers in San Salvador, a statement by one grower about the need to quell rural unrest in the style of the 1932 *matanza* elicited hearty applause. "Coffee growers should not anguish over the situation in El Salvador today," asserted a coffee oligarch. "There was a similar situation in 1932. If it was solved then, it can be solved now."[2]

From Oligarchs to the TNCs

TNCs form the links between the coffee business in Central America and the consuming nations. Two small groups of TNCs control the international trading, processing, and marketing of Central American coffee. Multicommodity trading TNCs buy coffee from Central American exporters and then sell it to the TNC roasters. Most of the largest roasters also do some of their own buying. Procter & Gamble and Coca-Cola, for example, buy part of their coffee supplies directly from Guatemalan exporters.

Three TNC traders—ACLI International, Volkart, and J. Aron— dominate the coffee trading business. ACLI International, a subsidiary of Cargill, trades about 10 percent of the world's coffee supply.[3] The conglomerate Cargill ranks as the world's top family-owned firm. The third-largest trader, J. Aron, is a subsidiary of Goldman Sachs, a New York financial-services corporation. Besides coffee, these firms also trade other commodities like sugar, cotton, and cocoa. These multicommodity traders count on a worldwide communications network that facilitates large-volume trading and allows them to set prices. Compared with small coffee exporting nations, these TNC traders are truly giants.

Six TNCs—General Foods, Nestle, Procter & Gamble, Consolidated Foods,

Standard Brands (part of R.J. Reynolds), and Jacobs—account for over 60 percent of the coffee-roasting business. Nestle's sales are higher than the GDPs of any one of the Central American economies. Sales of General Foods are 2.5 times the GDP of Costa Rica and 7 times higher than the country's annual budget.

Only rarely do the TNCs have direct investment in the coffee industry in third-world nations. They do, however, monopolize the instant-coffee business in the third world. Just two TNCs—General Foods and Nestle—process 75 percent of the world's instant coffee.[4] In Central America, Nestle and Coca-Cola operate plants that process low-quality beans not suitable for export into instant coffee for local consumers. Through pervasive advertising, these companies have persuaded Central Americans to drink coffee crystals instead of the "real thing."

Declining consumer demand and fluctuating coffee prices are straining Central American economies. In the last 20 years, the percentage of U.S. consumers drinking coffee dropped from 75 to 55 percent.[5] Central American countries depend on coffee exports as their leading source of foreign exchange, yet the ups and downs of the coffee market make life extremely difficult for government planners.

Inside the Banana Enclaves

Not until the late 1800s did North American entrepreneurs begin exporting bananas from the Atlantic coast to the harbors of New Orleans, Philadelphia, and New York. Soon the yellow fruit became a favorite in U.S. households. At first, local farmers sold their bananas to U.S. shipping companies, but U.S. investors rapidly gained control over the entire industry.

United Fruit and the Standard Fruit and Steamship Company (now owned respectively by United Brands and Castle & Cooke) in the early 1900s opened their own plantations around deep-water ports on the Atlantic coast of Honduras, Costa Rica, and Guatemala. Later the fruit companies extended their banana empire to Panama and Nicaragua as well as starting up new plantations on the Pacific side of Costa Rica and Guatemala.

Until the arrival of the banana companies, Great Britain ranked as the number-one foreign investor in Central America. U.S. banks had financed an occasional public utility or railroad and several U.S. firms had opened small mines, but banana plantations were the first substantial U.S. investment in Central America. By 1914, 60 percent of direct foreign investment in Central America came from the United States.[6] Unlike the coffee industry, in which production is locally owned, the region's banana industry came under total control by two foreign corporations.

Los Pulpos

Central Americans have many names for the banana companies, but one of the more common and appropriate nicknames is *pulpo* (octopus). It does seem that banana companies have their tentacles into just about everything. The companies acquired the sobriquet during the 1920s when they expanded their investments to include the region's principal utilities, railroads, ports, and communication systems. To provide for their isolated enclaves, the banana giants opened their own breweries, banks, shoe factories, restaurants, and general stores. Company-owned factories also manufacture cardboard boxes and plastic bags used to package the original product. All these subsidiary businesses later reached outside the banana enclaves to the national market.

In the 1960s, when the Central American Common Market (CACM) loosened up trade relations in the region (See Chapter 7), the fruit companies diversified into the food-processing industry. Both United Brands and Castle & Cooke converted areas of their huge estates into plantations of African palm trees. Palm oil production has made the banana companies the region's leading suppliers of cooking oil and margarine. The domain of the *pulpos* also includes vegetable and fruit-canning plants, pineapple farms, cattle ranches, and shipping companies.

In 1972, Del Monte (a subsidiary of R.J. Reynolds) became the third *pulpo* when it bought out United Brands' banana plantations in Guatemala. The three TNCs control 90 percent of the region's banana trade. The three banana giants supply 60 percent of the world market and 90 percent of the U.S. market.[7]

The Top Bananas

United Brands

United Fruit was formed in 1889 when Boston Fruit merged with three banana companies owned by the ambitious entrepreneur Minor C. Keith, who also owned International Railways of Central America. The company solidified its hold on the international banana market in 1930 when it bought out its main competitor in Honduras, the Cuyamel Fruit Company, from Samuel Zemurray. For the next 20 years, Sam "the Banana Man" Zemurray ran United Fruit, and by the time he stepped down the company owned more than 3 million acres throughout Latin America. Among its interests were sugar plantations in Cuba, where Angel Castro and his two famous sons, Raul and Fidel, worked.

United Fruit achieved international notoriety in 1954 when it encouraged the Eisenhower administration to overthrow the progressive government of Jacobo Arbenz in Guatemala. Five years later, after the Cuban Revolution nationalized its sugar plantations, the company began reducing its other landholdings, especially in South America. During the Bay of Pigs invasion, the company supplied two of its ships for use by the CIA-funded Cuban counterrevolutionaries. A U.S. antitrust action in 1972 precipitated the sale of its banana lands in Guatemala to Del Monte.

In 1970, United Fruit became United Brands, which is currently one of the world's largest producers, processors, and distributors of food products. In the United States, the company ranks number two in the banana industry, number three in meat packing, and number seven in food processing. Subsidiaries grow bananas in Panama, Costa Rica, and Honduras. Its plastic-manufacturing subsidiary Polymer operates 18 plants in Panama, Costa Rica, Honduras, Nicaragua, and Guatemala. Polymer also has a warehouse in El Salvador. The company's Numar Processed Food Group has facilities in Costa Rica, Honduras, and Nicaragua. United Brands owns 85,000 acres and leases another 45,000 acres in Central America.

United Fruit gained a reputation for its unusual (but highly successful) advertising campaigns. In the 1950s, Miss Chiquita Banana had a popular song in the U.S. hit parade and danced with an appealing banana United Fruit described as "a good eight inches along the outer curve, at least 1 1/4 inches across the middle, with the peel fitting tightly...sleek and firm." Miss Chiquita Banana lives in the 1980s as a teenage girl chosen each year to tour the United States promoting the nutritional values of United Brands' bananas.

The fruit company's expansion over the last few decades into a conglomerate food company has paid off handsomely. In its *1984 Annual Report*, United Brands told its shareholders that "sales and earnings at United Fruit Company for fiscal 1984 reached their highest level since United Brands Company was formed in 1970."

Castle & Cooke

This Hawaii-based TNC is the leading distributor of bananas in the United States. Founded by two missionaries in 1851, the firm is one of the largest landowners in Hawaii, where it cultivates sugar and Dole pineapples. Castle & Cooke acquired the Standard Fruit and Steamship Company in 1964. Besides being the top banana in the United States, the company is the nation's third largest tuna company and the leading pineapple corporation.

Like its competitors, Castle & Cooke has slowly moved away from direct ownership of banana production in Central America. Close to a half of its bananas come from associate growers. The company is "becoming more of a marketing than a farming firm," noted a Castle & Cooke official. It produces bananas in Honduras and Costa Rica. In 1983, the banana company suddenly pulled up stakes in Nicaragua, violating a 1980 agreement with the government. The company owns 41,000 acres in Central America.

R.J. Reynolds

In 1970, Alfred Eames, chairperson of Del Monte, a subsidiary of R.J. Reynolds, said, "Bananas are like money trees. I only wish we had more of them." Two years later, Del Monte acquired the banana plantations of United Fruit in Guatemala. It produces bananas mainly in Guatemala and Costa Rica, although in 1984 it entered into a business agreement with the Honduran government to manage banana production with local growers. Del Monte, one of the largest food processing TNCs in Central America, operates canning companies in Honduras, Costa Rica, and Panama.

Del Monte is the leading manufacturer of canned fruits and vegetables in the United States. While it is the smallest banana company in Central America, R.J. Reynolds ranks far ahead of either United Brands or Castle & Cooke in overall sales. The acquisition of Nabisco Brands in 1985 made R.J. Reynolds the world's largest consumer products corporation.

Modernizing the Banana Enclave

The attempted agrarian reform in Guatemala and a successful strike by banana workers in Honduras marked the end of enclave development. Ever since then, companies have been cutting their workforce to reduce labor problems. Through mechanization, new varieties of bananas, and use of herbicides, banana companies in Honduras managed to triple their per acre output while cutting their work force in half.[8]

Since the mid-1950s, the companies have also minimized production risks by relying on local farmers called associate growers to produce bananas for the company. Fully one-third of TNC bananas in the region are produced by these Central American contract growers.[9] Even with more land owned by associate growers, the banana enclaves still cover about 200,000 acres of the best land in Central America.

An official of Standard Fruit explained the trend toward more associate growers in Costa Rica: "Standard is not very interested in having its own production since the costs of production increase day by day."[10] Instead of growing the fruit themselves, the banana giants contract local growers, many of whom rent company land to grow specified quantities.

The corporation usually provides its associate growers with credit, technical advice, seeds, fertilizers, farm machinery, chemicals, aerial spraying of pesticides, irrigation equipment, plastic wrapping, and cardboard packing boxes. While the grower is guaranteed in advance a certain percentage of the purchase price, it is usually less than 25 percent. From that advance must come labor costs, taxes, and other expenses so that associate growers frequently come up short on corporate record books. Workers on locally managed banana farms often receive less pay and endure worse living conditions than workers on company plantations.

In the associate-grower arrangement, farmers bear the brunt of banana diseases and hurricanes that can ruin a year's harvest; and if the market is low, the companies simply reduce the quotas of production from their associates. This arrangement keeps banana land under company control without the expense and political difficulties of direct ownership. Asked about the company's sale of large portions of its estate to the Honduran government and associate growers, Bobby Walker, United Brands' production vice-president for Central America, said: "Actually we were glad to get rid of the land. We feel the more Hondurans we work with, the more secure our future is here."[11]

The banana companies also involve international financial institutions and the government in new projects. What the companies want is a three-way deal shared by 1) independent associate growers or agricultural cooperatives, 2) the state, and 3) themselves as the contractor and marketer. This strategy has worked well for the banana companies in Honduras, where the government has received funds from the Inter-American Development Bank (IDB) to develop African palm production for its agrarian reform program. The companies simply buy the African palm harvests from the farm projects without having to bear any of the initial investment in the project or to deal with the manifold problems of direct production.

Known as "triangulization," this strategy of bringing in the government and the international financial institutions is the perfect way for agribusiness TNCs to reduce the risks of actual production. It puts the government on the same side as the TNC and gives the agribusiness corporation access to low-interest development loans.

Bananas, Bribes, and Blackmail

In the mid-1970s, the region's banana-producing countries decided to form a cartel patterned after the oil producers' OPEC. After the founding of the Union of Banana Exporting Countries (UPEB) in 1974, the new group immediately encouraged imposition of an export tax of $1 for each 40-pound box of bananas. The companies protested that the tax would drive them out of business and they threatened to pull out of any country that legislated such a tax. None of the nations succeeded in setting the $1 tax. Costa Rica authorized the tax in 1975 but soon lowered it to 25 cents after the banana companies made noises about packing up. A UPEB representative charged that the companies had used "threats and blackmail" to keep the taxes low or nonexistent.

A turning point in this showdown between the companies and the governments came in 1975 when the president of United Brands dropped 44 stories from the Pan American Building to his death on the New York pavement. After his suicide, a federal investigation concluded that he had authorized a $1.25

million bribe to top officials in the Honduran government to persuade them not to raise the banana export tax. President Oswaldo Arrellano Lopez resigned as a result of the revelations. Another consequence of the affair, called Bananagate, was that the companies eased the pressure on Central American governments and higher taxes were imposed. Even though taxes never reached the original $1 goal, the governments did succeed in raising banana tax revenues from only $1 million in 1972 to $80 million by 1980.[12]

Although the countries do not want to lose the business, especially during these years of economic crisis, they contend they should be getting a better deal. The percentage value of the retail price that banana-exporting countries receive in the form of taxes and wages is only 14 percent, while foreign companies that ship, ripen, distribute, and retail bananas receive the other 86 percent.[13] And, due to inflation, the small share of value retained by governments in the form of taxes is shrinking.

Claims of financial crisis by the banana companies ring false in view of profit figures that appear on company ledgers. In the case of United Brands, bananas are 5 times as profitable as other company food sales. For R.J. Reynolds, the fruit accounts for 7 percent of corporate sales but 17 percent of profits.[14] Nevertheless, the Central American governments, which count on bananas as one of the top three earners of foreign exchange, have been cautious about calling the corporations' bluff. A 30 percent cut in Panamanian banana production and United Fruit's shutdown of its Pacific coast banana plantations in Costa Rica left over 5000 workers unemployed. In Honduras, over 10,000 workers depend on United Fruit for jobs. At a time when unemployment is approaching 50 percent in most Central American countries, those governments are anxious to keep TNC banana companies in the country even if it means lowering taxes and meeting other company demands.

Cotton and Sugar: Expanding the Plantation

In the 1950s and 1960s, two new cash crops—cotton and sugar cane—were introduced into the region's agro-export economy. As in the coffee business, TNCs are not directly involved in the production of cotton and sugar cane. But TNCs do finance sugar and cotton production, control world trade of these two commodities, and dominate the sugar-refining and textile industries. An advertisement by Citibank boasted that the "cloud-soft cotton of El Salvador is brought from boll to bale with the help of worldwide Citibank."[15]

When the Spanish forced their way into Central America, Mayans were already growing cotton for their own needs. It was not, however, until the 1950s that producers began exporting cotton from the region. Its expansion displaced thousands of small farmers and was accompanied by careless use of massive quantities of pesticides. In the hot coastal plains of Guatemala, El Salvador, and Nicaragua, growers produce about 6 percent of the world's cotton.

"The introduction of cotton in El Salvador is most tragic from the viewpoint of the country's displaced population," wrote Central American scholar Dr. Edelberto Rivas-Torres. Cotton produced foreign exchange for the well-established Central American producers at the cost of "a large margin of hunger and hopelessness" for *campesinos*.[16] Because the land used for the new cotton plantations had previously been used to produce staple food, food imports increased rapidly. In Nicaragua, food imports increased 5 times between 1960 and 1977—the same rate of increase as cotton exports.

Most cotton production in Central America came under the control of a new wing of the oligarchy. Investors from the cities bought up cotton plantations and mills with their accumulated profits. In Guatemala, only fifteen families account for 45 percent of total cotton production.[17]

Most cotton produced in Central America is purchased by one of 15 multi-commodity traders who then sell it to major textile firms.[18] Among the most influential are Bunge and Born (U.S.), Cargill (U.S.), Ralli Brothers (U.K.), Volkart Brothers (Switzerland), and Toyo Menka Kaisha (Japan).[19]

The sugar crops of third-world nations have been manipulated by the U.S. government in order to exert political pressure. Because of the Cuban Revolution in 1959, the United States switched Cuba's sugar quota to Central America. As a result, U.S. sugar imports from the region tripled in the 1960s. Sugar quotas were again increased when in the early 1980s the Reagan administration divided Nicaragua's share among its neighboring nations.

The world sugar market is the realm of four major TNC multicommodity traders: Sucre et Denrées (France), Tate and Lyle (U.K.), Englehard Phillips (U.S.), and EDF Man (U.K.)—which control over half the sugar on the international capitalist market. The trading TNCs buy unrefined Central American sugar and then sell it to a small group of TNC refiners that includes Gulf + Western, U.S. Sugar, and Amstar.

The main sugar producers in Central America are Belize, El Salvador, Guatemala, Nicaragua, and Panama. In the sugar industry, as in the cotton industry, the elite who own the mills (*ingenios*) extract the most profit from the business. Small growers forced to sell their sugar cane to one of the few *ingenios* have to accept low prices set by the mill owners. In El Salvador, for example, just three sugar mills control two-thirds of production.[20]

Pastures Over People

Most Central Americans do not eat much meat. The poorest half of the population consumes about 10 pounds per person a year.[21] In the United States, where billions of hamburgers are served each year, the per capita meat consumption is over 175 pounds.

Low meat consumption in Central America cannot be attributed to either the scarcity of cattle or to consumer preference for corn, beans, and rice. In the last 20 years, the cattle population almost doubled so that today there is a head of cattle for every two people in Central America. Pastures cover almost half the region's arable land. Most beef produced in Central America is not for the protein-starved population but for export, mainly to the United States. In Honduras, per capita beef consumption dropped 10 percent between 1965 and 1975, during which time that country's meat exports to the United States tripled.[22]

Since 1960, beef exports have ranked as one of the region's five major agro-exports. Between 1960 and 1980, meat exports increased seven times in Central America, and they now hold the third position among leading exports from Costa Rica and Honduras. In recent years, about 15 percent of U.S. meat imports came from Central America.

Unlike most U.S. cattle, Central American beef is grass-fed rather than grain-fed. As such, it is not as lean as American beef, but the U.S. fast-food chains, which buy most of the Central American meat, do not mind. Fast-food outlets have spread their neon signs and hamburger dining style throughout the world at a quickening pace. McDonalds sells *El Big Mac* in every Central American capital. In Panama, McDonalds serves local beef and decorates its restaurants with the traditional artwork of the Kuna Indians to complement its own "golden arches" motif.[23]

Back in the 1950s, beef was considered a nontraditional export. But with the assistance of AID, the World Bank, and the Inter-American Development Bank (IDB), the countries modernized and expanded their livestock sector. The World Bank noted in its 1975 sector policy paper on agricultural credit that "lending for livestock operations continues to be the single most important type of credit activity." In the case of Costa Rica, over 20 percent of the development loans from the IDB were for livestock programs, including the very first IDB loan to the country. As a result, thousands of 60-pound boxes of chilled beef regularly leave Central America to meet the fast-food needs of U.S. hamburger addicts.

While Central Americans are finding beef more and more expensive, U.S. companies have found that raising beef on the tropical forest land in Central America lowers their costs. The cost of a Central American steer is generally about 40 percent lower than that of a comparable U.S. steer.

A report done for the U.S. State Department called it "a quick and dirty business," where the U.S. investor extracts as much profit as possible from the converted forests before the land becomes eroded and worthless.[24] As landlessness and food deficits build, the use of half the region's arable land to graze cattle is harder to justify. Pastures are not even located on the worst land. In Honduras, cattle occupy 65 percent of the largest and most fertile landholdings.[25]

The land area required to graze only one or two steers, if converted to crops, could feed an entire family for a year.

The other question of land use associated with the cattle industry concerns the immense sections of tropical rain forests that are being destroyed to make way for more cattle. In the last several decades, two-thirds of these tropical forests have been cleared mainly for ranching. At the current rate of destruction, Central American rainforests will be gone by the end of the century.

Enter the Nontraditionals

In the 1970s, AID introduced a new twist to the agro-export system: the production of nontraditional exports like exotic flowers, shrimp, sesame seeds, and snow peas. This line of agro-exports are called nontraditionals because they move the nations away from their dependency on the traditional five cash crops. Nontraditional exports are backed by AID and the Central American governments because they provide an additional source of foreign exchange. Although different from the standard regional exports, vegetables, flowers, and shrimp exports are in the traditional mode of agricultural development in that they take land and resources away from local food production. Unlike the traditional agro-exports (except for bananas), the business of nontraditional agricultural products involves U.S. investors. But rather than getting directly involved in production, most investors contract local farmers to grow the vegetables. The U.S. companies buy the produce and export it to the United States.

Most of AID's money for nontraditional production flows through a consortium of TNCs called the Latin American Agribusiness Development Corporation (LAAD). LAAD is a consortium of 15 mainly agribusiness TNCs that were brought together by BankAmerica to invest in nontraditional exports from Latin America. LAAD has counted on over $50 million in low-interest loans from AID for its operations.

Central America is the heart of LAAD's business. From Belize to Panama, LAAD has an agribusiness portfolio of over 160 businesses (about 75 percent of its total investment). In its application for AID funding, LAAD said its two leading goals were 1) to improve the standard of living of Central American poor and 2) to stimulate economic and agricultural growth, create employment, and increase rural incomes.[26]

The unstated goal of LAAD is to bring home profits for its corporate shareholders—something that it does rather well. In 1984, profits rose a record 23 percent. Despite the sorry state of the region's economy, the TNC consortium can expect a rosy profit picture in years to come. One factor is the Caribbean Basin Initiative (CBI), initiated by the Reagan administration, which exempts companies like LAAD from paying import duties on produce shipped from the

Caribbean Basin. But the chief reason is the easy money it receives from the U.S. government.

LAAD gets its loan money from AID at 4 percent interest, then turns around and lends it to nontraditional export businesses at 12 percent or higher. Portions of the AID loans are also channeled into direct investments by LAAD. AID hails LAAD as an example of the way private business can develop Central America, but it is doubtful that LAAD or the entire strategy of nontraditional exports benefit the host countries.

Guatemala, which has over 60 LAAD-financed businesses, is the center of the consortium's operations in Central America. LAAD maintains close ties with BankAmerica and the country's American Chamber of Commerce—two organizations that have supported the military governments in Guatemala. Tom Mooney, the former president of the American Chamber of Commerce, serves as president of LAAD of Central America, which has its offices in Guatemala City. Concerning the political situation in the country, Mooney said: "The only way to stop Communism is to destroy it quickly. Argentina and Chile are nations which used this approach with considerable effectiveness and have gone on to become among Latin America's most stable and successful economies."[27]

TABLE 6B

LATIN AMERICAN AGRIBUSINESS DEVELOPMENT CORPORATION
1984 CORPORATE SHAREHOLDERS

Adela Investment	Deere & Co.
BankAmerica Intl. Finan. Corp.	Gerber Products
Borden	Goodyear Tire and Rubber
Cargill	Mellon Intl. Holdings Corp.
Castle & Cooke	Monsanto
Caterpillar Tractor	Rabobank Curaçao
Chase Manhattan	Ralston Purina
CPC Intl.	Southeast Bank

SOURCE: LAAD, 1984 Annual Report.

The most prominent LAAD project in Guatemala is Alimentos Congelados Monte Bello (ALCOSA). A subsidiary of Hanover Brands, ALCOSA processes and freezes broccoli, cauliflower, and okra grown by Indian farmers. In addition to providing financing for ALCOSA, AID funds numerous projects to persuade Indian farmers of the *Altiplano* (Highlands) to use their small parcels to grow vegetables for ALCOSA and other U.S. vegetable companies. One study found that crops of cauliflower displaced corn, beans, and cabbage cultivation by small farmers who produced for ALCOSA.[28]

After following AID's advice, many small farmers have discovered that vegetable farming is more expensive and riskier than traditional farming. "Nothing remains for us after we pay for transportation and for the fertilizer, and the insecticides the company requires us to use," said a member of the cooperative that produces Brussels sprouts. Indian farmers from the San Marcos area complained in 1984 that ALCOSA rejects about 30 percent of their produce—a fact they attribute to the overabundance of winter vegetables being produced by small farmers.

Small farmers throughout Guatemala have been told by AID that they should grow snow peas, cauliflower, and broccoli, but they frequently find that there is no one to buy their produce. AID can provide the technical assistance needed by small subsistence farmers if they are to switch to nontraditional exports, and it can tell them how much more they will make if they sell their produce to U.S. vegetable brokers. But what AID has not been able to do is to guarantee a market for their vegetables. In fact, the winter vegetable market has become increasingly competitive due to AID's promotion of nontraditional exports in all the countries of the Caribbean Basin.

Farmers that have been able to find a secure market for their vegetables have benefited from AID's promotion of nontraditional agribusiness. For the most part, these are not truly small farmers but medium-size farmers with experience in commercial marketing. Subsistence farmers depend on their corn harvests each year and have no room to experiment with crops they do not eat and may not be able to sell.

The Chemical Fix

Wherever you find cash crops in Central America, you will find ample evidence of pesticides. In the last 30 years, intensified use has made the countries of the region the highest users per capita of agrochemicals in the world. In 1981, Central America imported more than 12 pounds of pesticides for each person.

Central America became a proving ground for many pesticides in the 1950s and 1960s. At a Cotton Experiment Station set up by Nicaragua's dictator Anastasio Somoza, TNC chemical manufacturers tested their latest chemical concoctions and sent sales teams throughout Central America to hawk their eradicants as the cure-all for pest problems. Soon large producers were spraying their cotton fields 25 to 50 times a year with organochlorine pesticides like DDT, aldrin, and dieldrin. Cotton growers remain the best customers of the agrochemical companies, accounting for 80 percent of pesticide use in Central America, but all the other major agro-export producers also depend on pesticides.

From 50 to 75 percent of the pesticides applied by crop dusters never falls on the target crop.[29] The chemical fog descends on nearby homes, peasant families, streams, wells, and other crops. This careless and heavy use has created a host of health and environmental problems. Those who labor in the fields have suffered the most from unchecked application of pesticides. Each year thousands of workers suffer from skin burns and poisonings. Dizziness, vomiting, and general weakness are common symptoms of pesticide poisoning, symptoms that farm workers have learned to endure to keep their jobs. Those that suffer from chemical exposure rarely make it to a doctor; many die in the fields and are buried on the farms where they work.

Health experts now agree that the resurgence of malaria in Central America relates directly to heavy pesticide use. Overuse of chemicals has caused malaria-bearing mosquitoes to develop a biological resistance to most pesticides. Malaria rates have soared as a result. During the 1970s, reported cases of malaria infections increased 11 times in Guatemala, a pattern duplicated in neighboring nations.[30] The Central American Institute of Technology reports that incidence of the disease in the region is "clearly related to the percent of surface that is planted in cotton."[31] So direct is this relationship that an estimated 100 cases of malaria will result for every 2 pounds of pesticides added to the air.[32]

Agrochemicals take their toll on the natural environment of the coastal plains. *Campesinos* and fishermen report a severe loss of aquatic life that has come from aerial spraying that drifts over waterways or from contaminated irrigation water flowing into nearby streams. Costa Ricans charge that herbicides used to clear pastureland have almost extinguished the armadillo, crocodile, and fish population of the Guanacaste River. A Peace Corps volunteer in El Salvador studying the effects of pesticides on the marine life in Jiquilisco Bay reported these findings in 1976: "My nets came up filled with dead, decaying fish, crustaceans, and echinoderms. I didn't collect a single living fish that day. Bloated fish washed ashore in large numbers."[33]

Central America offers a major market for TNC agrochemical companies. Over one-quarter of the pesticides exported from the United States to Central America are not registered for use in the 50 states: when shipped from U.S. ports, they bear the ominous label "For Export Only."[34] The other 75 percent of U.S. pesticide exports to Central America include many chemicals that are heavily restricted for domestic use by the Environmental Protection Agency (EPA). For instance, the region imports close to 90 percent of the extremely toxic chemical methyl parathion exported by the United States. While this pesticide, closely related to a nerve gas developed by Nazi Germany, can be used only under restricted conditions in the United States, methyl parathion is sold freely on the shelves of stores even in remote parts of Central America.[35]

A notice placed in Costa Rica's leading daily, *La Nación*, by the environmental organization ASCONA expressed alarm at the ability of the TNCs to market banned pesticides in Costa Rica: "A series of pesticides prohibited in the United States are utilized with absolute liberty in our country and are within the reach of any consumer in many commercial establishments. [We use] aldrin, dieldrin, endrin, and heptaclor, as well as many mercury compounds that have practically disappeared in the United States. These pesticides are easily available to any person in our country."[36]

TNCs like Bayer, Monsanto, and Union Carbide trumpet their products as essential in the battle against world hunger. While pesticides do increase yields when used properly, the truth is that in Central America they are applied not on food crops but on cash crops. Of the 12 pounds per person of pesticides that are imported by Central American nations, only a few drops are used to grow food for local consumption. "The entire trade bypasses the need for more food," said David Weir, co-author of *Circle of Poison*.[37]

Careless chemical use is a problem that has come full circle back to the United States. The U.S. General Accounting Office (GAO) estimates that about 10 percent of U.S. food imports are dangerously contaminated by pesticides.[38] In the case of coffee imported from the region, residue tests show that 30 to 50 percent of the shipments of coffee beans show traces of chemicals banned in the United States like DDT, aldrin, and BHC.[39]

A poisonous cloud hangs over the rich farmland of Central America. Crop dusters, pesticide plants owned by Chevron and Monsanto, and the ever-present John Deere farm machinery are all signs that Central American agriculture is an outpost of U.S. agribusiness. Known in the past as Banana Republics, the countries now export much more: cotton, coffee, sugar, beef, vegetables, and flowers—headed to the United States. Meanwhile, there is less and less to eat in Central America, more and more pesticide poisoning, and at least as much government oppression. Whether producing traditional or nontraditional crops, U.S. agribusiness corporations continue doing business in Central America in the traditional Banana Republic way.

Taking Control of the Land

To improve agricultural production in Central America, there are many measures—like more irrigation, better pest management, and more agricultural extension services—that would help. But measures to increase production do not go to the heart of the problem of Central American agriculture: the dependence on the production of a few commodities that are drawing lower prices in the glutted international market.

International agreements to establish higher prices for agro-exports and a stable market would be a first step toward improving the grim outlook of the region's cash-crop economies. Unless the concentrated patterns of land and resource ownership change in these societies, an improvement in international trade relations would go mostly to the narrow class of oligarchs. Higher coffee prices would do little to improve the lives of coffee pickers who would continue to receive literally unlivable wages. Increased coffee prices under the present circumstances in most Central American nations would simply mean fatter Miami bank accounts.

Agriculture is the heart of Central American society and economy. For the region to develop, the agricultural sector has to be put on a new footing. A new agricultural development program for the region would necessarily involve profound agrarian reform, labor laws that permit farm-labor organizing, state control of international marketing, government coalitions with other agro-export-producing countries, emphasis on national food self-sufficiency, more agro-industry, and better integration between rural production and urban markets.

---

1 *Latin America Commodities Report*, April 4, 1980, p.7, and CEPAL, "America Latina y la Economia Mundial del Café" (Santiago), 1982. Figures are from 1977.
2 Eldon Kenworthy, "Is El Salvador a New Vietnam?" *In These Times*, March 23, 1983, p.16.
3 Fredrick Clairmonte & John Cavanagh, UNCTAD, "TNCs and Beverages" (study in progress for 1986).
4 CEPAL, "The Transnational Oligopoly in the Coffee Industry and the Case of Columbia" (Santiago), 1982, p.59.
5 Ibid., p.10.
6 CEPAL,"El Financiamiento Exterior de America Latina" (Santiago), 1964, p.16.
7 CEPAL, "Bargaining Position and Distribution of Gains in the Banana Industry of the Union of Banana Exporting Countries, Especially Honduras and Panama" (Santiago), 1982.
8 Frank Ellis, *Las Transnacionales del Banano en Centroamerica* (San Jose: Editorial Universiaria Centroamericana, 1983), p.364.
9 CEPAL, "Bargaining Position and Distribution . . .," p.115.
10 *Multinational Monitor*, July 1981, p.16.
11 *Los Angeles Times*, September 25, 1983.
12 CEPAL, "Bargaining Position and Distribution . . .," p.62.
13 Ibid., p.135.
14 Ibid., p.32.
15 Marc Herold, "From Riches to 'Rags': Finanzkapital in El Salvador, 1900–1980" (unpublished manuscript, University of New Hampshire, 1980).
16 Edelberto Torres-Rivas, "El Desarrollo de la Agricultura en Centroamerica," in Confederación Universitaria Centroamericana (CSUCA), "Documentos de Estudios" (San Jose), July 22–23, 1982; and CIERA and INIES, "El Subsistema del Algodón en Nicaragua" (Managua), 1983.
17 Calculations from data supplied by Granillo Bonilla and Rina Amelia, Universidad Centroamericana José Simeon Canas, "La Modernización del Cultivo del Algodón, Causas, y Consecuencias" (San Salvador), 1980, p.32.
18 UNCTAD, "Fibres and Textiles: Dimensions of Corporate Marketing" (Geneva), 1980, p.19.
19 Ibid.
20 Information from Instituto de Investigaciones Economicas, El Salvador.
21 Eric B. Ross, "Patterns of Diet and Forces of Production: An Economic and Ecological History of the Ascendency of Beef in the United States Diet," in E.B. Ross, *Beyond the Myths of Culture: Essays in Cultural Materialism* (New York: Academic, 1980), cited in "From Central American Pasture to North American Hamburger: The Effects of Beef Exports on Diet, Ecology, and Economy in Costa Rica," a paper presented by Marc Edelman to the Wenner-Gren Foundation for Anthropological Research Symposium No. 94 on "Food Preferences and Aversions" in October 1983.
22 James Nations and Daniel Komer, "Rainforests and the Hamburger Society," *Environment*, April 1983. Figures from a study of land use in Chiapas, Mexico.
23 Douglas Shane, US Department of State, Office of Environmental Affairs, "Hoofprints

on the Forest: An Inquiry into the Beef Cattle Industry in the Tropical Forest Areas of Latin America" (Washington), March 1980, p.27.

24 Ibid., p.68.

25 Jacobo Schatan, *La Agroindustria y el Sistema Centroamericano* (Mexico: CEPAL, 1983), p.46.

26 AID, "Agribusiness Employment/Investment Promotion," ROCAP Project Paper (Washington), May 15, 1981.

27 Jenny Pearce, *Under the Eagle* (London: Latin American Bureau, 1981), p.176.

28 AID, "The Social Impact of Agribusiness: A Case Study of ALCOSA in Guatemala," July 1981.

29 ICAITI, *An Environmental and Economic Study of the Consequences of Pesticide Use in Central American Cotton Production* (Guatemala), 1977, p.2.

30 Derived from data in PAHO, "1983 Annual Report to the Director," 1984.

31 ICAITI, op.cit., p.150.

32 Georganne Chapin and Robert Wasserstrom, "Agricultural Production and Malaria Resurgence in Central America and India," *Nature*, September 17, 1981, p.182.

33 Martin Wolterding, "The Poisoning of Central America," *Sierra Club Bulletin*, September/October 1981, p.65.

34 GAO, "Better Regulation of Pesticide Exports and Pesticide Residues in Imported Food is Essential" (Washington), 1979, p.8.

35 Shelley Hearne, *Harvest of Unknowns: Pesticide Contamination in Imported Foods* (New York: Natural Resources Defense Council, 1984), p.21.

36 Roberto Chediak, Tami Bensekry, Patricia Mora, Esther Lopez and Juan Carlos Del Bello, "Desarrollo de la Infrastructura y Capacidad de Planificacion en Ciencia y Technologia, A Report to the Government of Costa Rica" (Costa Rica), June 1983, p.32; *La Nación*, August 22, 1979.

37 Testimony by David Weir before the Subcommittee on Department Operations, Research and Foreign Agriculture, Committee on Agriculture, House of Representatives, *The Regulation of Pesticides*, Vol. 2, June 1983, p.204.

38 GAO, op.cit., p.31.

39 Hearne, op.cit., pp.2–3.

CHAPTER 7

Industry: Backyard Business

*The Salvadoran people are quite extraordinary. They are proud
of their reputation as the "Hong Kong of the New World."
Companies that have invested in our country know that Salvadorans are among the best workers in the world. They are
enterprising and hard working, they are private entrepreneurs
to their very souls.*
— President José Napoleon Duarte, excerpt from a 1984
speech to the Americas Society

THE REGION'S STEPS toward industrialization in the 1960s were regarded as
steps away from dependence on the United States and other developed capitalist
nations. Industrialization was also commonly considered an alternative to the
exploitative and backward cash-crop system. A quarter of a century after the
region embarked on its industrialization plans, Central America remains at least
as dependent on foreign industry as it was before.

What happened? Aren't there more factories in Central America than there
were in the 1950s? Don't the Central American nations now export manufactured
products like calculators, blue jeans, pesticides, and electronic relays? Doesn't
Central America now produce its own instant coffee, ketchup, bathroom fixtures,
and toilet paper?

In the last 25 years, the number of factories and the quantity of manufactured
exports have increased tremendously. But the facade of industrialization hides
its fraudulent nature. The following features of industrialization in Central America have undermined its worth as a vehicle of progress and modernization:

- TNCs took control of the most profitable manufacturing and food-processing industries.
- Investment by TNCs pushed large portions of the locally-owned industrial
sector out of business.
- Most new industries that produced for the local market were really "finishing-touch" industries that added very little value to imported goods.
- The increase of products manufactured in the region was accompanied by

an increase in the quantity of equipment and basic goods Central America had to import.

● Central America expanded its manufactured export industries, but TNC control resulted in very little positive effect on the local economy.

● Wages in manufacturing industries are only slightly higher than agricultural wages and do not cover the higher cost of urban living.

● Labor organizing in the TNC-owned manufacturing plants has been repressed to keep wages low.

Opening Up the Regional Market to TNCs

Central America was a latecomer to the movement toward industrialization in Latin America. Other Latin American countries like Argentina and Chile began to industrialize while the United States was in the throes of the Great Depression. Local entrepreneurs began to manufacture products that were previously imported. This strategy of industrialization is known as import-substitution. Latin America had another opportunity to chart its own development when the United States and European nations that traditionally dominated trade were busy with World War II.

Tight control by the banana companies and national agrarian elites kept Central America from moving ahead. Outside the banana enclaves and coffee plantations, few business opportunities were available.

By the 1950s, Central American society began to loosen up, with the rise of a small middle class and a group of modern capitalists who were ready for change. Business and government leaders sought to overcome the region's long-time dependence on a few agricultural commodities whose prices were steadily declining in relation to manufactured goods. The immediate obstacle stalling industrialization was the small-sized markets faced by manufacturers. Not only were the national populations relatively tiny (1 to 3 million), but the market for consumer goods was also constrained by the concentration of wealth among a small sector in each country.

An obvious solution to the problem was to widen the national markets by redistributing land and increasing wage levels. In Guatemala, where such reforms were tried with success, the reformist government was overthrown with the firm support of the coffee growers and U.S. investors. The oligarchies in each Central American country resisted all reforms that would allow a broader distribution of social wealth. In the mid-1950s, the United Nations Economic Commission on Latin America (ECLA) presented an attractive alternative. The UN planners offered an industrialization plan that would permit the modernization of the capitalist system without upsetting existing power relations. They proposed an import-substitution strategy based on an integrated regional market. Five Central American nations (Guatemala, El Salvador, Honduras, Nicaragua, and Costa

Rica) would form a customs union that would tear down trade barriers between the nations while erecting a regional external tariff to discourage manufactured imports. Local industries would then be able to market their goods throughout the entire region rather than being constrained to narrow national markets.

In 1958, the five nations signed a treaty that put the ECLA plan for a regional market in motion. The treaty called for 1) the gradual loosening of trade barriers between countries, 2) balanced development for each nation, 3) an emphasis on locally owned industries and controls on foreign investment, and 4) the creation of "integration industries."

To avoid duplication of production, a few integration industries would produce for the entire market without competition. They were to be parceled out among all five nations to allay the fears of the three least industrialized nations (Honduras, Nicaragua, and Costa Rica) that the treaty would favor the more developed countries of Guatemala and El Salvador.

The United States endorsed the idea of an integrated market in Central America but considered a common market primarily as an open door to the isthmus for U.S. trade and investment. President Eisenhower dispatched two diplomats to the region to steer the region away from the ECLA plan and toward an integrated-market concept that would facilitate U.S. manufacturing investment. The U.S. representatives proposed the immediate removal of all intraregional trade barriers, encouragement of foreign investment, elimination of mechanisms for regional industrialization planning, and subordination of balanced growth to unrestricted free trade.

With the promise of $100 million in economic assistance to support the region's industrialization, the United States lured the Central American nations away from the ECLA treaty. The General Treaty on Central American Economic Integration that established the Central American Common Market (CACM) was signed in 1961, superseding the ECLA-sponsored treaty of three years before.

To guide the new industrial development, the United States established a regional office of the Agency for International Development (AID) in Guatemala City. The regional office hoped to weaken the influence of ECLA in Central America by having regular contact with the new regional institutions that were being established in conjunction with CACM. From Guatemala City, the AID officials channeled U.S. technical and financial assistance throughout the region with the aim of improving the investment climate.[1]

The U.S. government guaranteed that the CACM would benefit U.S. interests by contributing the bulk of funding for CACM's planning, research, and financial agencies. The United States contributed 54 percent of the budget for the nine CACM agencies while 33 percent came from countries outside the region and only 13 percent of the annual budget came from the Central American nations themselves.[2]

One of the new institutions founded to serve regional integration was the Central American Bank for Economic Integration (CABEI). Rather than fostering regional industrialization, CABEI promoted U.S. investment and trade by funding infrastructure and communications. One loan of $1.1 million went to Phelps Dodge to expand its wire-manufacturing plant in El Salvador. Because the United States provided most of the bank's capital, it was able to specify that loans be used to purchase U.S. products.

The regional planning and financial institutions failed to protect local investors against the onslaught of TNCs during the 1960s and 1970s. The U.S. domination of the CACM institutions obstructed the development of "integration industries"—which were originally conceived as regionally-owned industries receiving special financing and trade protection. The three integration industries that did emerge were all controlled by TNCs. In Nicaragua, two plants with co-production arrangements were formed to manufacture pesticides and industrial chemicals, but they soon came under the complete control of Hercules Power and Pennwalt. The CABEI financed a Guatemalan company called GINSA (which was bought out by Goodyear) to produce tubes and tires for the region.

Before the creation of the common market, U.S. nonagricultural investment was limited to a few corporations like Coca-Cola and Sears, but CACM offered a regional market large enough to interest an array of transnational corporations. In 1950, over 95 percent of U.S. foreign investment in Central America was in nonmanufacturing activities. By the end of the first decade of regional integration, U.S. investment in manufacturing had increased 15 times.

Imported Industrialization

CACM achieved its purposes of expanding the regional market and promoting industrialization in Central America. But there were several underlying problems with the system. One major weakness was that it did not protect the market from the investment of outside capital. Corporations that had previously been exporting to Central America moved to the region to avoid high external tariffs and to take advantage of the low internal tariffs on goods manufactured within the region. Many of the new industries were only finishing operations for semi-manufactured goods.

A survey of products manufactured by 68 TNCs in Guatemala showed a foreign-import factor ranging from 70 to 85 percent.[3] The pharmaceutical industry in pre-revolutionary Nicaragua imported almost 90 percent of its raw materials. In El Salvador, only 5 to 20 percent of the manufacturing of "Salvadoran" products was actually done in the country. The factories in Central America put only the final touches on products such as cosmetics, pharmaceuticals, and home products. One Salvadoran company imported Worcestershire sauce in barrels, bottled it in a plant in San Salvador, and then marked it as a "Producto de Centroamerica."[4]

Many TNCs manufactured products that were not formerly imported. They took advantage of the regional market to introduce snack foods, cosmetics, and pharmaceuticals. With their enormous advertising budgets, they created a consumer demand for luxury goods, despite the fact that only a few Central Americans could afford these nonessential products.

The chairperson of International Flavors and Fragrances, explaining his company's marketing strategy, said: "How often we see in developing countries that the poorer the economic outlook, the more important the small luxury of a flavored soft drink or smoke . . . to the dismay of many would-be benefactors, the poorer the malnourished are, the more likely they are to spend a disproportionate amount of whatever they have on some luxury rather than on what they need. Observe, study, learn [how to sell in rural societies]. We try to do it. It seems to pay off for us. Perhaps it will for you too."[5]

After 10 years of industrialization, Central America had become even more dependent on industrial imports than it was when the import-substitution strategy was initiated. From 1960 to 1971, Central America's balance-of-payments deficit tripled. A high protective tariff did slow down the import of finished consumer goods, but the regional tariff on intermediate and capital goods (machinery and equipment) remained low, causing the imports of semi-manufactured products and machinery to skyrocket. The high import content of TNC manufactured goods reduced the real economic contribution of industry. Between 1960 and 1980, the value added by the industrial sector to the region's GDP increased only 4 percentage points.

TNC-led industrialization did very little to expand the employment opportunities of the Central American work force. Between 1962 and 1975, industrial employment as a percentage of total employment only increased from 9.6 percent to 10.3 percent. Since 1975, industrial employment has fallen to levels below those of 1962. By 1982, only 8.2 percent of the work force was employed in industry.[6] A study by SIECA, a CACM research organization based in Guatemala, observed that the contribution of industrialization to employment could have been greater if the integration planners would have limited the establishment of capital-intensive industries and encouraged the growth of small- and medium-size enterprises.[7]

The benefits of industrialization were further reduced by the rivalry between countries to offer the best incentives and tax breaks to new TNC investors. Tax benefits granted to foreign investors in El Salvador in 1975 equaled about 85 percent of all industrial wages. In the country's capital-intensive chemical industry, tax concessions to TNCs were twice the wages paid.[8]

The lack of central planning for industrialization resulted in the majority of the new investment flowing to El Salvador and Guatemala. The lesser developed countries were damaged when they stopped importing the lower-priced goods of the foreign industrial countries and had to buy the more expensive Guatemalan and Salvadoran products from the regional market.[9]

The circumstances of uneven development added to existing tension between

El Salvador and Honduras, culminating in the so-called Soccer War of 1969. Honduras began boycotting Salvadoran products and turned its anger on the Salvadoran immigrants within its borders. An attack by the Salvadoran army on Honduras initiated the six-day war. Honduras broke off all trade with El Salvador and withdrew from CACM, signaling the end of an open market for all five countries.

Reviewing the contribution of industrialization during the 1970s, SIECA found that the sector had been draining the region of its financial resources. The external deficit of the industrial sector grew from $370 million in 1970 to $1.6 billion in 1980. In 1980, the sector was exporting products out of the region valued at $900 million but was importing over $2.3 billion worth of intermediate and capital goods.

Also contributing to the deficit was the repatriation of TNC capital. Accounting for both new investments and profit repatriation by TNCs, the net contribution of foreign private capital in the 1970s was a negative $180 million— meaning that TNCs had taken out $180 million more than they put into the Central American economy.[10]

As the economic crisis took hold of Central America in the 1980s, governments began imposing heavier import duties and in some cases completely broke off trade relations with their neighbors on the isthmus. Political turmoil worsened the deterioration of intraregional trade, which declined almost 40 percent from 1980 to 1984.[11]

Buying Out Local Industry

Rather than starting a business from scratch, U.S. TNCs frequently acquire, partially or wholly, the assets of local companies. In Guatemala 20 of the 44 largest U.S. corporations operating in the country in 1970 started their operations by acquiring local firms.[12] When they go to Central America U.S. TNCs often leave their names at home and assume the name of the local company they purchase. About three-quarters of the "Central American" products traded in the region are currently produced by TNC subsidiaries.[13]

The flood of TNCs was resisted by some Central American industrialists and business groups, but most joined up with the corporations in joint ventures. They realized that without state protection it would be impossible to compete with the TNCs. Their business instincts overcame any nationalistic reservations about foreign intervention. They welcomed TNC representatives into their ranks and the American Chambers of Commerce became part of the local power structures. Joining the network of the social, economic, political, and military elites, TNC executives began to exercise significant influence in the national affairs of the Central American nations.

In El Salvador, 41 of the 55 foreign investments established after 1960 were joint ventures.[14] U.S. firms recognize that by associating with local firms they gain the knowledge and local market experience necessary for profitable businesses. A joint venture is an excellent way for a U.S. corporation to gradually absorb local wealth. It also has the effect of creating a dependent class of capitalists who are allied with U.S. political and business interests.

A study by the UN Center on Transnational Corporations stated that due to "the absence of regional or national policies with regard to foreign investment, TNCs met no opposition to their penetration of domestic markets and, in this manner, contributed to the progressive disappearance of the few pre-existing local groups of any importance." In conclusion, the UN study found that CACM "favored an increase in the dominating presence of transnational corporations . . . instead of stimulating the development of Central American productive forces."[15]

TABLE 7
INDICATORS OF LABOR CONDITIONS IN CENTRAL AMERICAN COUNTRIES

	BEL	CRA	ELS	GUA	HON	NIC	PAN
Organized Labor (% of labor force)	8	14	10 agric 7 urban	6	40 urban 20 rural	40	15
Organized Labor (thousands)	3	125	85 agric 60 urban	130	150 urban 120 rural	340	95
1980 Underemployment (% of EAP*)		27	49	51			46
Urban (% of urban EAP)		19	40	40			32
Rural (% of ag EAP)		43	57	60			73
1970–1980 Percent Change in Real Wages:							
Manufacturing		26	−7	−37	6 (a)	−26	−2
Agriculture		50	−15	−26	7 (b)	−25	35
Non Agriculture		13	7 (c)	−16	−22	−24	−13

*EAP—Economically Active Population; (a)1973–1980; (b)1974–1980; (c) 1970–1978.

SOURCES: Figures are abstracted and calculated from *World Factbook 1984,* USCIA; *Worldmark Encyclopedia of the Nations: The Americas,* 1984; *Statistical Abstract of Latin America,* Vol. 23.

Industrial Parks for Runaway Corporations

Once they had cornered the market on profitable consumer goods by the early 1970s, TNCs slowed down their new investment in the import-substitution sector. About the same time, another form of TNC investment began picking up.

Governments invited TNCs to use Central America as an export platform for their labor-intensive industries like electronics and clothing assembly. These export manufacturing plants are commonly called *maquiladoras* in Spanish. They are also known as offshore industries because (unlike import-substitution factories) they produce solely for the export market and have little to do with the local economy except for employing its cheap labor.

Industrial wages in Central America range from $3 to $9 a day, which compares with an average daily wage of $74 for a U.S. industrial worker. Central Americans not only work for much less but they also work an average of 46 hours a week.

The *maquiladoras* perform the labor-intensive portion of the manufacturing process. Companies ship the basic materials like patches of clothing or electronic parts to the *maquiladoras*, which assemble the pieces. The assembled products are then shipped back to the United States for additional manufacturing and distribution. This arrangement is ideal for TNCs worried about possible nationalization or the political instability of Central America. Having little or no investment in plant or equipment, a company can close up shop almost overnight and move on to a more secure and possibly cheaper part of the world.

There are two types of *maquiladoras* in Central America. Some companies, like Texas Instruments and Maidenform, operate their own assembly plants while other corporations contract a local firm to assemble goods that the U.S. corporation supplies. Even under the first arrangement, a U.S. company does not necessarily own its own plant. Companies frequently simply rent a factory shell provided by the government. Central American countries also provide electricity, telephone lines, factory maintenance, and workers. The TNC provides only the machinery and factory manager.

The second type of *maquiladora* or offshore business is known as subcontracting. Under this arrangement, the U.S. company does not even have to provide machinery or a manager. It simply contracts the production work out to a local company that specializes in assembly operations. U.S. corporations have no direct investment in the business, but they completely control the subcontractor because they supply the basic materials, financing, technology, and marketing. Without having to deal with the local labor force, U.S. firms receive products assembled according to detailed specifications from their subcontractors.

Although the TNCs gained from this development strategy, the Central American countries soon discovered serious disadvantages to it. Each country tried to undercut the other by offering more tax exemptions, better infrastructure, and a cheaper labor supply. With the exception of the Panama's Colon Free Zone, none of the industrial parks or free zones in Central America succeeded in attracting the expected number of "runaways." In 1981, the commercial officer at the U.S. Embassy in Honduras observed that Honduras was "losing its shirt on the Puerto Cortes Zone since it hasn't been able to attract enough industry to pay for the costs of establishing and building the zone."[16]

Despite this lack of success, the U.S. government is promoting *maquiladoras* as a solution to the region's current economic problems. It has pressured the countries to increase their exemptions and incentives for assembly industries. The Caribbean Basin Initiative (CBI) allows the duty-free import of many products that could be produced in *maquiladoras*.

In all the countries, both types of *maquiladoras* prefer to employ women. At the free trade zone in Puerto Cortes in Honduras, hundreds of women park their bicycles in front of a complex of unidentified buildings where they make baseballs, bras, and men's underwear for U.S. consumers. "The concentration of capital and resources affects everybody," commented Saralee Hamilton, coordinator of the Women's Network on Global Corporations, "but it affects women in particularly damaging ways, for it increases the subordination of women in the international division of labor. . . . Multinationals see women as a super-exploitable work force, and institute deliberate policies of preferential female hiring."[17]

A recent AID loan to promote export manufacturing in Honduras won the support of the Honduran-American Chamber of Commerce but drew fire from opposition politicians. The plan was based on an AID-commissioned report by International Parks Inc, which found that Honduras offered the best conditions for TNCs of any country in the Caribbean Basin except for Haiti. Honduras—which is also the poorest Caribbean Basin country after Haiti—not only offers low wage rates but also a comparatively stable political climate.

The Honduran School of Economists said implementation of the proposal would exempt U.S. firms from most taxes and duties, increase the country's dependency on the United States, raise the foreign debt, and convert national entrepreneurs into a "managerial bourgeoisie." Honduras will become "a kind of Singapore," said Christian Democrat Efraín Díaz Arrivillaga, "dedicated to the assembly of goods that are exported free of taxes and that would later be able to re-enter the Honduran market at elevated prices."[18]

MOLIDER, a faction of Suazo Córdova's Liberal Party, observed:

> The Suazo Córdova administration just signed a credit and donation agreement with the omnipresent Agency for International Development to establish manufacturing plants, or better said, industrial assembly enclaves to export products. This activity only benefits foreign capitalists

to the detriment of Honduras' business sector. . . . [The agreement] will lift import and export controls and favor tax evasion and smuggling. It stipulates the creation of tax free ports and areas throughout the country over which the government will have very little control.

This will create economic enclaves where Honduras will not be sovereign, in a setup that can be compared with the Regional Military Training Center. The independence of Honduras will be compromised by virtue of its greater vulnerability to outside sources. Also, the establishment of tax free areas in Honduras will imply high industrial infrastructure investments, increasing our foreign debt, and sidetracking funds that are needed for development programs.[19]

The Corporate Lobby

The first sign of rising corporate interest in the Caribbean Basin came with the founding of the Committee for the Caribbean during the last year of the Carter administration. The Committee for the Caribbean, together with the American Enterprise Institute and the Council of the Americas, sponsored in 1979 the first Miami Conference, to promote foreign investment in Central America and the Caribbean islands. At the conference, Robert West said that the U.S. private sector was "an untapped resource that can provide far more investment capital than all the aid the U.S. government can ever offer."[20]

The Committee for the Caribbean was the forerunner of a more powerful and better-funded organization called Caribbean Central America Action (CCAA). Robert West, chairperson of Tesoro Petroleum and the main organizer for Committee for the Caribbean, became the first president of CCAA.

Among the CCAA's 60 corporate sponsors are United Brands, Grace Foundation, Chase Manhattan, Maidenform, and BankAmerica. The founding committee of CCAA included not only corporate sponsors but also representatives of the National Security Council, U.S. Congress, and U.S. Information Agency.[21] It was launched with a $250,000 grant from AID and continues to receive AID support for its programs. Close cooperation with AID is a key to CCAA's strategy to increase U.S. investment in Central America.

Executive Director of CCAA Peter Johnson, who left the State Department to run CCAA, said that "CCAA is working with Central American private-sector leaders to create a region-wide vehicle for business leadership in development, and for channeling funds from AID and other donors directly into the private sector."[22]

In El Salvador, CCAA was instrumental in establishing a new private-sector organization called the Foundation for Social and Economic Development (FUSADES), which receives AID funds to promote the interests of the industrial sector. FUSADES was designed by CCAA and AID to be "the technical and research base of the country's private sector" and to work with the government and other agencies on "economic problems and opportunities."[23]

Executive Director Johnson described the role of CCAA as a broker arranging deals between U.S. firms and local business owners in the Caribbean Basin. He said, "Although multinational corporations account for much of the foreign investment in the region, CCAA will be emphasizing investments by small- to medium-sized U.S. businesses." The Miami Conference, which has become an annual event of the CCAA, puts U.S. investors in touch with Caribbean Basin politicians and business owners. The organization also co-hosts "telemission" conferences that provide direct television communication between U.S. corporate representatives and the private sector in the Caribbean.

Current CCAA chairperson is David Rockefeller, the former head of Chase Manhattan Bank. Rockefeller is a key figure in the corporate community's support of Washington's economic policies in the Caribbean Basin. A founder of the Caribbean Basin Coalition, a business group that lobbied for President Reagan's CBI program, Rockefeller directs several other corporate organizations concerned with Latin America. Rockefeller founded the Americas Society in 1981 as an umbrella group for corporate organizations concerned about Latin America. Under the aegis of the Americas Society are the Council of the Americas, the Center for Inter-American Relations, the Pan American Society, and CCAA. Not limited to economic concerns, the Americas Society serves as a political forum for U.S. corporations with interests in Latin America. To drum up corporate support for the *contras*, Rockefeller invited members of the civilian directorate of the anti-Sandinista Nicaraguan Democratic Front (FDN) to speak to the members of the Americas Society in 1984.

The relationship between the United States and other countries in the Americas is, according to Rockefeller, "not exclusively economic, but rather is based firmly in similar political aspirations." Supporting the formation of the Americas Society, Thomas Enders, U.S. Assistant Secretary of State for Inter-American Affairs, said, "As you know, the administration believes the private sector has a vital role to play in the hemisphere. So we are pleased that the Americas Society has been formed and we heartily endorse its objectives." Rockefeller said the organization will devote itself to cultural, public and business affairs.[24]

Representing the interests of U.S. corporations in Central America are branches of the American Chamber of Commerce of Latin America (ACCLA), which has offices in every Central American country with the exception of Belize. ACCLA is tied to CCAA through an AID grant for a joint program to attract new U.S. investment to the Caribbean Basin.

In Guatemala, the Chamber of Commerce has stood steadfastly behind the military governments and has supported continued U.S. military aid. Tom Mooney, president of the chamber in Guatemala, said, "The government of Guatemala, despite its numerous faults, is better than most governments of the world in terms of the very human rights grounds on which it is so severely attacked..."[25]

Former regional president of ACCLA, R. Bruce Cuthbertson, asserted that the entire future of Central America depends upon "neutralizing and eliminating terrorists" and on the "removal of the Sandinistas in Nicaragua."[26] Alexander Perry, Jr., the president of ACCLA, said: "Our opinion is sought after in Washington on many issues. We get involved not only in the relationship between the United States and Latin America but in their relationship with our administration in the United States."[27]

Industrialization Remains Part of the Solution

A quarter of a century of industrialization has done little to move Central America away from its underdeveloped and dependent state. Instead of decreasing imports and building a regional industrial sector, industrialization increased the region's balance-of-payments difficulties. It pushed local industrialists aside to make way for TNCs. What now passes for industrialization are industrial parks that advertise for runaway sweat shops. But there is no future in a sweatshop economy.

If Central America is ever to rise above its dead-end agro-export economy, industrialization must remain as part of the solution. It should be a process led by Central Americans themselves, not by the TNCs and AID. A program for self-sustaining industrial development would include the following elements: 1) use of regionally available basic materials, 2) labor-intensive production, 3) creation of larger internal markets by increasing incomes of the rural sectors, 4) support for public and private enterprises that manufacture products which meet basic needs, and 5) creation of an agro-industry that processes commodities for both the domestic and international markets.

1 Suzanne Jonas and David Tobis (eds.), *Guatemala* (Berkeley and New York: NACLA, 1974), p.89.
2 Donald Castillo Rivas, *Acumulación de Capital y Empresas Transnacionales en Centroamerica* (Mexico City: Siglo Veintiuno Editores, 1980). Information from Rene Poitevin, *El Proceso de Industrializacion* (Costa Rica: EDUCA, 1977).
3 C.V. Vaitsos, UNCTAD "Who Integrates, and with Whom, How, and for Whose Benefit," (Geneva), 1983, p.9.
4 Phillip L. Russell, *El Salvador in Crisis* (Austin: Colorado River, 1984), p.53.
5 Susan George, *How the Other Half Dies* (Montclair, N.J.: Allanheld, Osmun, 1977), p.143.
6 SIECA, *La Situacion Actual del Sector Industrial de Centroamerica y Algunas Propuestas de Medidas para su Reactivación*, (Guatemala: SIECA, 1983), p.5.
7 Ibid.
8 Russell, op.cit., p.55.
9 Marc Herold, "From Riches to 'Rags': Finanzkapital in El Salvador, 1900–1980" (unpublished manuscript, University of New Hampshire, 1980).
10 SIECA, op.cit., p.5.
11 Based on SIECA estimates of February 1985; *Central America Report*, April 19, 1985.
12 Jonas and Tobis, op.cit., p.132.
13 Edelberto Torres-Rivas, "Central America Today: A Study in Regional Dependency," in Martin Diskin (ed.), *Trouble in Our Backyard* (New York: Pantheon, 1983), pp.10–16.

14 Herold, op.cit., p.22.
15 United Nations Center on Transnational Corporations, "Measures Strengthening the Negotiating Capacity of Governments in Their Relations with Transnational Corporations" (New York), 1983, p.29.
16 Interview by Tom Barry, April 1982.
17 See "Ten People Who Aim to Tame the Multinationals" in *Multinational Monitor*, January 1982.
18 *Central America Report*, October 26, 1984.
19 *Honduras Update*, November/December 1984.
20 Philip E. Wheaton, EPICA, "Report of the Miami Conference on the Caribbean," November 1979.
21 Roger Burbach and Patricia Flynn (eds.), *The Politics of Intervention: The United States in Central America* (New York: Monthly Review, 1984), p.203.
22 See "Caribbean Investment: Following the Flag?" in *Multinational Monitor*, November 1981.
23 *CCAA in Action*, September/October 1982.
24 See "Rockefeller Launches Another Businessmen's Club" in *Multinational Monitor*, September 1981, p.3.
25 Bulletin of the American Chamber of Commerce in Guatemala, May 23, 1980, cited in Interfaith Center on Corporate Responsibility Brief, November 1980.
26 Robert H. Holden, "Corporate Officers Embrace Latin Dictators," *Multinational Monitor*, June 1982, p.12.
27 *Multinational Monitor*, June 1982.

PART THREE

CHAPTER 8

Belize

■

Trends
- Inability of political parties to win strong support of workers and peasants.
- Polarization between left and right.
- Possibility of British military withdrawal.
- Increased U.S. economic and military involvement despite national fears of becoming enmeshed in regional conflict.
- Expanding influence of Spanish-speaking population.

■

"NEWS FROM A new Central American nation in the heart of the Caribbean Basin." With that description of their recently independent country, the government-owned Radio Belize began its daily newscast in the months following independence from Great Britain in 1981. Belize is a country with a dual identity. While geographically Belize is sandwiched between Mexico and Guatemala on the Central American isthmus, culturally and economically the country identifies with the Caribbean islands.

Many studies of Central America do not even mention this sparsely populated country that was once known as British Honduras. Yet escalating conflict in the region makes it more difficult to separate Belize from its geographical circumstances. Salvadoran and Guatemalan refugees now flow across its borders, and Washington is attempting to incorporate the tiny nation into its geopolitical strategy for Central America.

Part of Belize's identity crisis arises from its cultural diversity. About the same size as El Salvador, Belize has only 160,000 inhabitants. Black Creoles, the country's largest ethnic group, make up 40 percent of the population and live mainly in Belize City. Spanish-speaking *mestizos* are the second largest group (35 percent) and live mostly in the northern sugar-growing areas around Orange Walk Town. Their numbers are growing because of the constant influx of Salvadoran and Guatemalan refugees. The Garifuna or Black Caribs live in southern Belize and comprise 8 percent of the population. Three Mayan groups (Yucatecan in the north, Mopan in the west and south, and Ketchi in the south) account for another 10 percent of Belizeans. A community of some 3000 Mennonite farmers, who speak a German *patois*, maintain a self-sufficient lifestyle in northern Belize. Many of the country's merchants are of Lebanese, Chinese, and East Indian descent.[1] One out of four Belizeans lives abroad, most in the United States.

English, the country's official language, is taught in Belize's classroooms, but a lilting English *patois* is the language of the streets. Spanish-speakers may soon become the majority, however, due to the steady exodus of Creoles and the equally steady immigration of Salvadoran and Guatemalan refugees. Native Belizeans leave to seek work or better wages while other Central Americans see opportunity in the uncleared backlands.

Black Belizeans are concerned about the cultural and ethnic identity of the country. Estimates of the number of aliens living in Belize run as high as 47,000. About one-half of the foreigners residing in Belize are refugees from El Salvador and Guatemala. Over 4500 legal Salvadoran refugees live in Belize under the supervision of the United Nations. The growth of the Spanish-speaking population represents "a serious threat to our Belizean heritage," said the country's Home Minister. Many Belizeans, however, including those in government, appreciate the hard work of Salvadorans in clearing the bush to expand the country's agricultural production.

Remittances from Belizean expatriates make up a full 25 percent of the national income. Another 15 percent comes from the presence of 2,000 British soldiers. Half the population is urban and only 15 percent of the arable land is farmed. The lack of roads into the interior and the lack of a good monetary system largely explain the undeveloped state of agriculture in Belize. Another reason is the historic dependence on imported food, which the British colonial system encouraged.

A History of Pirates and Slaves

The thick bush that covers most of Belize hides the ruins of the Mayan civilization, which began its decline about A.D. 900. No Spanish conquistadors ever marched across these tropical lowlands. British pirates seeking haven behind the barrier reef that runs along Belize's coast were the country's first colonists. In the 1600s, Belize was a favorite hideout for pirates who made their living attacking Spanish galleons.

Many buccaneers gave up piracy for logging the territory's mahogany forests. Known as the Baymen, they cut logwood and mahogany for the English market, using the labor of black slaves. A backwater of the British empire, British Honduras was not officially recognized as part of the British Commonwealth until 1862. Many slaves escaped the brutal conditions of the logging camps and the plantations.

The first stirrings of an independence movement came when black soldiers returned to British Honduras after having fought for the United Kingdom in World War I. They objected to the discrimination they experienced by the British colonial bureaucracy when they came home. "British Honduras should be a black man's country," said the black soldiers. Their protest, known as the Ex-Servicemen's Riot of 1919, was crushed by British police. As was the case on the English-speaking Caribbean islands, the labor movement in Belize provided the first viable challenge to British colonial rule. During the 1920s and 1930s, workers began to organize in Belize, but labor unions were not legalized by the colonial governor until 1941.

In 1949, the labor movement joined with the black middle class to form the People's Committee—which was the basis of the nationalist movement in the colony. The committee evolved into the People's United Party (PUP), the party that obtained self-government for British Honduras in 1964 and independence in 1981. The PUP, which had no coherent ideology aside from its nationalism, used the General Workers' Union (GWU) as its political base. In the process, the GWU's own politics of trade unionism and socialism were diluted. As the PUP became stronger, the labor movement in Belize grew weaker.[2]

On Independence Day, September 21, 1981, dancing and celebration filled the streets of Belize City. Independence, however, has not meant autonomous economic development. Like the other Central American economies, the economy of Belize stagnated in the early 1980s. Disillusionment and disappointment set in as unemployment increased.

Small Country Politics

Commonly regarded as the father of the country, George Price led Belize from self-government to independence and dominated its politics for over 20 years. A spartan man, Price lived in a one-room home and drove around the country in a beat-up Land Rover during his term (1980–1984) as Prime Minister. Price continues to preside over the PUP political party, which is characterized by its center-left politics.

The other leading party, the United Democratic Party (UDP), adamantly opposed independence. A center-right organization, the UDP is the darling party of the bourgeoisie in Belize. Both political parties are largely in the hands of middle- and upper-class sectors of Belizean society. Workers and the poor rural sector are not the priority focus of either party, nor do they have strong unions or associations to represent their concerns.

The December 1984 elections brought the era of PUP and one-man rule to an abrupt end. The UDP won a landslide victory over Price's PUP, catapulting the little-known Manuel Esquivel into the Prime Minister's office. During the election, the UDP took issue with what it called communist influence in the PUP administration and accused Price of being a follower of Castro. Slinging back the mud, Price charged that the UDP was a puppet of Uncle Sam and said that a UDP government would be a pork barrel for right-wing businessmen.

Although the UDP does lean more to the right than the PUP, little distinguishes one party's program from the other. Like the Price administration, Manuel Esquivel favors increased foreign investment as a solution to the languishing economy. Esquivel, a former teacher who has a reputation for being incorruptible, calls the UDP the "party of free enterprise."[3]

Although it agrees with many U.S. foreign-policy concerns, the Esquivel administration says its ties with the United States should be mainly economic. It craves the benefits of U.S. investment, a share of the U.S. market, and the largesse of U.S. foreign aid; but Esquivel has expressed reluctance at becoming one of Washington's strongholds in the region. At the beginning of his administration, Esquivel announced that he will seek closer ties with the Caribbean nations, which he says are "culturally and democratically closer to Belize." Under the UDP Belize probably will move farther away from the position of nonalignment that George Price tried to maintain. Despite promises to the contrary, the UDP's conservative politics are moving the newly independent nation closer and closer to the United States, both economically and politically.

In the Neighborhood

For several decades, Guatemala has claimed that Belize is really part of its national territory. Schoolchildren in Guatemala still learn that Belize is an administrative unit of their country, and a sign on the Belize border states that *"Belice es Guatemala"* (Belize is Guatemala). Guatemala contends that the Spanish colony of Guatemala included Belize and thus Great Britain had no claim.

Actual plans for an invasion of Belize have been drawn up several times by Guatemalan generals, but since 1981 the larger country has exhibited a somewhat more flexible attitude toward Belize. Guatemala still refuses to negotiate with Belize and insists that it have only observer status in negotiations conducted with Great Britain over Guatemala's demands for portions of its territory and for access to the Caribbean through Belize.

Great Britain has maintained a unit of 2000 soldiers and four Harrier aircraft in Belize to protect it against the imperialist designs of Guatemala. Belizeans get jittery when Great Britain talks of removing its troops, as it plans to do. Any withdrawal of British soldiers would probably make many Belizeans more willing to situate a U.S. military base in their country.

Belize is the Central American nation geographically closest to Cuba. Despite

Cuba's many offers of expanded political and economic relations, Belize, even during the Price administration, steered clear of establishing a bilateral agreement with Cuba. Belize has also avoided similar gestures from its Central American neighbor Nicaragua for fear of angering Washington. Commenting on this situation, the Belizean newsweekly *Disweek* said: "The two countries in the region—Cuba and Nicaragua—that have been most friendly to us—Cuba was the first and at that time the only country in Latin America to support us against Guatemala—are not allowed to have relations with us."[4]

Economic Doldrums

With its mahogany forests long since cleared, Belize now relies on sugar as its main legal agro-export. Exports of sugar earn over half the country's foreign exchange. Other agro-exports include bananas, citrus, cocoa, tropical hardwood, shrimp, and beef. Although it does not show up in official statistics, the leading cash crop is really marijuana. Estimated annual value of Belize's marijuana exports to the United States is about $100 million—more than the total value of all its legal agro-exports. In 1984, Belize ranked as the fifth largest exporter of marijuana to the United States, after Mexico, Colombia, Jamaica, and Bolivia.

Washington pressured the Price government to mount a national marijuana eradication campaign, which the government later discontinued because of widespread complaints about the use of the herbicide paraquat to destroy the marijuana fields. Sugar growers, in particular, claimed that the paraquat spraying was also killing their sugar cane.

"Almost everyone you meet in this country is at least tangentially involved in the marijuana trade," one Belizean told the *Washington Post*. "Most never see the stuff. But they may rent a plane or an airstrip to someone. Or a truck. They may lease out some land or ignore someone's use of it. It's so widespread the U.S. is crazy to try to stop it. It would be cheaper for them just to buy it and burn it. Marijuana has turned a very poor Caribbean country into a very stable one."[5]

Sinking prices and a steadily shrinking world market for sugar have hit Belize hard. In 1984, the British sugar giant Tate & Lyle announced that it was pulling out of the production and milling phases of the sugar cane industry. Tate & Lyle entered the country's sugar business in 1964. Ten years later, it sold most of its land to 4000 small sugar growers. Tate & Lyle retains a small interest (less than 20 percent) in the country's two sugar mills and controls the industry's management and marketing. The new UDP government has refused to honor an agreement made by the Price government with Tate & Lyle to buy out most of the company's interests in two major sugar mills. Hundreds of sugar workers were put out of work when the mills shut down.

Belize has a small manufacturing sector that produces beer, cigarettes, batteries, flour, fertilizer, nails, and roofing. Most other products are imported. Belize's foreign-investment law allows exemption from income taxes and import duties for as long as 15 years. One of the larger companies that enjoys the benefits is Williamson Company, which employs several hundred women to assemble Dixie Jeans for sale in the United States. Similarly, toilet-paper manufacturing in Belize involves little more than cutting huge rolls made in the United States into small rolls. Such industries do not contribute substantially to the economy, however, because most of them are the so-called "wrap and pack" or "screwdriver" industries that use Belize at the final stage of a long production line.

Substantial foreign investment is found in all parts of the country's agro-export business. Aside from Tate & Lyle in sugar, Hershey operates a cocoa plantation and Fyffes (a British subsidiary of United Brands) buys most of Belize's bananas. In 1985, Coca-Cola Foods entered a joint venture with two Houston investors to export citrus products from a 50,000 acre plantation known as Belize Estates. The property was described in *The New York Times* as "the largest single piece of potentially arable land in the whole of Central America." Other non-U.S. TNCs found in Belize include Nestle, Shell, Barclays Bank, Royal Bank of Canada, and Bank of Nova Scotia.

A minister in the PUP government said that 80 percent of the private property in Belize is owned by foreigners. Almost one-third of the U.S. investors in Belize own hotels or other facilities for tourists. One prominent U.S. investor in Belize tourism is film producer Francis Ford Coppola. Many entrepreneurs, both local and foreign, regard the tourism business with great expectations. The absence of quality hotels, restaurants, and entertainment facilities has kept the tourism industry from booming.

During the 1970s, Belize enjoyed a steadily expanding economy, but in the early 1980s it stagnated and the country failed to meet its debt payments. Declining government revenues and a slipping balance of payments caused Belize to appeal for standby financing from the International Monetary Fund (IMF) in 1984. In return for emergency financing from the IMF, the PUP government had to raise taxes and the price of utilities—measures that severely cut into Price's popularity.

The Yankees Move In

With U.S. hegemony in question in other parts of Central America, Washington saw the independence of Belize in 1981 as an opportunity to gain a secure ally in the region. Shortly after the independence celebrations had subsided, the United States began training officers of the Belize Defense Force (BDF) in Panama, sending Mobile Training Teams into Belize to instruct the entire 700-member army, and settling into housing at the British military base.

The Peace Corps has arrived in Belize, and with 100 Peace Corps volunteers scheduled for Belize in 1985, there will be one volunteer for every 1500 Belizeans. The staff attached to the U.S. Embassy number 47, up from seven at the time of independence in 1981. A large contingent of AID officials now works out of the AID Mission office in Belize City and administers an array of programs, most of which promote the development of the local private sector and attract new foreign investment.

More than anything else, television programs from the United States are drawing Belize and the United States together. In the last several years, station owners in Belize have been tapping satellite broadcasts to bring Belizeans everything from the six o'clock news to "Dallas." The streets and plazas of the major towns, previously crowded during the evenings, are now largely deserted as Belizeans crowd in front of TV sets to get their daily dose of U.S.-style news and entertainment.

Washington initiated talks with the Belize government over the possible location of a U.S. base or the U.S. Army School of the Americas in the country. One result of the talks was the 1984 placement of a Voice of America transmitter in southern Belize at Punta Gorda. Residents of Punta Gorda expressed concern that the 217-acre site where the transmitter is installed would eventually be used for a U.S. military base. Suggestions that U.S. troops could replace British troops now stationed in Belize are viewed with alarm by most Belizeans. "We don't think U.S. troops would be helpful," said Foreign Minister Dean Barrow. "We know their deployment here would suck us into the conflicts of Central America."[6]

---

1 Milton Jamail, "Belize: Will Independence Mean New Dependence?" *NACLA Report on the Americas*, July/August 1984, pp.13–16. See the two-part series by Milton Jamail in *NACLA* for a thorough examination of current political issues in Belize. The first part, "Belize: Still Struggling for Independence," was published in the May/June 1984 issue of *NACLA*.

2 See David Broad's "Belize: On the Rim of the Cauldron," *Monthly Review*, February 1984, pp.38–47 for an excellent summary of Belizean history.

3 *Central America Report*, December 24, 1984.

4 Cited in Jamail, op.cit.

5 Ken Ringle, "Mildewed Intrigue at Land's End," *Washington Post*, January 27, 1985.

6 *Los Angeles Times*, January 10, 1985.

CHAPTER 9

Costa Rica

■

Trends

- Growing government repression accompanied by stepped-up mobilizing of the right wing.
- Continued economic stagnation because of banana-industry cutbacks, constriction of local market, and failure to attract substantial new investments.
- Steady deepening of U.S.-led militarization of country.
- Sharpening of anticommunist sentiment.
- Widening disenchantment with Costa Rican government as more sectors feel disenfranchised by plitical system.
- Disorganized and largely ineffective leftwing movements.
- Continued but reduced government ability to co-opt poor and dissidents with economic concessions and social services.
- Loss of the epithet "Switzerland of Central America."

■

COSTA RICA HAS long been the exception to the region's history of repressive governments and utter poverty. Its high literacy rate, comparatively large middle class, democratic traditions, and lack of a standing army have distinguished Costa Rica from Latin America as a whole. But its reputation as a stable democracy committed to social reforms and neutrality is becoming less deserved.

The high per capita debt ($1600) has forced the country to bow to the dictates of the International Monetary Fund (IMF). Social services have been severely cut and wages held far below the rising cost of living. Its national currency was devalued 80 percent from 1981–1983. Government studies show that, as a result of reduced government services, literacy rates are declining and malnutrition is rapidly becoming commonplace.

The economic crisis makes the Costa Rican government more susceptible to pressure from the United States. In return for puppeting U.S. foreign policy, the country has benefited from over $600 million in U.S. economic aid from 1982 through 1985. This inflow of capital has prevented severe economic decline although not succeeded in putting the nation on the road to recovery. Although many Costa Ricans boast that their country has maintained its neutrality, elements of the government have allowed the country's northern border to be used as a base for destabilization efforts against Nicaragua and have permitted the Pentagon to militarize the country's police forces.

Social tensions are heating up, and Costa Ricans are getting a small taste of the repression seen elsewhere in Central America. Citizens risk arrest and police brutality for participating in solidarity demonstrations with the opposition movements of El Salvador. The Civil Guard blocks the celebration of masses or vigils commemorating assassinated Salvadoran Archbishop Oscar Romero. Paramilitary organizations in Costa Rica act in consort with the anti-Sandinista *contras* and guard against "antidemocratic" activity.

Although still a world apart from the extreme violence and repression found elsewhere in Central America, Costa Rica can no longer be considered the idyllic "Switzerland of Central America" that it once was. Yet Costa Rica's democratic traditions and social-welfare practices continue to distinguish it from other nations on the isthmus. These factors along with the enormous injections of U.S. economic aid keep Costa Rica relatively stable and explain the low degree of organized popular opposition.

History: Small Farmers, Coffee Oligarchs, and Bananas

During his fourth and final voyage, Christopher Columbus set his eyes upon Costa Rica. Yet for the Spanish, this territory failed to measure up to its original designation as the "rich coast." Costa Rica had neither precious metals nor a large exploitable Indian population essential for plantation agriculture. The Spanish who settled in Costa Rica generally lived on subsistence farms rather than on expansive haciendas like those in Guatemala. The size of the farm was limited to what a family could work itself. Even the governor of this southernmost part of Spain's New World colony farmed his own land.

The rise of coffee production in the early 1800s dramatically changed this nation of independent farmers. The country's fertile central mesa offered perfect conditions for coffee cultivation, and Europeans bought as much of that addictive bean as Costa Rican farmers could grow. Land became increasingly concentrated.

By the turn of the century, 5 percent of the growers produced more than 50 percent of the coffee exports.[1] By the late 1800s, 7 out of 10 rural families had become landless in a country that had once boasted of being a nation of "small farmers and democrats."[2] A new oligarchy was born, headed by a new class of *beneficio* owners and exporters. Coffee, as one author noted, was the "aristocracy's salvation and the peasantry's ruin."[3]

In 1871, the construction of the country's first railroad opened up the Atlantic coast to the banana business. An ambitious adventurer named Minor Keith imported black workers from Louisiana and the West Indies to lay the tracks for his International Railways of Central America. Thousands of workers died from tropical diseases and accidents to build the railroad that pushed its way into the jungle near the Atlantic port city of Limón.[4] Keith's ventures set the stage for the banana plantations later established by United Fruit and the Standard Fruit and Steamship Company. For many decades, their corporate enclaves on the Atlantic coast maintained closer ties to major U.S. ports like New Orleans than they did to San José.

The labor movement in Costa Rica emerged from the struggles between the banana workers and the companies. The communist *Bloque de Obreros y Campesinos* represented the workers, who fondly called it "the red union." The bloque was later integrated into the country's communist political party, known as the Vanguardia Popular.

In 1942, a Costa Rican named José Figueres Ferrer leapt into the public consciousness where he has stayed ever since. In a radio speech, Figueres denounced President Calderón Garcia for, among other things, seeking the alliance of the Vanguardia to strengthen the base of Calderón's National Republican Party. Calderón reacted to the speech of the previously unknown Figueres by exiling him, which transformed him into "Don Pepe," a public martyr and a hero to many middle class Costa Ricans.[5]

Figueres, who shared the anticommunist fervor of the United States, mounted what was later called the Revolution of 1948 against the National Republicans who had stayed in power despite questionable election results in that year. As he created an antigovernment force, Figueres counted on significant support from the United States, which was concerned about the growing power of the Vanguardia. When it became clear that the government's own troops were unable to repel Figueres and his followers, the government requested assistance from the Vanguardia, which summoned up its membership and supporters to defend the capital of San José.

During the week before Figueres' final move, the U.S. ambassador to Costa Rica visited him seven different times. On April 17, 1948, the U.S. government delivered a message to the Costa Rican government that U.S. military forces were on standby in the Panama Canal Zone, ready to come to San José to end "communist control" of Costa Rica. Figueres, with this powerful backing, threatened to march into San José. The government called off the Vanguardia forces and arranged for negotiations.

The resulting pact recognized Figueres' troops as victorious. Vanguardia's role in the negotiations brought about the inclusion of one of the seven points in the pact, which stated that "the social rights and guarantees of all employees and workers be respected and extended."[6]

"Don Pepe" Figueres, who served three times as president of Costa Rica, is the patriarch of the National Liberation Party (PLN). Still one of the country's most important politicians and national leaders, Figueres has lived in the United States, speaks fluent English, and jokes that he is "first Catalan, second gringo, and third Costa Rican." Figueres, who was good friends with Richard Nixon and Allen Dulles, has admitted to having had connections with the CIA.[7] An unabashed admirer of the United States and its way of life and business, Figueres has been criticized for encouraging the foreign tastes and consumer habits of the Costa Rican middle class. Yet Figueres has often been critical of U.S. foreign policy, and is closer to the Sandinistas than current PLN leadership.

From 1948 to 1982, Figueres and the PLN promoted a modern capitalist democracy with a substantial public sector. But the democratic society with its commitment to social welfare is losing ground because of the economic downturn and the region's political crisis.

Politics: Last Chance for Democracy

Costa Rica has been able to maintain a representative democracy and social peace largely because it has promoted reforms that blunted the sharp edges of its capitalism. As the economic crisis has set in, the emphasis has shifted from education and health programs to the well-being of the bourgeoisie. The truce between the classes has been called off, and the top-down reformism that once was a trait of Costa Rica's democracy is no longer considered economically viable.

Two main political organizations dominate political life in Costa Rica. The National Liberation Party, which has held power since 1982 under President Luis Alberto Monge, calls itself a social-democratic party and is a member of the Socialist International. During Monge's presidency, the party's right wing has held sway. Its 1986 presidential candidate, Oscar Arias, called for economic reforms but is generally regarded as belonging to the conservative and hawkish wing of the party. To secure the party's firm support, Arias, a political scientist, promised the party's liberal wing a small role in his administration. Elected in February 1986 as the new president, Arias will continue the economic and political policies of the previous administration.

The other main political grouping, the more conservative and stridently anticommunist Social Christian Unity Party (PUSC), is headed by Rafael Calderón Fournier, the son of ex-president Rafael Calderón Guardia. Calderón's Republican Calderonist Party has led this unity coalition of four conservative parties since its establishment in 1977. The avidly anticommunist PUSC represents many large landowners and business owners and gave strong support to the IMF program.

PLN also agrees with the austerity measures but thinks implementation should go slowly to avoid social upheaval. Aside from this and the degree of anticommunism, the two main parties offer little real choice to Costa Ricans.

In 1984, Costa Rica became the first Latin American country to have a political party that chiefly addresses environmental issues. Modeled after the green parties of Europe, the Costa Rican Ecological Party (PEC) criticizes unregulated pesticide use and the rapid deforestation of the country due to cattle grazing and aggressive exploitation of lumber.

Costa Rican leftists have been struggling to form a coalition behind which popular opposition could coalesce. A split in the Vanguard Party in 1984 severely weakened one shaky coalition called the Popular Unity Party. Members of the moderate wing of the Vanguard Party angered the more dogmatic leftists by saying that the main struggle is no longer for socialism in Costa Rica, but to keep democracy alive in the face of mounting anticommunism and conservatism. Except for banana workers, leftists have had a hard time finding a popular base in Costa Rica because of the country's successful welfare state policies.

Rise of the Right

Communism has become a major issue in Costa Rican politics. Many conservative politicians and business establishments have tried to blame the country's economic and social turmoil either on Nicaragua or on a domestic communist plot. In 1984, PUSC, together with a group of coffee growers and industrial magnates, forced President Monge to rid his administration of several PLN bureaucrats the PUSC group called "communist subversives." Monge replaced the progressive minister of public security with a leader of the right-wing Movement for a Free Costa Rica, closely associated with the paramilitary Blue Berets. Oscar Arias, who believes that Nicaragua is "a permanent danger to the region," has come under criticism from the PUSC and the far-right wing of the PLN for not being sufficiently anticommunist. The PUSC also accused the PLN of being soft on communism in 1983 when Monge pledged that Costa Rica would maintain "a permanent and active position of neutrality." Party leader Calderón charged that "in the face of Marxist-Leninist aggression, no Costa Rican should be neutral."[8]

Business has labeled all attempts by workers to protect their interests in the face of the economic crisis as "communist-inspired destabilization." The PLN has given support to this paranoia by saying that the outbreak of strikes in recent years has been "inspired by extremist groups foreign to our country." Much of the press has joined in this campaign. An editorial in the daily newspaper *La Nación* typifies the general tone of media coverage of union efforts:

The Workers' Unitarian Confederation (CUT), controlled by the communists, has initiated a series of strikes at key points of the public administration, whose apparent objective, for the masses that participate in good faith, is the immediate payment of the wage increase; but for the leaders of the movement the objectives go beyond simple economic demands, and its main purpose is political. . . . The promoters of strikes in the prisons, hospitals and other key points of the Costa Rican institutional system cannot hide their destabilizing aims.[9]

All the country's major dailies and most of the television and radio stations belong to the Costa Rica's right-wing upper class. Two radio stations, Radio Reloj and Radio Impacto (reputedly CIA-funded), regularly feature harsh ideological attacks against Costa Rican popular organizations, accusing them of working in conjunction with the "international communist conspiracy" now head-quartered, they say, in Managua and Cuba.[10]

The Costa Rican government, prodded by groups like the Costa Rican Association of Managers and Businessmen, created a national paramilitary organization called the Organization of National Emergencies (OPEN) in 1982. OPEN was given official status by a government decree that defined it as a "voluntary civilian force supporting the police forces of the country . . . composed of all those citizens of proven democratic creed, who are ready to submit themselves to the discipline and the political and civilian training that is required to support this force."

A number of other paramilitary groups associated with the Movement for a Free Costa Rica, like the Guanacaste Freedom Movement and the Blue Berets (or Tridents), also fervently support the *contras* and have attacked worker and peasant organizations in Costa Rica. Willy Solis, the founder of the Blue Berets, said his organization counters "the Communist subversives trained by Cuba and Libya that are hiding out in the jungles of Costa Rica waiting for the right time to overthrow the government."[11]

In response to President Monge's neutrality proclamation, anticommunist groups placed a full-page ad in *La Nación* that was entitled "Motherland Is in Danger! The Hypocrisy of the Pacifists." Another advertisement paid for by the Movement for a Free Costa Rica said: "On one side will remain the *Ticos* [Costa Ricans] who believe we should not lower our heads before a dictatorship [Nicaragua], and on the other the cowards. On one side there is true Costa Rican blood. On the other, the garbage that corrupts and shames our motherland."[12]

Two People, One Ideal

Costa Rica began to lose its traditionally liberal approach to foreign policy toward the end of the fumbling and inefficient Rodrigo Carazo administration (1978–1982). Pressured by Washington, which began to take more of an interest in the region after the successful revolution in Nicaragua in 1979, Costa Rica joined in the anti-Sandinista hysteria. Also in line with U.S. foreign policy, it joined coalitions with the governments of El Salvador, Guatemala, and Honduras, lending legitimacy to those governments and condemning the leftist guerrilla movements in the region. As its reward for toeing the U.S. line, economic aid to Costa Rica increased from $16 million in 1980 to well over $200 million in 1985.

Costa Ricans—the most pro-American of all Latin Americans—copy U.S. fads, follow U.S. sports and music, and many almost think of themselves as North Americans. Despite this and the fact that most of the population has a conservative view of regional politics, resentment is brewing over the interference of Washington in their country's foreign and domestic policies. In a 1984 poll that queried high school students about which country "interferes too much in Costa Rica's internal affairs," over 40 percent named the United States, with Nicaragua a distant second.

For President Reagan's visit in 1982, Costa Rica plastered a poster throughout the country that showed Presidents Monge and Reagan standing side by side. Underneath the photo was the slogan *"Dos Pueblos y Un Ideal"* (Two Nations and One Ideal). In contrast, in an incident ignored by most of the media, a Costa Rican legislator countered Reagan's speech with a statement that reflects the growing sentiment in Costa Rica:

> In Central America, the dilemma is not between democracy and totalitarianism. Here the dilemma is rather between oppression and submission on one hand and social justice and the people's right to self-determination on the other. . . . We believe that dignity and sovereignty are not negotiable and cannot be diminished in exchange for economic assistance.

A Bankrupt Democracy

Costa Ricans say that Mister *Fondo* runs their country. They refer to the International Monetary Fund (*Fondo Monetario Internacional*), which has been loaning money to shore up the debt-ridden economy. In exchange, the government must enforce a severe austerity program designed to reduce the government deficit, encourage exports, and foster foreign investment.

For the last three decades, Costa Rica had been living on borrowed money. The funds for its public services, infrastructure for agriculture and industry, and government bureaucracy came from foreign loans. By 1981, Costa Rica found that it was technically bankrupt. Burdened by one of the highest per capita debts in the world, the country shocked international creditors when the government announced that even after selling off all its gold reserves it could pay neither the principal nor the interest on its assorted foreign debts. Each year Costa Rica is required to pay about $550 million in interest on its debt, yet its annual export earnings are barely $1 billion.

Until 1980, Costa Ricans enjoyed the highest growth rate in the region. But then the development bubble burst. The immediate cause of the crisis was a drop in coffee prices, while other factors included higher oil prices, inflation, and rising interest rates. Its agro-export system was stagnating, and its inefficient industrial sector weighted the economy down with costly imports and under-capacity production. Thirty years of relative economic prosperity had ended, and Costa Ricans saw their country slipping into the same desperate economic circumstances that plagued its neighbors.

The IMF prescribed harsh medicine. The rural and urban poor had to swallow most of it in the form of wage controls, higher taxes, cuts in public employment, an end to price subsidies for basic foods, reduced social-service programs like health care, and higher utility rates. The Monge administration appealed to Costa Ricans to "tighten their belts" in order to save their democracy. In 1982, telephone rates jumped 55 percent, water and sewage rates increased 53 percent, and electricity rates went up by 87 percent.[13] After four years of austerity, many Costa Ricans are realizing that while they are forced to sacrifice, the upper class is benefiting from paying lower wages and receiving government incentives for export production.

In keeping with IMF goals, the legislature in 1984 passed a bill that accelerates depreciation allowances, lowers tariffs, gives business preferential access to credit, reduces interest rates, and guarantees insurance against political unrest. The bill was introduced by the Costa Rican Coalition of Initiatives for Development (CINDE), an organization funded by AID.

The United States has provided generous grants and soft loans to enable the country to balance its budget and pay off its foreign debts. On two occasions, however, AID held up promised funds until Costa Rica fully implemented portions of the IMF's austerity plan. In an interview with a Costa Rican newspaper, the outspoken U.S. Ambassador Curtin Winsor denied the accusation that the United States had used pressure tactics. "There is no political condition [to the aid]," he said. "We believe the modifications [to the monetary law] are necessary and that they will benefit the productive sectors. . . . I am sure that the Legislative Assembly will give its approval to the reforms so that the country will have access to the aid we want to give."[14]

Resistance Builds

There are few surprises over who has been made to pay for the economic crisis that has rocked Costa Rica since 1978. Between 1980 and 1982, the percentage of families below the poverty line increased from 40 to 70 percent, according to a study by the National University's Institute of Economic Investigations.[15]

A national protest against a sudden hike in electricity rates in 1983 was evidence that the Costa Rican poor were not going to quietly suffer the austerity measures imposed by the IMF. For two days, a protest by thousands of angry citizens blocked 35 major roads and forced the government to reduce the increase. Teachers, doctors, and government workers have also organized strikes and protests. While most large firms supported the new economic measures, the National Union of Small and Middle Producers charged that the program was driving many of them out of business. In the countryside, hundreds of land takeovers also signaled rising militancy among the traditionally passive peasantry.

Although popular resistance did expand in the early 1980s, the government prevented the riots and general strikes that have resulted from IMF austerity programs in other countries. Increasingly, it has relied on force and intimidation when dealing with strikers. While in keeping with the pattern of repression of popular movements in other Central American nations, these methods shatter Costa Rica's tradition of mediation and compromise in conflictive social situations. Despite this, the Costa Rican population has not moved markedly toward the left. As President Monge boasted, "Our medicine is bitter, but we have prevented the contagion."[16]

Because the PLN controls two of the three labor confederations, labor has not presented great opposition to the government's economic program. A history of antilabor judicial rulings has also kept the trade-union movement weak in most key sectors. The Democratic Workers Front (FDT) and the Confederation of Democratic Costa Rican Workers (CCTD) steer away from confrontation with business and government and carefully avoid association with the more militant leftist unions that are members of the Workers Unity Federation (CUT). The PLN has co-opted many trade unionists by integrating them into the party.

There appears to be no end to the country's economic problems and to government purse tightening. The country's politicians, its upper class, the IMF, the World Bank, and AID have all counted on the relatively complacent and unpoliticized Costa Rican populace to accept the austerity program without the kind of mass political resistance seen in other third-world countries. But as social services fall apart, Costa Rican workers and peasants in all likelihood will feel that they have been ignored by the political system and will form mass organizations to protect their interests.

Land Takeovers and Food Imports

Costa Rica is a lush country, capable of growing most crops. But it has to import more food than any other Central American nation. Although there have been some significant improvements in local grain production (notably rice), more than a quarter of the food Costa Ricans consume comes from the United States. The main reason for this imbalance is that most of the arable land is devoted to agro-export crops, mainly coffee, bananas, sugar, and cattle.

During the 1982 election campaign, Alberto Monge rallied rural Costa Ricans behind the PLN with the slogan, *"Volvamos a la Tierra"* (Let's Return to the Land). Once in power, Monge failed to follow through with the promise and his policies worsened the rural crisis. Rather than increasing credit and technical assistance to small farmers, Monge drastically cut the Ministry of Agriculture budget. The lack of funds and opposition by large landowners have prevented the implementation of a meaningful land distribution program. The austerity measures meant cuts in assistance to small farmers who grew much of the country's basic crops. The agricultural programs that the Costa Rican government has implemented in recent years have been advocated by the IMF and AID to promote more cash-crop production.

When Monge's government did return to the land, it was often with tear gas and bullets to evict groups of landless *campesinos* called *precaristas*. In Costa Rica, estimations of the rural landless population run as high as 60 to 75 percent.[17] Only 300 landowners control more than 25 percent of the country's agricultural land, while over 50,000 small farmers crowd on to less than 20 percent of the arable land.[18]

With less available land, more unemployment, and vanishing social services, more and more groups have taken over idle land. *Campesinos* in Limón occupied the offices of the government's National Agrarian Institute (IDA) in 1984 to demand that the government distribute the country's idle land and to break up the underutilized *latifundios*.

The Costa Rican government has stamped down hard on the land takeovers, using the Rural Guard to forcibly evict the *campesinos*. Hundreds of *campesinos* have been arrested, and several have been killed during the evictions.

Banana Business Slipping

From their long experience with TNCs, Costa Rica's banana workers have learned that standing behind the union and striking are the only ways to win concessions from the companies. Banana unions have not been able to count on support from the Costa Rican government, which has traditionally tried to break the leftist unions. All three banana TNCs do business in Costa Rica, but in the last couple of decades, they have been turning over most production to associate producers as a way of avoiding confrontations with workers and reducing their risks. United Brands also switched some of its production over to African palm, which employs fewer laborers.

Recent banana strikes have resulted in several deaths and numerous arrests of striking workers by the Rural Guard. In 1983, Del Monte workers went out on strike for two months to force the company to increase their 70-cents-an-hour wage. But it was the 1984 strike by 2500 United Brands workers on the company's Pacific coast plantations near Golfito that will be remembered for many years to come. As in the Del Monte strike, the government declared the strike illegal and tried to break it with its Rural Guard. United Brands even requested that the Monge government declare the Workers Unity Confederation (CUT) illegal. Monge labeled the banana strikes "negative efforts to harm Costa Rica" and said they were the result of "high level decisions of the Third [communist] International."[19]

Citing the losses suffered during the strike and poor market conditions, United Brands announced in late 1984 that it was shutting down its Pacific coast plantations. The announcement shocked the Monge government, which had supported the company during the strike and was counting on steady banana production to meet the export production target set by the IMF. The withdrawal of United Brands also broke a contract the company had signed in 1938 which stipulated that it would produce bananas on its 7500-acre leased property for 50 years. Minister to the Presidency Danilo Jimenez said the "social and economic consequences of this are enormous."[20]

Fearing riots and a wave of land takeovers, the government negotiated an agreement with United Brands whereby it would lease the land from the company for the next four years. Because the company had broken the contract, the government could have expropriated the land. However, under the provisions of the Caribbean Basin Initiative, expropriation of U.S. property would have resulted in the loss of U.S. aid. This placed the government in the ironic position of having to lease back its own land from a TNC that had just broken its contract. Now, as manager of a banana plantation, the government sells fruit to United Brands. The company also buys fruit from associate growers on the Atlantic coast.

Development in a Foreign Context

In the last 20 years, Costa Rica has become a semi-industrialized country—yet industry in Costa Rica is commonly owned by U.S. corporations. Industrialization has, according to former president of Costa Rica Balmorcich Francisco Orlich, "put the economic sovereignty [of Costa Rica] into a foreign context, in which decisions are made in accordance with the expansion of foreign enterprise and not the needs of Costa Rica, nor of the Central American regional economic whole."[21]

Foreign industry is finding Costa Rica increasingly attractive because of the devaluation of the *colon*. "Costa Rican labor costs are now among the lowest in Latin America," stated *Latin American Regional Report* in 1982. "Manufacturers who have been able to build markets in North America or Europe are placed to do extremely well. Government statistics show Costa Ricans working in the clothing industry for around 50 percent of their counterparts in Taiwan."[22] The U.S. Embassy says Costa Rica "has one of the best investment climates in the Caribbean Basin."[23]

The success of free trade zones in Hong Kong and neighboring Panama encouraged Costa Rica to open two free trade zones of its own in 1982. The corporations locating in these zones are offered duty free import of raw materials, components, machinery, and packaging material, plus 100 percent exemption from income taxes for the first five years and 50 percent for the following ten years.

Protecting local industry and promoting production of goods for the internal market are not among the priorities that the United States has for Costa Rica. A report by the Overseas Private Investment Corporation (OPIC) stated: "It is our belief that through application [of the Export Promotion Law], Costa Rica can move from the development stage which emphasizes a protected domestic market into a stage in which the national economy can prove its efficiency and the quality of its products in international competition."[24]

TNCs in Costa Rica

Over 300 U.S. firms and more than a dozen non-U.S. TNCs do business in Costa Rica. Over one-third of these TNCs are in the manufacturing sector. The top five U.S. pharmaceutical corporations have operations in Costa Rica. Many TNCs take advantage of the country's cheap labor to assemble products as diverse as nuclear gauges, golf carts, yachts, and bird cages. Movie Star Inc. produces underpants for export, Lovable manufactures a full line of women's underwear, and Consolidated Foods assembles bras. Costa Rica also has several clothing manufacturers that subcontract assembly work with large U.S. clothing companies. Over twenty TNCs either manufacture or distribute chemicals (mostly pesticides and fertilizers). Seven of the top twenty TNC food processors produce for the nation's internal market. Colgate-Palmolive markets toothpaste there and also manufactures candy, chocolates, and crackers through its subsidiary Pozuelo.

An impressive array of business equipment corporations, including IBM, Honeywell, Burroughs, ITT, and Xerox, market their products within the country. Five of the top eight accounting firms have offices, primarily to tend to the books of the other TNCs; and the top two U.S. banks—Citicorp and Bank-America—serve the TNCs active in the country. Also in the service sector are McDonalds, Kentucky Fried Chicken, and Pizza Hut.

All three banana companies have agribusiness operations. IU International has interests in sugar production, while Hershey and IC Industries are involved in the cocoa industry. Eight U.S. companies, including American Flower and Foliage Inc., dominate the ornamental flowers and plants business.

A Pawn in the Game

Democracy and neutrality are fading fast in Costa Rica. Its precarious economic situation has made the country vulnerable to foreign-policy pressure from the United States. Costa Rica has let itself be used as a pawn in the U.S.-directed destabilization of Nicaragua. Costa Ricans are bombarded with information supplied by U.S. intelligence agencies that Nicaragua is their number one enemy. The country has chosen to ignore its own worsening domestic conditions in favor of the frenzy of anticommunism. In the name of democracy, Costa Rica permits its territory to be used for terrorism. In the name of neutrality, it says it needs a U.S.-trained police force to protect its borders. Costa Rica serves the purposes of the Reagan administration well. But Costa Ricans may soon find that their country is little more than an expendable piece in a dishonorable game.

1 John P. Bell, *Crisis in Costa Rica* (Austin: University of Texas, 1971), p.6.
2 Mitchell A. Seligson, *Peasants of Costa Rica and the Development of Agrarian Capitalism* (Madison: University of Wisconsin, 1980), p.23.
3 Ibid., p.13.
4 Thomas McCann, *United Fruit: Tragedy of an American Company* (New York: Crown, 1976).
5 Bell, op.cit., p.37.
6 Ibid., p.151.
7 Alan Riding, "For Rudderless Costa Rica, a Quixotic Rescue Effort," *New York Times*, January 12, 1981.
8 *Central America Report*, March 1, 1985.
9 American Friends Service Committee (AFSC), "Report on Costa Rica: Summer 1984" (Philadelphia), 1984.
10 Ibid.
11 From a speech made on March 21, 1984, to a John Birch Society gathering. Reported by *People's World*, March 24, 1984.

12 AFSC, op. cit.
13 US Embassy, Costa Rica, "Foreign Economic Trends," 1983.
14 *La Nacion*, June 22, 1984. Cited in AFSC, op.cit.
15 Marc Edelman and Jayne Hutchcroft, "Costa Rica: Resisting Austerity," *NACLA Report on the Americas*, January/February 1984, p.38.
16 Ibid., p.40.
17 *Latin America Commodities Report*, October 14, 1983.
18 *AID Congressional Presentation FY 1980* and *Mesoamerica*, December 1982.
19 Joanne Omang, "Administration Worries as Banana Operation Closes in Costa Rica," *Washington Post*, January 16, 1985.
20 Edelman and Hutchcroft, op.cit., pp.37-40.
21 J. Edward Taylor, "Peripheral Capitalism and Rural-Urban Migration: A Study of Population Movements in Costa Rica," *Latin American Perspectives*, Spring/Summer 1980.
22 *LARR*, September 18, 1981.
23 US Embassy, op.cit.
24 Overseas Private Investment Corporation (OPIC), "Report on Costa Rica," 1985.

CHAPTER 10

El Salvador

∎

Trends

- Power in El Salvador to remain in the hands of Washington, private sector (oligarchy), and military despite the political victories of the Christian Democrats.
- Continued erosion of 1980 reforms and consolidation of oligarchy will prevent the initiation of new reforms needed to alleviate basic economic causes of war.
- Increased professionalization and effectiveness of U.S.-trained Salvadoran military.
- Greater reliance on air war, and growing numbers of displaced.
- Increased FMLN activity—both in the organizing of popular opposition and in antimilitary terrorism—in San Salvador.
- Inability of Christian Democrat-controlled government to improve situation of *campesinos* and workers will result in new popular challenges to their leadership.
- Increased trade-union organizing and possible resurfacing of mass organizations under new names.
- Expanding differences between armed forces and Duarte administration.
- Continuing commitment of FMLN to prolonged war strategy and its use of small units to attack the military and economic infrastructure.

∎

ORDERED BY CORTEZ to extend the conquest of Mexico to the isthmus, Pedro de Alvarado in 1524 marched into what is now El Salvador. After one of his first battles with the Indians there, Alvarado wrote that the "destruction we made amongst them was so great that in a short time none were left alive."[1] During the next 20 years, the Spanish completed their conquest, always encountering strong Indian resistance. Historians estimate that after 50 years of conquest, the Indian population of El Salvador declined from as many as 500,000 to about 75,000.

Indigo and cocoa were the first major agro-exports of El Salvador, but by the late 1800s coffee accounted for virtually all the country's exports. Great Britain was the major trade partner and the main source of foreign capital in the 1800s. In 1850, a Salvadoran newspaper, *El Progreso*, expressed what was a commonly felt hatred of the British consul: "There is a living curse which corrodes the vitals of Central America—and this is the . . . agent to England."[2]

By the turn of the century, U.S. capital and entrepreneurs began moving into El Salvador, and the United States soon overtook Great Britain as the principal foreign influence in the country. U.S. banana and railroad entrepreneur Minor Keith, in a self-serving financial deal, negotiated long-term loans in 1923 between American banking interests and the Salvadoran government amounting to $16.5 million. The terms provided that in case of default the U.S. bankers and the State Department would manage the country's international trade through a customs receivership.[3] The loans paid off El Salvador's debts to Keith and the British railway companies and funded several public works projects in San Salvador.

A History of Matanza

In 1931, a U.S. Army officer who was visiting the country was struck by the sharp contrasts he saw in San Salvador. He said: "There appears to be nothing between these high-priced cars and the oxcart with its barefoot attendant. There is practically no middle class. . . . Thirty or forty families own nearly everything in the country. They live in almost regal style. The rest of the population has practically nothing."[4]

Coffee provided the foundation of both the country's economy and the national oligarchy, often called the "Fourteen Families" (*Catorce Grande*). In 1931, historian David Browning wrote that, "Coffee was king. . . . It produced 95.5% of export earnings, paid the country's taxes, proportioned funds for central and local governments, financed the construction of roads, ports, and railroads, created permanent or seasonal employment for one part of the population and made the fortunes of a few."[5]

Unlike in Guatemala, where you can find beautiful handwoven textiles in many markets, it is difficult to find any evidence of the Indian culture and handicrafts in El Salvador. This and other sociological facts about the country can be traced back to 1932, the year Salvadorans remember as the time of the *matanza* (massacre).

By the 1930s, *fincas* had overtaken the western and central highlands of El Salvador. In the process, the Nahuatl-speaking Pipil Indians lost their communal lands and were forced to work on the plantations. Coffee prices began to drop because of the Great Depression. The growers halved the wages of their Indian coffee pickers and reduced production, so that many thousands of Indian families were left without work. In 1932, the Pipil Indians, armed only with their machetes, challenged the growers in the Izalco region.

The Indian uprising was planned to occur simultaneously with a workers' revolt in the cities organized by the Communist Party and its leader Augustín Farabundo Martí, a tireless organizer and committed revolutionary. The military government had refused to seat several popularly elected members of the Communist Party in the January 1932 elections. Martí and his fellow organizers were rounded up before the rebellion in the countryside even started. The army executed Martí and brutally crushed the Indian resistance.

Led by General Maximiliano Hernández Martínez, the army and bands of vigilantes massacred as many as 30,000 Salvadorans.[6] Tying their thumbs behind their backs (a common practice even today by the Salvadoran military), soldiers lined up row after row of Indian peasants behind the village churches and shot them. "The extermination was so great," wrote historian Thomas P. Anderson, "that they could not be buried fast enough, and a great stench of rotting flesh permeated the air of western El Salvador."[7]

During the rebellion, the United States stationed two destroyers and a naval cruiser with a complement of Marines off the coast of El Salvador. The U.S. Marine Air Group, stationed in Nicaragua, was also alerted.

After the *matanza*, the surviving Indian population discarded their traditional Indian dress and deliberately masked their culture to avoid a future genocidal bloodletting. Anderson, in his book *La Matanza*, wrote, "Indeed, the whole [subsequent] political labyrinth of El Salvador can be explained only in reference to the traumatic experience of the uprising and the *matanza*."[8]

Today, El Salvador's guerrilla army, the FMLN, bears the name of Farabundo Martí and its battalion in the area of Izalco is named after the Indian cacique, Jose Feliciano Ama, who led the peasant rebellion. General Martínez, who remained the country's dictator until 1944, has also been remembered. In the late 1970s, the Maximiliano Hernandez Martínez Brigade surfaced as one of the country's death squads.

Tensions Build

Between 1961 and 1975 the number of landless peasants increased from 11 to 40 percent of the rural population.[9] And while the manufacturing sector expanded 24 percent in the 1960s, manufacturing jobs only increased 6 percent. The conditions of landlessness, unemployment, poverty and the increased population density persuaded many *campesinos* to emigrate to neighboring Honduras—one of the least densely populated countries on the isthmus. By 1965, as many as 350,000 Salvadorans were living in Honduras and made up at least 30 percent of that country's banana workers.[10]

The Honduran agrarian and military elites blamed the Salvadorans for Honduran problems and resented the uneven industrial development of the two countries. The promises of balanced regional development of the early CACM proposals had fallen flat, and most industrial activity had located in El Salvador and Guatemala. By 1968, El Salvador accounted for a quarter of the regional manufacturing while Honduras contributed less than 10 percent.[11] Honduras' trade deficit with El Salvador grew steadily, and Honduran merchants responded with a campaign to boycott Salvadoran goods. Finally, in 1969, Honduras started deporting the illegal Salvadorans.

On July 14, 1969, war broke out between the two countries when the Salvadoran air force bombed Tegucigalpa, followed the next day by an invasion of the Salvadoran Army and National Guard. Called the "soccer war," the conflict lasted less than a week, but it took 3000 lives. It served both governments in uniting the populace around nationalistic slogans while undermining worker and peasant movements.

Before the war, emigration of Salvadorans to Honduras was an escape valve for the building rural tension in El Salvador. With that release gone and more landless peasants back in the country, the friction increased between the oligarchy and the workers and peasants.

Students, workers, women, *campesinos*, and church members created mass organizations to defend their rights and to stand up to the dictatorship. Although the hierarchy of the Catholic Church was an ally of the military and oligarchy, the priests and nuns working on the parish level helped create mass organizations. In reaction to the ecclesiastical activism, a death squad called the White Warriors Union in 1977 circulated flyers with the slogan "Be a Patriot, Kill a Priest!"[12]

The mass movements strengthened steadily, and by the mid-1970s, in the tradition of *la matanza*, the government was responding regularly with violence. In 1975, students in Santa Ana occupied the local campus to protest the government's expenditure of $1.5 million to stage the Miss Universe pageant in El Salvador. When students in San Salvador held a march in solidarity with the Santa Ana students, the National Guard opened fire. Scores of students were wounded and killed, and 24 disappeared. Government and right-wing violence has since become an everyday occurrence in El Salvador.

The new popular organizations that emerged during the 1970s replaced the electoral parties as the focus of political action. These mass organizations, which were coalitions of peasant, trade-union, professional, student, and slum-dweller groups, pressed for social justice. Their tactics included street demonstrations as well as occupations of public buildings, factories, and large estates.

Political Military Forces

The country's leftist guerrilla organizations began forming soon after the war with Honduras in 1969. They did not become a major force in El Salvador until the late 1970s when increased government repression under President Romero began driving activists from the mass organizations into hiding. In March 1980, four separate and, until then, frequently antagonistic guerrilla organizations formed the Unified Revolutionary Directorate (DRU) to coordinate their operations. In October 1980, DRU became known as the Farabundo Martí Liberation Front (FMLN). Since 1980, their forces doubled to an estimated 8,000 regular troops. In 1985, the FMLN had five components, which identify themselves variously as Marxist, Marxist-Leninist and Marxist influenced.

Several important changes have marked FMLN's development from 1980 to 1985. None of the guerrilla armies considers itself to be the vanguard of the revolution. All have expressed increasing willingness to negotiate an end to the war. The FMLN as a whole has demonstrated a new spirit of compromise evidenced in its willingness to be part of a government of "broad participation." The FMLN's combatants are better armed (largely with captured U.S. weapons) and function as a standing army with the ability to coordinate military actions throughout most of the country. Another change is the growing emphasis on both urban attacks and urban education.

The FMLN recognizes that the balance of forces in El Salvador and the country's geopolitical location make a complete military victory almost inconceivable. It also recognizes the need to share power with other social forces beyond the progressive democrats in the FDR. The FMLN considers that such an alliance could provide an acceptable framework within which the people could express their political will, satisfy their basic needs, and enjoy the rights to which they are entitled.[13] By early 1985, the FMLN controlled about 20 percent of El Salvador.

A noteworthy change in the FMLN is the increased participation of *campesino* elements in the organization's leadership. Commander Martinez of the People's Revolutionary Army in 1984 said: "Right below the top levels, our *comandantes* are now from rural areas. They fight by day and learn to read by night. Of our Central Committee, about 60 percent have urban roots and 40 percent are *campesinos*."[14]

Intensified bombardment of rebel-held zones has led the FMLN to pursue new tactics. In July 1985, Joaquín Villalobos, the FMLN's chief commander, said the guerrillas were waging a prolonged "war of attrition." Prevented by Washington from seizing political power through military victory, the FMLN has opted to fight a prolonged war aimed to sap the strength of the government, the army, and the economy while wearing down Washington's commitment to the war.[15]

In line with this strategy, the FMLN has escalated its war of economic sabotage. FMLN organizers are also active in the cities, backing strikes and demonstrations against government economic policies. Another element in their new strategy is the increase of small-unit assaults in San Salvador. Four U.S. Marines were machine-gunned down at a San Salvador restaurant in June 1985 as part of the new guerrilla presence in the capital. Soberly assessing the war, Commandante Villalobos said: "The war is cumulative. The question is who is able to destabilize and bleed the other side more."[16]

Working alongside the FMLN is the FDR. The FDR was formed in April 1980, shortly after the assassination of Archbishop Romero. The FDR represents the disenfranchised left-center political parties, trade unions, and the four major mass civic organizations. These organizations—BRR, LP-28, FAPU and UDN—were forced to stop public organizing because of government repression.

Guerrilla Armies

Popular Liberation Forces (FPL): Largest and oldest of the guerrilla groups, the FPL has close ties with the largest mass organization in the country, the People's Revolutionary Block. Formed in 1970 largely through the efforts of Salvador Cayento Carpio, who had been the secretary general of the Salvadoran Communist Party (PCS). Carpio became particularly dissatisfied with the party when it endorsed the government during the "soccer war." Greatly influenced by the Vietnamese experience, the FPL follows the line of "prolonged people's war" and has had success in the concept of popular organization linked to military struggle.

This guerrilla group performs public services such as building roads and digging wells in the Salvadoran zones they control, and it operates Radio Farabundo Martí. Since 1984, the FPL has been sending many of its members into San Salvador for the purpose of rebuilding mass organizations. The areas in which the FPL has most influence are Chalatenango, San Vicente, Usulatan, and Cabanas. Since the murder and suicide of Dr. Melida Anaya Montes (Comandante Ana María) and Carpio in 1983, the main spokesperson has been Leonel Gonzalez.

People's Revolutionary Army (ERP): ERP formed in 1971 and drew its members from disaffected members of the middle class and the Christian Democratic youth. Having strong ties with the People's League of February 28 (LP-28) mass organization, the ERP adopted more of a military approach than the FPL and was therefore more isolated from the people. Militarily, the ERP is the most impressive of the guerrilla groups. The ERP operates Radio Venceremos and wields most of its influence in Morazan, and its main spokespeople are Ana Guadalupe Martínez and Joaquin Villalobos.

Armed Forces of National Resistance (FARN): The FARN's major links are with the second largest mass organization, the People's Action Front (FAPU).

The FARN split from the ERP in 1975 over a disagreement between an emphasis on military action or on building a base of support. Poet Roque Dalton, who favored the building of a base, was murdered during the controversy. The ERP declared that Dalton was a CIA agent trying to undermine the movement and shot him. Dalton's followers withdrew and founded the FARN. Although it concentrates on mass work, the FARN is most well-known for kidnapping the executives and members of the "Fourteen Families." Its main spokespeople are Ferman Cienfuegos and Saul Villalta.

Central American Revolutionary Workers Party (PRTC): Founded in 1976, the PRTC emphasizes a regional focus to revolutionary work. While it has yet to develop into a major force, it is influential in small popular organizations. The PRTC's main spokesperson is Roberto Roca.

Armed Forces of Liberation (FAL): The military arm of the Salvadoran Communist Party, FAL didn't fully endorse the armed struggle until May 1980. It previously worked in electoral alliance with the Christian Democrats and opposed both the guerrilla struggle and the development of popular organizations like the Bloque and FAPU. Its main spokesperson is Jorge Shafik Handal.

Sources: Philip L. Russell, *El Salvador in Crisis*, 1984; *NACLA Report on the Americas*, "El Salvador—Beyond the Elections," March/April 1982.

Death Squads: Masked Repression

The *escuadrones de muerte* (death squads) began making their deadly rounds in El Salvador in the mid-1970s. They modeled themselves after their Guatemalan counterparts. One *escuadrón* even adopted the name of the most prominent Guatemalan death squad, La Mano Blanca.

The Salvadoran death squads were preceded by an organization formed in 1968 by General José Alberto Medrano known as ORDEN (National Democratic Organization). An official instrument of the Ministry of Defense, ORDEN kept watch on the progressive peasant organizations that were gathering strength in the rural villages. Medrano, who was a highly paid consultant to the CIA, said ORDEN was "the body and bones of the army in the countryside."[17] ORDEN functioned like a civil-defense patrol for the army. Its 50,000 plus membership acted as the eyes and ears of the armed forces and were rewarded with access to credit and jobs. Authorized to carry arms, they collaborated with the armed forces to terrorize and eliminate the leaders of the mass-based peasant associations. When ORDEN was formally prohibited in 1980, General Medrano reorganized it as the Nationalist Democratic Front.

The major death squads that formed after 1975 were the White Warriors Union, the White Hand, Anticommunist Forces for Liberation (FALANGE), the Organization for the Liberation from Communism (OLC), the Secret Anti-

Communist Army (ESA), and the Maximiliano Hernandez Martinez Brigade.

According to one U.S. official quoted in the *New York Times*, the members of the death squads belong to the Salvadoran Army, Treasury Police, National Guard, National Police, or are "the very sick young sons of affluent Salvadorans." It is a business "organized with salaries and a balanced account."[18] Rich members of the oligarchy, many of whom live in Miami, handsomely reward the death-squad members for their grisly work.

In early 1985, the ex-director of the military's Central Intelligence Institute, Colonel Roberto Santibánez, directly implicated ARENA's Roberto D'Aubuisson and high army officials in the crimes of the death squads, including the assassination of Archbishop Oscar Romero.

Washington finally let it be known in 1984 that military and economic aid would be cut if the disappearances by the death squads were not reduced. Death-squad violence did drop off dramatically. Several high officials in the armed forces who had been named as death-squad organizers were transferred to foreign posts in 1984 and 1985, but no officers were prosecuted for the thousands of murders attributed to the infamous death squads. One officer linked to the 1981 murders of the head of the Salvadoran agrarian reform program and two U.S. advisers was expelled from the National Guard, causing the brother of one of the murdered advisers to comment: "Since when is losing your job and pension considered appropriate punishment for a triple murder?"[19]

From Juntas to Elections

The year of the Sandinista victory in Nicaragua marked a time in El Salvador when the oligarchy and military hardliners began to lose their traditional hold on political power. Thousands of Salvadorans marched through downtown streets of the capital chanting, *"Romero y Somoza, son la misma cosa"* (Romero and Somoza are the same thing).

During the next six years of political maneuvering in El Salvador, the following patterns emerged:

- Washington attempted to create a centrist government and the decisive role of the U.S. Embassy in local politics became clear.
- All left-of-center elements were excluded from political power, and an alliance was forged by the United States between the center and the right to attempt to crush the popular opposition.
- The Salvadoran power elites realized that military and economic aid from the U.S. government would be endangered if they continued to refuse to share power with the Christian Democrats (PDC) or if they totally blocked reform measures.

- The Christian Democrats were not able to form a government strong enough to stand up to the military and the oligarchy.

In October 1979, a group of reform-minded junior officers ousted General Carlos Humberto Romero. The officers feared that the military government of El Salvador would face the same fate as the Somoza regime in Nicaragua if something was not done to gain popular support. The new junta government included three civilians and promised a series of reforms that would halt military repression and improve the nation's economy. The liberal junta expected but failed to receive firm backing from Washington.

The older, hard-line military officers led by Minister of Defense Colonel José Guillermo García permitted superficial changes but maintained control of the government. The junta could not stop the right-wing terror and military violence because, as civilian junta member Guillermo Ungo explained, "the army still views as the principal enemy not the oligarchy but the organizations of the left."[20] On January 3, 1980, Ungo resigned along with another civilian member of the junta, Ramón Mayorga.

The second junta formed on January 10 included two Christian Democrats, but the short-lived junta lasted only until the beginning of March. A conservative faction of Christian Democrats saw its chance to gain power by cooperating with the military in the junta government. Many other PDC members, however, abhorred the idea of joining hands with the military and eventually split from the party's conservative leadership. Some rank and file of the PDC moved directly to the popular opposition movement. On March 3, Christian Democrat Hector Dada resigned from the junta, saying, "We have not been able to stop the repression, and those committing acts of repression . . . go unpunished . . . The chance for producing reforms with the support of the people is receding beyond reach."[21]

PDC leader Napoleon Duarte took Dada's place in what became the third junta government. Duarte later became the country's president, and Jaime Abdul Gutierrez the vice-president and commander-in-chief. That government lasted until March 28, 1982, when D'Aubuisson gained political power. Duarte, more of a public relations agent than a true president, spoke of land reform, democracy, and the need to stop extremist violence, but the military held the real power. The United States moved quickly to support Duarte in the hope of thwarting a right-wing coup and of propping up a dwindling centrist political base. President Carter's ambassador, Robert White, arrived in El Salvador in early March and attempted to construct a center-left coalition, but it was too late. Violence by the military and the death squads was increasing, and only the old-guard conservative faction of the PDC would associate with the military.

Major Roberto D'Aubuisson, leader of the country's most right-wing party, the Nationalist Republican Alliance (ARENA), and his colleagues publicly threatened Archbishop Oscar Romero in February 1980 for Romero's criticism of military repression. On March 24, 1980, right-wing sharpshooters assassinated Archbishop Romero, who only the month before had asked President Carter to stop military aid to the junta. Romero's death was the catalyst for the creation in April 1980 of the popular opposition coalition called the Democratic Revolutionary Front (FDR). Virtually all the opposition groups in the country— political parties, religious-based communities, mass organizations, unions, and peasant groups—joined the FDR. Both Guillermo Ungo and Ramón Mayorga of the first military-civilian junta became the leading figures in the FDR.

On December 2, 1980, the country's security forces killed four U.S. churchwomen who were doing relief work among the growing number of refugees within El Salvador. The United States temporarily suspended military and economic aid to El Salvador. Another junta formed nine days after the murders, and the Reagan administration resumed aid in January 1981. In March 1982, the United States staged national elections to demonstrate the viability of the government. The FDR boycotted the elections, arguing that the government could not insure their safety.

The March 1982 elections gave birth to a new "government of national unity." As a candidate, D'Aubuisson had promised to abolish the U.S.-supported agrarian reform and to unleash the security forces on the opposition. When he became the president of the National Assembly, the United States in concert with the military prevailed upon D'Aubuisson to accept Alvaro Magaña as the country's provisional president. Magaña, a member of the coffee oligarchy, was a wealthy lawyer who had studied economics at the University of Chicago. As longtime president of the National Mortgage Bank, Magaña had authorized attractive loans to members of the military high command. The U.S. government thought that Magaña could provide a dignified, centrist image to the new government.

The triumph of D'Aubuisson and the appointment of General José Guillermo García as Minister of Defense put the most conservative political and military elements firmly in power. It signaled the end of the reform effort that the younger officers had attempted in October 1979. The conservative sector which gained power in March 1982 represented, according to NACLA, "the most ruthless, explicitly fascist and corrupt elements of the military, precisely those which the U.S. policymakers have tried to urge the Salvadoran government and military leaders to control."[22]

During President Carter's administration, government officials believed the revolutionary movement in El Salvador could be thwarted by forming a civilian/ military coalition apart from the oligarchy. It speculated that by redistributing some of the oligarchy's power and wealth, a new reform government could gain popular support. But the reforms were half-hearted and long overdue. The United States had overestimated the potential for a liberal, bourgeois government. By the end of Carter's term, human rights and reforms became secondary considerations for the United States as the guerrilla forces advanced.

Duarte Back in Office

In 1980, Guillermo Ungo, a member of the first junta and currently the leading FDR spokesperson, said the situation in El Salvador was "the crisis of a model imposed by the U.S. government that has failed and will continue to fail."[23] The political model that Washington has tried to install in El Salvador is that of a centrist democratic government that works with the military to crush the leftist opposition. The model also calls for reforms that reduce the dominance of the traditional ruling class and thereby give the lower classes a larger stake in society.

The success of elections in El Salvador proved to Washington that its model was viable. But many felt the model had not worked, considering 1) the undiminished economic power of the oligarchy, 2) the failure of reforms to better distribute income and land, and 3) the continued strength of the guerrillas.

The 1984 elections that brought Duarte back to the presidency were the most expensive in Central American history. Washington spent over $10 million and the political section of the U.S. Embassy became the largest in the world during the election process. The U.S.-backed UPD labor federation provided critical support for Christian Democrats during the 1984 presidential election.

The army high command and important sectors of the private sector threw their support behind Duarte. Despite their dislike for moderate politicians of Duarte's ilk, they knew from experience they could control him. They saw a victory for Duarte as the only guarantee to keep large amounts of economic and military aid flowing into the country.

The upper class and the military have kept Duarte in check. Even before the elections, the military let it be known that, regardless of the outcome, neither party could change the military. Immediately following Duarte's victory, Johnny Maldonado, a member of the oligarchy and president of the National Association of Private Enterprises (ANEP), warned: "The new administration must create a climate of stability, trust, respect for private property, and confidence in order to move to any kind of economic recovery. This must be done in contrast to the climate that prevailed in 1980 and 1981 [which was characterized by] threats of nationalization, total disrespect for private property and policies conducive to a socialist type of society."[24]

After the 1984–1985 election victories, Duarte and the Christian Democrats found themselves trapped between their populist promises and the private sector demands. As usual, the private sector had more pull. In addition, the IMF and AID pressured the government to promote the private sector. The Christian Democrats had little room for their own initiatives.

The 1985 elections insured the Christian Democrats of three more years of control, short of a coup. But their political leadership existed only within narrow parameters. The oligarchy still controlled the economy, the military was three times as large as it had been in 1979, and Washington held the keys to both the treasury and the arsenal.

Political Parties

The Center-Right

Christian Democratic Party (PDC): The major party of the center-right is Duarte's PDC. Formed during the beginning of industrial expansion in 1960, middle-class professionals created the party as the middle way between capitalism and communism. Imbued with the social reform ideology of the traditional Catholic Church, the party claimed that substantial reforms for the poor could be made within the capitalist system. The PDC is associated with the Christian Democratic International in Rome and the Konrad Adenauer Institute for International Solidarity of Bonn, Germany. It lost its left wing in the 1979–1981 period when it opportunistically allied itself with the military. Its strongest base of popular support has been the U.S.-supported unions and peasant associations which were organized by AIFLD. The PDC's credibility as a popular party slipped because of its failure to prosecute the death squads, stand up for the wage demands of urban workers, continue the agrarian reform, and stop the air war.

Democratic Action (AD): A small party led by René Fortín Magaña, the AD was formed by the Federation of Salvadoran Lawyers in 1981 to create "an ample center to weaken the PDC and FDR." Although it has supported dialogue with the opposition, it has not publicly criticized the military's conduct of war or challenged the extreme right.

The Right

Republican National Alliance (ARENA): ARENA first appeared as a political party in 1981 and since then has been led by the charismatic Roberto D'Aubuisson. ARENA's rural base of support originally came from the Nationalist Democratic Front, the reorganized version of the paramilitary organization ORDEN. Among the oligarchy, it counts on strong support from major business organizations. A violently anticommunist organization, ARENA stresses "the individual's right to acquire, maintain, and use property as a projection of human personality." It strenuously opposes all reforms that threaten property rights and rejects proposals for dialogue with the FDR/FMLN. ARENA has close ties with the National Liberation Movement (MLN) in Guatemala, which gave ARENA its colors (red, white, and blue) and its emblem (cross and sword) and taught it the basic rudiments of party organization. An ARENA-led coalition won the 1982 elections, but lost to the PDC in the 1984–1985 round of elections. The party's refusal to support a negotiated settlement to the war, plus new revelations about ARENA's involvement in the assassination of Archbishop Romero, have contributed to ARENA's reduced support. In early 1985, Hugo Barrera, a founder of ARENA, broke off to form another extreme right-wing party called Patria Libre. Later that year, D'Aubuisson stepped down as the head of the party. The new ARENA chief, Alfredo Cristiani, is a Salvadoran coffee producer who has headed the powerful association of coffee and cotton growers in the country. D'Aubuisson said he would start a new political institute associated with ARENA.

The Authentic Institutional Party (PAISA): Aligned with ARENA, PAISA is headed by retired Colonel José Escobar García. It was formed in 1982 as a splinter party of the PCN.

Party of National Conciliation (PCN): This was the official party of the military and oligarchy until 1979, and from 1961 had chosen each president from among military officers. Reflecting the military's move away from the oligarchy and toward Washington, it adopted a more moderate platform in 1981, criticizing "traditional economic interests" for opposing reforms and pointing to society's "unjust distribution of income, concentration of wealth, and minimal participation of the people in the political direction of the country." It has formed a voting block with the PDC but has lost significant numbers of its own members to parties with stronger right-wing tendencies. Its candidate in 1984 was Francisco José Guerrero.

Popular Salvadoran Party (PPS): This small right-wing party was founded in 1967 by dissidents from the PCN. It has strong support from sections of the oligarchy. Led by well-known rightist Francisco Quinónez Avila, PPS votes form a block with ARENA in the legislature.

The Left

The four traditional opposition parties in El Salvador are the Salvadoran Communist Party (PCS), the National Revolutionary Movement (MNR), the National Democratic Union (UDN), and the Christian Democratic Party (PDC). During the 1970s, the last three of these parties formed an opposition coalition that was denied office after two fraudulent elections. The Salvadoran Communist Party, which had been outlawed since 1932, did not have legal recognition and could not participate in elections.

The shape of the opposition changed substantially after the failure of the civilian-military juntas to stop the violence against popular organizations and opposition parties. The MNR and the UDN joined the Democratic Revolutionary Front (FDR), which united the popular mass organizations with the political left. The PCS directly joined the armed struggle, becoming a branch of the opposition army, and the PDC moved right.

The following describes the three political parties that compose the Democratic Revolutionary Front (FDR).

National Revolutionary Movement (MNR): Predominantly a party of intellectuals, the MNR is affiliated with the Socialist International and is a member of the Permanent Conference of Political Parties of Latin America (COPPAL). Its political tendency runs from social democratic to revolutionary, and its spokespeople are Guillermo Ungo (civilian member of the first junta formed in 1979) and Eduardo Calles.

Popular Social Christian Movement (MPSC): The MPSC was formed when members of the Christian Democratic Party withdrew in March 1980 protesting the PDC's association with the military government. Its main spokespeople, Hector Dada and Ruben Zamora, had both been appointed ministers of the first junta formed in 1979.

National Democratic Union (UDN): This is a legal political party that was formed as a front for the Salvadoran Communist Party in 1968. The UDN includes trade-union members, educators, and professionals, as well as *campesino* leaders. It maintains a socialist ideology, promotes self-determination for El Salvador, and is the political counterpart to the FAL, military arm of the Salvadoran Communist Party.

Negotiating for Peace

Responding to national and international pressure, Duarte announced the first peace talks with the FDR/FMLN in late 1984. From its conception, the FDR/FMLN had called for a negotiated settlement to the conflict. The oligarchy adamantly opposed negotiations that discussed anything but the unilateral disarmament of the guerrilla armies. The Salvadoran Association of Industrialists declared: "We cannot place peace before freedom, because through false hopes we could lose both peace and freedom." Opting for a military settlement, the business organization ANEP said that the "terrorist groups are the only beneficiaries of this breathing space in the military situation, which at this time is completely favorable to the Armed Forces."[25]

Duarte's offer at the first few sessions of peace talks in 1984 and 1985 included a general amnesty, guaranteed political participation, the return of displaced people to their homes, and measures to guarantee the return of the guerrillas to their homes and jobs. Duarte, however, refused to make any constitutional changes, a position criticized by Archbishop Rivera y Damas, saying, "If peace requires a change in the constitution, then the constitution should be modified."

President Duarte invited the FMLN to join the new democratic El Salvador. "This is not the same El Salvador that they left in 1978 and 1979. El Salvador has a new society today."[26]

The FDR/FMLN brought a different agenda to the peace talks. It represented portions of the earlier call in 1982 for a negotiated settlement that would establish a "government of broad participation." A political solution would require the following agreements:

- A direct sharing of power by the FMLN/FDR in a transition government that would include other political parties and the representative political groups of the middle class and the private-enterprise sectors not tied to the oligarchy.
- The purification of the army to include soldiers from the rebel army and some from the present army who have not been implicated in killings outside of combat.
- A mixed economy with rigorous reforms in the agrarian sector, financed by foreign trade.
- A nonaligned foreign policy, including a relationship of mutual respect with the United States. (The plan would also offer the United States as well as El Salvador's Central American neighbors a reciprocal security treaty. The FMLN/FDR recognizes that the United States has legitimate security interests in the region.)
- The right of El Salvador to choose its own political development free of foreign interference.
- Full rights of trade-union organization and assembly, a respect for human rights, and freedom of expression and movement.[27]

The FDR/FMLN disagreed with Duarte's contention that El Salvador was a new country. Most of the guerrillas had joined the FMLN not in 1978 or 1979 but while Duarte held office from 1980 to 1982—the time when government repression was at its peak. For the FDR/FMLN, the failure to prosecute death-squad members, the end of the agrarian reform, and the escalation of indiscriminate bombing of civilian areas were signs that the old El Salvador was alive and well.

For the Salvadoran government, the peace talks were more a public-relations strategy than a discussion of concrete ways to deal with the opposition's concerns. "There is no question of my agreeing to power with the rebels," said Duarte. "Power is not on the table."[28] As the *New York Times* observed: "The two initial meetings have shown that Mr. Duarte is not interested in arguing about fundamental points."[29]

Neither was the United States. According to Undersecretary of Defense Fred Ikle, the basic purpose of the 1984–1985 talks was to split the rebel forces. "You can use negotiations to bring over those associated with the insurgency who are willing to participate in the democratic process. You can shrink the insurgency, and that's very valuable."[30]

The 1984–1985 elections demonstrated a popular mandate for a negotiated settlement. Salvadorans voted for the Christian Democrats in such large numbers because they hoped that in contrast to ARENA they could bring the war to a halt by bargaining with the guerrillas. While the military has given its reluctant support to the initial talks, it seems convinced, like Washington, that a military victory is possible in the long run. Given the messages that the Christian Democrats were getting in 1985 from Washington and from the nation's own oligarchy and military, any wholehearted pursuit of a negotiated settlement by the ruling political party is unlikely despite the clear popular sentiment in favor of accommodation with the FDR/FMLN.

The Economy of War

After 1979 the Salvadoran economy began a dizzying downward spin. With massive infusions of U.S. economic aid, the decline leveled off in 1983. The aid has prevented the Salvadoran economy from completely disintegrating, but it has failed to turn around several dismal economic indicators that reflect the economy's decline since the civil war began:

- Twenty-five to thirty-five percent drop in the GDP.
- Twenty-five percent decline in per capita income.
- Rise of official unemployment from less than 10 percent to over 40 percent.
- Public investment was cut in half, while private investment dropped to one quarter of previous levels.
- The tax system covered less than one half of the government's budget by 1985.[31]

By 1985, Washington said that El Salvador was meeting its debt payments punctually and that the economy had stopped its negative growth. Little wonder, as the United States was pumping $1.5 million dollars a day into El Salvador. Without the $1.8 billion in aid from Washington since 1980, El Salvador's economy would have broken down completely as a result of the civil war and the massive capital flight of more than a billion dollars since 1979.

A 1984 study by the Institute of Economic Investigations concluded that the economy had changed from one that was afflicted by the war to one sustained by it. Instead of supporting development, most of the government's economic policy is oriented toward sustaining the military, whether directly or indirectly, and in "consolidating the political alliances that serve as the base of support for the war."

In 1982, Alberto Bonilla, president of the Central Bank, said that without U.S. aid "almost all our industries would stop and we would have at least 20 percent negative growth."[32] Two years later, he told the Kissinger Commission that El Salvador needed at least $1 billion a year to stay on its feet.[33] Commenting on this reliance on U.S. economic aid, a Salvadoran lawyer told the *Miami*

Herald: "We've never had such foreign dependence in our history. We can't pay for our own national budget. The U.S. government is even paying the salaries of our civil servants."[34]

The Reagan administration has defended its policies in the region by saying that three out of four dollars going to Central America promote "economic growth and development."[35] Studies by the Congress, the General Accounting Office, and AID's inspector general have found, however, that U.S. economic aid is not being used to resolve the country's deep-rooted economic problems. Instead, it is being lost through corruption, indirectly contributing to the country's defense budget, and subsidizing purchases by the nation's private sector.[36]

Most U.S. economic aid is included in a category called cash transfers or balance-of-payments support, which allows the private sector easy access to dollars to purchase U.S. goods. AID's import program for El Salvador was nonexistent before the Reagan administration's first term in 1980. It grew from only $9000 in 1980 to $195 million in 1985. Among the purchases subsidized with AID funds from 1982 to 1984 were: $1.6 million in TV sets and other electronic goods; $10,400 in candy; and a quarter of a million dollars worth of women's undergarments. "The whole thing is outrageous," a congressional staff member told the *Miami Herald*. "If you look at the enormous poverty in that country, and think that they are using foreign aid to buy consumer goods for the rich, you begin to understand why they have a civil war going on there."[37]

In the congressional study *U.S. Aid to El Salvador: An Evaluation of the Past, A Proposal for the Future*, investigators concluded that U.S. assistance to El Salvador for reform and development accounted for only 15 percent of total U.S. funding to the country from 1981 to 1985. The study noted that large parts of even this 15 percent could be judged "indirect war-related aid," because programs like agrarian reform fall under the government's pacification program.

Of all U.S. economic aid to the country, the study reported, 74 percent has been war-related aid. This includes the category of cash transfers, which help to cover the budget deficit, which was "clearly aggravated if not caused by the war." The study found that U.S. dollars "sustain the expanded Armed Forces" and have "enabled the government to shift its budget priorities to fight the war." The congressional report also found that economic aid replaced the over $1 billion lost to the economy from capital flight and balanced the country's budget each year.[38]

U.S. aid has also made up for declining taxes. The government raised $100 million less in taxes in 1985 than it did before 1980. In 1984, the government did increase taxes in line with recommendations from the IMF. But rather than imposing a progressive income or export tax, it increased the sales tax that is felt disproportionately by the poor.

By 1983 the civil war had cost the country over $600 million in damages to its infrastructure—much of which was quickly repaired by U.S. economic aid. Virtually none of the country's production of basic grains has been touched by

THE CENTRAL AMERICA FACT BOOK / 215

guerrilla actions. The FMLN argues that its attacks on coffee production or on power lines affect the ruling class substantially more than lower class Salvadorans. When the lights go out, only the 300,000 homes in the country that have electricity are affected.

As much as the civil war has damaged the economy, the losses accumulated have been slightly less than what has been lost due to capital flight. Even with all the U.S. economic aid flowing into El Salvador to boost the private sector, private investment failed to grow. Much of the aid that is pumped into the country is immediately sent back to the United States to buy condominiums in Miami or fatten the oligarchy's foreign bank accounts.

The Salvadoran economy is an artificial one swollen by AID dollars. "Our economy," said one Salvadoran business owner, "is like a junkie, waiting for the next hit from Uncle Sam."[39] By directing most of the aid to the private sector, Washington has shored up the very segment most resistant to the economic reforms that the country needs if it is ever to remove the root causes of the civil war. When asked about the role of U.S. aid in the economy, Minister of Planning Manuel Antonio Robles replied: "The problem is that we're trying to maintain the [same] economic structure that there was before the guerrillas because there is no new model for development."[40]

Labor Organizing: Through Peace and War

El Salvador has a long history of popular organizing. In 1929, at a time when San Salvador had a population of only 100,000, over 70,000 Salvadorans gathered in the central plaza for a May Day workers' march. Following the 1932 *matanza*, the government banned unions. After 16 years, the government permitted trade-union organizing again, but it continued the prohibition on rural organizing.

The origins of the 1970s militant trade-union movement date back to the founding of the General Confederation of Salvadoran Workers (CGTS) in the late 1950s. The U.S.-affiliated international trade-union federation ORIT formed a rival "democratic" union called the General Confederation of Trade Unions (CGS). In the 1960s, AIFLD trained the leaders of this pro-government CGS.

The country's largest demonstration occurred in 1968 when 150,000 gathered in support of a strike by the ANDES teachers' union. The military government called the strike "a premeditated plan by international communism" to destabilize the country. Repression of that strike and the solidarity exhibited by the diverse groups on strike were harbingers of things to come in the 1970s.

In the countryside, the Farmworkers Union (UTC) and the Christian Peasants Federation (FECCAS) began organizing in the 1960s, defying the government's ban on such endeavors. To counter these popular associations which both the Salvadoran and U.S. governments deemed leftist, AIFLD organized the Salvadoran Communal Union (UCS) and others. While the other *campesino* organizations were being viciously destroyed by the military and death squads, AIFLD associations were barely touched by the repression.

During the 1970s, the trade unions drew closer to mass organizations to protect themselves from growing repression. The demands of labor became inseparable from demands for political change. Following the killing of 20 demonstrators during a 1977 May Day demonstration, the Romero regime invoked the Law of Public Order to restrict union organizing. Between 1979 and 1982, more than 8000 Salvadoran trade unionists were murdered or abducted, disappeared, or were wounded. It was not until 1984 that unions again began to organize and strike. The confederation MUSYGES (Unity Movement of Labor and Trade Unions) grouped the remnants of the country's most important trade-union federations that had been associated with the FDR before being crushed by repression.

One union dissolved by the government was STECEL, the powerful and politically conscious union of hydroelectric workers. In 1979–1980, 18 of its members died at the hands of the death squads. After languishing in jail for four years, ten STECEL members were released in 1984. Before leaving the country for exile in the Netherlands, STECEL leader Hector Bernabé Recinos said: "We are not leaving our country by choice, but because the death squads force us to do so. Giving us our freedom is easier for Duarte than punishing those responsible for so many deaths."[41]

There has been a resurgence of union organizing since 1984, when repression eased up in the cities. On May 1, 1985, 20,000 workers marched through the streets of San Salvador—the largest popular rally in five years. Rather than citing the reappearance of union organizing as a sign of returning democracy, the Duarte government says the union activity masks an effort to assist the guerrillas. Referring to the wave of strikes that have hit the public and private sector, President Duarte said, "All these strikes, except for one or two small ones, are by unions managed by the Communists."[42]

Agriculture: Requiem for a Reform

In 1979, when civil war exploded, conditions in rural El Salvador were actually much worse than they were in 1932. Land was more concentrated, and landlessness had become the social condition of almost 60 percent of the population. The oligarchy had extended their coffee *fincas* into eastern El Salvador, pushing *campesinos* off their land around San Miguel and Usulatan. In the 1950s and the 1960s, expansion of cotton and sugar cane plantations along the Pacific coast resulted in yet more landlessness.

Institution of the minimum wage in 1965 hit the Salvadoran peasantry hard. Large landholders used the minimum-wage law as an excuse to evict the large sector of *colonos* (similar to sharecroppers in the United States) from the plantations and to rely solely on seasonal laborers. The *colonos* who formerly lived on the plantation during the entire year found themselves without a place to live or land to sharecrop.

The only part of El Salvador left for the *campesinos* was the northern provinces that sat on the mountain slopes along the Honduran border. Because of high population growth and a diminishing amount of land available for small farming, even their small plots shrank. By the late 1970s, 95 percent of small growers farmed plots too tiny to support one family. In contrast, six families of the oligarchy held more land than 133,000 small farmers.

El Salvador is one of the most environmentally devastated countries in the Western Hemisphere. A study by the Organization of American States found four-fifths of El Salvador's land area suffers from accelerated erosion—the result of skewed land ownership patterns that force the *campesino* population to work the same barren land year after year. The tropical deciduous forests that once covered 90 percent of the country have been totally destroyed by centuries of clearance for grazing, plantations, mining, charcoal manufacture, and intensive land cultivation.[43] El Salvador is so deforested that the country has to import firewood (the only fuel source for most Salvadorans) from Honduras.

In the 1960s, with the appearance of Christian base communities and the peasants associations like FECCAS and UTC, the landless and near landless, who had passively accepted their fate for almost three decades, began to demand justice. Many, feeling they had little to lose, joined the guerrilla army.

Agrarian reform had been on Washington's agenda for El Salvador since the 1960s. The U.S. government recognized unjust land distribution as one of the leading causes of revolution in Latin America. The U.S. government could not, however, persuade the country's generals and oligarchs to institute even a minor reform program until 1976.

At that time, President Arturo Molina saw the building rural tension and announced a land-reform program to be implemented jointly by the military, the new Agrarian Transformation Institute (ISTA), and the Salvadoran Communal Union (UCS). Standing behind ISTA and UCS was the U.S. Agency for International Development (AID). Even though the land distribution program called for by Molina involved only 4 percent of the nation's land, the oligarchy resisted the program with a virulent anticommunist campaign of propaganda and violence. Molina was replaced in a fraudulent election by the hard-line Minister of Defense Carlos Humberto Romero.

The 1979 progressive junta that overthrew Romero called for a more aggressive land-reform program. Washington, fearing that this junta was too far to the left, refused to throw its support behind the government, thereby allowing the oligarchy and the old military command to assume control once more. In March 1980, the U.S. government put its full support behind a government headed by Napoleon Duarte.

A new agrarian reform program of three phases was announced and pushed through without input from the peasant unions, the church, the university, or even the government's own ministry of agrarian reform, ISTA. Washington, which designed most of the program, saw land distribution as a way of 1) breaking the control of the oligarchy, 2) creating popular support for a centrist government, and 3) reducing peasant support for the FDR/FMLN.

According to AID, land reform in El Salvador was "a political imperative to help prevent political collapse, strike a blow to the left, and help prevent radicalization of the rural population."[44] The program's Phase Three was designed by Roy Prosterman, the man who had authored a similar program implemented during the Vietnam War. He saw agrarian reform as "an essential element of the pacification program" in El Salvador and regarded the Salvadoran program as "a chance to turn the tables on the guerrillas."

The involvement of the AIFLD unions was crucial to the success of the agrarian reform program as a pacification strategy. The reform created cooperatives from the members of the AIFLD-sponsored UCS union and organized the individual beneficiaries into peasant associations also run by AIFLD-trained organizers.

Both Phases I and II of the reform were designed to redistribute land belonging to the oligarchy and thereby reduce its hold on the nation's politics and economy. The land under both phases would be organized into cooperatives of farm laborers who had formerly worked as employees on the estates. Phase I covered the country's largest *latifundios*, which included much idle and pasture land. Phase II was the part of the program most threatening to the oligarchy because it included most mid-sized plantations that produced coffee.

Phase III allowed small farmers who were renting land to buy their parcels over a 30-year period. By making tens of thousands of *campesinos* small landowners, Washington hoped to give them a stake in the government. One AID official, commenting on the purpose of Phase III, remarked: "There is no one more conservative than the small farmer. We're going to be breeding capitalists like rabbits."[45]

Three years after the agrarian reform program began, the land distribution was effectively brought to a halt by the Salvadoran government in 1983 when the National Assembly passed a new constitution that stressed the virtue of private property. It declared that the government "recognizes, promotes, and guarantees the right of private property." There were to be no more land confiscations under either Phase I or III.

The short-lived agrarian reform failed to break the back of the oligarchy. A major reason for this failure was the inability and lack of resolve of the Christian Democrats under Duarte to implement Phase II—the heart of the land reform. Washington also proved ambivalent about Phase II which could have truly dissipated the power of the oligarchy. Phase I, while it did result in the distribution of land to over 100 cooperatives, involved mostly nonproductive land. Many large owners avoided having their best land expropriated under Phase I by switching titles to relatives. Others relied on connections with the military to maintain their property.

Through the agrarian reform, Washington came closer to realizing the goals of creating support for a centrist government and reducing the popularity of the guerrillas. The cooperatives and peasant associations organized by AIFLD did convince tens of thousands of *campesinos* that the Christian Democrats and the U.S. government offered them at least a little hope for a better life for their families.

The agrarian reform program did not succeed in meeting the pacification objectives of Washington for the following reasons: 1) the reform failed to address the needs of the landless *campesinos* who neither rented land nor who had steady work on large estates, 2) the small plots given to the *campesinos* under Phase III were too small to sustain a family, 3) the military, which originally promised to support the program, instead used the reform as a cover for a reign of violence against *campesinos*, 4) less than a third of the eligible *campesinos* received temporary titles, 5) the government provided little or no follow-up support for the new owners, and 6) the *campesinos* had no role in designing or implementing the program.

Instead of a carefully planned land distribution that would lead to rural development, the agrarian reform program was a hastily contrived program that was part of a larger plan of counterinsurgency. The program did succeed as a propaganda tool used by the Reagan administration to obtain increased military and economic aid from Congress. By 1984, the land-reform program was in ruins, and Washington turned to other pacification programs that were linked more closely to a military strategy against the insurgents. The Christian Democrats, the only party that has stood firmly behind the agrarian reform, won an electoral mandate in the 1984–1985 elections. It is unlikely, however, that President Duarte will risk alienating the military and the oligarchy by pushing for a substantial renewal of the land distribution.

TNCs in El Salvador

"El Salvador is a small and pleasant country, rich in natural beauty." That is how El Salvador's Foreign Trade Minister Manuel Morales Erlich described his country to the U.S.-sponsored Miami Conference on the Caribbean in 1984. With new incentives offered by the Salvadoran government and investment insurance offered by Washington, Morales Erlich expects "an avalanche of foreign investment" in coming years.[46]

El Salvador has traditionally been the region's most industrialized country. In the early part of the century, British and U.S. investors financed the country's roads, railroad, and utilities. In the 1960s, it was the first country to take advantage of the the Central American Common Market (CACM). With U.S. government encouragement, TNCs suddenly started flocking to the country, which had a good infrastructure, an industrious population, and willing Salvadoran business partners. Over 40 TNCs set up shop with Salvadoran junior partners during the 1960s.

Most large businesses in the industrial sector are backed up by some foreign capital, with the possible exception of the cement and beer industries. Many TNC executives have expressed their delight in the aptitude and hard work of their Salvadoran employees. "This is not a *mañana* country," said the vice-president of Taca Airlines, the Salvadoran national airline company that is largely owned by U.S. investors.[47]

TNCs from the United States accounted for more than half of foreign investment in the 1960s and 1970s. Japan, the second largest source of foreign investment, provided about 15 percent of El Salvador's foreign investment.[48] Almost all the investment by TNCs was in the manufacturing sector, especially in food processing, tobacco, bottling, and textiles.

As the regional market began to contract in the late 1960s, the Salvadoran government opened the San Bartolo Free Trade Zone and promoted the country as a center for assembly industries known as *maquiladoras*. In 1974, it officially entered the race to attract the world's runaway shops with introduction of the Export Promotion Law. Features of the law included the following incentives: total exemption on imports of machinery, equipment, and spare parts; a 10-year holiday from income and capital taxes; unrestricted repatriation of profits to the home country; investment guarantees against expropriation; and a specialized recruiting agency for labor. The law attracted many TNCs who were looking for cheap labor.

The year that Dataram closed down its operation in Malaysia, it established a plant in El Salvador; Texas Instruments shut down one plant in Curaçao and the same year moved to El Salvador; and both SmithKline Beckman and AVX Corporation previously had plants in Ireland before they expanded in El Salvador. Other firms attracted to the San Bartolo free zone in the 1970s were Bourns, Form-O-Uth, Eagle International, Delka, and Manexpo. The growth of *maquiladoras* resulted in the doubling of U.S. apparel imports from El Salvador between 1975 and 1978.

U.S. trade figures illustrate the results of the Export Promotion Law and other investment incentives. The top two nonagricultural U.S. exports to El Salvador are 1) electronic tubes, semiconductors, and integrated circuits and 2) synthetic fibers and yarns. Salvadorans do not need over $40 million in electronics and textiles from the United States. TNCs with assembly plants use these imports to manufacture finished products for export. Among El Salvador's top 10 non-agricultural exports to the United States are electronic products (second-largest export), capacitors and circuit boards (fifth), cotton towels (sixth), female and infant clothing (seventh), and bras (tenth).

No large TNCs have agribusiness operations in El Salvador. TNCs like General Foods, Coca-Cola, and Procter & Gamble buy Salvadoran coffee but have no direct foreign investment in the country. Through the Latin American Agribusiness Development Corporation (LAAD), there are nine agribusiness companies that produce mostly nontraditional agro-exports. One of the largest of these corporations is Quality Foods, which contracts farmers to grow okra for export. The country's internal market for chicken and turkey is dominated by two U.S. investors, while Cargill mills grain and produces eggs for the Salvadoran food market.

Three of the top five U.S. oil companies (Exxon, Texaco, and Chevron) are active in El Salvador. McDonald Servipronto serves hamburgers *pronto* for the sons and daughters of the middle and upper classes, who also have the choice of Hardees. The U.S. press corps has its headquarters in the Hotel Camino Real, which is owned by United Air Lines.

Managing San Salvador's office of the TNC advertising firm McCann-Erickson is Roberto Avila, a rightist alleged to have connections with the country's death squads. McCann-Erickson managed the highly successful 1982 advertising campaign of Roberto D'Aubuisson's ARENA political party. The publicrelations firm of MacKenzie McCheyne, which once tried to polish Anastasio Somoza's image, now represents the right-wing Salvadoran Freedom Foundation.

Like most other Central American nations, El Salvador has a manufacturing plant for women's underwear—Maidenform assembles bras for export to the United States. Levi Strauss also has a clothing factory in El Salvador. In early 1985, it considered moving the plant to Nicaragua but was dissuaded by the U.S. government's refusing OPIC insurance. An expanding area of U.S. investment in El Salvador is the business of road construction, engineering, and infrastructure repair.

Even in the unlikely event that El Salvador does experience "an avalanche of foreign investment," it will have a difficult time catching up to the level that existed before the civil war broke out in 1979. More than 35 TNCs have left the country. Some relocated after kidnappings of their executives, while others packed up after experiencing problems with El Salvador's Central Bank. The American Chamber of Commerce estimated that U.S. investment in El Salvador dropped from $150 million in 1979 to about $50 million in 1984.[49] A major blow was the shutdown of the Texas Instruments plant—the largest electronics firm in Central America—in late 1985.

Many foreign businesses, however, decided to stay in El Salvador. The president of the American Chamber of Commerce, one of the investors that stayed, owns a profitable importing business that is benefiting from U.S. economic aid which encourages U.S. imports to the country. In 1985, about 130 U.S. businesses were still doing business in El Salvador, including 48 large TNCs.

Caught in the Quagmire

The five-year flood of economic and military aid failed to win the battle against a peasant army that many Salvadorans fondly call "*los muchachos*" (the young ones) in El Salvador. During his first administration, President Reagan vowed to draw the line in El Salvador against leftist advances in Central America. "What we see in El Salvador," said President Reagan, "is an attempt to destabilize the entire region, and eventually move chaos and anarchy toward the American border."[50]

Although Reagan believed he could pull Americans out of the antiwar doldrums created by the Vietnam War, El Salvador increasingly resembles the Vietnam quagmire. As in Vietnam, ever escalating transfers of aid have kept the Salvadoran government from falling to pieces. Each new military tactic— from pacification programs and the training of Salvadoran troops to the U.S.-directed air war—has failed to bring peace and justice to El Salvador.

1   Pedro de Alvarado, *An Account of the Conquest of Guatemala in 1524* (Boston: Milfored House, 1972), pp.80–81. Cited in Philip L. Russell, *El Salvador in Crisis* (Austin: Colorado River, 1984).

2   A report for *El Progress* in 1850 cited in Mario Rodriguez, *A Palmerstonian Diplomat in Central America* (Tucson: University of Arizona, 1964), pp.316–317.

3   Marc Herold, "From Riches to 'Rags': Finanzkapital in El Salvador, 1900–1980" (unpublished manuscript, University of New Hampshire, 1980).

4   Quoted in Kenneth J. Grieb, "The United States and the Rise of General Maximiliano Hernandez Martinez," *Journal of Latin American Studies*, November 1971, p.152.

5   David Browning, *El Salvador: La Tierra y El Hombre* (San Salvador: Ministerio de Educacion, 1975), p.365.

6   Estimates of the numbers of Salvadorans killed during the repression range from as low as 8000 to 30,000. Thomas Anderson in his study *Matanza* said that the army did not have enough ammunition to kill many more than 10,000.

7   Thomas P. Anderson, *The War of the Dispossessed: Honduras and El Salvador, 1969* (Lincoln: University of Nebraska, 1981), p.24.

8   Thomas P. Anderson, *Matanza* (Lincoln: University of Nebraska, 1971), p.159.

9   Cynthia Arnson, *El Salvador: A Revolution Confronts the United States* (Washington: Institute for Policy Studies, 1982), p.7.

10 *Latin American Perspectives*, Spring/Summer 1980, p.129.

11 Susanne Jonas and David Tobis (eds.), *Guatemala* (Berkeley and New York: NACLA, 1974), p.99.

12 Penny Lernoux, *Cry of the People* (Garden City, NY: Doubleday, 1980), p.76.

13 *NACLA Report on the Americas*, March/April 1984.

14 *Los Angeles Times*, March 14, 1984.

15 *New York Times*, July 13, 1985.

16 Ibid.

17 Robert Armstrong and Philip Wheaton, *Reform and Repression: U.S. Policy in El Salvador 1950 Through 1981* (San Francisco: Solidarity, 1982), p.4.

18 *New York Times*, October 11, 1983.

19 *Mesoamerica*, January 1985.

20 Arnson, op.cit., p.45.

21 Ibid., p.49.

22 Ibid., pp.21–22.

23 Robert Armstrong, "El Salvador: A Revolution Brews," *NACLA Report on the Americas*, July/August 1980, p.11.

24 *In These Times*, May 30, 1984.
25 *Central America Report*, December 7, 1984.
26 *Central America Bulletin*, January 1, 1985.
27 *Christian Science Monitor*, May 7, 1984.
28 *New York Times*, December 12, 1984.
29 *New York Times*, December 6, 1984.
30 *Los Angeles Times*, November 16, 1984.
31 Figures from Representative Jim Leach, Representative George Miller, Senator Mark Hatfield, "US Aid to El Salvador: An Evaluation of the Past, A Proposal for the Future. A Report to the Arms Control and Foreign Policy Caucus" (Washington), February 1985.
32 *Multinational Monitor*, May 1983.
33 *LARR*, July 13, 1984.
34 *Mesoamerica*, July 1983.
35 Speech to joint session of Congress in April 1984. Cited in Ibid.
36 AID Inspector General, "Audit Report No. 1-519-83-8," April 20, 1983.
37 *Miami Herald*, December 23, 1984.
38 Rep. Jim Leach et al., op.cit. 39.
39 *American Banker*, March 3, 1984.
40 Christopher Dickey, "El Salvador: Economy of War," *Washington Post*, October 3, 1984.
41 *New York Times*, October 6, 1984.
42 *New York Times*, June 16, 1985.
43 Erick Eckholm, *Losing Ground* (New York: Norton for Worldwatch Institute, 1976), p.167.
44 Laurence R. Simon, "The Dismal Legacy of Land Reform," *In These Times*, July 11, 1984.
45 *New York Times*, March 11, 1980.
46 Andres Oppenheimer, "The Latest Country Courting Foreign Investors: El Salvador," *Miami Herald*, December 6, 1984.
47 Fred R. Bleakley, "Americans in Business," *New York Times*, March 25, 1984.
48 Fundación Salvaoreña Para El Desarrollo Económico y Social (FUSADES), "Investing in El Salvador" (San Salvador), 1982. FUSADES gives the following percentages for the period 1971–1981: United States (46.1 percent); Panama (can be included in the US figures because of pattern of US investors establishing tax shelters and holding companies in Panama) (14.1 percent); Japan (13.5 percent); West Germany (4.9 percent); and England (4.3 percent).
49 *New York Times*, May 2, 1976.
50 Address by President Reagan on Central America, May 9, 1984.

CHAPTER 11

Guatemala

∎

Trends
- New civilian role in government is unlikely to result in significant reduction in human-rights violations or in economic reforms.
- Widening divisions between military and private sector over economic planning.
- Unwillingness of military to retire from government and military controlled institutions.
- Severe economic decline that increases social tensions among all sectors.
- Increasing U.S. support for the Guatemalan economy and the military's pacification program.
- Failure of the pacification program to provide long-term economic alternatives to Indian population.
- Inability of military to crush guerrillas, who will prove capable of adapting to changing political circumstances.
- Resurgence of organizing among workers, urban squatters, and church groups.

∎

GUATEMALA IS A garrison state. The northernmost and most populated of the Central American nations, Guatemala is a nation ruled by military and right-wing terrorism. For the last 30 years, the garrison chiefs have presided over a war of elimination of all critics. Unable to quickly quell armed rebellion by leftist guerrillas, the military and the death squads have targeted labor-union activists, peasant organizers, students, university professors, left-of-center politicians, and liberal clerics.

Counterinsurgency advisors from the United States, Israel, Argentina, and Taiwan have coached the Guatemalan military in the techniques and philosophy of counterinsurgency. But the war of counterinsurgency is a war that never ends for the Guatemalan generals. Desperate living conditions and the lack of basic freedoms have kept popular opposition and armed resistance alive despite the most brutal repression.

In Guatemala City, unlicensed vans full of heavily armed men pull to a stop and in broad daylight kidnap another death-squad victim. Mutilated bodies are dropped from helicopters on crowded stadiums to keep the population terrified and passive in face of unrelenting repression. Those who dare to ask about "disappeared" loved ones have their tongues cut out.

The armed forces have divided the cities up into sections and subsections to facilitate their search-and-control operations. They have militarized the Indian provinces, forcing all teenage boys and men into civil patrols and forcing refugees into military-controlled "model villages." Americas Watch in 1984 called Guatemala a "nation of prisoners."

Three decades of repression have brought worsening living conditions for the Guatemalan poor. While scavenging for food, children die in city dumps, smothered under avalanches of falling garbage. Beggars in the streets of Guatemala City carry signs that say, "With your help, I will eat today." On mud wastelands at the city's edge, tens of thousands of families live in cardboard and corrugated tin hovels without running water or sanitation.

Nine out of ten Guatemalan farm families live on plots too small to provide for their subsistence, and the poorest 50 percent of Guatemalans get only a little more than half the calories they need. Guatemala's many peasants do not have shoes let alone mules or even carts to haul their fuel wood. Barefooted Indian *campesinos*, bent almost in half, carry immense burdens of wood to sell in town. Life expectancy for non-Indians, called *ladinos* in Guatemala, is 58 years, while Indians, who make up half the population, live an average of 44 years.[1]

The Indians of Guatemala are survivors. They have endured the scourges of colonialism and the barbarism of the Guatemalan army. These descendants of the Mayans speak 22 different languages and have over 250 distinct ways of dress. Indian activist Rigoberta Menchú attributes the survival of the Indian culture to the way its people have hidden many of the traditions from outsiders. "Our grandparents guard secrets and pass them on to their grandchildren who have the responsibility to pass them on, so there exists an expression completely enclosed in the Indian [tradition]." Guatemalan Indians have countered feelings of social inferiority by stressing their culture and communal identity.[2]

The Guatemalan oligarchy bears at least as much responsibility as the military for the country's misery. It has maintained an alliance with the Guatemalan generals, many of whom have joined the economic elite. The traditional base of the country's oligarchy is the agro-export system, but the modern oligarchy includes the elites from all main economic sectors. Describing this group, an AID-financed study said: "This is a very small group with very extensive influence in all areas of public and economic life—a group that must be led not pushed."[3]

Dictators, Reformers, and the CIA

The Spanish Crown regarded Guatemala as its most important colonial outpost in Central America. For the Spaniards, Guatemala was not a country to be developed but only a source of wealth for the royal coffers. Finding no gold, the Spanish colonizers turned to the land to make their fortunes. Expansive haciendas removed Indians from their land and used Indian slave labor to grow cocoa and produce indigo and cochineal dye for export. Then, as now, the ruling classes and the army in Guatemala did not value Indian life. Between 1519 and 1610, the Indian population dropped by two-thirds as a result of disease and brutality.[4]

Spain prohibited Guatemala from manufacturing products that would compete with its own trade to the Latin American colonies. Frustrated by this colonial control, the *criollos* (native-born Spanish) declared their independence from Spain in 1821. This new political independence neither ended the region's economic dependence on the European market nor improved the dire lot of the Indian population.

Cultivation and export of the coffee bean began in the mid-1800s and created an oligarchy of wealthy families, many of whom have passed on their riches and power to the present generation. From the outset, however, the financing, processing, and marketing of Guatemalan coffee was in the hands of outside interests, particularly Germans. During World War II, the Guatemalan government, forced by the U.S., confiscated German coffee interests and forced German citizens into confinement, allowing U.S. interests to gain hold of the coffee market.

U.S. investors first came to Guatemala not for coffee but for bananas. In 1904, dictator Manuel Estrada Cabrera granted United Fruit's affiliate, International Railways of Central America, a 99-year concession to finish the construction of Guatemala's principal railroad which ran from the capital to the Atlantic harbor of Puerto Barrios. In return for completing the railroad, United Fruit received a contract in 1906 for 170,000 acres of some of the country's best land for banana production on the Atlantic coast.

By the 1930s, the United Fruit Company had become the largest landowner, employer, and exporter in Guatemala. In 1936, the company signed another 99-year lease with General Jorge Ubico, then dictator of Guatemala, to operate a banana plantation on the Pacific coast.[5] "Ubico granted the company the kind of concessions to which it had become accustomed: total exemption from internal taxation, duty-free importation of all necessary goods, and a guarantee of low wages."[6]

Reflecting on the company's history and its significance in Guatemala, Thomas McCann, a former official of United Fruit, said: "Guatemala was chosen as the site for the company's earliest development activities at the turn of the century because a good portion of the country contained prime banana land and because at the time we entered Central America, Guatemala's government was the region's weakest, most corrupt and most pliable. In short, the country offered an 'ideal investment climate,' and United Fruit's profits there flourished for fifty years."[7]

In 1944, a popular coalition formed to break the power of the oligarchy and to modernize the country by instituting reforms.[8] The coalition, supported by 85 percent of the (literate male) vote, elected intellectual Juan José Arévalo as president, bringing more than one hundred years of dictatorship to an end. Arévalo initiated labor rights legislation, overturned the unfair vagrancy laws, and created a state bank to help small landowners.

In 1951, Jacobo Arbenz succeeded Arévalo as president with the promise to carry out a complete land reform to redistribute the country's idle land. Arbenz said: "First [we have] to convert our country from a dependent nation with a semi-colonial economy into an economically independent country; second, to transform our nation from a backward past with a predominantly feudal economy into a modern capitalist country; and third, to see that this transformation is carried out in such a way that it brings with it the highest possible elevation of the standard of living of the great masses of people."[9] The transformation of the country's feudal system and an end to economic dependency inevitably meant a confrontation with the interlocking U.S. corporations that dominated the country's commerce: United Fruit, International Railways of Central America, and Electric Bond and Share Company.

The Agrarian Reform Law of 1952 exempted all cultivated land no matter the size of the plantation. Chief target of the law was the United Fruit Company, which left 85 percent of its land idle. The largest single owner in Guatemala, United Fruit possessed more land than the combined holdings of 50 percent of the total population.[10] Expropriating 387,000 idle acres, the government offered to compensate the company $1.2 million based on the company's own tax declaration. But the U.S. State Department and United Fruit demanded $16 million compensation.

Reactions to the Guatemalan reforms were immediate. Nicaragua's dictator Anastasio Somoza and an attorney for United Fruit together attempted to pressure President Harry Truman for approval of "Operation Fortune." Without President Truman's consent this early plan to overthrow Arbenz foundered. United Fruit then mounted an extensive press campaign to discredit Arbenz, with claims that "an iron curtain" was falling over Guatemala.

U.S. Ambassador to Guatemala John Peurifoy said: "The candle is burning slowly and surely, and it is only a matter of time before the large American interests will be forced out completely." A. A. Berle of the State Department declared that Guatemala was "in the grip of a Russian-controlled dictatorship."[11] Arbenz was hardly the communist leader that United Fruit and the State Department claimed him to be. Though he did allow the Communist Party of Guatemala official recognition as a party, he himself rejected a class analysis in favor of a reformist ideology.

The Eisenhower administration approved a plan called Operation Success, which was organized, inspired, and financed by the CIA. In 1954, President Arbenz was overthrown by Colonel Carlos Castillo Armas, who had been trained at the U.S. Command and General Staff School in Fort Leavenworth and had served as director of the military academy under Ubico. Thomas McCann of United Fruit wrote that the company "was involved at every level" in the CIA's successful Guatemalan coup.[12]

United Fruit used its close connections in the Eisenhower administration to lobby for the coup. Secretary of State John Dulles had been a senior partner of Sullivan and Cromwell, United Fruit's New York law firm and its principal adviser on foreign operations; CIA Director Allen Dulles was also a former member of the law firm. John Moors Cabot, the assistant secretary of state on inter-American affairs, was the brother of Thomas Dudley Cabot, former president of United Fruit. Eisenhower's personal secretary, Ann Whitman, was married to Ed Whitman, director of United Fruit's public-relations department. General Walter Bedell Smith, a trusted adviser of Eisenhower and former CIA director, oversaw the destabilization of the Arbenz administration and then later joined the board of United Fruit.[13]

In her book *The Declassified Eisenhower*, Blanche Cook wrote that, "Guatemala represented a new level of political warfare, including a fully orchestrated cover-up and significant aerial bombing."[14] The cover-up hid the fact that Castillo Armas' army had trained on a United Fruit plantation in Honduras with arms flown in from a clandestine airport in Florida. On the day of the coup, Castillo Armas arrived in Guatemala City on a U.S. Embassy plane.

Castillo Armas attempted to dignify the coup by calling it the "Liberation." The name "Liberation" was meant to elicit sympathy in the United States by identifying the coup with the liberation of European countries from the German army. After the coup, the government launched a national anticommunist propaganda campaign led by the CIA-funded Liberation Radio. In the end, however, it was only United Fruit that could rightly declare that it had been liberated.

During and after the 1954 coup, over 9000 people were arrested and many tortured. Over 1.5 million acres were returned to the large landowners, including United Fruit, and the Armas government abolished 533 unions.[15] The 10-year Guatemalan experiment with political freedom and bourgeois democracy ended, only to begin a series of military dictatorships, each more repressive and bloodthirsty than the one before it.

Immediately following the coup, the United States rushed money and advisers to the Castillo Armas regime, increasing the number of personnel in its Guatemalan aid mission sevenfold.[16] U.S. salvage operations for the first few years after the coup, excluding military aid, cost $80 to $90 million—more than the entire funding for the rest of Latin America.[17] This assistance, in addition to funds from multilateral agencies, particularly the World Bank, financed massive infrastructure projects such as roads and electrical networks. A condition attached to these funds was that the roadbuilding contracts be given to private construction firms which were primarily U.S. companies.[18]

The sad consequences of the 1954 liberation can be summarized as follows: 1) repeal of agrarian reform, 2) destruction of trade-union and peasant movements, and 3) institutionalization of the right wing and the military in national politics. Mexican novelist and essayist Carlos Fuentes wrote: "It was an important year, 1954, because political development in Guatemala was not merely interrupted by violent foreign intervention; it has been continually perverted and poisoned to this very day."[19]

The Political Winter

One Guatemalan author referred to the 1944–1954 period as "ten years of springtime in the land of eternal dictatorship."[20] Since the 1954 coup, military dictatorships and fraudulent elections have been the political way of life in Guatemala. In the 1960s, a guerrilla group formed to challenge the string of military regimes. Guerrilla leader Marco Antonio Yon Sosa said that because of the 1954 experience of the military overtaking the elected government, he and others had chosen armed struggle. "The electoral path is barred in Guatemala," said Yon Sosa, "because the bourgeoisie cannot provide democratic elections and continue to remain in power."

To meet the guerrilla threat in eastern Guatemala, the Pentagon established a small counterinsurgency base in Izabal. There U.S. Green Berets and 15 specially trained Guatemalan officers instructed the Guatemalan army in the techniques of counterinsurgency. As many as 1000 U.S. Special Forces had joined the counterinsurgency campaign by the late 1960s. Not only did the campaign employ aerial bombing and scorched-earth assaults on communities suspected of aiding the guerrillas, but it also involved pacification programs that were being developed in Vietnam. AID officials worked alongside U.S. military/civic action teams in the departments of Izabal and Zacapa. At Washington's urging, the Guatemala army became one of the first armies in Latin America to develop its own military/civic action division.

During this counterinsurgency war, the Guatemalan death squads first appeared. U.S. Army Colonel John Webber acknowledged that he encouraged paramilitary groups associated with the large landowners in the area to collaborate with the army in the search for the subversives.[21] In 1968, Webber said: "That's the way the country is. The communists are using everything they have including terror. And it must be met." In an interview with *Time*, Webber said that it was at his instigation that "the technique of counter-terror had been implemented by the army."[22]

Colonel Carlos Arana Osorio earned the name "Butcher of Zacapa" because of the massacres of *campesinos* that regularly occurred during his 1966–1968 counterinsurgency campaign. Arana, who rose to the presidency in 1970, said, "If it is necessary to turn the country into a cemetery in order to pacify it, I will not hesitate to do so."[23] General Ríos Montt, who became president a decade later, served under Arana as chief of general staff and was personally responsible for several massacres of Indian villages. According to Amnesty International, even after the guerrillas were crushed, the right-wing paramilitary death squads "continued to operate, abducting and assassinating opposition leaders and their sympathizers and sometimes killing at random for the purpose of general intimidation. . . . Between 1966 and 1976, some 20,000 people had died at the hands of these paramilitary squads."[24]

The Armed Opposition

The early guerrilla movement arose out of an aborted military coup in 1960.[25] Three junior officers—Alejandro de Leon, Marco Antonio Yon Sosa, and Luis Turcios Lima—were upset by their low pay, government corruption, and the presence of Cuban exiles training for the Bay of Pigs invasion. They attempted a coup against President Miguel Ydigoras Fuentes. Four days after the military uprising began, it was crushed as the rebel-held areas were bombed by U.S.-trained Cuban pilots. Yon Sosa and Turcios Lima went into exile but returned to Guatemala in early 1962 to initiate guerrilla struggle.

Although they had no experience as guerrillas, they counted on their counterinsurgency training from the United States at Fort Benning and in the Canal Zone. The first guerrilla front was named the Alejandro de Leon November 13 Revolutionary Movement (MR-13) after their co-conspirator who had been killed during the attempted 1960 coup. This first guerrilla army and another one opened by the Guatemalan Communist Party (PGT) were quickly crushed. In late 1962, the remnants of the short-lived guerrilla fronts along with a student-based group (called the 12th of April Movement) formed the Rebel Armed Forces (FAR).

FAR, like other Latin American guerrilla movements of that period, adopted *foquista* tactics, which were based on those that proved successful for Castro and the Cuban guerrillas. Under this theory of warfare, guerrillas function as a predominantly military organization based in *focos* (centers) in the mountains. The successes of the guerrillas, the theory suggested, would ignite popular uprisings in the cities which would bring down the military regime. Although FAR was generally successful with its hit-and-run attacks on the military, it was never able to seriously threaten the armed forces with its poorly organized guerrilla army of 500 or less.

The military could not deal a death blow to the elusive guerrillas until late in the decade, but it did kill thousands of rural Guatemalans suspected of aiding FAR. A 1966–1968 reign of terror in the Zacapa and Izabal departments resulted in the deaths of 8000 people, mostly noncombatants. After briefly changing its targets to Guatemala City, FAR was by 1969 reduced to a few members.

In the next few years, the remaining members of FAR and other Guatemalan revolutionaries regrouped and separately reviewed their strategy for armed struggle in Guatemala. In the early 1970s, two new guerrilla groups—EGP and ORPA—emerged.

The two new groups considered the oppression of the Indian majority as a major social contradiction in Guatemala that had to be resolved in order to create a democratic society in the country. "We know that it is the Indians, half the population, who will determine the outcome of the revolution in this country," said EGP leader César Montes, adding that the guerrillas had "four centuries of justified Indian distrust of *ladinos* to overcome." In contrast to the guerrillas of the 1960s, ORPA and EGP recognized the need to establish a popular base of support before attempting military campaigns. Both guerrilla armies adopted the strategy of "prolonged people's war" rather than planning on a rapid military victory.

A new stage of unity in the armed struggle was reached in February 1982, when the four main guerrilla armies—EGP, ORPA, FAR, and the Guatemalan Labor Party-Nucleus (PGT)—formed a united military front called the Guatemalan National Revolutionary Unity (URNG). The URNG provided the disparate guerrilla armies with a structure to coordinate their military actions and to develop a consensus over the goals of the armed opposition.

The five main points of the URNG coalition are the following:

1) Elimination of repression and the guarantee of life and peace.

2) Distribution of property of the very rich, agrarian reform, price control, and the allowance of reasonable profits.

3) Guarantee of equality between Indians and *ladinos*.

4) Equal representation by patriotic, popular, and democratic sectors in the new government, equal rights for women, protection for children, and guarantee of freedom of expression and religion.

5) Self-determination, a policy of nonalignment and international cooperation.

Political/Military Organizations

Guerrilla Army of the Poor (EGP): Based in El Quiché, strongly Marxist and internationalist, its logo features a sketch of Che Guevara. This has been the largest of the country's recent guerrilla groups because of its large Indian following.

In a 1982 issue of its magazine *Compañero*, EGP defines its view of revolutionary struggle:

One of our basic political premises—perhaps the least orthodox within the programmatic objectives derived from the complexity of Guatemalan society and the problems posed by its revolutionary transformation—is the thesis that in Guatemala *the ethnic-national contradiction is one of the fundamental factors in all possible revolutionary change.* . . . We call the ethnic-national contradiction the domination of the Indian peoples and their ethnic-cultural identity by the dependent agro-export capitalist system which the ruling class has historically created in our country, and the need to eliminate the economic class and political base on which the domination rests.[26]

The momentum of EGP was seriously undermined by the Guatemalan army's bloody counterinsurgency campaign in the *Altiplano* (1980–1983). EGP has lost most of its popular base because of the ensuing pacification program. While the Guatemalan army was largely successful in separating EGP from its Indian base of support, it has not been able to substantially slow down EGP's military operations. Traditionally EGP has been active in El Quiché, Huehuetenango, Alta Verapaz, Baja Verapaz, Chimaltenango, Suchitepequez, Escuintla, Izabal, Chiquimala, Zacapa, and Guatemala City. In 1984–1985, its military actions were limited to Huehuetenango and El Quiché.

Organization of People in Arms (ORPA): ORPA, like EGP, sees a high potential for Indian involvement in armed struggle. After organizing themselves in Mexico, ORPA cadre entered Guatemala in 1972. They quietly organized a political base in the west-central mountains, primarily among Indian *campesinos* as well as an urban infrastructure to prepare for guerrilla war.

ORPA publicly announced its existence on September 18, 1979, with the takeover of the Mujulia farm in the coffee-growing region of Quezaltenango. In 1980, ORPA showed its strength by occupying the tourist center of Santiago Atitlán. Since 1980, ORPA has concentrated on military strategy rather than on mass organizing. Viewing the coffee-growing region of western Guatemala as the country's "spinal column," it believes that area to be the "strategic region" for guerrilla warfare.

ORPA attributes its endurance and hope in large part to the Indian culture. ORPA commander Gaspar Ilom (*nom de guerre* after the protagonist in Miguel de Asturias' famous novel *Hombres de Maiz*) said, "Again and again, we were told that the grandfather of a grandfather had said that one day men who were going to liberate the people would come down from the mountains. I think this has to be interpreted as an element of the tradition, the memory, the hope of a people, subjected to colonization, who created their own legends, their own expectations, to survive this situation." ORPA was seriously damaged in the last half of 1981 when the military, with the help of Argentine counterinsurgency specialists, destroyed its safe-houses in Guatemala City. Since then, it has recuperated and become the most aggressive of the guerrilla armies. It operates in San Marcos, Totonicapán, Quezaltenango, and Solola.

Rebel Armed Forces (FAR): Guatemala's oldest guerrilla organization, FAR faced near elimination in the late 1960s. FAR recovered and established itself as a small guerrilla band in Petén, remaining influential in urban areas and among the agricultural workers on the south coast. In the 1970s, FAR demobilized most of its guerrilla force to concentrate on union organizing among both urban and agricultural workers. It is currently active in Guatemala City, Chimaltenango, and Petén.

Guatemalan Labor Party-Nucleus (PGT): In the 1960s, the military committee of the PGT became the base of FAR, which evolved into an independent guerrilla force. More recently, in 1981, the Leadership Nucleus of the PGT broke away to open military actions and is now a member of the UNRG. As the remnant of the official Soviet-line communist party, the PGT has strong international links. Its base of support is within Guatemala City's labor movement and agricultural workers on the south coast. Recently PGT has not been identified with any military actions.

Popular Opposition

About the same time the guerrillas began establishing their bases of support in western Guatemala, there were stirrings of grassroots and union organizing. In 1973, the country's teachers struck for higher wages. Widespread and open support for the teachers forced the government to meet the teachers' demands. Soon union organizing, which had been stifled since 1954, spread to other sectors, and progressive labor leaders arose to lead a revitalized labor movement. After the 1976 earthquake, union organizing had another burst of energy. Over 60 unions agreed to form the National Committee of Trade Union Unity (CNUS) in 1976. The federation built union solidarity and gave individual unions the courage to confront repression.

The blossoming of city-based organizing was accompanied in 1977 by the courageous strike of the Mam Indian miners in the Highlands. A 250-mile march by the strikers and their supporters to Guatemala City sparked a massive demonstration of sympathy by 100,000 supporters in the middle of Guatemala City. For the first time, despite heavy repression, Indians and *ladinos*, workers and peasants, were marching at the same time. Other rural organizing by Indian *campesinos* working in church-sponsored grassroots organizations caused increased government repression and death-squad activity in the *Altiplano*.

The military's frustration with the spread of *campesino* activism broke loose when hundreds of Kekchi Indians from Alta Verapaz met in Panzós with the town's mayor to discuss their loss of land to large landowners. Troops and vigilantes surrounded the peaceful gathering and opened fire, killing more than 100 Indians. The massacre horrified the nation but did not slow the momentum of popular organizing. A march to protest the massacre brought together 60,000 demonstrators, including scores of nuns and priests. One onlooker commented: "This is what Guatemala has been waiting for from the Church—for over 400 years."[27]

In 1978, the Campesino Unity Committee (CUC) surfaced in the Guatemalan countryside. Its leadership rose from the Christian-based communities that were mushrooming across the Highlands. CUC's Indian leader Emeterio Toj said: "I joined the struggle because of my revolutionary convictions: that is because we ourselves have suffered in the flesh all that inheritance from the invasion of 1524." A national political front of unions, popular organizations, peasant groups, and left-of-center political parties called the Democratic Front Against Repression (FDCR) formed in 1979.

The level of violence during this period in Guatemala made international headlines when, on January 31, 1980, a group composed mainly of CUC members occupied the Spanish Embassy to protest the military occupation of El Quiché province. Thirty-nine protestors were burned alive inside the embassy.

Shortly after the conflagration, CUC showed its undaunted strength by organizing a two-week strike among sugar-cane and cotton workers on the south coast. The remarkable unity between Indian and *ladino* migrant workers forced the government to agree to a $3.20-a-day minimum wage for rural workers. A conservative journalist for a Guatemala City daily observed that the strike represented "an organized demonstration of salaried agricultural workers . . . [which] indicates a state of class consciousness. . . . We are witnessing a new scene with actors different from the Indian who removes his hat, places it over his chest and humbly asks his *patrón* for a few *centavos* more."[28]

CUC in 1981 joined with the most militant groups of workers, slumdwellers, Christians, and students to form the January 31 Popular Front (FP-31), named after the embassy protest the year before. The FP-31 called for "much more profound forms of struggle" and offered itself as "a unitary structure to deepen support and coordination between the mass organizations."[29] Government repression increased during this period, forcing most mass organizations like CUC and the progressive unions like CNUS underground.

War on the Highlands

During this same period, highly successful guerrilla organizing in the Highlands presented a serious challenge to the military regime of General Romeo Lucas García (1978–1982). In October 1981, Lucas García unleashed a scorched-earth campaign that was continued by his successor General Efraín Ríos Montt. Army officers upset with the corruption of the Lucas García administration and its poor relations with Washington staged a coup in June 1982 that prevented Lucas García's handpicked successor from taking office.

The Ríos Montt coup gave the Reagan administration the opening it needed to resume economic and military aid to the repressive Guatemalan government. During the Carter administration, there was no new military aid authorized. Immediately after the coup, Washington told Ríos Montt that it was looking forward to having a "friendly and fruitful" relationship with Guatemala. Because repression slowed down in the cities, it was easier to put forth an image of an improving human-rights situation. But the military escalated terrorism in the countryside, especially against Indian communities which it suspected of supporting the guerrillas. Ríos Montt, an avid Christian evangelist, regarded the counterinsurgency campaign in the Highlands as a holy crusade against atheism and communism. A 1985 report by the Washington Offic on Latin America on the military's ongoing counterinsurgency campaign said that the army destroyed 440 villages and caused the death or disappearance of 50,000 to 75,000 persons.[30]

"First they came in helicopters and gathered the people together," explained a Guatemalan refugee who fled to Mexico. "Then, one by one they took them away and killed them. As for my own family, they killed seven. They carry guns but they don't use them on the children. They kill them with their hands. My uncle saw them grab the children by their feet and smash their heads against a post, or take a rope, tied it around the child, and three pull in one direction and three in another."[31]

As many as 150,000 Guatemalans, mostly Indian *campesinos*, fled into Mexico from 1980 to 1984 to escape the military's campaign of terror in the *Altiplano*. About 50,000 of these refugees live in camps operated by the Mexican government, but they continue to be harassed by Guatemalan army patrols who have entered the camps.

The innovative part of Ríos Montt's counterinsurgency strategy was known at first as the "Beans and Rifles" plan. Its two components were food distribution and civil-defense patrols.[32] The military organized Indian boys and men into patrols that were sent out ahead of the military to engage the guerrillas. These patrols also monitored all population movement in their villages. They were our "eyes and ears," said an army officer. One of the 14 points of the Code of Conduct of the civil patrols states: "I will capture any suspicious-looking person who enters my community and I will inform the nearest military commander."

By 1985, the civil patrol network in the Highlands numbered over 900,000 teenage boys and men. "It is difficult to overemphasize," observed Americas Watch in its report *A Nation of Prisoners*, "the extent to which the civil patrol system allows the military to effectively monitor all movement in the rural areas."

The other component of the Ríos Montt pacification campaign was a food-distribution program for those who cooperated with the military. "If you are with us, we'll feed you," said a Guatemalan army officer. "If not, we'll kill you."[33]

After burning and massacring its way across the Highlands from 1981 to 1983, the military reduced the amount of bloodshed in 1984 and emphasized the pacification aspects of its counterinsurgency effort. Although Ríos Montt was successful in improving relations with Washington and containing the guerrilla armies, he angered many generals and oligarchs with his religious fanaticism. Ríos Montt, who conceived of himself as a populist, also upset the economic elite by trying to increase export taxes.

In August 1983, Ríos Montt was replaced in a military coup by his Defense Minister General Oscar Mejía Víctores, who had undergone counterinsurgency training in Panama and the United States. Only two days before the coup, Mejía Víctores met with his Salvadoran and Honduran counterparts and U.S. General Paul Gorman of SOUTHCOM (U.S. Southern Command based in Panama). Apparently, Mejía Víctores had already decided on the coup but was given approval by Washington. As the new chief of state, he directed the implementation of the Plan of Assistance to the Areas of Conflict (PAAC), an elaborate pacification strategy involving model villages, food-for-work programs, and rural development. The military called the broadened pacification plan *"Techo, Trabajo, y Tortilla"* (Housing, Work, and Food). In July 1984, Mejía Víctores ordered that all government ministries coordinate their operations with the military for the success of the PAAC pacification plan.

The military manages its pacification program through three different organizations: the army's Civil Affairs office, the Committee for National Reconstruction (CRN), and the National Coordinating Committee.

CRN was the organization formed to direct reconstruction work after the 1976 earthquake. Public-relations officer Oscar Gallegos said that CRN now concentrates on what he called "the human catastrophe" in the Highlands. It is staffed by civilian social workers and "rural promoters" but is directed by the military. The National Coordinating Committee brings together representatives of all the principal ministries under the command of the Minister of Defense. Similar coordinating committees on a department and local level are directed by the commanding officer of that area. This is known as the Inter-Institutional Coordination System. All rural development work in the areas of conflict is coordinated through this system. According to the 1985 study by the Washington Office on Latin America (WOLA):

> The Inter-Institutional Coordination System maximizes army control over public administration and development and may allow the army to maintain real if not formal control of development institutions and processes even after a civilian government is installed.[34]

The army's civil affairs office trains Guatemalan soldiers in the art of pacification and coordinates the army's psychological operations. Known as the S-5 Division, this office oversees the civil patrol system and the army operations in the model villages.

The PAAC, which relies on international food donations and development assistance, encompasses the following programs:

- Construction of tightly controlled model villages that shelter the displaced and former guerrilla sympathizers.
- Food-for-work programs that give the government cheap labor for the new

infrastructure of the Highlands (roads, model cities, government buildings, and community services) while keeping the population tied to the military which supervises the food distribution.

- Re-education programs designed to build anticommunism and "integrate the Indians into the life of the nation" by teaching Spanish and *ladino* customs.
- Substitution of the Indian "culture of corn" with a new agricultural base in nontraditional agro-export production supervised by consultants from the United States, Israel, and Taiwan.
- New roads and model cities that allow military penetration of isolated areas.

The PAAC plan is based on the military's analysis about the causes of the Indian rebellion and their support for the guerrillas. The government lost control of the Highlands, the military contends, because of the geographic and cultural isolation of the Indians. One section of the PAAC plan, called "Operation Ixil," states that it "is essential to include an intense, profound, and well-designed psychological campaign to capture the mentality of the Ixils to make them feel part of the Guatemalan nation." Specially trained army Civil Affairs units are responsible for the pacification program. "We are more like social workers than soldiers," said one of these officers stationed in Nebaj.[35]

The scorched-earth terrorism inflicted on the Highlands broke most of the links between the Indian villages and the guerrilla army. The ties that the Guerrilla Army of the Poor (EGP) had developed with the Indian villages of the *Altiplano* were largely cut off. The guerrilla armies had not been able to protect them against the genocidal tactics of the Guatemalan army. The army's food distribution and work programs encouraged many refugees and guerrilla supporters to come out of the mountains.

After experiencing the horror of the *kaibiles* (elite counterinsurgency troops), many Guatemalan Indians opted at least temporarily for survival over open rebellion. Given their long history of oppression, it is unlikely that the military's pacification programs will erase their memories of injustice. It also is unlikely that the military will be able to truly develop the Highlands without addressing the volatile issue of agrarian reform. As one Ixil elder said, "For years, they have stolen our sons to be soldiers, and our daughters for pleasure. It will take more than beans to atone for that history."[36]

On the Election Stage

In line with Washington's political stabilization plans for the region, Guatemala, like Honduras and El Salvador, has moved away from complete military control of the state political apparatus. Pushed by Washington toward "democratization," the Mejía Víctores regime authorized elections for a constituent assembly in July 1984 and for a new president in November 1985.

Politics in Guatemala is a Byzantine world in which generals and oligarchs plot for control of the presidency and the principal ministries. The 1984–1985 elections have added a new dimension to the complexity and intrigue of Guatemalan politics. The many political parties that registered to compete in elections presented a dizzying array of personalities and ever-changing alliances. Interparty vendettas have been responsible for several deaths. The high level of violence in Guatemalan politics has forced party leaders to travel in armor-plated jeeps with retinues of bodyguards.

The 1984–1985 elections were held in an atmosphere of fear and uncertainty, and the political contenders were far from representative of the varying political philosophies present in the country. As in El Salvador, the political left had been silenced by terrorism and did not participate. Even for the center and center-right political parties, politics is an extremely hazardous occupation in Guatemala.

Despite these serious drawbacks, the 1984 constituent assembly elections proved to some that Guatemala could take at least a small step toward democratization. But the military's tolerance of electioneering does not mean that it will allow an actual transfer of decision making from the military to an elected government. The British Parliamentary Human Rights Group predicted: "Even if a civilian president was elected in 1985, it is highly improbable that he would have any control over the Guatemalan military. The army will keep their hands firmly on the levers of power in the country as they have for 30 years." The human rights group also noted that political choices in the July 1984 constituent assembly elections were "severely limited," and that "none of the parties had proposed a change in the structure of power in the country."[37]

Another perspective on the "democratization" was offered in a May Day 1985 proclamation by a Guatemalan trade union: "What democratization can one speak of in Guatemala, when one has seen only murders and kidnappings and the high cost of living and our *campesinos* forced to work without compensation for the government in their Civil Patrols?"[38]

As in El Salvador and Honduras, the political process was designed to avoid stepping on the toes of the military. Despite rising popular pressure to initiate an Argentine-like inquiry into the military's role in "disappearances," the Christian Democrats backed away from any promises to prosecute those in the armed forces guilty of human-rights violations. "We think the past must be forgotten," said their leader Vinicio Cerezo Arévalo, who has also promised not to pursue an agrarian reform program. Many Guatemalans within the political process believe that the Guatemalan generals have tasted too much power and wealth to retire completely to their barracks.

In late 1985, the Guatemalan people elected Vinicio Cerezo to be their president. Financed in part by the United States, the presidential election paved the way for an influx of bilateral and multilateral aid. A civilian administration will bring international and (to a lesser degree) national legitimacy to government in Guatemala. But having already promised not to infringe on the considerable power of the military or to push for social and economic reforms, the significance of the Cerezo election is limited, even if he does manage to keep the presidential seat. Cerezo had only to look to the problems faced by his Christian Democrat counterpart in El Salvador, Napoleon Duarte, to appreciate his own tenuous and largely powerless position.

Cerezo, a consummate politician, has, however, been able to take some significant steps towards peace in Central America. He has refused to condemn Nicaragua, and has called for renewed peace negotiations. Within the country, he has requested that the military abandon the model villages and has called for the enforcement of the idle land tax. Forces on all sides threaten the stability of the Cerezo government: military, human rights advocates calling for prosecution of military criminals, the private sector's refusal to pay higher taxes, and increased trade union activity.

Political Parties
The Right

The leading parties of the extreme right are MLN and CAN while the key party of the center-right is UCN. Although the right-wing parties seek to work within the framework of government, they are not entirely separate from paramilitary operations.

National Liberation Movement (MLN): Headed by renowned anticommunist Mario Sandoval Alarcón, widely regarded as the father of Central American death squads. Formed immediately after the 1954 coup, the MLN is associated with death squads as far back as the 1960s. The MLN has close links with El Salvador's ARENA.

Its 1982 vice-presidential candidate Lionel Sisniega Otero once explained why the MLN is called "the party of organized violence": "Color organized is a painting. Sound organized is a melody. Violence organized is strength."[39] MLN's Mario Sandoval, who formed the organization in 1954 as the "party of liberation," has long harbored hopes of becoming president of Guatemala. He has links to the business community and the army, but his main base is in the traditional agricultural oligarchy.

Authentic Nationalist Central (CAN): Organized around former President General Carlos Manuel Arana Osorio (1970–1974), CAN is sometimes allied with the MLN. Its leader, Juan Carlos Simons, resigned in 1985 to form the New Right, which is said to be a mass movement—not just political—against corrupt and authoritarian government and calls for a "free society and free economy."

Party of Anticommunist Unification (PUA): Formed by Lionel Sisniega Otero, Mario Sandoval's running mate in the 1982 elections, PUA is strengthened by such prominent anticommunists as Luis Alfonso López, formerly of CAN, and Jorge Bonilla of the PID.

The Center and Center-Right

Union of the National Center (UCN): A center-right party recently formed by Jorge Carpio Nicolle, publisher of *El Grafico*. Carpio, who participated in the "Liberation Army" that overthrew Arbenz in 1954, characterizes himself as a member of a "new breed" of business owners. A firm supporter of the United States, Carpio says, "If it wasn't for them, Guatemala would be a socialist country now." While Carpio has offered his party to the Guatemalan public as the party of moderation, the UCN maintains close ties to the military. It promised both the private sector and the military that it would not pursue any reforms that would alter the present economic structure. Numerous reports of CIA and armed forces support of the UCN circulate in Guatemala. One report said that Carpio Nicolle received loans totaling $3 million on easy terms from the Bank of the Army.[40]

Democratic Party of National Cooperation (PDCN): Headed by born-again evangelist Jorge Antonio Serrano, this new party hopes to win 75 percent of the evangelist vote. Serrano, a rising political star in Guatemala, calls the country's neutral stand on Nicaragua "infantile."

Guatemala Christian Democratic Party (DCG): This was the most progressive of the centrist parties in the 1960s but was seriously damaged by the fraudulent defeat of its candidate General Efraín Riós Montt in the 1974 presidential elections. It was later decimated by the exit of many leaders who formed the FDC-5. The party was further weakened by the assassination of its most progressive members and the abandonment of the party by many of its younger leaders. The DCG affirmed its conservative position during the 1985 election campaign when it promised not to embark "on banking or land reforms nor on the nationalization of privately-owned enterprises or property." It also announced that if it came to power it would not seek to prosecute civilian or military officials for corruption or human-rights abuses. Vinicio Cerezo Arévalo, who has been the target of several assassination attempts, leaves his heavily guarded home only with a squad of bodyguards. He favors accommodation with the military and the private sector. While he professes to hold the banner of the popular opposition, raised in the late 1970s by Manuel Colom Argueta and Alberto Fuentes Mohr, Cerezo and the DCG tend toward center-right politics.

The Center-Left

Democratic Socialist Party (PSD): This center-left party disbanded following the assassination of PSD founder Alberto Fuentes Mohr and 15 other party leaders during the Lucas García regime (1978–1982). PSD's leaders returned from exile in Costa Rica in early 1985 to prepare the PSD for the November 1985 elections.

By campaigning for fairer distribution of wealth, the PSD slate, headed by Mario Solorzano, hoped to garner the huge protest vote.

United Front of the Revolution (FUR): This center-left party is headed by two leaders widely respected in reformist circles, Edmundo López Durán and Augusto Toledo Peñate. This was the party of Colom Argueta, the popular former mayor of Guatemala City, who was assassinated in 1979.

Closer Ties with Washington

The Guatemalan military and right-wing politicians have a friend in Washington. President Reagan is regarded as one of the few U.S. politicians who understands the situation in Guatemala. Guatemalan generals and rightists called Reagan's election in 1980 a victory of anticommunism over communism. As Roberto Alejos Arzu, a right-wing agro-industrialist, said: "Reagan is one of the few people in the high political sphere who understands what is going on down here."[41]

The U.S. involvement in the 1954 coup gave Washington a special interest in Guatemala. As a House of Representatives report concluded in 1957, the United States was more than a simple observer in Guatemala. It was "a strategic country for the defense of the Western Hemisphere."[42] After 1954, Washington promoted Guatemala as a "showcase of democracy." The initial enthusiasm for the "liberated" country, however, waned over the next two decades as the United States grew increasingly more uncomfortable with the gross human-rights violations of the military governments. The human-rights policies of the Carter administration led to the halt of military aid to Guatemala.

The Reagan administration was not so circumspect about embracing Guatemala as a friend and ally. In 1983 Reagan sought a restoration of Guatemala's eligibility status. Military aid officially resumed in 1985 in the amount of $300,000 with $4.8 million more approved for 1986. The staggering increase in economic aid, from $20 million in 1984 to over $100 million in 1985, was slated for programs in the Highlands.

Along with food donations of the UN's World Food Program (most of which is PL480 food from the United States), AID funds provide the principal support for the military's pacification plan for the Highlands. AID offers five main kinds of support: 1) food, distributed by the UN and PVOs in food-for-work programs, 2) bilingual education programs, schools, and health clinics in the military-controlled areas, 3) roadbuilding, 4) funds for nontraditional agricultural and agro-exports, and 5) reconstruction- and rural-development programs channeled through PVOs that work with the military's Committee for National Reconstruction (CRN).

In its 1986 strategy statement for Guatemala, the AID Mission in Guatemala City said that the priority should be "to improve the current economic situation and address the political unrest in the *Altiplano*." It noted that it could implement all its own goals, such as agricultural diversification, while simultaneously supporting the Guatemalan government's "commitment to provide for the previously disadvantaged population in the *Altiplano*." Moreover, the AID Mission observed: "The government views AID as the best source of assistance in the development of the *Altiplano*, and consequently AID can have a major impact in shaping programs undertaken there."[43]

In 1984 President Reagan appointed Alberto Piedra as the new ambassador to Guatemala. In his book *Guatemala: A Promise in Peril*, Ambassador Piedra, a right-wing Cuban American, defends the 1954 CIA-backed overthrow of the Arbenz government. Piedra served on the advisory board of the Council for Inter-American Security, a Washington-based group that seeks to reverse what it says is the military decline of the United States and to forge a new alliance "in order to protect freedom and our country's southern flank."

Human-Rights Improvement Questionable

The U.S. State Department has claimed that the human-rights situation in Guatemala has been improving since 1983. While death-squad activity in the cities did let up during the Rios Montt regime, the level of repression resumed during the reign of Mejía Víctores. A report issued in 1985 by the British Parliamentary Human Rights Group stood in contrast to U.S. State Department statements about improving human rights. The report *Bitter and Cruel* summarized Guatemala's political reality: 100,000 killed since 1960, 100 political assassinations a month in 1984, 10 disappearances a week in 1984, and the presence of 100,000 orphans and 500,000 displaced in Guatemala.

An organization composed of relatives of the disappeared formed in 1984 to protect human rights. The Mutual Support Group (GAM) formed when several relatives of the disappeared started talking at the city mortuary while looking for the bodies of family members. According to 1984 figures from the GAM, over 3000 persons disappeared and over 10,000 children were orphaned during the first year and a half of the Mejía Víctores regime.

President Mejía Víctores called the Mutual Support Group "a pressure group which is being manipulated for subversion." Two weeks after Mejía Víctores made that statement, two of the leaders of the human-rights group were found murdered. Its publicity director, Hector Gomez, was kidnapped and his body found later with his tongue torn out. The 24-year-old secretary of the group, María del Rosario Godoy, was killed with her son and brother four days later in what the military said was a car accident.[44] Godoy had spoken at Gomez's funeral and blamed the military regime for his death. "The assassination of our leaders will not intimidate us," she stated. "On the contrary, it drives us to struggle with more strength so that our loved ones may be returned to us alive."[45]

Economic Crisis Threatens Stability

Since 1980, the Guatemalan economy has been in the doldrums. Like the other Central American economies, Guatemala has been hit hard by the bearish world market and high interest rates. The regional crisis has also hit Guatemalan industrialists hard. Their traditional domination of the Central American Common Market is now sagging. In 1983, the IMF began telling Guatemala that it had a fiscal crisis that needed immediate attention. In line with IMF recommendations, the Ríos Montt regime imposed a 10 percent sales tax, but Mejía Víctores angered the IMF by reducing that tax to 7 percent in 1984.

It was in 1984 when Guatemala really began to feel the crunch. Government income that year was a gaping 40 percent below projections, and by year's end, the government was forced to recognize the parallel foreign-exchange market. Although the government refused to alter the official exchange of one-to-one parity with the dollar (the rate established in 1925), the quetzal was allowed to float on the parallel market. The country's international reserves fell so low by early 1985 that the government considered selling off all its gold reserves. When it hesitated, rumors circulated that the nation's gold—like so much else in Guatemala—had been stolen by the generals.

Another blow to the economy that came in 1984 was the breakdown of the Chixoy hydroelectric dam. The dam, which was originally slated to cost $360 million, had already cost Guatemalans $860 million by 1984. The announcement that the dam would cost several million to repair because of faulty construction work led to angry charges by the private sector that the military's inefficiency was bleeding the country dry.

One difference between IMF's recommendations for economic stabilization for Guatemala and those for other Central American nations is the larger burden that falls on Guatemala's industrial and agro-export sectors. Military regimes in Guatemala have historically squeezed the poor for the revenues to run government, leaving the wealthy to pay only small amounts of income, production, and export taxes. In Latin America, only Haiti has a lower tax rate.

Exporters in Guatemala are notorious for evading the few taxes that do exist. As of 1983, export tax collection had dropped by three-fourths from 1978. Direct taxes on property and income in Guatemala are among the lowest in the world. Another major problem that the IMF wants the government to address is the vast capital flight to the United States. Between 1980 and 1985, Guatemala lost over $1.1 billion in foreign exchange just to the United States.[46]

Guatemala's economic crisis has created a serious inter-ruling-class split between the private sector and the military. The Committee of Agricultural, Commercial, Industrial, and Financial Associations (CACIF) speaks for most sectors of the country's economic elite. It blames the military's corruption and mismanagement for the financial crisis. The military regime responds that the private sector must shoulder more of the costs of running the government if the economy is to get back on its feet.

Divisions between the two factions began to surface in early 1984 when the National Center for Economic Research (CIEN), an organization tied financially to the private sector, published an analysis of the government's 1984 budget. "The national budget," said CIEN, "is a masterpiece in the art of concealing figures." According to CIEN, over half the budget will be lost to "corruption, debt, squandering, and confidential disbursement." CIEN said the most shameful thing about the budget was the "confidential disbursements that are used to pay government-sponsored paramilitary groups and death squads, maintain clandestine jails, and bribe delegates, politicians, journalists, ex-triumverates, union leaders, and one or another business leader."[47]

The split deepened in 1985 when the military prohibited CACIF from publishing a newspaper ad that attributed the economic crisis to excessive public spending. CACIF demonstrated its power when it responded to several government controls by dramatically raising food prices. Consumer anger was directed at the government, and the Mejía Víctores regime called off the financial controls and acceded to CACIF demands that two key cabinet members be fired.

Guatemala's rising debt burden and expanding government deficits together with pressure from the IMF are pushing the government to take measures to cut capital flight and increase government revenues through taxes. In 1985, the Mejía Víctores regime announced that the budget of most ministries would be cut and that there would be no increases except for the ministry of defense, which received a 10 percent budget increase. The budget for defense has jumped from 10 percent of the total government in 1975 to 22 percent in 1985. The prospects for a resolution of the country's economic crisis, without massive infusions of foreign aid, are not good.

The powerful and unrelenting private sector will resist any attempts to cut into its profit levels and will count on factions of the high echelons of the military to support their position. It has already shown that it will resort to the manipulation of popular pressure for its own ends—no matter if the tactics lead to large jumps in unemployment and hunger or to increased military repression.

Coca-Cola and Union Organizing

Coca-Cola is the best known and most scorned TNC in Guatemala. On two occasions, Coca-Cola has been at the center of labor controversy that brought worldwide attention to the company's operations in Guatemala.

In the mid-1970s the resurgence of union organizing reached a critical level when workers of Coca-Cola's franchise Embotelladora Guatemalteca tried to form a union in 1975. Workers knew it would be a difficult struggle because the franchise owner, John Trotter, was known for his extreme right-wing politics.

Trotter, a Houston businessman, was a leader of the anticommunist Guatemalan Freedom Foundation, which reputedly maintained close connections with the military and the death squads.

In March 1974, Trotter fired 152 labor activists, an action which angered workers enough that they occupied the plant. Trotter called in the police, who stormed the factory and evicted the workers by force. A week after the eviction, over 60 unions formed the National Committee of Trade Union Unity (CNUS) to defend the rights of the Coke workers and other unions being attacked by combined private-sector and government repression. During the next four years, CNUS organized labor solidarity throughout the country.

Backed by CNUS, the Coke workers organized a hunger strike and other protests outside the bottling plant. Popular support of the Coke workers pushed the government to intervene in the dispute and legally recognize the union. Trotter then tried to break the union by subdividing the operations of the factory. Repression was stepped up. From 1978 to 1980, the union leadership was systematically eliminated. Death-squad violence cut down eight union leaders of the Coca-Cola union. Pedro Quevado was shot in his delivery truck. Manuel Lopez had his throat slit while making deliveries. Arnulfo Gomez had his lips and tongue cut off before being shot in the head.

These brutal attempts to crush the union only increased popular support for the Coke workers. Coca-Cola posters and billboards were defaced to read: *"Coca— Chispa de muerte"* (Spark of death). One U.S. investor in Guatemala told *Newsweek*: "Coca-Cola is becoming a leading brand name of oppression here, and believe me, they've got heavy competition."

In early 1980, the International Food and Allied Workers (Geneva) called an international boycott against the Coca-Cola company. The worldwide support campaign for the Guatemalan workers mushroomed to involve union-led boycotts in 50 countries. International pressure from unions and churches persuaded Coca-Cola officials in Atlanta to sign an agreement to buy out Trotter's contract and to manage the unionized plant for five years. The settlement was a testimony to the steadfast courage of the Guatemalan workers and to the power of international solidarity.

By 1983, however, Coca-Cola in Guatemala City was again trying to break the union by splitting up its operations and declaring bankruptcy at the unionized central plant. Workers said the supposed financial crisis at Embotelladora Guatemalteca was a ruse to break the union. As the *Financial Times* noted: "The very thought of Coca-Cola [in Guatemala] going bust is, of course, absurd."[48] When the company closed its operations in February 1984, its 400 workers occupied the plant to block the removal of the equipment to other locations.

A new labor federation called the Coordinator of National Trade Union Unity (CONUS) formed in 1984. In many ways it replaced the earlier federation CNUS, which had been decimated by repression. CONUS offered financial and material support to the occupiers of the Coca-Cola plant. The bottling plant was a symbol to Guatemalan workers of the possibilities of trade union solidarity. "If we don't help the Coca-Cola union," asserted one union member, "then we won't survive. If Coca-Cola fails, we all fall."[49]

Once again the plight of the union attracted widespread support from outside the country. Another international boycott forced Coca-Cola to the bargaining table, and the TNC agreed to reopen the plant under new ownership and to respect all union rights. Significantly, Coca-Cola also agreed to provide compensation to the families of murdered union activists. The reopening of the plant in March 1985 was a tremendous victory for the Guatemalan labor movement, which had been rejuvenated by the resolve of the Coke employees.

The history of the Guatemalan labor movement is a history of martyrs. In the cafeteria at the Coca-Cola plant, the framed photos of the eight murdered union leaders hang on the wall in commemoration. Each union has its own list of members that have been kidnapped and killed. The new surge in labor activism that began in 1984 has added further names to that list. But through innovative ways of organizing and a bold approach, the union movement has made steady advances.

TNCs in Guatemala

Three decades of political violence have not frightened off U.S. investors. The American Chamber of Commerce, which moved its office after a bombing, still has a healthy membership list in Guatemala. Over 400 U.S. businesses operate in the country, including 90 of the top 500 U.S. corporations. In a report on the labor situation, the Chamber reported in 1980 that none of the U.S. businesses it contacted was "experiencing or expecting to experience any unmanageable labor problem." It said that the "general feeling is that political agitation is imported rather than internal."[50]

The TNCs carry out their business with the full cooperation of the military. "We guarantee your investments," said former Army Chief of Staff General Benedicto Lucas García. "The government has said so. The president has said so. Those in charge of the security of the country have said so. I want all North Americans to come and invest in Guatemala."

Foreign investment has diversified substantially since the days of United Fruit. TNCs now have investments in finance, manufacturing, services, and mining as well as agriculture. Del Monte (a subsidiary of R.J. Reynolds) bought out United Fruit's banana subsidiary in 1972. In 1983, a Venezuelan banana company named Covenco became a partner in Del Monte's Bandegua banana operations near Puerto Barrios. In early 1985, Richard Stone, President Reagan's former roving ambassador in Central America, successfully negotiated Bendegua's demand that it not process its funds through the country's Central Bank. As a result of the negotiations, General Mejía Víctores also agreed to loan $30 million to Bandegua, which employs 5500 workers and claims annual export sales of $75 million.[51]

The other U.S. TNC with plantations in Guatemala is Goodyear, which has several rubber plantations that cover over 63,000 acres. Ralston Purina has an animal feed mill, grows ornamental plants, and owns restaurants. Guatemala is the country with the largest number of businesses that receive financing from the Latin American Agricultural Development Corporation (LAAD). LAAD agribusinesses mainly produce and process nontraditional exports like broccoli and snow peas. Recently, LAAD has financed cardamom exports.

The principal founder of LAAD, BankAmerica, is a powerful force in Guatemala. Many of the country's most powerful landowners, industrialists, and generals have been among its clients. It extended a personal loan to the nation's president, General Lucas García, to allow him to purchase his 7000-acre cattle estate in the Northern Transverse Strip. BankAmerica has financed the meat-packing firm PROKESA, which is owned by Fred Sherwood, a former president of the American Chamber of Commerce and vigorous supporter of the military government.

Sherwood, who was involved in early attempts in the 1960s to form death squads in Guatemala, said: "Why should we do anything about the death squads? They're bumping off the commies, our enemies. I'd give them more power. Hell, I'd give them some cartridges if I could, and everyone else would, too. They're bumping off our enemies, which are also the enemies of the United States."[52] Among those "bumped off" were six of PROKESA's employees in 1980 who were trying to organize a union.

BankAmerica, which began operating in Guatemala one year after the 1954 coup, also has provided direct support to the military government by maintaining accounts with the government itself, the military-controlled ministry of telecommunications, and the *Instituto de Prevision Militar*, the army's retirement fund.[53] BankAmerica official Keith Parker, in a 1980 interview, said, "When you've got a situation like you have here, you need the strongest government you can get. If you use human rights in a country with guerrillas, you're not going to get anywhere."[54]

On the outskirts of Guatemala City is the country's pharmaceutical strip. Seventeen of the top twenty U.S. pharmaceutical firms are active in Guatemala. In 1985, Guatemalan dailies reported that these companies enjoyed profit margins of up to 300 percent for some of their products. Of the eight top accounting firms, seven maintain offices in Guatemala. Three of the top five U.S. food and beverage companies have processing operations in the country: Beatrice manufactures snack foods and Coca-Cola produces instant coffee.

Another food processing giant, Warner Lambert, considers Guatemala its principal location for the manufacture of Chiclets and health-care products like cough drops. Its subsidiary in Guatemala City, Productos Adams, recently closed down one of its plants and reopened under another name to block union organizing. U.S.-based Philip Morris produces cigarettes for Guatemala's smokers. All top ten U.S. chemical companies have branches in Guatemala for pesticide manufacture and distribution.

The four leading car rental firms have outlets in Guatemala City and three hotel chains—Sheraton, Ramada Inn, and Westin Hotels— help make tourists feel at home. In downtown Guatemala City, McDonalds and Pizza Hut (PepsiCo) serve up their famous fast food. All the top five U.S. oil firms are also active in Guatemala, mostly in distribution. Foreign investment in the petroleum exploration and production sector in 1985 was over $30 million. A new company with U.S. capital, Peten Petroleum, joined four other companies that have signed contracts under the 1983 Hydrocarbons Law: Texaco Exploration, Hispanoil, Petrobas International, and Texaco Canada Resources.[55] The new law, in an attempt to breathe new life into the industry, lowered government production-sharing requirements.

Oil production is about 6000 barrels per day (about one quarter of national consumption), but the government is optimistic about a greatly expanded petroleum sector. For the last several years, U.S. government officials have regarded the country's supposed oil resources as the salvation of the economy. The State Department once called Guatemala "the plum of Central America" because of its petroleum potential. The slow rate of discovery, however, has caused enthusiasm to dissipate.

In 1983, Eximbal, a U.S.-Canadian nickel mining venture closed because of high fuel costs and low international nickel prices. There were signs in 1985 that the company, which is a joint venture between International Nickel Corporation (Canada) and Hanna Mining, was interested in resuming its mining operations. When it shut down the mine, it owed the government $5.9 million in back taxes.

Resistance Won't Disappear

Three decades have passed since the United States in a fit of anticommunism overthrew a democratically elected government in Guatemala. Ever since then, the Guatemalan people have been subject to horrific violence and unrelenting repression. All attempts to renew the reforms of the Arbenz period have been ruthlessly crushed. Describing the nature of death-squad violence in Guatemala, the popular center-left politician Alberto Fuentes Mohr said: "Every single murder is of a key person— people in each sector or movement who have the ability to organize the population around a cause." Several days later, Fuentes Mohr fell to a hail of bullets in the streets of Guatemala.

Despite this constant violence, the resistance continues in Guatemala. Union leaders and students disappear but their relatives march in protest. The Catholic Church, which blessed the military officers who "liberated" the country in 1954, has also raised its voice against military and death-squad terrorism. Each time that the military declares that it has wiped out the guerrillas they resurface to challenge military rule. The generals and the oligarchs of Guatemala have been trying for 30 years to quiet all forms of popular opposition. It is a testament to the courage and democratic principles of the Guatemalan people that so many continue to oppose the repression that was installed in 1954.

1 AID, *Congressional Presentation FY85, Latin America and the Caribbean, Vol. 2*, p.88.
2 Jonathan L. Fried et al. (eds.), *Guatemala in Rebellion: Unfinished History* (New York: Grove, 1983).
3 Instituto de Ciencias Ambientales y Technologia Agrícola (ICATA), "Perfil Ambiental de la República de Guatemala," April 1984. Report contracted by AID Mission in Guatemala City.
4 Eric Wolf, *Sons of the Shaking Earth* (Chicago: University of Chicago, 1959), pp.31,195.
5 Stephen Schlesinger and Stephen Kinzer, *Bitter Fruit: The Untold Story of the American Coup in Guatemala* (Garden City, N.Y.: Doubleday, 1982), p.70.
6 Ibid.
7 Thomas McCann, *An American Company: The Tragedy of United Fruit* (New York: Crown, 1976), p.45.
8 Susanne Jonas and David Tobis (eds.), *Guatemala* (Berkeley and New York: NACLA, 1974), p.49.
9 Blanche Cook, *The Declassified Eisenhower: A Divided Legacy of Peace and Political Warfare* (Garden City, N.Y.: Doubleday, 1981), p.224.
10 Thomas and Marjorie Melville, *Guatemala, The Politics of Land Ownership* (New York: Free, 1971), p.51.
11 Cook, op.cit.
12 McCann, op.cit.
13 Jonas and Tobis, op.cit.; Cook, op.cit.; Schlesinger and Kinzer, op.cit.; Lars Schoultz, "US Policy Toward Guatemala" (unpublished paper, University of North Carolina, 1981).
14 Cook, op.cit., p.278.
15 Jonas and Tobis, op.cit., p.75.
16 Ibid., p.81.
17 GAO, "Report: Examination of Economic and Technical Assistance Program for Guatemala, International Cooperation Administration, Department of State, 1955–1960," (Washington), 1960, p.19; Jonas and Tobis, op.cit., p.81.
18 Jonas and Tobis, op.cit.
19 Carlos Fuentes, "Three Dates of Change," in Marvin E. Gettleman et al. (eds.), *El Salvador: Central America in the New Cold War* (New York: Grove, 1981).
20 Luis Cardoza y Aragón, *La Revolución Guatemalteca* (Montevideo: Ediciones Pueblos Unidos, 1956), p.74.
21 Penny Lernoux, *The Cry of the People* (Garden City, N.Y.: Doubleday, 1980), p.186.
22 Jenny Pearce, *Under the Eagle* (London: Latin America Bureau, 1981), p.68.
23 James Y. Bradford, American Friends Service Committee, "Guatemala: A People Besieged," January 1978.
24 Amnesty International, "Memorandum Presented to the Government of the Republic of Guatemala Following a Mission to the Country from 10 to 15 August 1979" (London), 1979.
25 Description of the armed opposition groups and their history drawn largely from George Black, "Guatemala: The War is Not Over," in *NACLA Report on the Americas*, March/April 1983, pp.9–10, and Fried, et al., op.cit.
26 *Compañero: The International Magazine of Guatemala's Guerrilla Army of the Poor (EGP)*, 1982.
27 Black, op.cit., p.5, and *Latin America Political Report*, October 6 and 13, 1978.
28 Cited in *Inforpress*, February 28, 1980.
29 Black, op.cit., p.8; interview with the FP-31 in *ALAI*, March 27, 1981, and founding communique of the FP-31, January 31, 1981.

30 Chris Krueger and Kjell Enge, *Security and Development Conditions in the Guatemalan Highlands*, (Washington: Washington Office on Latin America, 1985), p.v.

31 Americas Watch, "Human Rights in Guatemala: No Neutrals Allowed," November 23, 1982, p.13.

32 Mario Sandoval Alarcón is said to be the originator of the civil patrol system. The plan was held in reserve until Defense Minister Benedicto Lucas, brother of then-president Lucas García, launched it in late 1981. The Patrullas Auto-defensas Civles (PACs) became a leading element in the counterinsurgency strategy of Ríos Montt.

33 *New York Times*, July 18, 1982.

34 Krueger and Enge, op.cit.

35 Interview by Tom Barry, May 1984.

36 *Newsweek*, December 13, 1982.

37 Interim Report of the British Parliamentary Human Rights Group, "Bitter and Cruel," November 1984, p.29.

38 Statement of the Central American Glass Works Union (STICAVIA) on May 2, 1985; *Enfoprensa*, May 17, 1985.

39 Cited in the Canadian Broadcasting Corporation's program, "Fifth Estate: Guatemala," aired October 1, 1980.

40 *SIAG Press*, August 31, 1984.

41 *Green Revolution*, Winter 1981, p.50.

42 Foreign Affairs Committee, House of Representatives, "Report of the Special Study Mission to Guatemala," March 1957, p.15.

43 AID, *Country Development Strategy Statement for 1984*.

44 *LARR*, June 8, 1984.

45 *Barricada International*, April 18, 1985.

46 Statement of Minister of Economy reported in *Enfoprensa*, April 19, 1985.

47 *Enfoprensa*, February 24, 1984.

48 IUF/North American Trade Union Delegation, "A Special Report on the Occupation of the Coca-Cola Bottling Plant in Guatemala," p.11.

49 *Labor Notes*, January 1985.

50 Association of American Chambers of Commerce, *AACCLA Outlook*, Fourth Quarter, 1980.

51 *Washington Report on Latin America*, March 5, 1985.

52 Allan Nairn, "To Defend Our Way of Life: An Interview with a U.S. Businessman," in Fried et al., op. cit. Fred Sherwood told John Chancellor of NBC: "A number of us thought that we could stop the movement (leftist) through the organization of something of the style of the vigilantes or night attackers. For example, there was a group that tried to bring some Puerto Ricans and Cubans. They proposed the business of killing or assassinating 12 communists for $50,000. We did what was possible to raise this money, but we only managed to collect a part of this sum so that this affair never happened. The US government helped with its power these small groups and helped organize the groups of resistance." Cited in "The Science of Spying," aired on NBC May 4, 1965.

53 *Multinational Monitor*, October 1982.

54 Allan Nairn, "Bank of America Asked to Explain its Support for the Guatemalan Death Squads," *Multinational Monitor*, March 1982, p.14.

55 *Business Latin America*, November 21, 1984.

CHAPTER 12

Honduras

∎

Trends
- **Imposition of austerity programs will threaten the stability of government.**
- **No real economic growth.**
- **Military in consultation with U.S. Embassy makes major economic, political, and military decisions even though civilians are officially in charge.**
- **Willingness of Washington to provide aid even if government slips into military hands.**
- **Growing resistance to U.S. military presence and interference in national politics.**
- **Continued acceptance of *contras* and U.S. militarization if Washington agrees to maintain high levels of aid.**
- **Mounting tensions between *contras* and Hondurans.**
- **Increased politicization of workers and peasants.**
- **More militant land occupations.**

∎

OF THE CENTRAL American nations, Honduras best fits the label of Banana Republic. Two corporate banana giants have cast their shadow over the country's political and economic life for over 80 years. Despite this long exposure to the ways of U.S. business, Honduras remains the third poorest country of the hemisphere, following Haiti and Bolivia. Banana enclaves prospered while national development was ignored.

Statistics indicate the staggering magnitude of underdevelopment in Honduras. Only 10 percent of rural Hondurans (who make up over 60 percent of the population) benefit from electricity. Seven out of ten Hondurans live in conditions of desperate poverty, and less than 15 percent of rural Hondurans have access to drinking water. Eight out of ten rural Hondurans live in wretched hovels, and fifty children die each day from preventable diseases.

Since 1980 Honduras has changed quickly from a Banana Republic to a U.S.

military outpost. Formerly a remote outpost on the U.S. geopolitical frontier, Honduras has been chosen to play a central role in Washington's plan to roll back revolution in Central America. Washington found a willing accomplice in President Suazo Córdova. With the right amount of military and economic aid to keep the generals content and his political associates smiling, the Honduran president adopted U.S. foreign policy as his own. "Due to its geopolitical situation," said the Honduran president in 1982, "[Honduras] is of fundamental strategic importance in pacifying the region and stabilizing democratic, economic, and social progress in Central America."[1]

A Banana Republic Is Made

In the early 1500s, the Spanish *conquistadores*, lured by precious metals, trampled over the fading Mayan civilization based at Copan and the pine-covered mountains of Honduras. In the 1570s, they were rewarded by the discovery of a major silver lode that ran below what is now the capital city of Tegucigalpa.

In 1821, the Central American region gained its independence from Spain. The Federal Republic of Central America, a chaotic experiment, split apart in 1838 and Honduras became its own nation. For the balance of the nineteenth century, creole *latifundistas* sat tight on their cattle ranches and depended on communities of sharecroppers to produce the food they needed. Other Central American nations developed an agro-export economy baed on the production of indigo, cocoa, and coffee, but Honduras missed even this distorted form of development.

Loans, primarily from the British, set the stage for the eventual domination of Honduras by U.S. financial interests. At the turn of the century, U.S. financiers assumed the servicing of European debts under a plan formulated by President Taft whereby the debts would be guaranteed by a U.S. customs receivership. This creditor/debtor type of arrangement placed the U.S. government in an ideal position to manipulate Honduran politics.

In other parts of Central America (Guatemala, El Salvador, and Costa Rica), national oligarchies arose in the latter part of the nineteenth century with the development of the coffee industry. As the region's first agrarian capitalists, the coffee growers and exporters oversaw the construction of the infrastructure they needed. But the coffee boom bypassed Honduras because there was no group of business-minded entrepreneurs to push this type of agricultural development forward.

The first banana concession in Honduras was granted in 1899, when the Vacarro brothers of New Orleans moved into the Valle del Aguan on the Atlantic coast. By 1914, the Vacarro concessions totaled 100,000 acres, but their chief competitors in the country—Samuel "Sam, The Banana Man" Zemurray and the United Fruit Company—were busy amassing an even more immense banana empire.[2] These two fruit kingdoms soon dominated both the politics and the economy of Honduras.

After less than 15 years of business, the banana companies accounted for two-thirds of Honduran exports and ended up with control of the national railroad. The banana enclave had swallowed up the country's weak national economy and political system. Honduras became the quintessential Banana Republic. The banana companies' ownership of over a million acres of the country's best land meant that Honduran *campesinos* had little hope of improving their lives.[3]

The banana companies added a new dimension to political intrigue and power-brokering in Honduras, but they were only one part of the country's rocky political history. In the 61 years between political independence and 1900, Honduras was ruled by 64 separate presidents.[4]

Zemurray, commenting on United Fruit's way of business, said: "In Honduras, a mule costs more than a deputy." Political life settled down a bit in the 1930s and 1940s, when dictator Tiburcio Carias Andino, who was backed by banana companies, occupied the National Palace. During 16 years of martial law (1932–1948) Carias used a heavy hand to fashion the central institutions and infrastructure that made Honduras look more like a modern state.

A transitional epoch for Honduras began in the 1950s when new forces started to challenge the traditional balance of power maintained by the large landowners and the banana companies. A new bourgeoisie began to emerge, and workers and peasants started to speak out and organize.

A successful strike in 1954 by the banana workers of United Fruit sparked widespread organizing for the first time among the country's other workers. By the end of the decade, *campesinos*, encouraged by the Catholic Church, also organized to demand agrarian reform and better wages.[5] The *New York Times* called "the awakening and mobilization of the peasantry the most important social phenomenon in Honduras since independence from Spain in 1821."[6]

Taking the Alliance of Progress rhetoric seriously, President Villeda Morales in 1962 drew up an agrarian reform act. Contrary to the instructions from Washington, the president authorized the moderate reform program before it had been reviewed by the State Department and United Fruit. The banana company retaliated by slowing down production and eliminating jobs, forcing government officials to travel to Washington to formulate an even milder land reform program.[7]

The backward nature of Honduras was revealed to the world during a 1969 four-day war with El Salvador. After Honduras deported tens of thousands of illegal Salvadorans, the Salvadoran army retaliated and ran over the untrained foot soldiers the Honduran generals shoved to the front lines. Afterwards, sectors of the oligarchy and factions of the military were determined that Honduras should finally enter the twentieth century by modernizing its economy and armed forces. In 1972, General Oswaldo López Arellano seized power and announced the country's first National Development Plan. He nationalized the rapacious timber industry and revived the agrarian reform program.

Although López Arellano did not follow through with many of his promises to Honduran workers and *campesinos*, his programs did spark popular organizing by raising worker and *campesino* expectations of reform. López Arellano fell from power in 1975, after the famous "Bananagate" scandal in which the country's financial minister was shown to have received a $1.25 million bribe from United Brands (the conglomerate that owned United Fruit).

Stepping into the power vacuum created by López Arellano's sudden departure was a corrupt clique of military officers headed by the unsavory Colonel Juan Alberto Melgar Castro, who quickly moved to smother rural organizing. Hondurans remember Melgar Castro for the Massacre of Los Horcones, in which several peasant leaders and two foreign priests were tortured and killed in 1975 and the brutal destruction by the military of the Las Isletas banana cooperative in 1977. With Melgar Castro in power, military corruption as well as military repression was on the upswing. There was scarcely a member of the military's high command by the late 1970s who had not become a millionaire.[8]

Behind the military government stood an economic elite, whose wealth was great compared to Honduran peasants but not as impressive as the fortunes of the oligarchies in other Central American nations. The main elements of economic power in Honduras were: the landholders tied to the domestic market (the traditional *latifundistas*); the landholders tied to foreign markets (coffee, cotton, tobacco, and sugar exporters); and the industrial and financial entrepreneurs who were generally tied to foreign investment. In this latter group was a mercantile class dominated by an immigrant sector from the Middle East called the *turcos* or *árabes*.

While the agro-exporters and the non-agrarian bourgeoisie were prodding the Honduran economy toward modernization during this period, the traditional landholders and the banana companies slowed the progress by obstructing agrarian reform. Occasionally, the military encouraged national development but its corruption and ambivalent feelings about worker and peasant organizing kept the economy from moving ahead.

In 1978, when a three-man junta headed by General Policarpo Paz kicked the repressive government of Melgar Castro out of office, it seemed as if Honduras would be saddled with another corrupt and inefficient military government. But events in neighboring Nicaragua set Honduras on a new course of political development.

Democracy on Trial

Representative democracy in Honduras was more the result of external pressures than of internal momentum to restore civilian political control. The success of the FSLN guerrillas in Nicaragua was a signal to Washington that it had better shore up the political systems in other parts of Central America or face the loss of its traditional hegemony in the region. Washington wanted a politically secure base in Honduras, which borders revolutionary Nicaragua and embattled El Salvador. The U.S. Embassy in Tegucigalpa let the Honduran military know that their time in the National Palace was up. The democratization strategy began in 1980 when deputies were elected to the National Assembly and began drawing up a new constitution. In 1981, a presidential election put Roberto Suazo Córdova in the National Palace.

The 1981 presidential election made the Liberal Party's Roberto Suazo Córdova, a doctor and rancher from the Comayagua Valley, the nation's chief executive and commander-in-chief of the armed forces. He received widespread support for his promise to address the needs of the nation's workers and *campesinos* and to keep the military out of national politics. The Liberal Party won firm control of the National Assembly, which also had members from the conservative National Party, the centrist Innovation and Unity Party, and the center-left Christian Democratic Party.

Political Parties

Liberal Party (PL): For many years, the *caudillo* (strongman) Modesto Rodas presided over the party. When Rodas died in 1979, leadership passed to Roberto Suazo Córdova. Traditionally the antimilitary party, the Liberal Party under the Suazo Córdova government (1981–1985) adopted a decidedly pro-military stance. The party is wracked by internal dissension. The Suazocordovistas include the most conservative elements of the party. This is the minority but most powerful wing of the Liberal Party. The opposition within the Liberal Party broke ranks with Suazo Córdova in 1984. The two main factions of the Liberal Party opposition are ALIPO, a moderate group of business people, and MOLIDER, a social-democratic splinter group. The Liberal Party has three candidates running for president: Oscar Mejía Arellano (Suazocordovista), Carlos Roberto Reina (MOLIDER), and José Azcona del Hoyo (ALIPO and MLR). Oscar Mejía, the president's personal choice, lost to José Azcona, who won 25 percent of the total vote in the November 1985 presidential election. Azcona, 58, is an engineer who was born in Spain. He served as campaign coordinator for Suazo Córdova in 1981, and he is deputy in the National Congress. If the military sees fit to support him as president, Azcona, a center-right politician, will probably not deviate from the political direction set by Suazo Córdova. He did, however, promise to prevent the *contras* from maintaining bases in the country, but he is by no means a friend of Managua.

National Party (PN): The more conservative of the two main Honduran political parties, the PN traditionally has counted on close ties with the generals. Many Hondurans dismiss it as merely a civilian wing of the military. The party's patriarch is Ricardo Zuniga Augustinus, who suffered a crushing defeat as the

PN's presidential candidate in 1981. Its own internal divisions and its lack of a clear political program prevented it from offering strong opposition to the government of Suazo Córdova. After Zuniga's electoral defeat, the party began a search for a *caudillo* to replace Zuniga. By 1985, a less conservative wing of the party even joined Liberal Party dissidents, minority parties, and trade-union leaders in a coalition against the Suazo Córdova government.

The 1985 standard-bearer of the National Party was Rafael Leonardo Callejas, who won more than 40 percent of the total votes. Callejas, 42, is a businessman and economist who attracted the youth vote with his capable campaigning. Like Azcona, Callejas is a center-right politician who posed no threat to U.S. policy in Honduras. During the military government in the late 1970s, he served as Minister of Natural Resources, and then ran as the vice-presidential candidate for his party in 1981.

Innovation and Unity Party (PINU): A moderate opposition party that won only a single assembly seat in the 1981 elections. This is the only party that has offered candidacies to peasant and labor leaders, notably Julín Méndez of the ANACH peasant association.

Christian Democratic Party of Honduras (PDCH): A small progressive party that has been extremely critical of the Liberal Party's role in the militarization of Honduras, the PDCH is led by the highly respected Efraín Díaz Arrivillaga who became the party's one representative in the National Assembly in 1981. The party has been unable to offer a candidate with sufficient charisma to attract the opposition vote.

Patriotic Front: This is a coalition that includes the following leftist parties: Revolutionary Party of Honduras (PRH), Communist Party of Honduras (PCH), Marxist-Leninist Party of Honduras (PCMLH), and the Socialist Party (PS).

As Suazo Córdova neared the end of his first term in office, the four-year-old government looked very fragile. The president's cooperation with the United States in militarizing the country, his servile relationship to the generals, his failure to back the demands of worker and peasant groups, and the government enforcement of harsh austerity programs reduced Suazo Córdova's support inside his own party.

Four years in power turned the country doctor into an autocratic politician who took his orders from the military and U.S. Embassy. In 1985, when the president tried to handpick the right-wing political bureaucrat Oscar Mejía Arellano as his successor and to block legislative measures for electoral reform, a political crisis of historic proportions broke loose in Tegucigalpa. The president went so far as to order the arrest of the chief of the Supreme Court and four other justices appointed by an anti-Suazo Córdova coalition in the national assembly.

An unprecedented national alliance named CODECO (Democratic and Constitutional Coordinator) of all sectors stretching from factions of the National Party to the progressive political factions and the unions formed to break Suazo

Córdova's control of the political process. Threat of a general strike by peasant and workers' unions forced the government to back down. As the crisis escalated, General Walter Lopez, the military chief, stepped into the fracas, giving critical backing to the widespread demands for the naming of an entirely new Supreme Court and for the prohibition of politicking by either the president or the heads of the judicial and legislative branches of government.

During Suazo Córdova's term as president, elements of the National Party drew closer to the popular opposition. It accused the government of violating constitutional and human rights in its efforts to control worker and *campesino* organizations. "Although it is called democracy in Honduras, President Suazo Córdova has turned it into a totalitarian government," said Rafael Callejas, a National Party leader.[9]

Despite all the government's problems, a military coup is unlikely. The bounty of economic and military aid flowing from the United States is the best guarantee that Honduras will continue with its weak civilian rule. In late 1984, then U.S. Ambassador John Negroponte reminded Hondurans that "local political conditions have always been an important factor affecting our ability to provide economic and military assistance."[10]

Politics in Honduras is more a matter of personality and influence, than of ideology. The 1985 presidential election brought little change to Honduras.

The lack of a strong progressive opposition left the two traditional parties to split the vote. Rather than demonstrate the stability of the democratic process in Honduras, the November 1985 election illustrated its instability. A 1985 election law, supported by the military and the Liberal Party, awards the presidency not only to the candidate with the most votes but to the leading candidate of the party whose candidates jointly won the most. Under this law, the Liberal Party's Azcona is scheduled to assume the presidency in early 1986, despite widespread popular opposition. But whoever is president in Honduras, it is the military that holds supreme power as the nation's watchdog and arbitrator.

Only God and the United States Can Help

Whatever small economic advances Honduras made after the 1969 war with El Salvador were lost in the early 1980s. "Only God can save the national economy," lamented Minister of Economy Gustavo Alfaro in 1982.[11] The setback suffered by Honduras in the last half decade has not differed substantially from the economic whiplash experienced by its Central American neighbors. Inflation, rising debt payments, lower coffee prices, an expanding balance-of-payments deficit, and a threefold jump in unemployment occurred throughout the region. When the crunch came, most Hondurans were already living in deprivation as the third poorest people in the hemisphere.

Seeing the medieval-like poverty of the Honduran countryside or the thousands of hovels that cover the dusty hills around the capital city, it may seem little wealth could be squeezed out of Honduras. But the economic elite has found a way, and most hard currency they earn in agro-export and industrial profits rapidly leaves the country. Estimates of capital flight from the country range from $500 million to $1 billion since 1979.[12] It has been estimated that more than 500 Hondurans maintain bank accounts in Miami alone.[13]

Honduras fell into the grip of the IMF in 1981 when it could no longer meet its debt payments. The IMF's austerity program put even more of a hardship on Hondurans, most of whom were already close to absolute poverty. "Produce more, export more, consume less, and spend less," exhorted Suazo Córdova. After four years of austerity, the economy continued to stagnate. IMF's answer: more austerity. But higher taxes, devaluation, and government budget cuts have exacerbated tension between the government and just about all other sectors, with the exception of the military which receives all the funds it requests.

The government has few places to turn. It urgently needs IMF assistance to pay its debts but faces increasing labor militancy every time it tries to impose another austerity measure demanded by the IMF. The threat of a general strike makes the government reluctant to follow through with IMF measures. It has become dependent on economic assistance from AID, but these funds come only if the government buckles under IMF's dictates. As a result, the government in 1984 cut the national health and education budget for the first time. But the austerity program did not extend to the military, which saw its budget increase.

The College of Economics at the National University issued a statement in 1984 that said the IMF-AID austerity plan is a dead-end road for Honduras. They said it is a program of the right wing, and one that has already failed in other parts of Central America. The university economists said that the government needs to better distribute the crisis among all sectors, not just the poor and middle class. If the country were truly concerned about the economy, said the university economists, it would tackle the soaring military and government budgets.

Besides Belize, Honduras is the least industrialized Central American nation. Even though it is small, the industrial sector has been hard hit by the economic crisis, which has resulted in less money in the local market to buy its goods. After the 1969 war, the government bolted from the Central American Common Market (CACM) to protect the country's industrial sector from lower priced imports from elsewhere in Central America, particularly El Salvador. Industry did make some strides forward during the 1970s, but Honduras still refuses to join CACM. Operating at 50 percent or less capacity, the industrial sector will likely sink into deeper recession before moving forward again.

God has not come through for Honduras, but AID has. The $572 million in U.S. economic assistance from 1980–1985, known by Hondurans as the *lluvia de dólares* (rain of dollars), came in exchange for allowing its national territory to be used as a garrison for the Pentagon and a haven for the *contras*.

Philip Shepherd, a professor at Florida International University, warned Congress that U.S. aid is creating a dependency that Honduras may not be able to shake. "The Honduran elite," he said, "has staked its entire political-economic fortunes on a massive economic bailout by the U.S." Their future is "mortgaged" to the United States.[14]

After the ouster of General Gustavo Alvarez as head of the military in 1984, Honduras began to demand more economic and military aid. For the right to use Honduran territory for its military build up and as a haven for the *contras*, Honduras insisted that Washington substantially increase its economic aid. But the country had become so dependent on the rain of dollars that it could not seriously threaten to go it alone if Washington refused to meet its demands. Confident that Honduras would continue to acquiesce to U.S. foreign policy, Washington in 1985 denied the country's requests for an augmented aid program.

Disappearances Increase with Democracy

The ascent of Argentina-trained General Gustavo Alvarez Martínez to the role of chief of the Honduran armed forces in 1982 marked the beginning of grave human-rights violations in Honduras. Alvarez, who expressed admiration for the military's "dirty war" in Argentina, created an infrastructure of secret-police terror in Honduras. Before his appointment as military chief by President Suazo Córdova, Alvarez directed the Public Security Forces (FUSEP), which put him in control of the feared DNI secret police.

The violence that took place under Alvarez was not dissimilar to the right-wing vigilante terror found in El Salvador and Guatemala. According to the Committee in Defense of Human Rights in Honduras (CODEH), 138 individuals of different nationalities, mainly Salvadorans and Nicaraguans, disappeared in Honduras between 1981 and 1984. During that same period, 85 Honduran labor and *campesino* leaders were executed by alleged clandestine death squads, and 9 priests were murdered.

While the number of political assassinations decreased after the departure of Alvarez in March 1984, CODEH said the number of persons "disappeared," "temporarily disappeared," and those taken as "political prisoners" and "tortured" actually increased. Amnesty International said in 1985 that Honduran authorities were "apparently trying to link nonviolent groups, such as trade unionists, religious groups, peasants, and members of legal opposition parties... with armed groups, often on the basis solely of statements extracted under torture."

The *contras* have also been implicated in the surge of human- rights violations since 1979. Former National Guardsmen became members of a paramilitary group based in Choluteca called the Honduran Anticommunist Movement (MACHO). According to CODEH, one ex-guardsman, Ricardo "El Chino" Lau was involved in the torture, disappearance, and murder of several dozen victims in Honduras.[15] In 1985, the Honduran military acknowledged that its own investigations revealed the involvement of the *contras* in the disappearance of at least 18 Hondurans.

Ramón Custodio, president of CODEH, casts part of the blame on the United States for the deterioration of human rights in Honduras:

> The military presence of the North American troops has endangered, and indeed aborted, the democratic process. Every time a military solution is chosen for political problems, the human-rights situation deteriorates. We have a right to claim that the people most responsible for these violations of human rights by the armed forces are the American advisers, because they are the people who train the Honduran officers. They have a moral responsibility more than anything else. There's also the definite influence of the American ambassador and this influence hasn't proved to be for the best in the past.

Denationalizing Honduras

Hondurans say that it may be debatable who is the second most powerful figure in their country—the president or the head of the armed forces—there is no doubt who holds the number one spot: the U.S. ambassador.

In addition to the quick buildup of U.S. military presence in Honduras in the 1980s, the AID Mission tripled its staff. The U.S. Embassy in Tegucigalpa suddenly became the largest in Latin America after Mexico and Brazil. The Peace Corps contingent of almost 300 volunteers ranks Honduras the largest host nation in the world.

Syndicated columnist Jack Anderson reported on the U.S. geopolitical designs in Honduras only months after the Sandinista victory in 1979: "The president seems determined to add still another chapter to the chronicle of Yankee imperialism in Central America. The [Carter] administration apparently has chosen Honduras to be our 'new Nicaragua'—a deplorable satellite bought and paid for by American military and economic largesse."[16]

When Brigadier General Gustavo Alvarez was kicked out of the country in 1984, the United States lost a committed anti-Sandinista and a reliable strongman in Honduran politics. No dramatic changes in U.S.-Honduran military relations occurred after the ouster of Alvarez, but the Honduran military did begin to express some reservations about U.S. designs in Honduras.

The new military chief General Walter López was a bit more concerned about national sovereignty and the welfare of Hondurans than he was about a Sandinista blitzkrieg attack on Tegucigalpa. "We have stopped being your yes men," López told the *New York Times*. "Our social problems are the biggest thing facing our country. If people are out of work and hungry, that's when the external threats become important; that's what makes it easy to have revolutions."[17]

López is not a populist, but neither is he the fanatic anticommunist that Alvarez was. "The overthrow of the Sandinistas may be our hope," said López, "but it is certainly not our objective."

Another important difference between López and his predecessor is that López, who was a hero in the 1969 war with El Salvador, fears that the U.S.-trained Salvadoran army may eventually turn its guns again on Honduras. For that reason, López objected to the use of the Regional Military Training Center (CREM) at Puerto Castilla to train Salvadoran troops. In 1984, the new military chief went so far as to tell the Pentagon that it could no longer train Salvadorans in Honduras. Since that was the reason CREM was constructed, the United States shut down the center in mid-1985.

Tension also persists between Honduras and El Salvador because of border disputes between the two nations. The 1980 treaty signed by Honduras and El Salvador at the insistence of the United States specified that their claims on border territories would be worked out by the end of 1985. Their continued failure to resolve the land dispute has frustrated the United States, which wants the two countries to unite their armies to crush the FMLN guerrillas.

Despite U.S. military civic action and medical programs, Honduran opposition to the U.S. military presence grows each year. "Yankee Go Home" has become an oft-heard demand raised at worker and peasant rallies. Jorge Arturo Reina, a leader of the Liberal Party's center-left wing, said that even the military became more resistant to complete subservience to U.S. foreign-policy demands than did the Liberal Party government. In early 1985, it came to the point, he said, where "the armed forces [were] more moderate than the civilian government."

While the military was hardly telling the Yankees to go home, it did successfully stand up to the Pentagon on the issue of Salvadoran training, whereas the Suazo Córdova government was woefully unsuccessful in its negotiations with Washington. So submissive did the Suazo Córdova government become that Reina said that in Honduras, "It's no longer a question of nationalizing the banana plantations or the banks or commerce, but simply nationalizing government."[18]

The two most sensitive issues in Honduran-U.S. relations have been the harboring of the *contras* and the training of Salvadoran troops. The presence of a 12,000 member counterrevolutionary army inside Honduran borders is clearly not in the country's self-interest. Until 1984, Honduras tolerated their presence but officially denied that it gave them sanctuary. As the money started running out and the war turned decidedly against the *contras*, Honduran politicians and generals began to worry about having thousands of out-of-work mercenaries roaming around their country.

Country Faces Its Own Guerrilla Movement

In 1980, Honduras became the fourth Central American country to face a leftist guerrilla movement. On the day that the Honduran government signed a treaty with El Salvador, the Lorenzo Zelaya Front attacked the U.S. Embassy in Tegucigalpa. The group said the United States had promoted this treaty as a part of its planned militarization of Honduras.

By 1983, five other guerrilla organizations had announced their presence with terrorist actions, most of them aimed at U.S. government and U.S. corporate targets. Bombings occurred at Le Volcanic, a Tegucigalpa discotheque frequented by U.S. soldiers, and the offices of Texaco and Rosario Resources (AMAX). A joint statement by the six groups in April 1983 asserted that Honduras "has been turned into a blind instrument of Reagan's policy of intervention and war in Central America."

The four principal guerrilla organizations are Morazanist Front for the Liberation of Honduras (FMLH), Revolutionary Workers Party of Central America (PRTCH), Popular Movement of Liberation (MPL "Cinchoneros"), and the People's Revolution Forces (the Lorenzo Zelaya Front—FPR). The guerrillas have for the most part confined their operations to a series of isolated terrorist acts.

The most sensational guerrilla action was the 1982 takeover of the meeting of the San Pedro Sula Chamber of Commerce by the Cinchoneros. In 1983, the PRTCH did try to establish a military front of 100 guerrillas in Olancho, but they were rapidly eliminated by the Honduran army's elite Cobra division under guidance of U.S. counterinsurgency experts.

Within the guerrilla movement, there has been much dispute about the timeliness of armed opposition in Honduras. The FPR, the first extreme left group to engage in terrorism, acknowledged in 1983 that many previous guerrilla operations had been "at the margin of the mass movement." After 1983, members of the various guerrilla groups decided to forego armed rebellion in favor of attempts to educate the trade-union and peasant movements politically.

Although armed struggle has not gained momentum in Honduras, the guerrilla organizations have not disbanded. In early 1985, the Cinchoneros called for the creation of an anti-interventionist guerrilla front to confront the U.S. military presence in Honduras.

Unions Take a Stand

Although virtually nonexistent in Honduras until 1954, worker and peasant unions have become a powerful force in Honduran society. In the last 30 years, the upsurge in labor and rural organizing has distinguished Honduras from other

Central American societies. Aside from revolutionary Nicaragua, Honduras has the highest percentage of organized rural and urban workers.

Continuing tension in the Honduran labor movement arises from the strong influence of AIFLD over two major peasant and trade-union federations (ANACH and CTH). Largely because of AIFLD, the Honduran labor movement had steered clear of political involvement through the last decade.

The Confederation of Honduran Workers (CTH), created in the aftermath of the 1954 strike against United Fruit, represented the combined effort of the banana TNCs, the Honduran government, and Washington to put the lid on militant union organizing. Initially, the AIFLD-linked CTH threw its support behind the U.S. militarization of the country. Its chief, Víctor Artíles, was a member of the now-defunct APROH, a right-wing coalition of the business elite formed in 1982. In the 1980s, this apolitical approach to organizing changed rapidly due to the general politicization of the Honduran environment that came with increased U.S. presence in the country.

Other factors that sparked the unions to take more of an active role were the sharp economic downturn and the stepped-up repression of union organizing. Most union federations blame CTH for breaking the solidarity of Honduran workers. It refused to join a 1984 May Day rally to protest the kidnapping of a prominent union activist. As political and economic tensions intensify, the CTH will have an ever more difficult time justifying its pro-U.S. stance to its members.

The two other major federations are the Workers General Central (CGT), affiliated with the Christian Democrats, and the Unitary Federation of Workers (FUTH), founded in 1981 and the most militant of the three. Calling for the departure of U.S. troops and a negotiated settlement to the conflicts in Central America, these two unions have been persecuted by government security forces.

Numerous labor leaders have "disappeared" and been jailed since 1980. But the repression leveled against the unions did not cause the labor movement to moderate its tactics. Instead, the unions became bolder. Victories in pushing back taxes and blocking a massive firing of union members strengthened their resolve. Ability to call general strikes and mobilize tens of thousands of Hondurans make unions a powerful force that the government and military have to reckon with.

Campesino Unions Demand More Land

No other country in Central America has such active *campesino* unions. Since 1962, when the first agrarian reform law was passed, the peasant groups have been struggling to ensure that large agro-exporters and ranchers do not block land redistribution in Honduras. Dissatisfied with the progress of land redistribution, *campesinos* have occupied hundreds of idle landholdings since 1980.

The most militant, and consequently most repressed, of the peasant associations is the National *Campesino* Union (UNC). The other two major *campesino* associations are the AIFLD-affiliated National Association of Honduran Peasants (ANACH) and the Agrarian Reform Cooperative Federation (FECORAH), which represents *campesinos* who have received land. Both take a more moderate approach to agrarian reform, although all three have led land occupations.

Over 40 percent of rural Hondurans are landless, and 80 percent suffer from malnutrition. These factors have also contributed to rising urban problems. With no land of their own to farm, more than 2000 people stream into Tegucigalpa from the countryside every month.[19]

All three *campesino* associations insist that the answer to many of the country's rural and urban problems is a stepped-up land-redistribution program. They point out that vast stretches of fertile land are underutilized. As much as 65 percent of the country's richest land is used to raise cattle for export. Almost 50 percent of all arable land in Honduras is used as pasture, and another 26 percent lies fallow.[20]

UNC's Esteban Enriquez commented on the slow pace of land distribution in Honduras: "The legal paperwork to get idle land through the agrarian reform takes five years or more. After that long wait, the courts usually refuse to give the land to the *campesinos*." Once a petition for land is in the legal system, the law and the petitioning *campesinos* usually lose out to "the influence and bribes of the landowners."

After more than two decades of agrarian reform, only 10 percent of rural Hondurans have benefited, leaving as many as 125,000 families still petitioning for land.[21] When the government does enforce the agrarian reform, it is frequently following pressure from *campesino* federations like the UNC. "We have discovered that the only way to get the land is to take possession of it physically in actions we call *recuperaciones de tierra* (land recoveries)," said UNC's Enriquez.[22] "In Honduras, we are the agrarian reform," affirmed another peasant leader.

As economic problems persist and landlessness grows, Honduran *campesinos* are becoming ever more aggressive. At the same time, landholders have become more intransigent. Although rural tensions do not yet approach those in Guatemala and El Salvador, the confrontation over land in Honduras may evolve into a highly political conflict. Already many UNC members have been killed. UNC leader Esteban Enriquez says the government is using its Anti-Terrorist Act, which was supposedly designed to fight guerrilla terrorism, to arrest *campesinos* who are demanding rights to idle land.

TNCs in Honduras

While the U.S. banana TNCs have dominated the Honduran economy, they have had company. A study by the National University's Institute of Economic and Social Research found that U.S. TNCs control 100 percent of the country's five largest firms, 88 percent of the 20 largest, and 82 percent of the 50 largest companies.[23] The book value of U.S. investment in Honduras was estimated to be $235 million in 1984. Close to 300 U.S. firms do business in Honduras, including about 60 of the top 500 corporations in the United States.

Honduran agribusiness has more U.S. investment than that of other Central American nations. All three banana TNCs have operations: United Brands and Castle & Cooke have a long and less than glorious history in Honduras, while Del Monte (R.J. Reynolds) recently began producing and buying bananas in Honduras.

According to a report in the daily *El Heraldo*, the advent of Del Monte in Honduras was accompanied by violence. The newspaper cited a case in which members of the Honduran armed forces along with officials of the Tela Railroad Company (United Brands) destroyed the packing equipment of an independent banana packer. The businessman had signed a contract with Del Monte that gave him a better price than what he had received from Tela.[24]

Besides growing bananas, Castle & Cooke also produces pineapples, citrus, and African palm, and is experimenting with the production of nontraditional exports like cucumbers. United Brands has African palm plantations and cattle ranches in addition to its extensive banana estates.

Outside the banana enclave, U.S. Tobacco operates a plantation and produces cigars and cigarettes. Seven other smaller U.S. tobacco corporations also either grow or manufacture tobacco products in Honduras. Nine U.S. firms raise and package shrimp, and there is considerable U.S. investment in the country's meatpacking industry. Robinson Lumber, a contributor to the Honduran-based *contras* through the right-wing Council on National Policy, exports wood from Honduras. An estimated 10 percent of the smaller (not in the top 500) U.S. corporations are active in logging, milling, and production of wood or wood products.

With the assistance of AID, several U.S. firms have recently invested in nontraditional agriculture in Honduras. Foodpro, a subsidiary of National Starch and Chemical (a U.S. subsidiary of the British/Dutch corporation Unilever), has an AID contract to grow snow peas and broccoli near Tegucigalpa. A visit to their operations revealed that they were paying workers less than the minimum wage. In the Comayagua Valley in central Honduras, hundreds of Honduran women and children, working for other projects sponsored by AID, pick cucumbers and other nontraditional crops slated for export to the United States.

The top three U.S. banks—Citicorp, BankAmerica, and Chase Manhattan—do business in Honduras. Citicorp has interests in the Banco de Honduras, while Chase Manhattan owns part of Banco Atlantida, the major competitor of Banco de Honduras.

In the manufacturing sector, Kimberly-Clark makes toilet paper, Beatrice Foods produces snack foods, Sterling Drugs manufactures pills, United Brands produces plastics and vegetable oil, and Castle & Cooke is the country's beer and soft-drink processor.

Puerto Cortés, an hour's drive from the country's industrial center of San Pedro Sula, is the site of the major free-zone industrial park in Honduras. The Industrial Incentive Law offers tax exemptions and the duty-free importation of material and equipment used by the labor-intensive assembly plants located in the Cortés Free Zone. A dozen U.S. corporations employ hundreds of Honduran women for a few dollars a day to produce bras, men's underwear, boots, and softballs for export. A fifth of the softballs pitched in the world are sewn together by rows of women working for the Tennessee-based Worth Sports Company.[25] Other U.S.-owned plants rely on Honduran labor to assemble stop-smoking kits for U.S. consumers to manufacture shoe soles, and to stitch together outfits for U.S. babies.

While it may not be categorized technically as a Banana Republic, Honduras still receives Banana Republic treatment. In the last few years, disputes have developed with the four most active U.S. TNCs concerning their contributions to the economy and their conduct in labor-management matters. In one case, a bill was introduced in the House of Representatives that called for the termination of all economic assistance to Honduras until the country paid a construction company for services the government said were never completed.

The few advances the Honduran government has made to extract benefit from the banana industry have been whittled away by the TNCs which continually threaten to fire workers and leave the country if their demands are not met.

A recent example of this type of economic coercion came in late 1984 when Standard Fruit threatened to fire 500 workers because it said it was losing money. But the workers' union said the company was doing fine financially and only wanted to avoid paying a wage hike scheduled in the union contract. The union also charged that Standard Fruit switched its pineapple operations over to another corporate division as a way to break its contract with the union. Standard Fruit, which had not paid its land taxes for three years, finally agreed to retain the 500 workers after the government said it would suspend the TNC's entire tax obligations for a year.[26] About the same time, the government signed an agreement with United Brands that exempted the company from export taxes on its first several shipments of bananas each year.

Rosario Resources, the gold- and silver-mining subsidiary of AMAX, laid off 120 union employees in 1985. The company blamed the layoffs on increasing production costs and falling prices, but the union interpreted the dismissals a bit differently. Manuel Guerrero, president of the Syndicated Mineworkers Union, charged that the company pushed out unionized workers to hire cheaper temporary workers. After getting rid of the Honduran employees, Rosario turned around and hired 60 Nicaraguans, among them former members of Somoza's National Guard. Mine director Walter Smith and several other top management employees of Rosario formerly worked at the company's mines in Nicaragua during the Somoza regime.

Union leader Guerrero said the company's economic woes were exaggerated and that it simply was trying "to destroy the organization of the union" by laying off the unionized miners. He said the layoffs violate various clauses in the workers' contract, one of which prohibits the dismissal of permanent union employees to hire cheaper temporary workers.[27]

Since 1982 the Honduran government has had an ongoing dispute with Texaco, which runs the country's only oil refinery. The company refused to pay the import taxes it owed the government. When Texaco came to Honduras almost 20 years ago, it was granted a five-year exemption from taxes. After that initial grace period was over, the oil giant never began paying its taxes despite frequent government protestations. Texaco has also angered the government by stopping refinery operations on several occasions to force the government to raise the maximum legal price for petroleum sold in Honduras. In 1981, closures of the refinery caused severe fuel shortages and paralyzed up to 95 percent of transport within Honduras.

Christian Democrat legislator Efraín Díaz Arrivillaga, a U.S.-trained economist, complains that U.S. business has created a separate economy that is oriented to the outside, not to Honduras. "Most of the resources," he said, "have not benefited Honduras in the sense of creating Honduran capital to develop the country."[28]

1 *Central America Report*, July 23, 1982.
2 Steve Lewontin, "Outpost of the Banana Empire," *Honduras Update*, July 1984.
3 Walter LaFeber, *Inevitable Revolution: The United States in Central America* (New York: Norton, 1983), p.45.
4 Thomas Anderson, *Politics in Central America* (New York: Praeger, 1982).
5 James Morris and Marta Sanchez Soler, "Factores de Poder en la Evolucion del Campesino Hondureño," *Estudios Sociales Centroamericanos*, January–April, 1977.
6 *New York Times*, November 30, 1975.
7 LaFeber, op.cit., p.178.
8 Washington Office on Latin America (WOLA), "Honduras: A Democracy in Demise," February 1984.
9 *Financial Times*, February 2, 1985.
10 *New York Times*, November 24, 1984.
11 *Central America Report*, January 7, 1983.
12 *Mesoamerica*, October 1984.
13 *Boletin Informativo Honduras*, September 1984.
14 Hearings on HR 4931 before Subcommittee on Military Installations, Committee on Armed Forces, House of Representatives, March 1984, pp.997–999.
15 *CODEH*, "Violaciones a los Derechos Humanos Cometidos por los 'Contras' o Somocistas en Honduras," March 1985.
16 *Washington Post*, March 23, 1980.
17 John B. Oakes, "What Honduras Wants from US," *New York Times*, January 1, 1985.
18 *Guardian*, February 6, 1985.
19 AID, "Honduras: Progress Under US-Honduras Economic Cooperation," August 1984.
20 AID, "Honduras: A Country Profile," June 1981.
21 *Mesoamerica*, May 1983; *Inforpress*, January 26, 1984.
22 Interview by Deb Preusch, August 1984.
23 Antonio Muiga Frassinetti, "Concentración Industrial en Honduras," *Economía Politica*, No. 9. pp.70, 85–86.
24 *El Heraldo*, February 23, 1984.

25 Mike Edwards, "Honduras: Eye of the Storm," *National Geographic*, November 1983.
26 *El Tiempo*, December 6, 1984; *El Tiempo*, December 27, 1984.
27 *Mesoamerica*, February 1985.
28 Charles U. Hanley, "Ties to Central America in a State of Flux," *Los Angeles Times*, September 25, 1983.

CHAPTER 13

Nicaragua

∎

Trends
- Increasing economic difficulties in the face of destabilization and the *contra* war.
- Continued U.S. economic destabilization.
- Reversal of initial social and economic advances.
- Growing dissatisfaction with government in face of declining quality of life.
- No serious effort by United States for a negotiated settlement, despite the continued willingness of Nicaragua to do so.
- Possible limited U.S. military involvement in the form of aerial raids to push back alleged Nicaraguan aggression against its neighbors.
- Continued absence of unity among counterrevolutionary elements.
- Failure of *contras* to advance inside Nicaragua and secure territory.
- Possible direct U.S. training of *contras* and resumption of C.I.A. and military assistance.

∎

AFTER THE REVOLUTION, the Sandinistas no longer had to rely on wall paintings to communicate with the Nicaraguan people. Their messages were plastered across the country on highway billboards. Each ministry and popular organization had the opportunity to advertise their own themes.

Some of the first bright billboards to appear on the revolutionary landscape urged all Nicaraguans to join the literacy crusade, either as students or as teachers. Not to be outdone by the education ministry, the health-care department began erecting a series of *carteleras* promoting its preventive health-care program aimed at cutting child mortality caused by dehydration from diarrhea. The Sandinista police, not having the squad cars to patrol the streets, kicked off its own billboard campaign against drunken and careless driving, stressing safe motoring as a revolutionary virtue. Other billboards portrayed the Sandinistas' image of the

"New Nicaragua" by projecting images of strong-looking women, cooperatives, and the young working alongside the old.

In 1984, new billboard themes emerged. The government brought the war at the borders home to Managuans with the slogan of the times: "Everything for the Combatants, Everything for the War Fronts." In the midst of this state of war, Nicaraguans also saw the new political process played out on competing billboards. The different parties petitioned the recently registered voters to give them a chance to chart a new political course for Nicaragua.

The government in 1985 erected a billboard with a message not for the Nicaraguan people but for Washington. Directly across from the main entrance of the U.S. Embassy in Managua, the new *cartelera* displayed the text of a note sent by Nicaraguan patriot Augusto César Sandino to the U.S. Marine captain who had demanded his surrender in July 1927:

> I have received and understood your communication of yesterday. I will not surrender, and I await you here. I want a free country or death. I am not afraid of you. I count on the patriotism of those who are with me.

More than the content of its billboard advertising distinguishes Nicaragua from other Central American countries. The differences are apparent immediately upon crossing the border. The country's *aduana* buildings have been destroyed by *contras*, forcing Nicaraguan immigration officials to work from battered trailers located a mile or more from the border.

Politics abound in Nicaragua. Fierce political discussions are heard in Managuan bars and cafés. Every day *La Prensa* newspaper airs a new attack against the Sandinistas. Criticism is also found in the government's daily, the *Barricada*, which raises public complaints about failures and inefficiencies of various ministries. Those foreigners previously convinced that Nicaragua is a totalitarian society find vigorous dissent from the vendors of the Mercado Oriental to the Constituent Assembly. But even more striking is the patriotic fervor of Nicaraguans and the widespread support for the Sandinistas. This spirit is felt at funeral processions for combatants killed at the front or farmworkers murdered by the *contras*. Cries of *no pasarán* (they won't cross the border) are heard through the country.

Then there is the lighter side of Nicaragua. It seems that every other Nicaraguan is a poet. Even the Sandinista police have a regular poetry contest. On Sundays, many *campesino* men and boys put down their machetes, pick up their baseball gloves, don their cherished Dodgers or other U.S. baseball caps, and set out to play ball. The movie houses in Leon are crammed every night, with people munching on homemade sweets sold by vendors on the sidewalks outside.

Nicaraguans are rightly proud of the fine taste of the country's Victoria beer and world-renowned Flor de Caña rum.

Having lived through 40 years of cruel dictatorship, a bloody civil war, and a half-decade of counterrevolution, Nicaraguans yearn for peace. But like Sandino, Nicaraguans also value their national *dignidad* (dignity), and large numbers of them honestly prefer a *"Patria Libre o Morir"* ("a free country or death").

History of Intervention

Nicaragua fell into the hands of the Spanish in 1523. In his writings about Spain's treatment of Central American Indians, Bartolome de las Casas described the subjugation of the "perfectly happy province of Nicaragua." The Spanish bishop said that the Nicaraguans "suffered as much as possible the tyranny and bondage which the Christians imposed upon them . . . [and] subjected to so much evil, butchery, cruelty, bondage, and injustice that no human tongue would be able to describe it."

The Spanish succeeded in colonizing the Pacific plains but failed to incorporate the Atlantic region because of the stubborn resistance of the Carib Indians. The Miskito Coast, as this region was called, came under the control of the British. It was not until 1894 that the eastern half of Nicaragua became truly integrated into the nation.[1]

The history of U.S. intervention in Nicaragua dates back to the 1830s when U.S. businessmen started formulating plans to construct an interoceanic canal across Nicaragua. In 1837, President Van Buren sent a representative to the country to negotiate a right-of-way for the proposed canal. But the presidential representative consulted with U.S. businessmen in Nicaragua, not with Nicaraguans. This early canal proposal failed, although shortly afterwards investor Cornelius Vanderbilt had a plan to establish the Accessory Transit Authority (ATA) to finance, build, and operate a canal in Nicaragua.

In 1854, after an anti-United States protest attacked the U.S. Foreign Ministry in San Juan del Norte, the U.S. warship *Cayne* shelled that Nicaraguan port. Four times in the 1850s, the U.S. military invaded Nicaragua: 1850, 1853, 1854, and 1857.

In 1855, one ambitious U.S. adventurer, William Walker, came to Nicaragua with a band of mercenaries and declared himself president of Nicaragua. Walker retained his title for a year, until investor Cornelius Vanderbilt, with an army of Nicaraguans and Costa Ricans, forced Walker to surrender to the U.S. Navy. Following two more military excursions to Central America, the adventurous Walker was finally captured and shot by Hondurans.[2]

After the Civil War, the United States turned its attention to domestic affairs and did not interfere in Nicaragua again until the turn of the century. In 1912,

U.S. Marines hit the shores of Nicaragua to back a Conservative Party revolt against President José Santos Zelaya, whose nationalism threatened Washington. The Marines stayed on intermittently through the next 20 years. During the occupation, U.S. financial advisers managed the nation's fiscal policies and established the *cordoba* as the national currency. The cause for U.S. intervention in 1926 was a Liberal Party revolt against the U.S.-supported Conservative Party leader. The U.S. occupation army, which had left in 1925, came back the following year to enforce a political settlement.

Finding this settlement dishonorable and unsatisfactory, Augusto César Sandino organized an anti-imperialist army of peasants, which had the support of the progressive urban population. The U.S. Marines mounted the region's first counterinsurgency war in Nicaragua, but they could not defeat Sandino's Defensive Army of National Sovereignty.[3]

The Marines finally withdrew in January 1933. Popularly known as the "General of Free Men," Sandino had basically achieved his main objective of chasing the Yankee army out of Nicaragua. But before their departure, the U.S. Marines established the National Guard as its watchdog under the leadership of the English-speaking Anastasio Somoza García.

Somoza's first task was clear. He told a council of Nicaraguan officials in February 1934: "I have come from the United States Embassy where I have had a conference with Ambassador Arturo Bliss, who has assured me that the government in Washington supports and recommends the elimination of Augusto César Sandino for considering him a disturber of the peace of the country."[4] Soon thereafter, Sandino accepted a fateful dinner invitation at the Presidential Palace, ostensibly to discuss the future of Nicaragua. On his way home after the dinner, Somoza's men assassinated him.

Having taken care of his main competitor, General Somoza then ousted the president of Nicaragua, Juan Bautista Sacasa, in 1936. With the U.S. blessing, Somoza initiated the longest, most corrupt dictatorship in Latin America. Twenty years later, Nicaraguan poet Rigoberto López Perez shot the Somoza patriarch in the town of Leon. The White House ordered a helicopter from the Canal Zone to transfer its wounded ally from Leon to Managua, where the head of the U.S. Army Walter Reed Hospital tried unsuccessfully to treat him. Somoza's eldest son, Luis Somoza Debayle, became the new state power and, upon his death in 1967, his brother Anastasio "Tacho" Somoza Debayle inherited the family dictatorship.

In 1934, the Somoza family had owned practically no land; but dictatorship is good business, and by the 1950s the family was the country's largest landholder. In its book on Central America published in 1964, the Life World Library reported that the Somoza family controlled "about one-tenth of the cultivable land in Nicaragua, and just about everything else worth owning, the country's only airline, one television station, a newspaper, a cement plant, textile mill, several sugar refineries, half-a-dozen breweries and distilleries, and a Mercedes-Benz agency."

The Politics of a Revolution

To renew the struggle begun by Sandino, a small group of Nicaraguans founded the Sandinista Front for National Liberation (FSLN) in 1961. From that time, the FSLN was at the forefront of the movement to overthrow Somoza. In 1978, the guerrilla war against the National Guard was joined by mass insurrections by the residents of Leon, Masaya, Esteli, and Managua that forced Somoza to flee the country. Comandante Humberto Ortega, the present defense minister, said that the FSLN had "thought of the masses . . . as a prop" for the military campaign. But, "Reality was quite different: guerrilla activity served as a prop for the masses, who crushed the enemy by means of insurrection."

Leaders of the FSLN were united in their conviction that armed struggle was needed to overturn the Somoza dynasty. In the mid-1970s, however, the FSLN commandantes were divided into three political factions, preventing them from functioning as a team. In January 1979, the guerrilla commandantes created a nine-person directorate which united three political factions of the Sandinistas.[5]

The *Proletarios* (proletariats) emerged from the urban guerrilla front in 1975. Led by intellectuals and academics like Jaime Wheelock Román, Carlos Núñez Tellez, and Luís Carrión Cruz, the *Proletarios* sought to broaden the anti-Somoza movement by organizing in factories and poor neighborhoods. Other factions criticized *Proletarios* for excessive "propaganda" and adherence to traditional Marxist line.

The *Guerra Popular Prolongada* (prolonged people's war—GPP) was heir to the original FSLN rural organization. With both urban and rural operations, the GPP, led by Bayardo Arce, Henry Ruíz Hernández, and Tomás Borge, preferred the cautious strategy of accumulating forces. Other factions criticized it as being too careful militarily and prone to isolate itself from the daily life of the people.

The *Tercistas* (third force), which appeared in 1976, has also been called the *Insurreccionales*. Ideologically heterodox, the *Tercistas* relaxed the Marxist rigor of the original FSLN and rapidly increased their ranks with social democratic and bourgeois recruits. Militarily bolder than the other factions, in 1977–1978 the *Tercistas* pressed urban and rural insurrection with vigor. Other factions criticized them for excessive boldness and for lack of ideological purity. Its leaders were the brothers Daniel and Humberto Ortega Saavedra and Víctor Tirado López.

The Elections

The Sandinistas ousted Somoza July 19, 1979, and in 1980 promised to have elections by 1985. They bested their original promise by holding the presidential and constituent assembly elections in November 1984.

In early 1983, the Council of State (the legislature composed of representatives of all major economic and political sectors) formed an electoral commission to develop the country's election laws. The commission had representatives from the Social Christian Party and the Conservative Democratic Party as well as the FSLN. Delegations were sent to Spain, France, Finland, Federal German Republic, Sweden, Mexico, Costa Rica, Venezuela, Colombia, Peru, Ecuador, and Canada to study the electoral systems in their countries. A delegation requested permission to study the U.S. system, but the Reagan administration denied the members visas.[6]

Nicaraguans were obviously enthusiastic about the elections as over 90 percent of eligible voters registered—with no reports that citizens were in any way forced to register. All parties, including those of the right-wing opposition, were given $300,000 in state funds to pay for their publicity campaigns, and each was given regular prime TV time to broadcast its political messages. The U.S. press focused on the opposition rallies being stormed by "mobs" of Sandinista supporters, but the National Electoral Council reported that only 5 of the some 250 opposition rallies were disrupted. In no case were there any dead or wounded— a marked contrast with election campaigns in El Salvador and Guatemala, where political candidates have been assassinated.[7]

Three conservative parties of the CDN coalition did not participate in the elections and called for voter abstention. Although the Reagan administration presented the CDN as a highly popular opposition group, most Nicaraguans were barely familiar with the political coalition. Despite much publicity, the CDN was only able to draw crowds of several hundred supporters for speeches by conservative spokesperson Arturo Cruz.

In December 1983, Cruz announced the CDN's refusal to participate in the elections unless the FSLN agreed to direct talks with the U.S.-sponsored *contras*. Although the government met other CDN demands regarding electoral safeguards, Cruz withdrew in July 1984—just four days after declaring his candidacy—still demanding direct talks between the government and the *contras*.

Even with the withdrawal of the conservative opposition, about 80 percent of the registered voters turned out for the elections to choose among candidates from seven parties. The elections proved a clear vote of confidence for the FSLN leadership. Over 60 percent of the voters chose Daniel Ortega for president and Sergio Ramirez for vice-president. Nationally, the FSLN won 61 of the 96 assembly seats. The two centrist parties (PLI and PCD) and the center-left PPSC together received 29 percent of the vote, even though the PLI presidential candidate withdrew his name ten days before the election. With the support of almost one-third of the electorate, these three parties gained significant power in the constituent assembly.

The three left-wing parties, which are characterized as "ultra-left" by the FSLN, shared 3.5 percent of the vote.[8] Considering the Reagan administration's characterization of the elections as being "Communist-style," it is ironic that the communist parties were the big losers in the elections. The left-wing parties previously had each held three seats in the council of state. After the election they were left with only two seats each in the newly formed constituent assembly.

The *Columbia Journalism Review* said that the U.S. television networks "all but ignored the Nicaraguan election" compared to the comprehensive coverage they gave of the 1982 Salvadoran election. International observers of Nicaragua's voting process called it "exemplary." The Latin American Studies Association (LASA) found that the elections were conducted in a fair and efficient manner. In its report, the prestigious academic group reported that the percent of adults voting in the Nicaraguan election was higher than comparable elections in 12 other Latin American nations.[10] Among other conclusions of the LASA observers were: "vote was truly a secret ballot," "Sandinistas made major concessions to opposition forces on nearly all points of contention," and "no major political party was denied access to the electoral process."[11]

Political Parties

Extreme Left

Nicaraguan Socialist Party (PSN): The PSN, founded in 1944, opposed armed struggle until 1977 and is critical, yet supportive, of FSLN. Its labor federation (CGTI) is second only to the CST of the FSLN.[12]

Communist Party of Nicaragua (PCdeN): This party was formed from a split in the PSN in 1970. Initially strongly anti-FSLN, its confrontations with government have lessened considerably. It favors deepening of agrarian reform. The Party's leadership was jailed in 1980 for allegedly fomenting strikes.

Popular Action Movement/Marxist-Leninist (MAP/ML): Founded by ex-FSLN members in 1970, MAP/ML has had confrontations with the FSLN government stemming from MAP/ML's ultra-left politics. It is linked to Frente Obrero trade union, and feels pace of nationalization should be quickened. Calls for suppression of all bourgeois parties.

Left

Sandinista National Liberation Front (FSLN): Founded in 1961 and named after Nicaraguan nationalist Augusto César Sandino. The FSLN emerged in the 1970s as the leader of the movement to overthrow Somoza. It has organized unions, with a combined membership of 175,000, in virtually all sectors of the work force. It has also organized mass organizations such as youth and women's groups. Its Sandinista Defense Committee has more than 300,000 active members.

Popular Social Christian Party (PPSC): Founded in 1976, PPSC split from right-wing PSC. It advocates socialism based on Christian principles. Its leader Mauricio Díaz was elected to serve as one of the three vice-presidents of the National Constituent Assembly.

Center

Independent Liberal Party (PLI): Founded in 1944 as a split-off of Somoza's Liberal Party, the PLI has conditionally supported the FSLN government. The party has its base in middle-class and intellectual groups as well as traditionally liberal peasant families. Its candidate, Virgilio Godoy Reyes, withdrew shortly before the election, but his name was still on the ballot. The PLI's membership and most of its base disagreed with Godoy's decision, thereby dividing the party. Godoy was minister of labor until he resigned to participate in the elections.

Democratic Conservative Party (PCD): Descendent of the traditional conservative/liberal split of the nineteenth century. PCD identifies with conservative parties of Europe. This center-right party calls for negotiations with the *contras*. Before a February 1984 split over issues of support for the FSLN government, its membership included opposition spokesman, Arturo Cruz. Its leader Clemente Guido was elected to be one of three vice-presidents of the national constituent assembly.

Right

Nicaraguan Democratic Coordinator (CDN): Three conservative parties formed this coalition in 1980. The liberal Constitutionalist Party (PLC) describes itself as "devoted to the reconciliation of the Nicaraguan family." The strongest CDN member is the Social Christian Party (PSC), which has close links with other Christian Democratic parties, such as those in Costa Rica and El Salvador. It suffered a loss in popular membership when the PPSC bolted from its ranks in 1976. The third founding party of the CDN is the Social Democratic Party (PSD), formed in 1979 after the Sandinista triumph. PSD sought but was denied membership in Socialist International, which generally supports the FSLN government. PSD leader Luis Rivas is president of CDN, which has affiliations with the following organizations: the daily newspaper *La Prensa*, COSEP (Superior Council of Private Enterprise), and CTN and CUS trade-union federations (of Social Christian and AIFLD allegiance, respectively). It has been "inoperative" since the 1984 elections due to internal disagreements about the decision not to participate in the electoral process and about cooperation with *contra* organizations.

The Armed Counterrevolution

Thousands of members of Somoza's National Guard fled Nicaragua after the

Sandinista triumph. A group of around 60 exiled former guardsmen created a terrorist force called the "15th of September Legion" in Honduras. A few short months after the revolution, they commenced their war of terrorism against Nicaragua. Soon Argentine military experts were advising these Honduran-based guardsmen.

In late 1981, prospects for the Somocistas quickly improved. The leader of the guardsmen, Colonel Enrique Bermúdez Varela recalled that time. Suddenly, he said, "I could feel the steps of a giant animal."[13] The giant animal was the Central Intelligence Agency, which took control of the counterrevolutionary war. In the next three years, the CIA fashioned the motley group of guardsmen into a counterrevolutionary army which the CIA labeled the Nicaraguan Democratic Force (FDN).

At first, President Reagan told Congress that covert aid to the *contras* would be used to help interdict arms flowing from Nicaragua to El Salvador. Unable to prove that arms were being shipped from Nicaragua, the president said later the aid would put pressure on the Sandinistas to change their style of government. By 1985 President Reagan admitted that U.S. aid was being given so that the "freedom fighters" would "remove" the Sandinistas.

A 1985 study entitled *Who Are the Contras?* by the Arms Control and Foreign Policy Caucus of the U.S. Senate revealed the degree to which the FDN was a reincarnation of Somoza's National Guard. The study found that 46 of the FDN's 48 military leaders had been members of the *guardia*. Chief military commander, Enrique Bermúdez Varela, served as Somoza's military attaché in Washington until June 1979.

While President Reagan called the FDN *contras* "freedom fighters" and the "moral equivalent to our Founding Fathers," congressional critics of aid to the *contras* saw them as little more than terrorists. In opposing the administration's aid requests, Senator Tom Harkin noted that the *contras* "have promised to bring to Managua a reign of terror that will make the French Revolution look like a Labor Day picnic. Their methods are those of the Marquis de Sade, not the Marquis de Lafayette."[14] A FDN member told *Newsweek* in November 1982, "Come the counterrevolution, there will be bodies from the Honduran border to Managua."

Edgar Chamorro, who was dumped from the FDN's civilian directorate in 1984 for criticizing human-rights abuses by the former guardsmen, told *News-week* that the *guardia* have no political agenda beyond a desire to restore a Somoza-like regime. Chamorro said they just want "to return to the way things were before" and "to settle accounts" with the Sandinistas.[15]

The Practices of the "Freedom Fighters"

A 1984 report by the Council on Hemispheric Affairs condemned the *contras* as being one of the "worst human-rights violators" in Latin America. A study by Americas Watch and the Lawyers Committee for International Human Rights provided gruesome details of *contra* terrorism. Below is an excerpt from an interview with a *contra*. The authors of the West German book, *La Contra*, said the purpose of the book's interviews was to let the *contras* reveal who they really are in their own words.

Eduardo López Valenzuela, member, Nicaraguan Democratic Force (FDN), spoke about attacks upon civilians:

> We arrived at the road at 4:30, and proceeded at once to set up our roadblock. A blue jeep with 13 people appeared. The 13 people got out and lined up in front for us. Among them were three nurses. Jimmy Leo, Polo and Ruben proceeded to rape all three. The women pleaded with them to stop but no one paid any attention to them. After the rape, they fired salvos of 20 shots from their FALs [a type of automatic rifle—eds.] in the breast and head of each woman.
>
> Then Jimmy Leo went up to one of them who looked like a foreigner, who said, "Stop this shooting, we are civilians. I am a doctor from Germany. Don't murder us!"
>
> Jimmy paid no attention to this, and as the foreigner once more cried, "Don't murder us," Jimmy proceeded to fill him with lead from his FAL, from his head down to his chest. After he shot him, Jimmy turned to me and said, "Now it's your turn." So I went and killed a person wearing blue pants and a white shirt. One shot after another from the machine gun, five in the head and five in the chest.
>
> When they were all dead, we were satisfied. We were happy, and shouted out many times: "With God and Patriotism we will overthrow the communists" and "Long live the FDN."[16]

The Contras

Nicaraguan Democratic Force (FDN): In August 1981, the CIA formed the FDN from disparate groups of Somoza *guardia* and the next year the CIA formed a civilian directorate of FDN to broaden support and improve its public image. This directorate, however, has little control over the military command. Adolfo Calero (former president of the Nicaraguan Chamber of Commerce and owner of the country's Coca-Cola franchise) is the chief political representative while Colonel Enrique Bermúdez Valera runs military operations. In 1985, the FDN claimed 12,000 fighters. Bolstered by new U.S. aid and the disintegration of ARDE, the FDN began to relocate some of its forces to Costa Rica in 1985.

Nicaraguan Opposition Union (UNO): UNO was an organization set up by Washington in an attempt to represent the entire counterrevolutionary movement. Its principals are known as the three 'A's: Adolfo Calero, Alfonso Robelo, and Arturo Cruz. It calls for a government of reconciliation. The United States channels its "humanitarian" aid through UNO. The FDN is the military arm of UNO. All U.S. official "humanitarian" aid is being channeled through UNO.

Revolutionary Democratic Alliance (ARDE): This coalition was formed in early 1982 in Costa Rica among Alfonso Robelo's MDN and two armed guerrilla groups: the Nicaraguan Democratic Union (UDN) and the Revolutionary Front of Sandino (FRS). The latter group was a creation of the former Sandinista hero Eden Pastora, who commanded the ARDE forces. His ambivalent attitude about cooperating with former guardsmen in the FDN resulted in reduced U.S. support in 1984. The Misurasata (see below) was allied with ARDE but withdrew support when ARDE began cooperating with FDN. The millionaire Alfonso Robelo also backed out of ARDE, but he threw his support to the FDN. ARDE never had more than about 2000 combatants. Lack of progress in the war and money problems caused hundreds of ARDE members to petition for refugee status within Costa Rica in late 1984.

MISURA: A force of about 1000—mainly Miskito Indians—in Honduras formed by Steadman Fagoth, who has publicly declared his alliance with the CIA. The group is allied with the FDN. It says it is fighting for Indian rights as part of a war against Sandinismo.

Misurasata: A guerrilla army based in Costa Rica of about 1500 Miskito Indians commanded by Brooklyn Rivera, who says the focus of the war is justice for Indians, not the military defeat of the Sandinistas.

Indian Opposition

The Atlantic coast was incorporated into the Republic of Nicaragua in 1894, but it has always remained separate from the country's political and economic life. The region's main resources—wood, gold, fish, and bananas—were developed by U.S. firms in partnership with the Somoza family. There was only scant participation by the Atlantic coast population in the uprising against Somoza. Aware of the special problems of the Atlantic coast, the Sandinistas stated in their 1969 program that the revolution would "wipe out the odious discrimination to which the indigenous Miskitos, Sumus, Zambos [Garifuna or Carib blacks], and blacks of this region are subjected."[17]

When the victorious Sandinistas came to the Atlantic coast, its residents tended to distrust the olive-clad Sandinistas as the new "Spanish" rulers. The FSLN representatives sent to the region compounded this tension by assuming that only one genuine national question faced Nicaragua—that of the Nicaraguan nation as a whole—rather than recognizing the national identities of the Indian population.[18]

In 1979, William Ramirez, FSLN's political secretary for northern Zelaya, commented on these early problems. "There were no Sandinista Miskito leaders who could head up and guide the population," Ramirez recalled, "and we who arrived were people of the Pacific, [and] unable to communicate with the population. We didn't know the language, and we also didn't know the customs, the characteristics, the way of life, the religious problem, the ethnic problem."[19]

Tensions between the Sandinistas and the Miskitos worsened considerably in late 1981, when Honduras-based *contras* launched "Red Christmas"—a plan designed to create a secessionist movement among the Miskitos. In November 1981, *contras* attacked Miskito villages along the Rio Coco border area. The CIA-funded *contra* radio station "September 15" sparked panic among the entire Miskito population by broadcasting that Sandinista planes were coming to bomb their villages. Steadman Fagoth and the other *contras* said that the Sandinistas believed all Miskitos were in revolt and were coming to punish them. Largely as a result of this misinformation, as many as 10,000 Miskitos fled to join relatives in Honduras and 2000 went to Costa Rica.

In January 1982, the Sandinistas told the Miskitos that they had to move inland, away from the Rio Coco, so the Sandinistas could protect them against *contra* terrorism and forced recruitment into the *contra* armies. About 12,000 Miskitos were moved in a series of forced relocations in 1982–1983 by the Nicaraguan government.

Americas Watch concluded "that the serious attacks across the border in November and December 1981, events known as 'Red Christmas,' provided reasonable grounds for the decision to evacuate the border area to be justified by military necessity." Americas Watch did criticize the manner in which the relocation was conducted—because the Miskitos had no part in the decision and were given very short or no notice at all.[20]

The Moravian Church, to which most Miskitos belong, also recognized the need for the evacuation of approximately 35 border villages: "We lament the natural difficulties which were produced by the evacuation of the Rio Coco to the interior of the country because given the situation in the [Rio Coco] area, it is impossible to live in peace. We support our government in the work of evacuation and the efforts to normalize activities in the region as a whole."[21]

Several U.S. Indian groups condemned the manipulation of the Miskitos by the *contras* and Washington, although others support the armed anti-Sandinista opposition. The International Indian Treaty Council stated:

> Although the relocation was difficult for the Miskito, the government of Nicaragua has provided health care, transport, and arable lands for farming in the new location. . . . Our greatest concern is for those Miskitos who have been manipulated into crossing the border and are now being used by the anti-government forces. We remember clearly the minorities who were used by the CIA in Laos and Vietnam, and who later became outcasts among their own people once the CIA didn't need them anymore.[22]

In 1984, the International Justice Fund, a project of the National Center for Immigrants' Rights in Los Angeles, reached the following conclusions in a report on the Miskito issue in Nicaragua:

- The U.S. government played a principal role in creating dangerous conditions which precipitated Miskito relocations.
- After the relocation, the United States engaged in a disinformation campaign, falsely charging Sandinistas with violations of human rights.
- Nicaragua acted in compliance within international legal standards in its relocation program.
- The government is making good faith efforts to work with Miskito people and restore peace.[23]

By 1985, relations between the Miskitos and the Sandinistas had begun to improve as a result of a series of government initiatives to develop the Atlantic coast and to grant limited autonomy to the Indian people. The government promoted bilingual education, opened new development projects in the severely depressed region, and granted amnesty to Miskito *contras*. The Sandinistas began repatriating Miskitos to the Rio Coco area in June 1985.

Among the features of the autonomy are: a regional assembly, two government administrations dividing Zelaya into north and south, regional government involvement in the naming of federal ministers to work in the region, and control over natural resources by regional governments.

"As the benefits of the revolution arrive in Northern Zelaya," said the FSLN's William Ramirez, "the propaganda of the counterrevolution crashes into the reality of the deeds that people see."

These efforts, along with the government's willingness to meet other demands from Indian groups, softened opposition leader Brooklyn Rivera's criticisms of the Sandinistas. During a visit to Nicaragua in late 1984, he said that the Sandinista revolution made mistakes in these areas, "but the situation was exploited by foreign forces to discredit the revolution and manipulate the Miskitos. We disagree with that, because we are a people of peace."[24]

Nicaraguan Indian Groups

Miskitos, Sumus, Ramas, and Sandinistas United (Misurasata): This group was organized by the Sandinistas a few months after their victory. Among those chosen to lead Misurasata were two of the small number of formally educated Miskitos: Steadman Fagoth and Brooklyn Rivera. Rather than developing into a mass organization that would support the goals of the revolution, Misurasata became an opposition group that was deeply critical of the Sandinistas.

In early 1981, the Sandinistas jailed the Misurasata leadership. It quickly released all the Miskito leaders except for Fagoth, who was accused of being a CIA accomplice. The government released a letter found in the files of Somoza's secret police which described Fagoth's earlier work as a spy for the secret police. After being conditionally released in May 1981, Fagoth fled to Honduras. In January 1982, Fagoth declared "open war against Sandinismo." He joined forces with the original *contra* group of former guardsmen called the "Legion of September 15." Fagoth soon thereafter formed his own band of counterrevolutionaries called Misura.

Brooklyn Rivera split with Fagoth in 1983 and revived Misurasata as an army of Miskito Indians who were allied with the ARDE *contra* group in Costa Rica. Rivera had strong reservations about working with former guardsmen. In 1984, when ARDE did start collaborating with the FDN, Rivera withdrew his support of the ARDE *contras*. That year Misurasata also began negotiating with the Sandinistas. Unlike Fagoth's Misura, Misurasata says it is not anti-Sandinista, only pro-Indian rights.

In mid-1985, Rivera tried to extend his influence over Miskitos in Honduras by calling for the formation of a unified pan-Atlantic Coast indigenous organization called Asla (Miskito for unity). Asla intends to be a "united political, diplomatic, and military front."

Miskitos, Sumus, and Ramas Together (MISURA): Indian *contra* army allied with the FDN and led by Jan Steadman Fagoth Muller. He worked alongside the CIA and the FDN in the "Red Christmas" terrorist operation, causing thousands of Miskitos to migrate to Honduras by warning Miskitos that they would be massacred by the Sandinistas. Fagoth was expelled from Honduras in January 1985 after declaring at a press conference that he would order the execution of 23 captured Nicaraguan troops if the Sandinistas tried to rescue them. After several years of collaborating with the FDN and CIA, Fagoth lost the majority of his following among the Miskito people.

Nicaraguan Indian Coast Unity (KISAN): A new Indian group formed in late 1985 to act as a channel for U.S. humanitarian assistance to the *contras*. KISAN is simply another name for MISURA, although it says it represents all Indians.

Misitan: A pro-Sandinista Miskito organization formed in 1984. Its two founding goals were to reunite the estimated 13,000 Miskito refugees in Costa Rica and Honduras with their families in Nicaragua and to promote bilingual programs for the Indian and Creole population. Misitan praised the government's proposals for coastal autonomy which were introduced to the constituent assembly in 1985. No previous example is available for the autonomy of indigenous groups in Latin America.

Church Hierarchy Opposes Revolution

Within Nicaragua, two sectors—the Catholic Church hierarchy and private business—present the most serious opposition to the revolution. The success of the elections and the patriotic unity forged by the *contra* war of aggression and U.S. imperialist actions have undermined the strength of domestic opposition to the Nicaraguan government. After six years, the private sector and the government have moved toward accommodation and understanding. The Catholic Church hierarchy, however, has moved into the forefront of the domestic opposition and has lent considerable moral support to the violent counterrevolution.

Archbishop (now Cardinal) Miguel Obando y Bravo supported the movement to overthrow Somoza but was not a FSLN sympathizer. In much the same way as the private sector, the Catholic Church recognized the leading role of the Sandinistas in the revolution but expected that more moderate elements would assume political power after the triumph. During the 1970s, the Catholic Church was close to the Social Christian Party but felt its political role diminished when the progressive wing of the party split off to establish the Popular Social Christian Party.

About the same time the *contra* war began heating up, the Sandinista government also encountered rising opposition from the Catholic Church hierarchy. As Obando y Bravo's criticisms sharpened, the divisions within the church widened. By 1984, the church establishment, supported by the Vatican, had become part of the internal counterrevolution. While even leading anti-Sandinistas in the private sector protested Washington's role in the expanding *contra* terrorism, the archbishop remained silent.

In June 1984, a major crisis arose when a close associate of Obando y Bravo's, Father Luis Armando Pena, was accused by Nicaragua's State Security of trafficking arms and explosives in collusion with the FDN. The government presented videos as proof of Pena's guilt, but the archbishop refused to examine them. Instead, the archbishop led a march in solidarity with Father Pena, after which the government responded by expelling 10 foreign priests who had participated in the march.[25]

Making use of the archbishop's opposition to the Sandinistas, the U.S.-based right-wing Institute of Religion and Democracy (IRD) sponsored Obando y Bravo on a speaking tour throughout the United States. He also linked up with the corporate right wing, which channeled money to the Catholic Church's training program in Nicaragua. J. Peter Grace of W.R. Grace & Company, a pillar of the elite Catholic men's organization Knights of Malta, arranged for contributions to the Catholic Church's anti-Sandinista popular educational organizations from his Sarita Kennedy East Foundation. In a memorandum about his meeting with the archbishop, John J. Meehan, an executive of W.R. Grace, said, "The archbishop has been working on a 'development plan' to thwart the Marxist-Leninist policies of the Sandinistas."[26]

Nicaraguan Vice-President Sergio Ramírez calls Obando y Bravo "the spiritual leader of the right wing." It is the FSLN's opinion that the archbishop considers the days of the Sandinistas numbered, but that he will eventually recognize that the revolution is not going to be toppled. "History shows," said Ramírez, "that the church ultimately comes to terms with all forms of power. Monseñor Obando is going to be archbishop of Managua until he is 75 years old, and during that time, we intend to continue exercising revolutionary power here."[27]

The Nicaraguan government also counts on strong religious support both within and outside the country. The Vatican tried to break these ties by ordering that all priests holding government positions resign. Father Edgar Parrales, ambassador to the Organization of American States, said: "I have been asked to choose between the exercise of my priestly functions and the betrayal of my people." Parrales and the other priests serving with the Sandinistas declined to obey Rome.

Ernesto Cardenal, a former Trappist monk, stayed on as the minister of culture. Fernando Cardenal, his brother, is minister of education, and was expelled from the Jesuit order (which was pressured by the Pope) for refusing to leave his position. Father Miguel D'Escoto, a Maryknoll priest, is minister of foreign relations. Because of their refusal to step down from their appointed government positions, the four Sandinista priests are not allowed to perform priestly functions by decree of Pope John Paul II.

Building a People's Economy

In 1979, the Sandinistas inherited a devastated economy. According to the United Nations, over 25 percent of Nicaragua's factories suffered damage to plant and inventory during the insurrection, and over 90 percent closed completely during the final stages of the war. The war cost Nicaragua $500 million in physical damage, $200 million in lost cotton exports, and $700 million in capital flight, as well as a 25 percent reduction in its cattle herd. Unemployment was 40 percent at the time of the victory, and inflation was 80 percent.[28] The Somoza family had plundered the national banks, leaving only $3.6 million in the national treasury and a national debt of $1.6 billion.

In 1979 the new government set out to reconstruct the country and to create a new economic system that would for the first time meet the needs of the country's peasants and workers. Xabier Gorostiaga, a Jesuit economist who worked in the Nicaraguan ministry of planning, described the Sandinista philosophy this way:

> Our strategy differs from other models of economic development whose first priority is to establish a model of accumulation. Our first objective is to satisfy the basic needs of the majority of the population. This creates a new logic, which we call the "logic of the majority"— the logic of the poor. Instead of organizing the economy from the perspective and interests of the top 5 percent, as was done during the Somoza dynasty, we are trying to organize the economy from the perspective of the majority.[29]

The Sandinistas were not utopian in their economic vision. Minister of Agriculture Jaime Wheelock described the state of underdevelopment facing the new government. "What are we? A country of cotton pickers, coffee pickers, and cane cutters, with a small administrative structure of bookkeepers."[30] Nonetheless, the FSLN brought with them a conviction that they could put Nicaragua on the path of development. "With the revolution," said Wheelock, "Nicaraguans can begin to decide something as basic as what to produce. We can develop a new type of trade and consider other markets."[31]

The first few years after the revolution brought improvements for most *campesinos* and workers. In 1983, Nicaragua had the highest rate of economic growth of any Latin American country. But as the *contra* war intensified, and Washington's war of destabilization began to work, the economy deteriorated in 1984 and further in 1985.

To deal with the crisis, President Daniel Ortega announced an austerity plan in early 1985. Nicaragua's self-imposed austerity program included the following measures: devaluation through a staggered exchange rate that penalizes importers of nonessential products; end of government subsidies of many staples controlled through state distribution channels such as eggs and milk; periodic increase in wages to offset higher prices; freeze on state spending; and opening of state foreign-exchange houses at free-market rates to boost the state's supply of dollars and curb the black market.

The government promised to take the following steps to boost the economy:

- Production of goods for popular consumption to minimize imports.
- Increase of public investment programs to stimulate growth.
- Incentive programs for highly productive workers.
- Price hikes and other incentives for efficient producers.
- Reaffirmation of the principle of a mixed economy.
- Redirection of social services from the cities to rural sectors.

President Ortega, while acknowledging that the government's previous economic policies had weaknesses, pinned much of the blame for the decline in the economy since 1984 on the war with the *contras*. Nicaragua expanded its 1985 defense budget in the hope of being able to deal a serious blow to the *contras* and thereby reduce the attacks on its agricultural production. Because of the cost of the war, Ortega also included among his economic priorities a commitment for an urgent search for peace negotiated with the U.S. government.

Since the private sector did not initiate much new investment after 1979, the government tried to push the economy forward with its own ambitious new investment projects. Mostly agro-industrial complexes, these include a huge sugar-refining complex, a fruit and vegetable processing plant, dairy farms, and a thread plant in Esteli. But the Sandinista government is still hoping that private enterprise will increase its stake in the new Nicaragua.

In 1985, Ortega promised to "protect the private sector and put all possible resources at its disposal." Industries that fulfill defense requirements and produce essential consumer goods for domestic consumption will get preferential access to foreign exchange. New initiatives by the Sandinistas to address the economic demands of the private sector were favorably received by business owners.

Asked about the possible socialism of the Nicaraguan economy, Dionisio "Nicho" Marenco, minister of commerce and industry, offered this pragmatic response: "Put briefly, socialism in Nicaragua is at this moment mathematically impossible." Because of chronic underdevelopment and resulting massive unemployment, Marenco explained, Nicaragua evolved into a country populated with small vendors and businessmen. "Whenever you buy something on the street or in the market, you can be sure it has passed through five or six sets of hands. Our problem isn't socialism or capitalism. Our problem is trying to figure out how to take the thousands of people you see on the street selling snowcones and homemade cookies and incorporate them into productive factory work even though we have no factories."[32]

War of Economic Destabilization

In October 1980, the right-wing Heritage Foundation published a report by former CIA agent Cleto DiGiovanni that discussed the prospects of an economic war against the Sandinistas. "Nicaraguan workers," said the Foundation, "continue to have an emotional attachment to the revolutionary movement. This attachment can be expected to weaken as the economy deteriorates. . . . There are some indications of growing broadly based support to take to arms to overthrow the Sandinist government, and this support could increase as further economic problems develop." The foundation report, which became the blueprint for President Reagan's policy, suggested that "economic shortcomings might provoke at least limited civil unrest" as early as the summer of 1981.[33]

The financial damage done by the *contras* from 1981–1985 was accompanied by an open war of economic aggression by Washington. Using trade and assistance, the Reagan administration tried to force the Sandinistas to "say uncle," as Reagan hoped publicly in early 1985. Finally, in May of that year, President Reagan imposed a trade embargo on Nicaragua under the provisions of the International Emergency Economic Powers Act. The president said that he found "that the policies and actions of the Government of Nicaragua constitute an unusual and extraordinary threat to the national security and foreign policy of the United States." The embargo was opposed by 25 Latin American nations, with only Honduras and El Salvador supporting Washington.

Nicaragua has been hurt by the following U.S. measures: 1) restricting trade, 2) cutting off bilateral aid, 3) blocking multilateral aid, and 4) discouraging foreign investment and commercial bank lending. Combined, these measures succeeded in halting the economic progress the Sandinistas had made in their first two years. But the economic pressure did not have the immediate political effect hoped for by Washington.[34]

As William Leo Grande, professor at American University, pointed out: "It's exactly the same dynamic that you saw in Cuba. The economic blockade made people's ordinary lives very difficult, and yet it made Fidel Castro politically stronger. The problems of the people's daily lives were sacrifices in the struggle against imperialism. And they saw them that way. So they didn't blame the government for the economic problems." Leo Grande predicted that the same thing would happen in Nicaragua.[35]

Richard Feinberg, an economist at the Overseas Development Council, said that the destabilization is primarily aimed "to create discontent in the middle class" and thereby add to the counterrevolutionary sentiment within Nicaragua. "Without foreign exchange," said Feinberg, "not only can reconstruction not take place, but the government can't afford to import the goods the middle class needs."[36]

Reagan's Economic Weapons

Trade and Credits

One of the first weapons used by the Reagan administration to force Nicaragua to "say uncle" was the cut-off of all trade credits from Eximbank and the Commodity Credit Corporation. Without the guaranteed export and import credits offered by Washington, U.S. corporations were reluctant to trade with Nicaragua. Specific measures taken by the Reagan administration to make trade more difficult and costly for Nicaragua included the cancellation in 1981 of a "Food for Peace" credit line to purchase U.S. wheat, the suspension in 1983 of 90 percent of Nicaragua's sugar quota with the United States, and the trade embargo imposed in May 1985. Largely as a result of these policies, U.S.-Nicaraguan trade dropped from $400 million in 1977 to $170 million in 1984.[37]

Bilateral Aid

When the Sandinistas assumed control of the government in 1979, the country was ripe for aid. Washington granted $75 million in economic assistance to the devastated nation but restricted most of the money to the private sector. Shortly after Reagan became president in 1981, he blocked the remaining $15 million of the promised $75 million in economic aid and cancelled an AID-managed credit line to purchase U.S. wheat. He also cut off all new bilateral aid to Nicaragua except for $7.5 million that was to go to the private sector. Nicaragua rejected this aid, which was earmarked for the major and predominantly antagonistic private-sector business organizations.

According to the State Department's Otto Reich, the aid was a "symbol of moral and political support" for Nicaraguans who "desire to be free."[38] The

Sandinistas said that aid to such openly hostile organizations as the Superior Council of Private Enterprise (COSEP) had "political motivation designed to promote resistance and destabilize the revolutionary government." As a whole, Nicaragua has been conspicuously excluded from the regional development recommendations of Reagan's Caribbean Basin Initiative and the Kissinger Commission.

Multilateral Aid

Multilateral aid from International Financial Institutions (IFIs) like the World Bank, the International Monetary Fund, and the Inter-American Development Bank (IDB) has been repeatedly blocked by the United States, which can strongly influence multilateral lending patterns because of its control of a large percentage of IFI votes. (See Table 2I.)

Asked what single step made by the U.S. government, aside from supporting the *contras*, has been most damaging to Nicaragua's economy, Jim Morrell, research director of the Center for International Policy, said, "There has been nothing more troublesome than the pressure the United States has exerted on the international lending institutions."[39] During the first two years after their victory, Nicaragua did receive its fair share of international lending, but since 1983 the government has been receiving only a small fraction of the amount going to other countries in the region.

The United States has a policy of voting against all international loans to Nicaragua. Because most other countries support Nicaraguan loan proposals, it has been able to receive some multilateral lending. In the case of the Special Operations Fund of the IDB, the United States has been able to block all lending because of its strong veto power over that "loan window" of the bank. In 1985, the United States threatened to withdraw all its funding to the IDB if it approved any more loans to Nicaragua. While most Latin American countries have expressed their disapproval of Washington's pressure of the bank, they have been reluctant to confront their giant colossus to the north.

Pressured by the United States, the World Bank stopped funding Nicaragua after 1982. Relations between the International Monetary Fund and the Sandinistas were strained even before the FSLN triumphed in July 1979. Only two months before the Sandinista's victory, the IMF promised Somoza $66 million, rejecting the FSLN's protests that Somoza would use the funds to continue the brutal repression of the mass insurrection. Somoza absconded with the initial payment of the loan, $22 million, and left only $3.6 million in the national treasury. The IMF demanded immediate repayment of its loan by the financially strapped Sandinista government. No new loans from the IMF have been forthcoming, although Nicaragua is expected to negotiate a repayment in 1985.

Banks and Corporations

Washington's refusal to issue insurance from the Overseas Private Investment

Corporation (OPIC) discourages new foreign investment in Nicaragua. This decision acts as a disincentive for current TNC investors to expand their operations in Nicaragua. The June 1983 closing by Washington of Nicaragua's six consulates in the United States made it all the more difficult for potential investors and traders to contact Nicaraguan officials. Washington also hampered the country's ability to obtain commercial financing. As one U.S. banker explained: "We think the U.S. government is going to push Nicaragua into a default whether it's by backing exile invasion or cutting off their access to credit."[40]

The overlap between the U.S.-directed *contra* war and economic destabilization was made clear by the spring 1984 mining of Nicaraguan harbors. The CIA's purpose was to intimidate international shippers, thereby disrupting trade and worsening Nicaragua's oil shortage. After the mining, Exxon, which operates the country's only oil refinery, informed the government that it would no longer allow its own ships to enter Nicaraguan waters. A U.S. official explained that the mines were placed by the CIA to "wake up the folks in Lloyd's of London."[41]

"Companies with operations in the region are intensely anticommunist," said Gary Springer, an analyst for Business International Corporation, the publisher of *Business Latin America*. "But there is a feeling that what Reagan is doing is not good for business, and that economic aid is [what is] needed down there. ...Businessmen are worried that they will end up bearing the brunt of an invasion."[42]

Violations of International Law

Washington's economic war against Nicaragua has violated numerous international laws and treaties, including the following:

Organization of American States Charter: "No State may use or encourage the use of coercive measures of an economic or political character in order to force the sovereign will of another state." (Article 19)

UN Charter of Economic Rights: "Every State has the sovereign and inalienable right to choose its economic system as well as its political, social, and cultural systems ... without outside interference, coercion, or threat." (Article 1)

"No State may use or encourage the use of economic, political or any other type of measures to coerce another state in order to obtain from it the subordination of the exercise of its sovereign rights." (Article 32)

General Agreement on Tariffs and Trade (GATT): In October 1983, GATT (of which the United States is a member) concluded that the United States had violated its charter and suggested that it allocate a sugar quota consistent with GATT's criteria on fair trade.

Agreement Establishing the Inter-American Development Bank: "The Bank ... shall not interfere in the political affairs of any member, nor shall they be influenced in their decisions by the political character of the member or members concerned. Only economic considerations shall be relevant...." (Section 5)

Source: Institute for Policy Studies (IPS), "The Economic War Against Nicaragua," March 1985

The Question of Soviet Aid

Since 1981, Washington cut Nicaragua off from all bilateral aid and has blocked numerous multilateral loans. When President Daniel Ortega traveled to Moscow in 1985 to seek development aid, Washington pointed to the trip as proof that Nicaragua was indeed a Soviet-bloc nation. Yet Nicaragua was hardly the first Latin American nation to seek Soviet aid. According to State Department figures, 15 other noncommunist Latin American nations preceded Nicaragua in the receipt of Soviet economic aid, including Brazil and Argentina.

Nicaragua first received Soviet aid in 1980, when it signed an agreement with Moscow for assistance to agriculture, fisheries, mining, and energy. Separate agreements were signed for military assistance. Soviet aid peaked in 1982 at about $250 million, falling to about $150 million for each of the two following years. After the 1985 U.S. trade embargo of Nicaragua, Soviet aid returned to the 1982 level. Soviet aid to Nicaragua has frequently picked up where U.S. aid left off. When the United States canceled PL480 food shipments in 1981, the gap in food aid was filled by the Soviet Union, Bulgaria, and East Germany.[43]

Noncommunist donors have also stepped in to provide economic assistance when Washington blocked multilateral lending to Nicaragua. After the United States vetoed a proposed $2 million loan by the Inter-American Development Bank (IDB) for a rural roads project in 1983, Nicaragua turned to the Netherlands for the necessary financing. Similarly, Nicaragua successfully appealed to Canada when the IDB failed to act on its request for help with a hydropower development project.[44] Nicaragua has sought broad support for its economic development. Italy has made a financial commitment for a project that will produce electricity from volcanic gases, and France has granted a loan for improvement of Nicaragua's telecommunications system.

Striving for a Mixed Economy

The Sandinistas are committed to a mixed economy, meaning one where private enterprise, cooperatives, and the state sector all produce and market their goods. Immediately after the revolution, the state role in the economy increased dramatically from the confiscation of the property owned by the Somoza family and their close associates. Those appropriations made the government the owner of about 20 percent of the farmland and a large collection of agro-industries and manufacturing plants including sugar mills, cement factories, and fishing businesses.

Because of the enormous difficulties of managing such a large economic sector, the FSLN encouraged the private sector to stay in Nicaragua and participate actively in the country's economic growth. But the new government insisted that the private sector would not be given political power—which they said would be in the hands of those who represent the interests of peasants and workers, namely, the FSLN and the mass organizations.

Peter Marchetti, Jesuit sociologist who works at the government's land-reform institute, summed up the FSLN's position: "The Sandinistas are saying to the economic elite, 'We'll protect your private property, but you can no longer translate wealth into political power. The great majority of our people are very poor. This is a government that is going to respect their needs.'"[45]

Many wealthy business owners did not appreciate being excluded from political decision making and became part of the counterrevolution. The base of the private-sector opposition has been the Superior Council of Private Enterprise (COSEP), the business organization that unites the richest elements of the country's agricultural, service, and industrial private sector. COSEP helped establish the anti-Sandinista political coalition CDN and is among its most conservative elements. Many COSEP members have become open supporters of the *contras*.

Two other groups of large producers exist in Nicaragua. One group, which is allied with the political center, continues to produce but complains that the FSLN is destroying the country's business climate. The other group, known as the "patriotic producers," has pushed output to an historic level and is at least mildly sympathetic to the aims of the Sandinistas. The most frequently cited example of a "patriotic producer" is the San Antonio sugar mill, the country's largest agribusiness, which employs 7000.[46]

In terms of the sizeable participation of the private sector in the country, Nicaragua can hardly be labeled a "communist state." The government accounts for about 40 percent of the GDP—a lower percentage than countries like Mexico and Brazil. State control of the economy varies from complete control of domestic banking, financing, insurance, external marketing, mining, and utilities to 16 percent of domestic agricultural production. Percentage of state control in other sectors are export agriculture (24), cattle (25), agro-industry (28), fishing (72), and manufacturing (32).[47]

The Nicaraguan government has tried to keep the state sector from growing because of its difficulty in managing what it already has. As part of the austerity measures announced in early 1985, Minister of Agriculture Wheelock said that state enterprises would be shut down if they did not make a profit. In keeping with Nicaragua's innovative approach to economic issues, Wheelock described the state enterprises as "new forms of social production where the laws of the market still strongly predominate."[48]

Agrarian Reform

The agricultural sector exemplifies Nicaragua's mixed economy. After the initial confiscation of Somoza's land, the government did not redistribute more land until 1981 when it passed an agrarian reform law allowing for expropriation of land only after judicial proceedings. Grounds for expropriation are failure to use land productively.

The Sandinistas call their approach to agrarian reform a system of a "mixed economy under popular hegemony." "More than control of the means of production," explained Minister of Agriculture Jaime Wheelock, "we are interested in controlling the economic surplus in order to distribute justly the nation's wealth."[49] While insisting that all external marketing be government controlled, the Sandinistas have encouraged even the large capitalist farms and ranches to increase their participation. Contrary to the image of Nicaragua propagated by the Reagan administration, private agricultural production is quite common in the land of Sandino.

Agrarian reform has radically changed the patterns of land ownership in Nicaragua. The three major changes are the decrease in the number of large private farms, the increase in agricultural cooperatives, and the emergence of a sizeable state sector. During the Somoza era, owners with over 850 acres controlled over one-third of the arable land. Their control has been cut to about one-tenth of total farmland. Cooperatives were practically nonexistent in Somoza's Nicaragua, but today almost one-fifth of the country's farmland is held by either Sandinista production cooperatives (9 percent) or credit/service associations (10 percent). The new state farms control about one-fifth of Nicaraguan cultivable land.

Together, large and medium-size private farms cover more than half the agricultural land. The total private sector accounts for just over 70 percent (including 62 percent unassociated individual producers and 10 percent who are members of 665 credit cooperatives) of Nicaragua's farmland.

The agrarian reform program ensured *campesino* support for the Sandinistas. The majority of landless *campesinos* benefiting from the land redistribution have expressed their trust in the revolution. "Before the land was for the colonels and the very rich. We were hired to cut the weeds and pick the cotton," said a member of a land-reform cooperative near León. "Now we get money from the bank to grow our own cotton and we own the land."[50] Describing the agrarian reform program in *Newsweek*, Jacobo Timerman wrote: "For many years, when peasants asked for land, they were answered with bullets. To be sure, today many peasants lack seeds, tractors, combines, and fertilizers. They still wait for better times, but at least they are waiting on their own land."[51]

The land reform program was cited as a major reason for solid *campesino* backing for the FSLN in the 1984 elections. Ramón Tellez, an ex-cotton-picker and current member of a 1500-acre cotton cooperative, recalled the election campaign: "Sure the politicians came around. Some said agrarian reform was a farce . . . that we didn't own the land . . . that the Sandinistas owned it and were simply the new *patrones*. Then the Communists came and told us the Sandinistas were making us into bourgeois peasants, dividing us from our brother farmworkers so we couldn't make a real socialist revolution. But we all voted for the Frente Sandinista because that is how we overcame the 'days of the rich.'"[52]

TABLE 13

SOCIAL PROGRESS IN NICARAGUA, 1978–1984

	1978–1979	1983–1984
Health Indicators		
Infant Mortality		
(per 1000)	121	74
% of Population with Access to		
Medical Care	28	80
Primary Care Units	172	446
Case of Disease:		
Measles	901	104
Polio	36	0
Tuberculosis	1,645	950
Education Advances		
Illiteracy	50%	13%
% GNP for Education	1%	5%
# of Children in Preschools	9,000	70,000
Total School Population	501,000	1,127,428
Organized Labor		
% of Workforce Organized	6	40

SOURCES: *Central America Bulletin*, Nov. 1984; Oxfam America, "Facts for Action: Nicaragua Development Under Fire," No. 8, 1984; Institute for Food and Development Policy, *What Difference Could a Revolution Make*, 1985; *American Journal of Public Health*, October 1984.

The Progress of the Revolution

The Sandinistas inherited a country with the worst life expectancy in Central America and one of the highest infant mortality rates. The health-care and education programs of the new government brought the Sandinistas international acclaim.

Some indicators of the advances made by the Nicaraguan revolution in its first four years include:

- World Health Organization (WHO) and the UN Children's Fund (UNICEF) both gave Nicaragua their awards for best health achievement in the third world.
- Nicaragua was unanimously chosen by the UN Education, Scientific and Cultural Organization (UNESCO) in 1980 for its Grand Prize in recognition for the country's National Literacy Crusade.
- After three years, Nicaraguans were eating 30 to 40 percent more rice, beans, and corn than before 1979.
- Diarrhea, the leading prerevolutionary cause of infant mortality, fell to fourth among causes by 1983.
- In recognition of its advances in health care, a Nicaraguan was elected as the president of the Pan American Health Organization in 1982.[53]

Setbacks Caused by Contra War, 1981–84

The war with the *contras* undercut many of the advances that the Sandinistas had made in their first several years to improve the social and economic condition of Nicaraguans:

- Infrastructure damage that cost the country more than $375 million.
- Over 150,000 Nicaraguans displaced or relocated.
- Defense budget increased from 7 percent of GDP in 1980–1981 to 40 percent in 1985.
- Forty-one health-care centers destroyed by *contras* and termination of popular health brigades in war zones because of death toll of health workers.
- Fifteen rural schools partially destroyed, construction of 27 interrupted, and 138 primary and 647 adult education centers closed in war zones.
- Twenty-three primary school and 135 popular education teachers murdered by *contras*.
- Close to 3000 Nicaraguans killed by *contras*.

Referring to slow progress in recent years, Nicaragua's Interior Minister Tomás Borge commented: "Some foreigners say we Sandinistas have recouped the property of Somoza. That's true, but what we really have recouped is the right to have hope."[54]

TNCs in Nicaragua

During the Somoza era, Nicaragua featured one of the region's most attractive foreign investment laws. TNCs came to Nicaragua in the 1960s to take advantage of the country's favorable investment climate and its "stable" political system under the Somoza family. Foreign investment in Nicaragua, however, did not approach the level of investment found in countries like Guatemala or Panama. The revolution immediately frightened off some foreign investors, but the San-dinistas encouraged the many who stayed on. The only expropriations were mining and lumber companies, industries that controlled the country's national resources. Nicaragua nationalized (with compensation) the gold and silver mines of Asarco, Rosario Resources (AMAX), and Noranda Mines—all of which had been abandoned during the insurrection.

Although the Sandinista government did not threaten other corporations with expropriation, there has been a gradual exodus of TNCs which have complained of the foreign-exchange crunch and the shrinking domestic market for their goods. The inability to secure trade guarantees and investment insurance from the U.S. government has also discouraged continued business operations in Nicaragua. TNCs also complain that the Sandinistas have been slow to announce a promised investment code that would delineate the rules for doing business in Nicaragua.

Only 30 of the top 500 U.S. corporations are still in the country. The largest of these are Exxon (oil refinery), General Mills (flour mill), Hercules (chemical and pesticides manufacturer), Texaco (petroleum distribution), Quaker Oats (food processing), and Nabisco Brands (food processing). Citicorp and BankAmerica maintain offices in Nicaragua as do five of the top U.S. accounting firms. A number of TNCs like IBM and NCR distribute and service office products. Over 75 smaller U.S. corporations are active in services, manufacturing, and mar-keting. At least three of these smaller firms run chemical fabrication plants. Five non-U.S. TNCs still have business operations in Nicaragua including British American Tobacco (BAT) and Nestle.

Most of the TNCs operate at reduced capacity (as they do in other Central American nations) and complain about their inability to repatriate profits because of the shortage of dollars. After Castle & Cooke broke its agreement with the government and precipitously pulled out in 1982, the only remaining agribusiness firm in Nicaragua was BAT. Exxon, the largest TNC in Nicaragua, has main-tained its refinery. After the mining of the harbors, however, it refused to use its ships to bring fuel into the country. When the U.S. trade embargo was announced in 1985, *Business Week* asked Exxon if it intended to stay in Nicaragua. "We've been in Nicaragua 60-odd years, with and without revolutions," said company spokesperson Jeffrey S. Higgins. "We will stay as long as it is opportune in a business sense, our employees are safe, and we're permitted to operate without excessive restriction on private enterprise."[55]

Threat of an Example

President Reagan seems determined to rid the hemisphere of the Sandinistas by the end of his term in office. He has called this small nation of three million "an extraordinary threat" to the U.S. national security. The Sandinistas are not a threat to the national security of the United States, says Tomás Borge, but "the threat of a good example." While Ronald Reagan would scoff at the description of Nicaragua as a *good* example, he might agree that Nicaragua is an example of a political experiment that challenges the economic and political position of the United States in Latin America.

To many Nicaraguans, perplexed by the Reagan administration's hatred of their country, the "good example" explanation makes a good deal of sense. "You know," one Nicaraguan told the *Village Voice*, "we do represent a threat: the sort of threat a worker represents to an enterprise which is breaching the labor laws. If all of a sudden one worker speaks up, the owner begins to worry. Nicaragua is not only challenging the U.S. It challenges the belief that there could not be another revolution in Latin America for the rest of this century. If people believe something cannot be achieved, they will not attempt it. We are becoming a stimulus to other Latin American countries, just by being. Therefore I believe that the U.S. has concluded we must be stopped."[56]

Nicaragua's extraordinary achievements during the first few years of revolution were summed up by Jaime Belcazar, a Bolivian who was director of the United Nations Development Program (UNDP) from 1979–1984. He said:

> In all my 25 years with the UN, I have never worked in a country where the government was really doing something effective about poverty and development until now. The government officials are dedicated to eliminating inequalities. In the first several years of their administration, they have made extraordinary advances in health, education, and agriculture.
>
> It's given me enormous satisfaction to serve in such a country where your efforts really benefit the needy. The tragedy of course is the U.S. war against Nicaragua. Much of the excellent groundwork in social and economic programs is now suffering. Nicaragua was providing an alternative development model for the third world, a pluralistic model that offered concrete lessons to others—invaluable lessons—with its mistakes, successes, failures, and hopes. Now that experiment is being un-

dermined by the United States. Innocent people are being killed, development projects destroyed, and we are all the losers because of it. Why do the American people stand for such a desecration of their principles?[57]

1 Henri Weber, *The Sandinist Revolution* (London: Verso Editions, 1981).
2 Lars Schoultz, "Nicaragua: The United States Confronts a Revolution," in Richard Newfarmer (ed.), *From Gunboats to Diplomacy: New US Policies for Latin America* (Baltimore: Johns Hopkins University, 1984).
3 Yvonne Dilling and Philip Wheaton, *Nicaragua: A People's Revolution* (Washington: EPICA, 1980), pp.1–2.
4 John Gerassi, "America's Hit List," *Mother Jones*, June 1981.
5 This section on the FSLN tendencies is taken directly from an excellent study by John Booth, *The End and the Beginning: The Nicaraguan Revolution* (Boulder: Westview, 1982), pp.143–144.
6 *Central America Bulletin*, November 1984.
7 Marc Cooper, "Nicaragua: Waiting for Uncle Sam," *Village Voice*, November 27, 1984. See this excellent article for a comparison between the Nicaraguan and Salvadoran elections.
8 William Gasperini and Jeffrey Gould, "How the Vote Broke Down," *In These Times*, January 9, 1985.
9 Composition of the Constituent Assembly after 1984 elections: FSLN (61 seats), PDC (14), PLI (9), PPSC (6), PCdeN (2), PSN (2).
10 Latin American Studies Association, "The Electoral Process in Nicaragua: Domestic and International Influences," November 1984.
11 Ibid.
12 Description of political parties drawn from *Central America Bulletin*, November 1984.
13 Doyle McManus and Robert C. Toth, "The Contras: How US Got Entangled," *Los Angeles Times*, March 4, 1985.
14 Presentation by Sen. Tom Harkin, "Contras or Contadora: Military Solution or Negotiated Political Settlement," March 26, 1985, cited in *Washington Report on the Hemisphere*, April 16, 1985.
15 *Newsweek*, April 29, 1985.
16 Dieter Eich and Carlos Puicon, *La Contra* (Hamburg: Konkret Literatur Verlag, 1984).
17 Ellen Kratka, "Revolution Advances on Atlantic Coast," *Intercontinental Press*, February 18, 1985.
18 CIDCA (Centro de Investigaciones y Documentación de la Costa Atlántica) reported the Atlantic Coast population in 1983 to be the following: Mestizos, 182,000 (64.5 percent); Miskitos, 67,000 (23.8); Criollo blacks, 26,000 (9.1); Sumo, 5000 (1.7); Carib blacks, 1500 (0.5); and Rama, 650 (0.2).
19 Kratka, op.cit.
20 Ibid., p.85.
21 Cited in International Justice Fund, "Report on the Relocation of Miskito Indians by the Nicaraguan Government" (Los Angeles), 1984.
22 Ibid., p.27.
23 Ibid.
24 *Barricada*, November 8, 1984.
25 *Central America Bulletin*, October 1984.
26 Philip Taubman, "Managua Cleric is Said to Train Sandinista Foes," *New York Times*, August 1, 1984.
27 Stephen Kinzer, "Nicaragua's Combative Archbishop," *New York Times*, November 18, 1984.
28 George Black, "Challenges of Reconstruction," in *Nicaragua*, newsletter of the National Network in Solidarity with the Nicaraguan People, May/June 1982, p.1.
29 Quixote Center, "Nicaragua: A Look at the Reality," February 1985.
30 *Intercontinental Press*, December 12, 1983.

31 *Intercontinental Press*, May 21, 1984.
32 Marc Cooper, *Village Voice*, November 27, 1984, op.cit.
33 C. DiGiovanni, "U.S. Policy and the Marxist Threat to Central America," *The Heritage Foundation Backgrounder*, October 15, 1980, pp.3–5.
34 See an excellent report by the Central American Historical Institute entitled "US Economic Measures Against Nicaragua," in *Update*, April 1, 1985. This summary of economic destabilization measures relied heavily on that report. Other sources: Institute for the Study of Militarism and Economic Crisis, "Reagan's Covert Intervention Strategy: Economic Effects of US Aggression Against Nicaragua," April 1985; Joy Hackel and John Cavanagh, "Squeezing Nicaragua's Economy," *Washington Post*, March 25, 1984.
35 Nancy Strogoff, "Nicaragua: The Other War," *The Progressive*, January 1984.
36 Ibid.
37

NICARAGUA-U.S. TRADE, 1977–1984
(millions $U.S.)

	1977	1984	% change
Exports (to U.S.)	$180	$58	−68
Imports (from U.S.)	220	109	−50

38 Statement of Otto Reich, Assistant Administrator of AID, House Committee on Appropriations, June 23, 1982.
39 See interview with Jim Morrell in *Multinational Monitor*, April 1985.
40 *Business Week*, January 10, 1983.
41 *New York Times*, March 7, 1984.
42 *New York Times*, August 15, 1983.
43 Center for International Policy, "AID Memo: The Ortega Trip to Moscow" (Washington), May 5, 1985.
44 Ibid.
45 Oxfam-America, "Facts for Action," November 8, 1984.
46 Chris Norton, "Behind US War of Economic Attrition," *In These Times*, November 21, 1984. Cites analysis of private sector by Xavier Gorostiaga, director of CRIES in Managua.
47 Information from Ministerios de Desarrollo Agropecuario, Industria, and Planificación, at end of 1983. *Inforpress*, December 8, 1983.
48 *Central America Report*, May 10, 1985.
49 Joseph R. Thome and David Kaimowitz, manuscript for *Nicaragua: Five Years Later*, (to be published, 1985).
50 Interview by Tom Barry at the UNAG cooperative of La Florencia, September 1984.
51 Jacobo Timerman, "Haunted by a Vision of Reagan," *Newsweek*, August 13, 1984.
52 Gasperini and Gould, *In These Times*, January 9, 1985, op.cit.
53 Jay Levin, "Preparedness or Propaganda," *San Francisco Bay Guardian*, January 1, 1985; Oxfam-America, *Facts for Action*, No. 8; State Department, "Country Reports on Human Rights Practices for 1983."
54 Marc Cooper, "Whose Revolution Is This Anyway?" *Village Voice*, August 9, 1983.
55 Larry Boyd, "The Nicaraguan Embargo: Multinationals Aren't Packing," *Business Week*, May 20, 1985.
56 Alexander Cockburn and James Ridgeway, "What Reagan is Giving Nicaragua for Christmas," *Village Voice*, December 27, 1983.
57 Statement of Jaime Belcazar of UNDP, April 12, 1985.

CHAPTER 14

Panama

■

Trends
- Military interference in national politics.
- Escalation in urban violence related to rising unemployment.
- Steady movement by politicians and military away from the populism of the Torrijos era and movement toward closer alignment with U.S. policies.
- Increasing importance of the private sector in policy making.
- Growing resistance among the general population in reaction to austerity measures.
- Manipulation of popular discontent by right-wing parties.
- Continued economic decline as past economic development strategies wear thin with no alternatives in sight.

■

PANAMA IS FACING what one politician called "the worst moment in its history."[1] One of two workers living in the decaying slums of Colon and Panama City has no job and little hope of finding one. The service industry, which kept Panama's economy booming until recently, is on the skids. The country's hopes for democratization were deflated in 1984 by a presidential election universally believed to be fraudulent. The military stands in the dark shadows of the government—ready to move in whenever it deems that politics are out of control.

Unlike other countries on the isthmus with primarily agrarian economies, Panama is a service economy. Trading, financial, and transportation services account for three out of five GDP dollars.

Its position as a global crossroads distinguishes Panama from the other nations on the isthmus. It is a mostly urban society, with over half of its two million people living in the two cities— Panama City and Colon—that sit at either end of the Panama Canal. The Canal, which splits the country in half geographically, has also been at the center of Panamanian politics and the economy.

A Red, White, and Blue History

Boasting of his role in the making of the Panama Canal, President Theodore Roosevelt said, "I took the Canal, and let the Congress debate."[2] Official arrogance toward Panama has continued into modern times. As presidential candidate, Ronald Reagan, echoing a common U.S. conservative slogan, said: "We bought it, we paid for it, we built it, and we intend to keep it."[3]

The California Gold Rush of 1848 first brought Panama into the realm of interest of the United States. Tens of thousands of adventurers from the east coast sailed to the narrowest part of the continent to trek through Panama on their way to the riches of California, preferring that route to the arduous, often dangerous transcontinental trip across the United States. Recognizing the importance of the isthmus, New York financiers secured an exclusive concession from Colombia to construct a railroad across its territory of Panama.[4] The railroad, completed in 1855, substantially reduced the cost of transporting goods, raw materials, and passengers from one ocean to the other. The U.S. Army intervened five times between 1856 and 1865 to protect the railroad from possible attacks by the Panamanian independence movement.[5]

The Spanish-American War of 1898 marked the birth of the United States as an imperial power. U.S. military leaders, concerned that their gunboats had to travel the long route around Cape Horn, lobbied for the construction of an interoceanic canal across Panama. The Senate of Colombia rejected a U.S. petition in 1903 to build a canal through Panama, but their vote did not stop the United States or President Roosevelt. The *U.S.S. Dixie* and the *U.S.S. Nashville* sailed to Panama to prevent Colombia from squashing a U.S.-instigated revolt. A major figure in these machinations was William Nelson Cromwell, founder of the prestigious New York law firm Sullivan & Cromwell. Cromwell represented and owned stock in the French Canal Company and was a director of the Panama Railroad.

Only five days after securing Panama's independence from Colombia, the first canal treaty was signed with the United States. Signing the treaty for Panama was Frenchman Philippe Bunau-Varilla, who, like Cromwell, was interested in selling the remaining assets of the French company that had earlier tried to build a canal.

The treaty gave the United States the right to intervene in the internal affairs of the new country, which became an unofficial protectorate of the United States. U.S. government and military leaders supervised Panama's national elections in 1908, 1912, and 1918. Unlike other sectors of the population, the Panamanian oligarchy supported the U.S. presence in Panama and often requested the intervention of U.S. forces to control popular protests and uprisings. In 1918, a detachment of Marines arrived in the province of Chiriqui and stayed for two years to maintain public order. In 1925, 600 U.S. Army troops marched into

Panama City to break a rent strike. For twelve days, American troops patrolled the streets to keep order and guard U.S. property.[6]

Popular opposition forced the Panamanian government to reject a largely concessionary treaty with the United States in 1926. It was not until the General Treaty of Friendship and Cooperation in 1936 that the United States relinquished the right to unilateral intervention in Panama's political affairs. In that treaty, the United States obtained access to additional lands and waters for the defense and modernization of the canal. In 1942, the U.S.-Panama Base Convention allowed the United States over 100 new military and telecommunications facilities in Panama, beginning the extensive and permanent U.S. military presence in the Canal Zone. In 1947, popular protests prevented the authorization of increased U.S. military presence, but the Treaty of Mutual Understanding and Cooperation of 1955 permitted the United States to locate another large military base in Panama in exchange for increased commercial access to the Canal Zone by the local elite.[7]

Pent-up resentment against the United States surfaced in the Flag Riots of 1964 when U.S. authorities prevented Panamanian students from raising their national flag alongside the U.S. flag at a high school in the Canal Zone: "Within hours, 30,000 Panamanians were in the streets of Panama City, confronting U.S. troops who had orders to fire warning shots before shooting to kill. The riot soon spread to Colon, on the Atlantic side of the Zone, then deep into the interior. . . . By the time this explosion of anti-Yankee fury was contained, over $2 million in property had been burned or otherwise destroyed—almost all of it American. Twenty-eight people had been killed, 300 wounded, and 500 arrested, almost all of them Panamanian."[8]

When the government of Panama reacted by breaking relations with the United States, the United States agreed to raise the Panamanian flag at the Canal Zone high school and to negotiate a new canal treaty. After three years of negotiations, the United States proposed a treaty that was soundly rejected by Panamanians. Finally in 1977, under the leadership of Brigadier General Omar Torrijos Herrera, Panama and the United States reached an agreement over the ownership and operation of the Panama Canal.

Torrijos said: "Mr. President [Carter] . . . I want you to know that this treaty, which I shall sign and which repeals a treaty not signed by any Panamanians, does not enjoy the approval of all our people, because the 23 years agreed upon as a transition period are 8395 days, because during this time there will still be military bases which may make our country a strategic reprisal target, and because we are agreeing to a treaty of neutrality which places us under the protective umbrella of the Pentagon. This pact could, if it is not administered judiciously by future generations, become an instrument of permanent intervention."[9]

Since the first treaty in 1903, the United States had resisted attempts by Panamanians to obtain more control over the canal and the Canal Zone. In the 1960s, however, U.S. military analysts reported that they no longer considered the canal of strategic military importance since at least 24 of the largest U.S. aircraft carriers could not fit through the canal.[10] Military experts also noted that the most likely threat to the operation of the canal would come from within Panama by insurgents frustrated with continued U.S. domination of the canal and the Canal Zone. The military generally agreed that the best defense of the canal would be a cooperative, protective contract involving Panama's National Guard (now called the Panamanian Defense Forces).

Provisions of the 1977 agreement include:

- Right of the United States to manage and operate the canal until the year 2000.
- Perpetual U.S. authority to protect and defend the canal.
- All key bases and training areas operated by the United States to remain under U.S. control until the year 2000.
- Appropriation of territorial jurisdiction by Panama in 1982 over the Canal Zone (five-mile area on either side of the canal).
- The perpetual right of the United States to build a new sea-level canal ten miles to the west.
- An increase of toll fees received by Panama from $2.3 million to approximately $70 million annually.
- Establishment of a nine-member canal commission, composed of five U.S. members and four Panamanian members, to manage the canal (in 1989, to change to four U.S. and five Panamanian members).

"The United States basically won on the treaties," commented Mario Galindo, a lawyer in Panama who led the local opposition to their ratification. "In fact, the new treaties make us more subservient to the Americans than ever. The 1903 treaties at least pretended Panama was sovereign. The 1977 treaties give the U.S. the right to intervene here without even asking permission."[11]

The Neutrality Treaty has no termination date. Under its provisions, the United States and Panama both guarantee the neutrality of the Canal "in order that both in time of peace and in time of war it shall remain secure and open to peaceful transit by the vessels of all nations on terms of entire equality." Attached to the treaty was the DiConcini Condition stating that "if the Canal is closed, or its operations are interfered with, [the United States and Panama shall each] have the right to take such steps as each deems necessary . . . including the use of military force in the Republic of Panama, to reopen the Canal or restore the operations of the Canal."

The U.S. enclave in what was known as the Canal Zone still exists but is considerably smaller. Most of the U.S. citizens that had been involved in the municipal functions of the Canal Zone have left, but about 7000 U.S. nationals still remain. The "zonians," as they are called, have remained extremely isolated from Panamanian life. Few speak Spanish or have any social dealings with Panamanians.

Even though U.S. influence has diminished in Panama, resentment about the privileged way of life and supercilious attitudes of the zonians remain—particularly among the Panamanian employees of the canal. In 1984, the canal commission voted 5 to 4 to increase the canal budget by $15 million to provide higher salaries to the U.S. employees of the canal. The five U.S. members of the commission argued that the U.S. employees needed higher salaries because they no longer enjoyed privileges at the U.S. commissary. That Panamanian canal workers were not granted a raise and 500 were fired for budgetary reasons sparking sharp complaints in Panama City that the nondiscrimination clauses of the canal treaties were being violated.

Politics of Democrats and Defense Forces

General Omar Torrijos instilled nationalism and populism into Panamanian politics. He became the country's Supreme Commander in 1968 in a coup by the National Guard that threw Dr. Arnulfo Arias Madrid, a member of the Panamanian oligarchy, out of the presidential office. The coup set the reformist leadership of the National Guard against the traditional oligarchy.

To gain a power base outside the oligarchy, Torrijos initiated a populist program that involved increased government services, support for agrarian cooperatives, and better government relations with the labor movement. The popular general soon won the base he sought among the lower classes, particularly the rural poor. Photos of Torrijos, who was killed in a 1981 airplane crash, are still given places of prominence in the tens of thousands of Panamanian homes. Many suspected CIA involvement in the plane crash because of Torrijos' nationalist politics and his friendly relations with Cuba.

The death of Torrijos marked the end of Panama's reform era and maverick international politics. But even before the plane crash, politics had been moving steadily to the right. In the late 1970s, Torrijos and the government's Revolutionary Democratic Party (PRD) had begun to edge away from the alliance with workers, peasants, and political reformers. After having gained his popular base, Torrijos began to swing the nation's politics back toward the bourgeoisie.

Before Torrijos, an oligarchy dominated political and economic life in Panama. The oligarchy, known as the *Rabiblancos* (white-tailed birds), comprised the *Veinte Familias* (Twenty Families) who had been intermarrying and concentrating economic power since before the turn of the century. According to the Life World Library (1964), "the *Rabiblancos* constitute less than 1 percent of Panama's population, but they own half of all the land not owned by the government. They own the banks, the breweries, the newspapers, the radio, the television stations, the sugar mills, the coffee plantations, the insurance companies, the construction industry, the luxury shops for tourists. Many represent U.S. companies that do business in Panama. On every board of directors one finds the same names. . . . The Panamanian oligarchs not only dominate the economy of the country; they also dominate its politics."

The political domination of the oligarchy was interrupted by the 1968 coup, which threw the oligarchy out of politics but did nothing to challenge its privileged economic position. During the Torrijos years, the oligarchy modernized with the growth of the International Finance Center and the country's expanding industrial sector. By the late 1970s, the country's elite began to reassert itself in government through powerful new business organizations. Sections of renovated oligarchy worked their way into Torrijos' PRD and in the 1980s began pushing the party to the right.

Politics after Torrijos

Since the sudden death of strongman Torrijos in 1981, politics has been a volatile and unpredictable affair. Through 1984, there were three different heads of state (Aristides Royo, Ricardo de la Espriella, and Jorge Illueca), three chiefs of the defense forces (Florencio Flores, Rubén Darío Paredes, and Manuel Noriega), four attorney generals, and continual cabinet changes.

To run in the 1984 elections, the military and the PRD chose Nicolas Ardito Barletta, a former World Bank vice-president, University of Chicago-trained economist, and friend of George Shultz and Henry Kissinger. Backing Ardito Barletta was a PRD-led grouping called the National Democratic Unity Coalition (UNADE) which consisted of PRD, two right-wing parties, the Liberal Party, and a splinter group from the main opposition party. Ardito Barletta became the first elected president in 16 years.

The vote count took place behind closed doors, and it was widely suspected that the military fixed the vote totals. The country's Roman Catholic bishops called the election a "serious step backward on the path to democratization and a deterioration of our country's image abroad." So tainted was the election by fraud charges that many Panamanians referred to the president as Fraudito Barletta. Adding to the election controversy was the revelation that AIFLD and the PRODEMCA (two AID-funded organizations) contributed $20,000 to Ardito Barletta's campaign.

Leading the opposition in 1984 was the 72-year-old Dr. Arnulfo Arias Madrid. A sworn enemy of the military, Arias has held the presidency three times, most recently in 1968 when he was kicked out by Torrijos. Arias, who has close links to the traditional oligarchy, heads the Authentic Panamanian Party (PPA), which is the nation's second largest political party. The PPA led the opposition coalition known as the Opposition Democratic Alliance, which grouped the PPA and several center and right-of-center parties.

It is difficult to categorize the country's political parties according to class divisions. The parties tend to be grouped around personalities, not politics. The PRD includes both the very wealthy who have benefited from the military's corrupt rule and the very poor who continue to support the Torrijista party. Blacks, who compose a large portion of the military, also back the PRD largely because of the racist policies of Arias during his previous presidencies.

The constituency of the PPA and the Alianza comes from diverse classes but with its greatest backing from middle-class sectors tired of continued military control and government corruption. By no means, however, is the PPA a party of social reform. Seven political parties—including the three leftist parties—were abolished after the 1984 elections because of their failure to achieve the minimum percentage of votes required to retain legal standing.

The leftist parties failed to capture the opposition (antimilitary and PRD) vote, which went instead to the rightist Arias. The combined vote of the three leftist parties was less than 10,000.

The principal arbiter of politics in Panama, the Panamanian Defense Forces (PDF)—formerly called the National Guard—is closely tied to the ruling political party. The two leading figures in the military are Colonel Manuel Antonio Noriega and Colonel Rubén Darío Paredes. Known to have psychological problems, Noriega is the country's most powerful figure. Some describe the PDF as a "family" that cares for its own, which means both the business community that pays its dues to the military and the lower classes that make up its ranks.

The PDF maintains integral ties with local business. "To get anything done," Panamanians say, "you have to put a colonel on your payroll." That includes the business of the "*narcotraficantes*" (narcotics traffic dealers) who count on safe conduct across the isthmus if they pay the right bribe.

The major challenge that Ardito Barletta faced when he took office was his need to implement an austerity budget without fanning too much civil discontent and upsetting his military patrons. His lack of political skills and a secure base of political support made that a difficult chore. By late 1984, the president was failing miserably. The PDF removed Ardito Barletta in September 1985, replacing him with Vice-President Eric Arturo Delvalle. Delvalle is a key member of the rightist Republican Party which is composed primarily of businessmen. An industrialist, he is president of one of the largest sugar companies as well as nine other companies, most of them investment businesses.

Ardito Barletta's failure to consult other members of his party before he announced his austerity program made it impossible for him to push the plan through the national legislature. The budget, which included the proposed imposition of a steep services tax, unleashed a wave of popular opposition that brought hundreds of thousands to the streets to protest. The president backed down initially, but pressure from the World Bank and IMF kept the austerity measures on the political agenda.

The PDF provided strong backing for Ardito Barletta's bid for the presidency. Unprecedented popular anger with the president's austerity program caused his military support to wane, though the military still promised that it would not interfere in government. Attacks on government corruption (which frequently involves the PDF) and cutbacks in government hiring by Ardito Barletta have also caused increased military displeasure with his government. It was his announced intention, however, to investigate the torture-murder of a popular doctor by the PDF-linked death squad called F-8 Terrorista that ensured his removal.

A rising political star in Panama is Ricardo Arias Calderón, a shrewd academic who leads the Christian Democrats and has succeeded Arnulfo Arias as the leader of the Panamanian opposition. Referring to the PRD and Ardito Barletta, Arias Calderón said: "The opposition can only accept the destruction of the system that took him to power." The Christian Democrat leader believes that "the problem of ethics has led to a stagnation of political life. But to tackle that would mean to tackle its source: military leadership."[12]

Economy Moves toward Austerity

Panama stands far ahead of the other Central American countries in per capita income. The relatively high wages of canal employees and the large white-collar work force in the service industry as well as the country's comparatively small agricultural labor force contribute to Panama's above-average personal income. Use of the dollar as the national currency also partly explains the country's high per capita income. Although income levels are higher, so are the prices of basic necessities like food, housing, and transportation. Prices in Panama are often on the same level as those in the United States.

While Panamanians are generally better off than their Central American neighbors, the nation's economic situation is looking increasingly grim. The problems started in the 1970s, when the government began borrowing immense sums to sink into large public investment projects and to cover budget deficits. This borrowing spree, which TNC banks encouraged, combined with a global recessionary trend, have resulted in Latin America's highest per capita debt ($1,775). The IMF in 1979 declared: "Panama has arrived at a relationship between indebtedness and national income without precedent in the Western Hemisphere."

To remedy the debt crisis, the IMF and World Bank imposed a series of austerity measures as conditions for more lending. Although Washington agreed with those measures, concern that increased unemployment and fewer social services would destabilize the economy led the U.S. government in 1985 to increase its economic-aid commitment dramatically. The Reagan administration apparently realized that it had a reliable ally in the government of Ardito Barletta and feared his government would crumble in the face of mounting class tension.

The new economic austerity program calls for the state to sell such state assets as sugar mills, cement plants, and hotels. This "privatization" is in perfect consonance with AID's push for increased private-sector control over Central American economies. The sale of state investments marked the end of a period of state-led industrial development in Panama. Starting in 1974, the ruling PRD tried to move the country toward industrialization by investing in agro-industries, mining ventures, and an oil pipeline. These investments as well as an ambitious attempt to become energy self-sufficient pushed Panama deeper into debt.

The private sector backed the austerity program that included the promotion of private enterprise and foreign investment. Presence of the "business wing" of the PRD in the president's cabinet and the almost complete absence of the party's liberal faction ensured that the Ardito Barletta government would favor the business sector.

In contrast, labor unions in Panama feel under attack by the latest political developments. They have adamantly objected to plans to revise the highly progressive labor code—the only vestige of Torrijos era reforms. In mid-1985, an umbrella group of labor unions called a successful general strike that forced Ardito Barletta to promise not to touch the labor code. They have also led massive protests against wage cuts and lay-offs of government employees. "No worsening of the current conditions of Panamanian workers," warned the National Workers Central, "will resolve the economic crisis."[13]

The contribution of the new transisthmus oil pipeline, which transports Alaska North Slope crude between two marine terminals, has been the only positive aspect of the Panamanian economy. The U.S.-built pipeline, which has caused ecological havoc, somewhat compensated for falling revenues from other parts of the economy. Banks are closing down in the country's International Finance Center, the Colon Free Zone is losing tenants, and revenues from the Panama Canal are down. Other indicators of the economic crisis are that 60 percent of the population lives below the poverty line and the unemployment rate is 45 percent. In 1984, the World Bank said that the country's economy would have to increase over 7 percent annually just to keep pace with the normal increase of the work force.

International Finance Center

In 1970, Panama passed a banking law that created the ideal conditions for an international finance center. Bank deposits are not taxed, no reserves are required for foreign operations or exchange controls, and profits are exempt from income tax. What really attracts international bankers, though, is that the U.S. dollar is Panama's unit of exchange, meaning that there is no currency devaluation and that the inflation rate matches that of the United States.

More than 130 banks (not including local branches) from over 30 nations have operations in Panama. Bank assets surpass $25 billion. One airport arrival in every four is connected with the banking business.[14] The bulk of the finance center's business is offshore banking, meaning that it does not touch the local economy. Most of the transactions in the finance center serve TNCs.[15]

Little of the profit from this huge banking complex stays in Panama. Like the Canal, offshore banking dollars just flow through the country. Because the banking business is not taxed, the only benefits Panama can count on are from increased white-collar employment and from the boom in the construction industry, which, until recently, was building one bank after another along Via España.

The future of international finance in Panama is uncertain. The growing importance of Miami and increased concern about Panama's stability have caused assets to drop. From 1982 to 1984, foreign deposits in Panama dropped from $36 billion to $26 billion. Panama's bank secrecy law still represents an important advantage to some banks who benefit from drug traffic known as "narco-dollars." Secrecy is also important to generals and oligarchs who have personal accounts in Panama holding millions of dollars in illegal "capital flight" deposits.

A One-Crop Country

The United Nations categorizes Panama as a one-commodity country because more than 50 percent of its export earnings (not counting free-zone trade) come from bananas. Large-scale banana production began in the 1880s in Panama, and today United Brands operates two-thirds of the nation's banana farms with the balance owned by independent producers under contracts with the corporation. In recent years, the TNC has been selling its banana lands to the government, which then leases the land back to United Brands.[16]

Since the mid-1970s, banana taxes have been the government's second largest source of revenue. In the last several years, United Brands successfully pushed the banana export tax down, creating additional economic difficulties for the country. United Brands refused to cooperate with the government when Panama joined the Union of Banana Exporting Countries (UPEB) and its marketing arm, Comunbana.

Initially, the company signed an agreement with Comunbana to market its bananas through that organization whenever Comunbana had a cargo ship available. Then in 1981, the Chiriqui Land Company, a subsidiary of United Brands, violated this agreement by refusing to load its bananas on a Comunbana-chartered boat. The government fined the company and charged that United Brands was waging an "unfair and unjustified campaign," including attempts to pressure small producers not to sell to Comunbana.

United Brands official Bobby Walker saw the situation differently. He said that government taxation and international marketing organizations like Comunbana are leeching off the company, which bears all the production risks. Comunbana, Walker threatened, "is going to lose [its] behind trying to cash in on the banana trade." He added that United Brands has more capital invested in Panama than any other company. "We employ 10,000 people, 99.8 percent of them are Panamanians. If that's colonialism, I don't know what their problem is," said Walker.[17]

Other important agro-exports are shrimp, tobacco, rice, cattle and sugar.

Drastic reductions in the U.S. sugar import quota together with sagging international prices have brought hard times to the nation's sugar industry.

With the exception of Belize, the agricultural sector in Panama is the region's most underdeveloped. Although land is abundant, only 7 percent is cultivated, with the balance left fallow or in pasture. Most small farmers do not own the plots they farm. About two-thirds are squatters on state or private land, and only 10 percent of the farms have clear property titles. The state owns over 80 percent of the country's land, and private agricultural property is highly concentrated. Of the 105,000 private farms, 224 account for 20 percent of the farmland. One-half of these plantations are operated by absentee landlords. The owners of the 22 largest plantations, with more than 6500 acres each, control more land than the total amount held by all the nation's small farmers.[18]

Because so much land is left uncultivated and because such a high percentage of the cultivated land is used to grow cash crops, Panama has to import about a third of its food. In the late 1970s, the government announced an agrarian reform program and rural development projects to improve local food production, but budget deficits and other priorities prevented the government from giving the agricultural sector needed attention.

Free-Zone Development

Panama boasts many features that make it an ideal spot for light assembly plants and manufacturers interested in easy access to a wide international market. The International Finance Center facilitates trade, the country is an ideal location for transportation, and a large free zone in Colon offers an array of tax incentives for new manufacturing plants. Panama's low minimum wage of 75 cents an hour is higher than wage rates in the rest of Central America, but makes it attractive compared to industrialized countries.

The Colon Free Zone (CFZ), located at the Atlantic terminus of the canal, hosts about 600 foreign companies (half of which represent trading operations). It is the largest free zone in the hemisphere, and the second largest in the world. Panama's free convertibility with the dollar and the absence of controls on remittance of dividends and interest payments also attract companies to the free zone. The commercial business of the CFZ is aimed primarily at Latin American and Caribbean markets, with over 5 percent of Latin American sales now moving through the zone.

"Paper" companies are yet another type of offshore business found in Panama. Over 50,000 nonfunctioning companies are registered in the country. Within a few hours, a registered company can be available to corporations with the aid of local lawyers. The Latin American Agribusiness Development Corporation (LAAD) has its "paper" headquarters in Panama to escape U.S. taxation. These "paper" companies facilitate bookkeeping manipulations which enable companies and individuals to avoid taxation in their home countries.

TNCs in Panama

Thousands of foreign companies are officially registered in Panama but only a small portion actually have business activity in the country. Even excluding "paper" companies and financial investments, Panama has more foreign investment than any other Central American nation. Over 130 of the top 500 U.S. corporations do business in Panama. Ten of the top 20 U.S. food corporations are active here. General Mills has a flour mill, Borden produces dairy products, and Beatrice manufactures Swift-brand foods in Panama. Besides United Brands, only one other large corporation is active in the agricultural sector. That one is Ralston Purina which operates a 10,000-acre shrimp farm.

Six of the top ten oil companies are found in Panama, three of which— Mobil, Phillips, and Texaco—own oil refineries. Two U.S. firms, CBI Company and Northville Industries, are involved in a joint venture with the government to operate a 78-mile oil pipeline. The pipeline allows supertankers that are too large for the canal to transfer their crude oil to supertankers at the other end of the pipeline.

Over 300 non-500 firms also do business in Panama. About a third of these have manufacturing plants that export such products as paper doilies, swimming-pool covers, artificial Christmas trees, and Bestform and Jordache clothing. Non-U.S. TNCs operating in Panama include BAT Industries, Lloyds Bank, Nestle, Kuwait Petroleum Company (oil exploration), and Shell.

TNCs have regarded Panama as one of the less risky third world countries. The presence of the Canal Zone and the U.S. bases were a guarantee that Panama would never drift too far away from Washington. Yet it is this very proximity to U.S. military power that has engendered a deep-seated anti-imperialist sentiment in Panama that may someday explode. Successful negotiation of the canal treaties diffused some of this nationalism.

But as the economy worsens and unemployment expands, political tension may again build in Panama. The United States has increased economic aid to Panama and integrated the Panamanian Defense Forces into its war games to encourage the rightward drift of Panamanian politics. Yet, little can be counted on in the world of politics in Panama. The country's stance toward the United States has flip-flopped too many times in recent years for Panama to be counted on as a firm ally of U.S. foreign policy in Central America.

---

1 *Latinamerica Press*, April 25, 1985.

2 Eduardo Galeano, *Open Veins of Latin America* (New York: Monthly Review, 1973).

3 Committee for the Ratification of the Panama Canal Treaties, "Panama Canal Treaties."

4 Richard F. Nyrop (ed.), *Panama: A Country Study* (Washington: American University, 1981), p.18.

5 EPICA, "Sovereignty for a Land Divided," (Washington), 1976, p.11.

6 Nyrop, op.cit., p.198.

7 *NACLA Report on the Americas*, September/October 1979, p.13.

8 Ibid., p.3.

9 Nyrop, op.cit., p.166.
10 *NACLA Report on the Americas*, September/October 1979, op.cit., p.4.
11 Ibid.
12 *LARR*, October 26, 1984.
13 *Central America Report*, November 16, 1984.
14 Study by the Panamanian Tourist Institute in 1982.
15 Michael Kolbenschlag, "Going for Profits," *Forbes*, March 17, 1980, p.91.
16 Karen DeYoung, "Gentle Banana Center of Dispute in Central America," *Washington Post*, June 10, 1978.
17 Ibid.
18 *Latinamerica Press*, April 25, 1985.

Central America
Chronology, 1900–1985

1901 United Fruit becomes first transnational corporation (TNC) to arrive in Guatemala.

1903 Colombian Senate refuses to permit United States to build a canal through its territory of Panama.

1904 Panama establishes monetary system based on U.S. dollar.

1905 U.S. troops land in Honduras for the first of five times during next 20 years.

1908 U.S. troops land in Panama for first of four times within next decade.

1911 United States places Nicaragua under customs receivership and controls Nicaragua's trade revenues for next 38 years.

1912 U.S. Marines begin 20 years of repeated occupations in Nicaragua.

1914 Panama Canal completed.

1918 Over the next two years, President Wilson determines who will govern Costa Rica and develop oil resources in Costa Rica and Guatemala.

1919 Labor unions in El Salvador, Nicaragua, and Honduras join short-lived Pan-American Federation of Labor, sponsored by American Federation of Labor.

1920 President Coolidge announces Evart Doctrine to justify intervention in internal affairs of Latin American countries to protect U.S. foreign holdings.

1921 President Coolidge pressures Guatemala to overthrow President Carlos Herrera, enabling United Fruit to expand.

1926 Augusto Sandino, "General of Free Men," leads seven-year opposition against U.S. Marines' occupation of Nicaragua.

1929 International Railways of Central America, a United Fruit affiliate, connects Guatemalan and Salvadoran railways. IRCA also operates banana railroads in Costa Rica and Honduras.

1931 Dictators Jorge Ubico in Guatemala and Carias Andino in Honduras receive immediate support from U.S. government. In El Salvador, dictator Maximiliano Hernandez takes power.

1932 Farabundo Martí leads peasant uprising in El Salvador. U.S. warships stand by during massacre of 2 percent of Salvadoran population.

1933 President Franklin Roosevelt announces Good Neighbor Policy for Latin America and declares U.S. opposition to armed interventions.

1933 United States sets up National Guard with Somoza Garcia as commander-in-chief before Marines withdraw from Nicaragua.

1944 Industrialized nations create World Bank and International Monetary Fund.

1945 Export-Import Bank Act enables U.S. government to provide credit for purchase of U.S. exports.

1945 Juan José Arévalo is elected president of Guatemala, initiating a decade of reforms.

1947 Rio Pact, sponsored by United States, emphasizes cooperation against external attacks.

1948 Anticommunist revolution successfully led by José Figueres in Costa Rica. Figueres, three-time president of Costa Rica, later admits his CIA connections.

1948 President Truman sends first U.S. military training mission into El Salvador.

1948 Organization of American States (OAS) is founded.

1949 U.S. Army School of the Americas (sometimes derisively called the School of Coups) is founded to train Central American military officers.

1950 U.S. direct investment in Central America totals $313 million.

1951 Mutual Security Act passage by U.S. Congress makes funds available to strengthen Latin American armies for hemispheric defense.

1951 Inter-American Regional Organization of Workers (ORIT) forms with backing of U.S. Department of State.

1953 Colon Free-Trade Zone created in Panama based upon proposal by a vice-president of National City Bank of New York.

1953 Government of Jacobo Arbenz in Guatemala confiscates 400,000 acres of uncultivated United Fruit Company land and begins redistribution.

1954 President Eisenhower approves Operation Success to permit CIA-directed coup d'état in Guatemala which ousts Arbenz. Land reform reversed and thousands are killed.

1954 Successful strike by Honduran banana workers leads to widespread organizing among other Honduran workers.

1957 Eisenhower establishes Office of Public Safety (OPS) to train Latin American police.

1958 David Rockefeller starts U.S. Inter-American Council to promote private-sector development in Latin America.

1959 Inter-American Development Bank (IDB) forms as channel for multilateral grants and loans to Latin America.

1959 Fidel Castro leads guerrilla army victory in Cuba.

1960 U.S. direct investment in Central America doubles during decade, reaching $747 million.

1960 United States stages invasion of Cuba from Guatemalan and Nicaraguan soil in what was known as the Bay of Pigs operation.

1960 Panama Canal Zone becomes center for U.S.-sponsored counterinsurgency training.

1961 Central American Common Market (CACM) is established. U.S. corporate investment in Central America increases dramatically.

1961 Alliance for Progress is created by President Kennedy to promote Latin American economic development.

1961 Central American Bank for Economic Integration (BCIE) is formed.

1961   Foreign Assistance Act states that U.S. aid should assist U.S. economy. Agency for International Development (AID) is established.

1961   OPS expands after transfer to AID.

1961   National Sandinista Front for Liberation (FSLN) forms in Nicaragua.

1962   Operation Brotherhood (forerunner to CONDECA) military exercises involve U.S., Honduran, Guatemalan, Nicaraguan, and Salvadoran troops.

1962   American Institute for Free Labor Development (AIFLD) is founded to "respond to threat of Castroite infiltration and eventual control of major labor movements within Latin America."

1964   Twenty-eight killed and more than three hundred wounded during suppression of Flag Riots protesting U.S. dominance in Panama.

1964   United States sponsors formation of CONDECA to coordinate Central American military action against internal subversion.

1964   ADELA forms "to promote economic and social progress in Latin America by encouraging development of the private-enterprise sector."

1965   United Brands acquires Numar, a Costa Rican margarine plant, as it, along with Standard Fruit and R.J. Reynolds, continues to diversify.

1966   U.S. Special Forces participate in Operation Guatemala, a counterinsurgency campaign which kills more than 8000 people.

1967   Association of American Chambers of Commerce in Latin America (AACCLA) is founded.

1968   Salvadoran Communal Union (UCS) forms with AIFLD assistance.

1968   General Omar Herrera Torrijos comes to power in Panama.

1969   Inter-American Foundation is created to "strengthen the bonds of friendship" between Latin America and the United States.

1969   War breaks out between Honduras and El Salvador. CACM collapses.

1970   U.S. direct investment in Central America reaches $1.732 billion, again more than doubling during the decade.

1970   Council of the Americas supersedes U.S. Inter-American Council and supports International Finance Center in Panama.

1970   U.S. corporations form Latin American Agribusiness Development Corporation (LAAD) to promote production of nontraditional exports from Latin America.

1971   Three separate guerrilla movements begin a four-year period of organization in El Salvador.

1971   Overseas Private Investment Corporation (OPIC) begins to insure and guarantee U.S. investments.

1974   Discovery that police are being taught torture techniques leads U.S. Congress to abolish OPS.

1974   Five Central American countries start Union of Banana Exporting Countries (UPEB) to increase control in international banana market.

1975   United Brands pays $1.25 million bribe in Honduras to lower banana tax. Company saves $7.5 million in taxes.

1975   Offshore light assembly industries begin to locate in Central America, taking advantage of cheap labor and tax incentives.

1975   Harkin Amendment prohibits U.S. foreign assistance to governments with gross human-rights violations.

1977   Successful Las Isletas banana cooperative destroyed by Honduran soldiers who arrive in Standard Fruit's railroad cars.

1977   El Salvador and Guatemala reject U.S. aid because of human-rights attachments.

1977   Comunbana becomes marketing arm of UPEB. In Panama, United Brands refuses to load Comunbana ships and government threatens nationalization of United Brands acreage.

1979   Panama Canal Treaties provide for joint Panama-U.S. control over Panama Canal.

1979   President Carter sets up Airborne Caribbean Task Force.

1979   FSLN triumphs over dictator Anastasio Somoza Debayle in Nicaragua.

1979   Military coup in El Salvador results in series of short-lived juntas.

1980   U.S. direct investment over last decade more than doubles to a new total of $4223 million.

1980   Amigos del Pais and Guatemalan Freedom Foundation hire U.S. public-relations firms to launch a campaign in the United States praising the Guatemalan government.

1980   AIFLD sponsors agrarian reform program in El Salvador.

1980   Two guerrilla organizations come into public view in Honduras.

1980   Nicaragua conducts literacy campaign which reduces illiteracy rate from 50 percent to 13 percent in five months.

Jan.   Civilian members of El Salvador's ruling junta resign due to continued military repression.

Feb.   El Salvador's Archbishop Oscar Romero writes to President Carter asking the United States to stop military aid to El Salvador.

Mar.   Right-wing terrorists murder Romero. One week later, United States approves $5.7 million in military aid.

Apr.   In El Salvador, over 50 mass organizations join together in Revolutionary Democratic Front (FDR).

Apr.   AID funds Caribbean/Central American Action (C/CAA) to promote private-sector interest in the region.

May   Six hundred Salvadoran peasants are massacred by Salvadoran and Honduran troops while crossing the Rio Sumpul.

Aug.   Workers in Guatemala win a five-year union struggle against Coca-Cola.

Nov.   Farabundo Martí Liberation Front (FMLN) becomes the umbrella for five guerrilla organizations in El Salvador.

Dec.   Four U.S. churchwomen are raped and killed by the Salvadoran army. United States stops military aid.

1981   Three-year civilian death count in El Salvador reaches 35,000.

1981   Nicaragua conducts health-care campaign which reduces infant mortality by 40 percent from prerevolutionary figures.

Jan.   United States resumes military aid to El Salvador. Reagan bypasses Congress to send additional military aid and advisors to El Salvador.

Feb.   United States sponsors peace treaty between El Salvador and Honduras.

Mar.   Army kills 1500 Indian *campesinos* in Chimaltenango Province, Guatemala, in two-month period.

Mar.   United States suspends aid to Nicaragua with claim that Cuban arms pass through Nicaragua en route to El Salvador.

Jun.   United States "White Paper" alleging Cuban intervention in El Salvador is discredited.

Jul.   President Torrijos killed in Panama plane crash.

Aug.   Twenty-one U.S. military advisors arrive in Honduras.

Aug.   Americas Society becomes umbrella to coordinate private-sector development organizations in Latin America.

Sep.   Belize gains independence from United Kingdom.

Nov.   United States authorizes $19 million to destabilize Nicaraguan government.

Nov.   Suazo Cordova elected first civilian president in Honduras in more than two decades.

Dec.   Atlacatl, U.S.-trained Salvadoran brigade, murders 1000 civilians during search-and-destroy missions.

1982

Jan.   Reagan administration brings first of 1600 Salvadoran military to United States for training.

Jan.   President Reagan proposes Caribbean Basin Initiative (CBI) to increase U.S. economic aid to Central America and asks for increased military aid to the region.

Jan.   Administration uses $20 million for the *contras* from CIA contingency funds.

Feb.   Four Guatemalan guerrilla groups form Guatemalan National Revolutionary Unity (URNG).

Mar.   Roberto D'Aubuisson, with help from a large U.S. public-relations firm, becomes president of the national assembly and Alvarado Magana becomes president of El Salvador.

Mar.   Military coup d'état takes place in Guatemala.

May   Luis Alberto Monge replaces Rodrigo Carazo as president in Costa Rica.

Jun.   General Efrain Rios Montt declares himself president and commander-in-chief of Guatemala and initiates the "beans and bullets" campaign.

Jul.   Ricardo de la Espriella enters as president of Panama, marking a move to the right with increasing influence of the National Guard.

Aug.   UN High Commission on Refugees reports 287,000 registered refugees in Mexico and Central America.

Aug.   Congress adds $200 million economic aid and $12 million military aid to CBI and military appropriations for FY82.

Aug.   World Council of Churches reports Guatemalan government responsible for the deaths of over 9000 people in last five months.

Oct.   Standard Fruit violates its agreement to administer banana industry until 1985, leaving 3500 unemployed when it suddenly pulls out of Nicaragua.

1983

Jan.   Costa Rican foreign debt soars 40 percent in seven months to $4 billion.

May   Reagan dubs the *contras* "freedom fighters."

Aug.   General Mejías Víctores takes power in a Guatemalan coup and institutes the "model villages" program.

Sep.   Contadora Peace Plan for the Central American region is proposed by Mexico, Columbia, Panama, and Venezuela.

Oct.   U.S. invasion of Grenada shocks the world and heightens tensions in Nicaragua.

Nov.   U.S. Congress approves $24 million in covert aid to the *contras*.

Nov.   Guatemalan military kill two AID employees. United States cuts off economic aid to Guatemala.

1984   Salvadoran military strategy changes to "air war" and bombings take place regardless of civilian presence. Refugees now total over 25 percent of the entire population.

1984   U.S. military aid to Honduras has increased 20 times since 1980.

Jan.   Kissinger Commission recommends $8 billion developmental aid to Central America; increase in arms to Honduras, El Salvador, and Guatemala; and continued support of *contras*.

Mar.   United States helps *contras* mine Nicaraguan harbors in violation of international law. Seven ships are damaged. Nicaragua takes case to World Court, but United States refuses to accept World Court jurisdiction.

Mar.   Internal military coup ousts General Gustavo Alvarez Martínez in Honduras.

May   With CIA support, José Napoleon Duarte is elected President of El Salvador.

Jul.   Nicaraguan government's agrarian reform program has redistributed 2,400,000 acres of land to 45,000 land-poor families in previous five years (more than ten times the land owned by peasants under Somoza).

Sep.   Two members of Civilian Military Assisatance, a right-wing U.S. group aiding the *contras*, are shot down in a helicopter flying over Nicaragua.

Sep.   Nicaragua agrees to Contadora peace plan. United States asks Honduras, El Salvador, and Costa Rica to demand changes in plan.

Sep.   Official economic and military aid to Guatemala resumes.

Sep.   School of the Americas closes in Panama and relocates to Fort Benning, Georgia, four months later.

Oct.   Secret CIA guerrilla warfare instruction manual for *contras* becomes public.

Oct.   First peace discussion between the government and the FMLN-FDR occurs in El Salvador.

Nov.   Nicaragua has its first free elections in history. Sandinista Daniel Ortega is elected president. United States denounces elections as a sham.

1985

Jan.   United States government indicts 16 North Americans and arrests 60 Central Americans in major crackdown on church sanctuary movement.

Feb.   *Contras* linked to 200 death-squad killings in Honduras.

Feb.   Reagan says Nicaragua must "say uncle."

Feb.   Pope ousts five Nicaraguan priests.

Mar.   Coca-Cola plant in Guatemala City reopens after yearlong worker occupation and international union pressure.

Mar. Duarte elected president in El Salvador.

May Reagan imposes embargo on trade with Nicaragua.

Jun. Congress approves $27 million in "humanitarian" aid to the *contras*.

Jun. Four U.S. Marines and two U.S. businessmen among those killed in rebel attack on swank San Salvador restaurant.

Aug. Private aid to *contras* from private right-wing organizations almost equals U.S. government aid.

Aug. Congress approves foreign aid funding for Central America that authorizes programs and funding levels (more than $1 billion a year through FY89) recommended by Kissinger Commission.

Sep. Gen. Noriega, chief of Panamanian Defense Forces, forces president to resign and installs industrialist Eric Arturo Delvalle in office amid growing popular discontent.

Oct. FMLN kidnapping Duarte's daughter and the negotiation for her release further weaken the president's standing with military.

Dec. Leading Liberal Party candidate José Azcona declared winner of presidential election in Honduras, although National Party candidate gains most votes.

Dec. Christian Democrat Cerezo wins presidential election in Guatemala, setting stage for increased U.S. aid.

U.S. Transnational Corporations and Their Subsidiaries Operating in Central America, 1985

The following is a list of the major U.S. corporations along with their branches, subsidiaries, and affiliates in Central America. The list includes only the largest U.S. corporations, which are ranked among the top 500 industrial and service corporations in the United States, and the top 100 private firms. Not included in this listing are the many businesses in Central America owned by smaller U.S. firms. See Table 2G for a complete breakdown of U.S. investment in Central America by category of business, and Tables 2C and 2D for a breadown of U.S. TNCs most active in Central America.

Major U.S. Corporations in Central America

Parent Corporation Subsidiary Company	Corporate Rank Kind of Business	Location *
ABC International Worldvision	S14	CR
AH Robins Co Industrial Santa Agape	404 Dog collar & leash mfgr	GU

Parent Corporation Subsidiary Company	Corporate Rank Kind of Business	Location *
AMAX Inc	153	ES
New York and El Salvador Mining		
Rosario Resources	Silver, lead & zinc mining	HO
Abbott Laboratories	131	
Abbott	Pharm	ES
Abbott Laboratorios	Pharm mfgr	GU
Abbott Laboratories	Pharm mfgr	PA
Alexander & Alexander Services Inc	F98	
Alexander & Alexander de Centroamerica	Insurance brokerage	GU
Allegheny International	154	
All State Welding Alloys	Industrial products	CR
Allied Corp	26	
Atico		CR
Refinadora CR de Petroleos	Oil refinery	CR
Quimica Aliada de Centro-america		ES
Marco Castillo	Chem & plastics	GU
Union Texas Petrolera de Guatemala	Petro products	GU
Mergenthaler		PA
Aluminum Co of America (ALCOA)	62	
ALCOA of Costa Rica	Aluminum products	CR
Aluminos de Centroamerica (ALDECA)	Aluminum products	ES
Pan-Ore Transportation	Transportation	PA
ALCOA	Aluminum products	PA
American Cyanamid Inc	100	
Cyanamid Inter-American Corp	Pesticides & pharm	CR
Cyanamid Interamerican Corp	Pesticides & pharm	GU
Shulton	Cosmetics	GU
American Express Co.	F2	
American Express	Credit card svcs	GU
American Express	Credit card svcs	HO
American Express	Travel & financial svcs	PA
American Home Products Corp	78	
Anakol de Costa Rica	Pharm & cleaning products	CR
Fort Dodge Laboratories	Pharm	HO
Productos del Hogar	Pharm & cleaning products	GU

Parent Corporation Subsidiary Company	Corporate Rank Kind of Business	Location *
American Intl Group	F18	
American Life Insurance	Insurance	ES
Edificio de Hanover	Insurance	ES
La Seguridad Salvadorena	Insurance	ES
Administradora Atalaya	Insurance	GU
American Intl Underwriters	Insurance	GU
La Seguridad de Centroamerica	Insurance	GU
American Intl Underwriters	Insurance	HO
Hanover Insurance	Insurance	HO
Administradora Atalaya	Insurance	PA
American Life Insurance	Insurance	PA
La Seguridad de Panama	Insurance	PA
Natl Union Fire Insurance	Insurance	PA
American Motors Corp	91	
Auto Tecnica	AMC auto dealership	CR
Financiera de America	Financing	CR
American Standard Inc	123	
Indus Ceramica Costarricense	Bathroom fixtures mfgr	CR
American Standard		ES
Indus Centroamerica de Sanitarios	Bathroom fixtures mfgr	GU
Industria Ceramica	Bathroom fixtures mfgr	NI
Trane Western Hemisphere	Air conditioning mfgr	PA
Arthur Andersen & Co	A2	
Arevalo, Perez y Asociados	Accounting	GU
Arthur Andersen	Accounting	HO
Arthur Andersen	Accounting	PA
Arthur Young & Co	A8	
Fernando Fumero y Asociados	Accounting	CR
Despacho Oscar Rene Marroquin	Accounting	CR
Lizarralde, Ayestas y Asociados	Accounting	GU
Mendieta y Asociados	Accounting	HO
Arthur Young	Accounting	PA
Atlantic-Richfield Co	12	
ARCO	Oil exploration	BE
Avon Products Inc	127	
Mallinckodt Inc		GU
Productos Avon de Guatemala	Cosmetics	GU
Productos Avon	Cosmetics	HO
BF Goodrich Co	115	
BF Goodrich Quimica		CR
BOC [1]	265	
Gases Industriales	Industrial gases	HO

Parent Corporation Subsidiary Company	Corporate Rank Kind of Business	Location *
Baker Intl Corp	199	
Tri-State Oil Tool	Oil field machine mfgr	PA
Bank of Boston Corp	B16	
Corporacion Intl de Boston (CIBSA)	Financing	CR
Financiera de America	Financing	CR
Servicios Comerciales e Industriales	Industrial financing	GU
Compania de Credito	Credit svcs	HO
First Natl Bank of Boston	Banking	HO
Banco de Boston	Banking	PA
BankAmerica Corp	B2	
Bank of America	Banking	CR
Bank of America	Banking	GU
Bank of America	Banking	HO
Bank of America	Banking	NI
Bank of America	Banking	PA
Financiera Bamerical	Banking	PA
Bankers Trust New York Corp	B10	
Bankers Trust	Banking	PA
Baxter Travenol Labs	207	
Travenol Laboratories	Medical products	CR
Travenol Laboratories	Medical products	PA
Beatrice Companies	36	
Avis Rental Office	Car rental	CR
Max Factor	Cosmetics	CR
Avis Rental Office	Car rental	GU
Avis de Guatemala	Car rental	GU
Chitos Intl	Snack food mfgr	GU
Fabrica de Productos Alimenticios	Snack food mfgr	GU
Max Factor	Cosmetics	GU
Boquitas Fiestas	Snack food mfgr	HO
Max Factor	Cosmetics	HO
Quimica Stahl Centroamericana	Industrial chem mfgr	NI
Targa Sasso Rent-a-Car	Car rental	NI
Alimentos del Istmo	Snack food mfgr	PA
Avis Rent-A-Car	Car rental	PA
Swift	Food processing	PA
Becton, Dickinson & Co	286	
Becton, Dickinson	Medical svcs & supplies	PA
Bemis Co Inc	358	
Bemis de El Salvador	Paper bag mfgr	ES
Bemis Bijao de Honduras	Paper bag mfgr	HO

Parent Corporation Subsidiary Company	Corporate Rank Kind of Business	Location *
Compania de Sacos Centroamericana	Cloth sack mfgr	HO
Fabrica Textile Bemis Handal	Textile mfgr	HO
Black & Decker Mfg Co	232	
B & D de Costa Rica	Power tools	CR
Black & Decker de El Salvador	Power tools	ES
Black & Decker Interamerica	Power tools	PA
Borden Inc	81	
Lactaria Costarricense	Dairy products mfgr	CR
Diadema	Dairy products franchise	ES
Broex		PA
Compania Chiricana de Leche	Dairy products mfgr	PA
Compania Internacional de Ventas	Food products	PA
Fabrica de Productos Borden	Beverage mfgr	PA
Helados Borden	Ice cream & dairy products mfgr	PA
Quimica Borden	Chem products mfgr	PA
Borg-Warner Corp	99	
Borg-Warner	Air conditioners	PA
Bristol-Myers	92	
Empresas Bristol de Costa Rica	Cosmetics & pharm	CR
Compania Bristol-Meyers	Cosmetics & pharm	ES
Bristol-Myers de Centroamerica	Cosmetics & pharm	GU
Unitek de Centroamerica	Dental supplies	GU
Bristol-Myers de Centroamerica	Cosmetics & pharm	HO
Bristol-Myers de Centroamerica	Pharm	NI
Brislab	Pharm	PA
Bristol Laboratories Intl	Pharm	PA
Bristol Pharm Information Center	Pharm consulting	PA
Compania Bristol-Meyers	Cosmetics & pharm	PA
Brown-Forman Corp	336	
Lenox de Centro America	Plastic dinnerware mfgr	ES
Brunswick Corp	239	
Brunswick	Marine, medical, recreational equip	CR
Brunswick	Medical & hospital equip	GU
Burroughs Corp	76	
Burroughs de Centroamerica	Business equip	CR
Burroughs	Business equip	PA
CBI Industries Inc	310	
Belize Steel	Industrial gas	BE
Petroterminal de Panama	Oil storage & shipping	PA

Parent Corporation Subsidiary Company	Corporate Rank Kind of Business	Location *
CBS Inc	58	
Industria de Discos Centroamericana	Recorded music	CR
Mundo Musical		CR
Distribuidora Guatemateca de Discos	Records	GU
CIGNA Corp	F4	
Tecni Seguros de Centroamerica	Insurance	CR
Compania de Seguros Cruz Azul	Insurance	GU
Constabilidad Mecanizada	Insurance	GU
Seguros el Roble (AFIA)	Insurance	GU
INA	Insurance	PA
CPC Intl Inc	87	
Productos de Maiz y Alimentos	Milled corn products mfgr	GU
Alimentos del Istmo	Corn starch & veg oil mfgr	HO
Capital Cities Communications	313	
Televisora de Costa Rica (ABC)	Media broadcasting	CR
Cargill Inc	P1	
Adria		ES
La Sultana		ES
Termicar	Poultry & egg production	ES
Cargill Americas	Animal feed	GU
Industria Timba		GU
ALCON	Animal feed mfgr	HO
FANALCO	Animal feed mfgr	HO
Castle & Cooke Inc	932	
Compania Financiera	Financing	CR
Envases Industriales	Plastics mfgr	CR
Standard Fruit & Steamship	Banana & pineapple shipping	CR
Standard Fruit	Banana & pineapple production	CR
Bananera Antillana	Banana production	HO
Banco del Comercio	Financing	HO
Cerveceria Hondurena	Beer & soft drinks mfgr	HO
Compania Agricola Industrial	African palm & margarine	HO
Dole Pineapple of Honduras	Pineapple processing	HO
Envases Industriales Hondurenos	Metal container mfgr	HO
Fabrica de Manteca y Jabon	Veg oil, soap, animal feed	HO
Industria Aceitera Hondurena		HO
Manufacturas de Carton	Cardboard box mfgr	HO
Nacional Immobiliaria	Finance	HO
Pina Antillana	Pineapple production	HO
Plasticos	Plastic bag mfgr	HO
Servicios de Investigaciones	Data processing	HO

Parent Corporation Subsidiary Company	Corporate Rank Kind of Business	Location *
Standard Fruit & Steamship	Banana & pineapple shipping	HO
Standard Fruit	Banana, pineapple, citrus production	HO
Caterpillar Tractor Co	52	
Caterpillar Americas	Tractor dealership	BE
Celanese Corp	120	
Celanese de Guatemala	Chem & plastics	GU
Champion International	70	
Empaques Multiwall Ultrafort	Packaging materials & paperboard	NI
Envases Industriales Nicaraguenses	Cardboard box mfgr	NI
Chase Manhattan Corp	B3	
Atlantic Bank	Banking	BE
Banco Atlantida	Banking	HO
Casa Propria	Financing	HO
Inversiones Atlantida	Financing	HO
Chase Manhattan Bank	Banking	PA
Chemical New York Corp	B6	
Marpan One		PA
Chesebrough Pond's Inc	197	
Chesebrough Pond's Intl	Cosmetics	GU
Cosmeticos Honduras	Cosmetics	HO
Casa Comercial Ahlers	Cosmetics	NI
Cosmeticos	Cosmetics mfgr	PA
Chevron Corp	11	
Gulf Costa Rica	Petro & petro products	CR
Quimicas Ortho de California	Pesticides mfgr	CR
Compania Petrolera Chevron	Petro & petro products	ES
Compania Petrolera Chevron	Petro & petro products	GU
Petroleos Gulf de Guatemala	Petro & petro products	GU
Compania Petrolera Chevron	Petro products	NI
Chevron Chemical Intl		PA
Gulf Petroleum	Petro & petro products	PA
Citicorp	B1	
Citibank	Banking	CR
Citibank	Banking	ES
Citibank	Banking	GU
Diners Club de Guatemala	Credit card franchise	GU
Banco de Honduras	Banking	HO
Diners Club de Honduras	Credit card franchise	HO

Parent Corporation Subsidiary Company	Corporate Rank Kind of Business	Location *
Citibank	Banking	NI
Citibank	Banking	PA
Diners Club de Panama	Credit card franchise	PA
Clark Equipment	268	
Atlas Electrica	Kitchen appliance mfgr	CR
Atlas Electrica	Kitchen appliances	GU
Atlas Electrica	Kitchen appliances	HO
Cluett, Peabody & Co Inc	311	
Arrow Inter-America y Compania	Shirt mfgr	GU
Coca-Cola Co	46	
Coca-Cola	Beverage franchise	BE
Coca-Cola Interamerican	Beverage mfgr	CR
Embotelladora Salvadorena	Beverage franchise	ES
Embotelladora Guatemalteca	Beverage franchise	GU
Industria de Cafe	Soluble coffee mfgr	GU
Coca-Cola de Panama-Cia Embotelladora	Beverage mfgr	PA
Columbia Pictures of Panama	Motion pictures	PA
Colgate-Palmolive Co	73	
Colgate Palmolive (Costa Rica)	Soap & toothpaste mfgr	CR
Pozuelo	Candy & cracker mfgr	CR
Colgate Palmolive Central America Inc	Soap & toothpaste	ES
Agencias Maritimas de Guatemala		GU
Alimentos Kern de Guatemala	Canned fruit processing	GU
Colgate Palmolive (Centro America)	Cosmetics & pharm mfgr	GU
Helena Rubinstein de Centroamerica	Cosmetics	GU
Colgate Palmolive (West Indies)	Soap & toothpaste	HO
Colgate Palmolive Central America	Soap & toothpaste	NI
Colgate Palmolive	Soap & toothpaste	PA
Kendall	Pharm	PA
Colt Industries Inc	195	
Industrias Fairbanks Morse	Pump mfgr	GU
Combined Intl Corp	F62	
Rollins Health Intl	Insurance brokerage	PA
ConAgra	121	
Armour de Panama	Food products	PA
Consolidated Foods Corp	49	
Manufacturera de Cartago	Bra mfgr	CR

Parent Corporation Subsidiary Company	Corporate Rank Kind of Business	Location *
Continental Corp	F22	
Comercial Afianzadora	Surety bonds	GU
Comercial Aseguradora Suizo Americana	Insurance	GU
Promotora Continental		GU
Seguros Universales	Insurance	GU
Continental Insurance	Insurance	PA
Coopers & Lybrand	A3	
Ceciliano	Accounting	CR
Rosales Chavez y Associados	Accounting	GU
Davila, Oscar D	Accounting	NI
Chandeck y Bosquez	Accounting	PA
Core States Financial Corp	B34	
Banco Internacional de Panama	Banking	PA
Crown Cork & Seal Co Inc	246	
Crown Cork Centroamericana	Container mfgr	CR
Crown Cork Centroamericana	Container mfgr	HO
Crown Zellerbach Corp	129	
Convertidora Nacional de Papel	Paper products mfgr	CR
Cummins Engine Co	155	
Servicios Unidos	Heavy equip distrib	CR
Salvador Machinery	Heavy equip distrib	ES
Maquinaria y Equipos	Heavy equip distrib	GU
Comercial Laeis Honduras	Heavy equip distrib	HO
F Alfredo Pellas	Heavy equip distrib	NI
Cumins Panama	Heavy equip distrib	PA
Dart & Kraft Inc	33	
Kraft Foods	Food processing	PA
Data General Corp	279	
Data General Costa Rica	Computers	CR
Deere & Co	86	
Deere	Heavy equip distrib	HO
John Deere	Heavy equip distrib	PA
Deloitte Haskins & Sells	A5	
Deloitte Haskins & Sells	Accounting	CR
Deloitte Haskins & Sells	Accounting	GU
Donkin y Arguello	Accounting	NI
Deloitte Haskins & Sells Intl	Accounting	PA
Digital Equipment Corp	65	
Digital Equipment Panama	Computers	PA

Parent Corporation
  Subsidiary Company
	Corporate Rank
	  Kind of Business
		Location *

Donaldson Lufkin & Jenrette Inc	F33	
Internacional de Comercio (ACLI)	Commodities brokerage	GU
Dow Chemical Co	25	
Dow Quimica de Centroamerica	Plastics mfgr, pesticides distrib	CR
Tecnica Petroquimica de Centroamerica	Pesticides & pharm	GU
Coral Navigation	Oil field svcs	PA
Dow Chemical Intl	Financing	PA
Dowell Schlumberger	Oil field svcs	PA
EI Du Pont de Nemours & Co	7	
Conoco	Oil refinery	CR
Continental Oil Co of Guatemala	Oil exploration	GU
Quimica DuPont de Centroamerica	Chem & pesticides	GU
Refineria Panama	Oil refinery	PA
Eastern Airlines Inc	T8	PA
Eastern Airlines	Air transportation	PA
Eastman Kodak Co	30	
Kodak Panama	Photo finishing	PA
Eaton Corp	138	
Cutler-Hammer Centroamericana	Electrical controls mfgr	CR
Cutler Hammer	Electrical controls	HO
Economic Laboratories	379	
Soilax Caribbean	Cleaning products	PA
Eli Lilly & Co	130	
Industrias Quimicas		ES
Eli Lilly de Centroamerica	Pharm	GU
Emerson Electric Co	93	
Skil Centroamericana	Electrical & electronic products	CR
Emery Air Freight Corp	T33	
Movicarga	Air freight	PA
Ernst & Whinney	A6	
Ernst & Whinney	Accounting	PA
Esselte Pendaflex Corp [2]	413	
Esselte Pendaflex	Filing equipment & supplies	CR

Parent Corporation Subsidiary Company	Corporate Rank Kind of Business	Location *
Exxon Corp	1	
Esso Standard Oil	Petro & petro products	BE
Essochem de Centro America	Chem products	BE
Essochem de Central America	Chem products	CR
Esso Standard Oil	Petro & petro products	ES
Essochem de Centro America	Chem products	ES
RASA		ES
Refineria Petrolera Acajutla	Oil refinery	ES
Esso Standard Oil	Petro & petro products	GU
Essochem de Centro America	Chem products	GU
Esso Standard Oil	Petro & petro products	HO
Essochem de Centro America	Chem products	HO
Esso Standard Oil	Oil refinery	NI
Essochem de Centro America	Paint stripper mfgr	NI
Esso Marine Supply Co		PA
Esso Standard Oil	Petro & petro products	PA
Essochem de Centro America	Chem products	PA
FMC Corp	119	
FMC Intl	Pesticides	CR
FMC Guatemala	Pesticides	GU
Intertrade Transportation Specialists	Freight, courier svcs	PA
Firestone Tire & Rubber Co	95	
Industria Firestone de Costa Rica	Tire & rubber products mfgr	CR
Super Servicios	Tires	CR
Firestone Interamerica	Tire & rubber products	PA
First Chicago Corp	B10	
First Chicago de Panama	Banking	PA
Fluor Corp	59	
Fluor Panama	Mgmt & public relations	PA
Foxboro Co	455	
Instrumentos Industriales Centro America	Instrumentation equip	CR
GD Searle & Co	266	
GD Searle	Pharm & sweeteners	GU
GTE (General Telephone & Electronics)	U1	
Compania General de Directorios	Phone book printing	CR
GTE Sylvania	Lighting products mfgr	CR
GTE Sylvania	Lighting products	ES
GTE Sylvania	Lighting products mfgr	GU
GTE Sylvania	Lighting products mfgr	HO

Parent Corporation Subsidiary Company	Corporate Rank Kind of Business	Location *
GTE Sylvania	Lighting products	NI
GTE de Panama	Lighting products	PA
General Electric	9	
Muebles Metalicos Prado		ES
General Mills Inc	64	
Industria Harinera Guatemalteca	Wheat flour processing	GU
Industria del Maiz	Corn flour processing	GU
Programacio y Computacion	Computer programming	GU
Triticus	Grain mill products	GU
Agua Finca de Camarones	Shrimp production	HO
Industrias Gemina	Flour mill	NI
General Mills de Panama	Flour mill	PA
Harinas y Cereales	Wheat flour processing	PA
Panalimentos	Grain mill products	PA
Productos de Trigo	Grain mill products	PA
Semolas de Panama	Wheat production	PA
General Signal	210	
New York Air Brake Intl	Hydraulic pump mfgr	PA
Gerber Products	350	
Productos Gerber de Centroamerica	Baby foods mfgr	CR
Gillette Co	160	
Productos Distribuidos	Cosmetics, pens, razor blades	CR
Gillette de Centroamerica	Cosmetics, pens, razor blades	GU
Compania Interamericana Gillette	Cosmetics, pens & razor mfgr	PA
Goodyear Tire & Rubber Co	31	
Goodyear Export	Tires, rubber products	CR
Goodyear Tire & Rubber		ES
Plantaciones de Hule Goodyear	Rubber plantation	GU
Goodyear Export	Tires, rubber products	PA
Goodyear de Panama	Tires, rubber products	PA
Gran Indus de Neumaticos (GINSA)	Tire mfgr	GU
Great Northern Nekoosa Corp	194	
Envases Industriales de (ENVACO)	Cardboard box mfgr	CR
Industria Panamena de Papel	Cardboard box mfgr	PA
Greyhound Corp	527	
Financiera Greyhound	Financing	PA

Parent Corporation Subsidiary Company	Corporate Rank Kind of Business	Location *
Gemini Greyhound Leasing (Panama)	Leasing	PA
Gulf + Western Industries	77	
Paramount Films of Panama	Motion pictures	PA
HB Fuller Co	473	
Alfombras Canon	Rug mfgr	CR
Deco Tintas	Ink mfgr	CR
HB Fuller Costa Rica	Adhesive mfgr	CR
Kativo Chemical Industries	Paint mfgr	CR
Kativo Commercial	Paints	CR
Reichhold de Centroamerica	Plastic mfgr	CR
Synteticos	Vinyl materials mfgr	CR
Kativo de El Salvador	Paints	ES
Adhesivos Industriales de Guatemala	Adhesive mfgr	GU
Alfombras Canon de Guatemala	Rugs	GU
HB Fuller Guatemala	Adhesives	GU
Kativo de Guatemala	Paint mfgr	GU
Kioskos de Pinturas	Paints	GU
Pinturas Fuller de Centroamerica	Paint mfgr	GU
Punto de Viniles	Vinyls	GU
Adhesivos Industriales	Adhesive mfgr	HO
Aerosoles de Centroamerica		HO
Alfombras Canon	Rugs	HO
Comercial Kioskos de Pintura	Paints	HO
Comercial Punto de Viniles	Vinyls	HO
HB Fuller Honduras	Adhesive mfgr	HO
Kativo Comercial	Paints	HO
Kativo de Honduras	Paint mfgr	HO
Punto de Viniles	Vinyl materials mfgr	HO
Industrias Kativo de Nicaragua	Paints	NI
Mercadeo Industrial	Adhesive mfgr	NI
Kativo Comercial	Paints	PA
Kativo de Panama	Adhesives & paint mfgr	PA
HJ Heinz Co	98	
Star-Kist Intl	Food products	PA
Halliburton Co	56	
IMCO Services	Oil drilling fluids	GU
Brown & Root	Engineering	HO
Hearst Corp	P89	
King Features Syndicate	Newspaper cartoons	CR
Hercules Inc	144	
Hercules de Centroamerica	Pesticides	GU
Hercules de Centroamerica	Pesticides mfgr	NI

Parent Corporation Subsidiary Company	Corporate Rank Kind of Business	Location *
Hershey Foods Corp	190	
Hummingbird Hershey	Cocoa production & training center	BE
Agricola Huntro	Cocoa	CR
Hewlett-Packard Co	60	
Cientifica Costarricense	Electronic products	CR
IPESA	Electronic products	GU
Electronic Balboa	Electronic products	PA
Foto Internacional	Electronic products	PA
Hilton Intl	588	
Panama Hilton Intl	Hotel	PA
Holiday Inn	533	
Posadas de America Central	Hotel	HO
Posadas de America Central	Hotel	PA
Honeywell Inc	56	
Honeywell Sistemas de Informacion CR	Business machines	CR
Hospital Corp of America	S13	
Centro Medico Paitilla	Hospital	PA
Household Intl	R10	
Natl Car Rental System	Car rental	CR
Natl Car Rental System	Car rental	GU
Natl Car Rental System	Car rental	PA
Hughes Tool Co	271	
Superser de Guatemala	Oil exploration equip	GU
IBM World Trade Corp	6	
IBM de Costa Rica	Computer supplies mfgr	CR
IBM World Trade	Business machines	ES
IBM de Guatemala	Business machines	GU
IBM de Honduras	Business machines	HO
IBM World Trade	Business machines	NI
IBM de Panama	Business machines	PA
IC Industries	90	
Costa Rican Cocoa Products	Cocoa & chocolate processing	CR
Compania America de Refrigeration	Commercial refrigeration mfgr	GU
IU/Intl Corp	S20	
Cariblanco	Sugar production	CR
Agronomicas de Guatemala	Cardamom, coffee, nut production	GU

Parent Corporation Subsidiary Company	Corporate Rank Kind of Business	Location *
Empresa Agricol el Pacayal		GU
Empresa Agropecuaria Patzulin		GU
Industria Guatemalteca de Macadamia	Macadamia nut processing	GU
Monte de Oro	Cardamom, coffee, nut production	GU
Namolco (Panama)	Sugar production	PA
Internorth	S3	
Distribuidora Centroamer de Gas (DIGAS)	Liquid gas	GU
Interpublic Group of Companies Inc	S92	
McCann-Erickson	Advertising	CR
McCann-Erickson	Advertising	ES
Publicidad McCann-Erickson	Advertising	GU
McCann-Erickson Centroamericana	Advertising	HO
McCann-Erickson de Panama	Advertising	PA
Intl Telephone & Telegraph Corp (ITT)	21	
ITT de Costa Rica	Business machines	CR
Compania Hotelero Salvadoreno (Sheraton)	Hotel	ES
ITT de Centroamerica	Communications equip	ES
Isel de El Salvador (Sheraton)		ES
Conquistador Sheraton Hotel	Hotel	GU
ITT de Guatemala	Communications equip	GU
ITT Telecommunication Products	Communications equip	HO
ITT Standard Electric of Panama	Communications equip	PA
JWT Group	AD1	
APCU Thompson Asociados	Advertising	GU
Johnson & Johnson	57	
Johnson & Johnson de Costa Rica	Health care products mfgr	CR
Johnson & Johnson		ES
Johnson & Johnson de Centroamerica	Health care products mfgr	GU
Ethnor del Istmo	Health care products	PA
Johnson & Johnson Panama	Health care products mfgr	PA
Joseph E Seagram & Sons [3]	238	
Seagram's de Costa Rica	Liquor mfgr	CR
Kellogg Co	143	
Kellogg de Centroamerica	Cereal mfgr	GU
Kimberly-Clark	108	

Parent Corporation Subsidiary Company	Corporate Rank Kind of Business	Location *
Kimberly-Clark de Centroamerica	Disposable hygiene products mfgr	ES
Kimberly-Clark de Centroamerica	Disposable hygiene products	GU
Kimberly-Clark Intl	Disposable hygiene products mfgr	HO
Kimberly-Clark Intl	Disposable hygiene products	PA
Koppers Co	202	
Impregnadores de Madera	Poles & railroad tie mfgr	GU
Maderas del Norte	Timber production	GU
Nello L Teer Co de Centroamerica	Contracting	GU
LTV Corp	48	
Importavia	Small aircraft	GU
Lear Siegler Inc	187	
Rapistan Division of Lear Siegler Inc	Conveyor systems & casters mfgr	CR
Levi Strauss	149	
Centro Industrial de Ropa	Clothes mfgr	ES
Litton Industries Inc	75	
Royal MacBee de Guatemala	Accounting	GU
Western Geophysical Co of America	Geophysical seismic exploration	GU
Lockheed	43	
Lockheed Air Terminal		PA
Loews Corp USA	F16	
Loews Hotels	Hotel	CR
Louisiana Land & Exploration	249	
LLE Petroleum	Oil exploration	HO
MGM/UA Entertainment	S86	
Metro-Goldwyn-Mayer de Panama	Motion pictures	PA
Management Assistance	487	
MAI de Costa Rica	Computers	CR
Manhattan Industries	491	
Confecciones Istmenas	Clothing	CR
Confecciones Istmenas	Clothing	GU

Parent Corporation Subsidiary Company	Corporate Rank Kind of Business	Location *
Industria Nacional de Confecciones	Men's clothing mfgr	PA
Manville	204	
Ricalit	Fibrous cement products mfgr	CR
Marine Midland Banks [4]	B17	
Crece	Banking	CR
Marine Midland Bank	Banking	PA
ATLAPA Panama Center	Convention Center	PA
Marriott Corp	R26	
Cosinas y Servicios Turisticas	Tourism svcs	GU
ATLAPA Panama Center	Convention Center	PA
Inversiones Turisticas Aeropuerto Panama		PA
Marriott Caesar Park Hotel	Hotel	PA
Panmar Construction		PA
McCormick & Co Inc	353	
McCormick de Centroamerica	Food seasonings mfgr	ES
McCormick de Centroamerica	Food seasoning	GU
McDonald's Corp	R28	
McDonald's Costa Rica	Fast food restaurants	CR
McDonald Servipronto de El Salvador	Fast food restaurants	ES
Servirapido de Guatemala	Fast food restaurants	GU
McDonald's Panama	Fast food restaurants	PA
McGraw Edison Co	218	
Alberto L Arce	Electric generators	CR
Worthington Centroamericana		CR
Compania Importadora de Maquinaria	Auto & machinery	ES
Guatemala Tecnica	Electric generators	GU
Casa Comercial Matthews	Construction machinery	HO
Guardia	Electric generators	PA
McGraw-Hill Inc	245	
Editoriales Pedagogicas Asociadas	Publishing	GU
Editorial McGraw-Hill Latinoamericana	Publishing	PA
McKesson Corp	S10	
Comercial Farmaceutical Interamericana	Pharm	CR
Comercial Interamericana		ES
Corporacion Bonima	Pharm mfgr	ES
Comercial Interamericana	Pharm	GU

Parent Corporation Subsidiary Company	Corporate Rank Kind of Business	Location *
Calox Panamena		PA
Capitales Asociados		PA
Distribuidores Especialidades		PA
Intercal	Pharm	PA
Vehiculos Italianos		PA
Merck & Co	110	
Merck, Sharp, & Dohme	Pharm mfgr	CR
Merck, Sharp, & Dohme	Pharm	GU
Fregenal Holdings		PA
Merck, Sharp, & Dohme (Panama)	Pharm	PA
Merrill Lynch & Co	F6	
Merrill Lynch Intl	Investment brokerage	PA
Miles Laboratories [5]	281	
Miles Chemicals Overseas de Costa Rica	Chem	CR
Miles de Costa Rica	Chem & pharm	CR
Laboratorios Miles	Pharm mfgr	GU
Cutter Laboratories Intl	Pharm	PA
Minnesota Mining & Manufacturing (3M)	45	
3M Centroamerica	3M consumer products mfgr	CR
3M Interamericana	3M consumer products	ES
3M Interamericana	3M consumer products	GU
3M de Panama	Business machines	PA
Mobil Oil Corp	3	
Mobil Oil	Petro products	GU
Superior Oil Guatemala	Crude oil & natural gas	GU
Mobil Exploration Honduras	Oil exploration	HO
Mobil Oil	Petro products	HO
Mobil Refining	Oil refinery	PA
Monsanto Co	51	
Monsanto de Costa Rica	Ag technical svcs, pesticides	CR
Monsanto de Guatemala	Pesticides	GU
Monsanto	Medical equip	HO
Monsanto Agricola de Nicaragua	Farm mgmt	NI
Chemstrand Overseas	Investments	PA
Monsanto Centroamerica	Pesticides	PA
Monsanto Overseas	Investments	PA

Parent Corporation
  Subsidiary Company
	Corporate Rank
	  Kind of Business
		Location *

Morrison-Knudsen Co	S29	
Consortio Lami	Engineering	GU
Intl Morrison-Knudsen	Engineering	PA
Motorola Inc	67	
Motorola de Centroamerica	Radio assembling	CR
Murphy Oil	167	
Deep Submergence Systems Corp	Oil field diving svcs	PA
Ocean Contract Services	Oil well drilling	PA
Ocean Nihon Drilling	Oil well drilling	PA
Odeco Intl	Oil & gas extraction	PA
Odeco JILD Offshore Exploration	Oil exploration	PA
Odeco Nihon	Oil well drilling	PA
Odeco Odyssey	Oil well drilling	PA
Poseidon Industries	Oil field diving svcs	PA
Subagua Services Intl	Oil field diving svcs	PA
Submersible Systems	Oil field diving svcs	PA
Westminster Marine (Panama)	Oil well drilling	PA
NL Industries Inc	248	
Baroid		GU
Nabisco Brands Inc	54	
Golden		CR
Pan American Standard Brands	Food products	CR
Dely	Butter mfgr	GU
Pan American Standard Brands	Teabags, sauces, Royal desserts mfgr	GU
Salvavidas de Guatemala	Candy & gum mfgr	GU
Industrias Nabisco Cristal	Biscuit mfgr	NI
Marcas Alimenticias Intl (Marinsa)	Royal desserts mfr	PA
National Cash Register Corp (NCR)	97	
NCR	Accounting machines	ES
NCR Azmitia	Accounting machines mfgr	GU
NCR	Accounting machines	NI
NCR de Panama	Accounting machines	PA
National Semiconductor Corp	225	
Control Electronico	Semiconductors & computers	CR
National Starch & Chemical [6]	342	
Foodpro de Honduras	Vegetable exporter	HO
Northwest Industries Inc	242	
Microdot-Costa Rica	Auto electric equp mfgr	CR

Parent Corporation Subsidiary Company	Corporate Rank Kind of Business	Location *
Velsicol de Centroamerica	Pesticides	CR
Velsicol de Centroamerica	Pesticides	GU
Occidental Petroleum Corp	18	
Belize-Cities Services	Oil exploration	BE
Interior Productos Quimicos- Agricolas	Fertilizers	CR
Occidental de Honduras	Oil exploration	HO
Olin Corp	178	
Ramset de Guatemala	Construction materials	GU
Owens-Illinois Inc	112	
Premadas	Wood products mfgr	GU
Owens-Illinois Intl		PA
Pan American World Airways Inc	T10	
Lineas Areas Costarricenses (LASCA)	Air transportation	CR
Pan American World Airways	Air transportation	CR
Panatravel		ES
Pan American World Airways	Air transportation	GU
Agencia Warren	Air transportation	HO
Pan American World Airways	Air transportation	PA
Parker Hannifin	256	
Parker Hannifin	Auto parts mfgr	HO
Parker Pen Co	S85	
Manpower-Servex	Temporary help svcs	PA
Peat, Marwick, Mitchell & Co	A4	
Peat, Marwick, Mitchell	Accounting	CR
Peat, Marwick, Mitchell	Accounting	ES
Praun, Reyes, Aldana & Asociados	Accounting	GU
Peat, Marwick, Mitchell	Accounting	HO
Peat, Marwick, Mitchell	Accounting	PA
Pennwalt Corp	297	
Electroquimica Pennwalt	Caustic soda mfgr	NI
PepsiCo Inc	40	
Pizza Hut	Fast food restaurants	CR
Embolletadora La Cascada		ES
Taco Bell		ES
Comidas	Pizza Hut restaurants	GU
Comigua	Pizza Hut restaurants	GU
Pepsi Cola Interamericana	Beverage bottling	GU

Parent Corporation Subsidiary Company	Corporate Rank Kind of Business	Location *
Compania Interamericana de Servicios		PA
Navpan (North American Van Lines)	Ocean transportation	PA
Puerta (Pizza Hut, Taco Bell)	Fast food restaurants	PA
Perkin-Elmer Corp	275	
Analitica de Centroamerica	Optical instruments	CR
Pfizer Inc	101	
Pfizer	Pharm mfgr	CR
Pfizer Sucursal Guatemala	Chem & pharm	GU
Howmedica Intl Inc	Hospital products	PA
Pfizer Chemical	Chem	PA
Pfizer	Pharm	PA
Pfizer Intl Corp	Chem & pharm	PA
Phelps Dodge Corp	306	
Conducen	Electric wire mfgr	CR
Conductores Elec de Centroamer (CONELCA)	Electric wire mfgr	ES
Facelec	Electric wire mfgr	GU
Electroconductores de Hond	Electric wire mfgr	HO
Alambres y Cables de Panama (ALCAP)	Electric wire mfgr	PA
Philip Morris Inc	32	
Seven-Up	Beverage franchise	BE
Mendiola	Cigarette mfgr	CR
Tabacalera Costarricense	Cigarette mfgr	CR
Tabacalera Centroamericana (TACASA)	Cigarette mfgr	GU
Tabacalera Nacional	Cigarette mfgr	GU
Tabacalera Nacional	Cigarette mfgr	PA
Phillips Petroleum Co	17	
Productos Plasticos	Plastic products mfgr	CR
Intl Petroleum Sales	Petro & petro products	PA
Phillips Petroleum Intl	Chem products	PA
Phillips Petroleum Intl	Oil refinery	PA
Phillips Petroleum Management	Mgmt svcs	PA
Pillsbury Co	94	
Molinas Modernos	Flour milling	GU
Productos Alimenticios Imperial	Jams, flavorings, soups mfgr	GU
Polaroid Corp	263	
Polaroid Interamerican	Photo equip	PA

Parent Corporation Subsidiary Company	Corporate Rank Kind of Business	Location *
Price Waterhouse & Co	A1	
Price Waterhouse	Accounting	CR
Lopez Salgado	Accounting	ES
Price Waterhouse	Accounting	GU
Price Waterhouse	Accounting	HO
Price Waterhouse	Accounting	NI
Price Waterhouse	Accounting	PA
Procter & Gamble Co	22	
Orange Crush de Costa Rica	Beverage bottler	CR
Embotelladora Istmena (Orange Crush)	Beverage franchise	PA
Quaker Oats Co	118	
Quaker de Costa Rica	Food products	CR
Quaker de El Salvador	Food products	ES
Quaker de Guatemala	Food products	GU
Quaker Honduras	Food products	HO
Quaker de Centroamerica	Food products	NI
RCA Corp	S2	
Hertz-Rentautos	Car rental	GU
Hertz de Panama	Car rental	PA
RJ Reynolds	23	
Banana Devel Corp of Costa Rica (BANDECO)	Banana production	CR
Canada Dry Bottling Co of CR	Beverage franchise	CR
Compania Bananera Carmen	Banana production	CR
Corp de Desarrollo Pinero de Costa Rica	Pineapple production	CR
Frutera Atlantica	Banana production	CR
Kentucky Fried Chicken	Fast food restaurant	CR
Embotelladora Miguelena (Canada Dry)	Beverage franchise	ES
Corrugadora Guatemala	Cardboard box mfgr	GU
Desarrollo Bananero de Guat (BANDEGUA)	Banana production	GU
Del Monte	Contract ag production	HO
Amherst Shipping	Banana shipping	PA
Cerveceria Nacional (Canada Dry)	Beverage franchise	PA
Del Monte Intl	International marketing	PA
Del Monte de Panama	Fruit drinks mfgr	PA
Federal Transport	Banana shipping	PA
Princeton Shipping	Banana shipping	PA
Ralston Purina Co	72	
Autocafes Purina	Restaurants	GU
Distribuidora Dedo Verde		GU

Parent Corporation Subsidiary Company	Corporate Rank Kind of Business	Location *
Invernaderos Tropicales		GU
Plantadores Ornamentales Unidos	Ornamental plant production	GU
Purina de Guatemala	Animal feed mfgr	GU
Agromarina de Panama	Shrimp farming	PA
Ramada Inns Inc	S97	
Hotel Ramada Antigua	Hotel	GU
Ramada Intl	Hotel	HO
Ramada Intl	Hotel	PA
Revlon Inc	152	
Armour Farmaceutica de Centroamerica	Pharm	GU
Exporpon		PA
Reheis Intl	Pharm mfgr	PA
Revlon (Panama)	Cosmetics mfgr	PA
Richardson-Vicks Inc	261	
Richardson-Vicks Interamericas	Pharm	ES
Richardson-Vicks Interamericas	Pharm mfgr	GU
Richardson-Vicks Interamericas	Pharm	PA
Rohm & Haas Co	179	
Laboratorios Quimicos Industriales	Fertilizer & pharm mfgr	CR
Rohm & Haas Centroamerica	Pesticides mfgr	CR
Rorer Group Inc	450	
Rorer de Centroamerica	Pharm	ES
Rorer de Centroamerica	Pharm	GU
SC Johnson & Sons Inc	P26	
SC Johnson de Centroamerica	Insecticides mfgr	CR
SCM Corp	185	
Bodega Hopec		CR
Compania Agricola Myristica	Food processing	CR
Exportada Hopec		CR
Glidden Intl.		CR
Holterman	Business association	CR
Lordan International	Cosmetics & pharm mfgr	CR
Pinturas Centroamerica CR	Plastics & resins mfgr	CR
Plastikart	Plastics	CR
Services Inter-Americanos de Computacion	Data processing svcs	CR
Clorinadora Industrial		GU
Galvanizadora Centro-Americana	Galvanized sheeting mfgr	GU
Pinturas Centroamericanas	Paint mfgr	GU
Servicios Minimax		GU

Parent Corporation Subsidiary Company	Corporate Rank Kind of Business	Location *
Glidden de Honduras	Plastics & resins mfgr	HO
Fabrica de Pinturas Glidden	Resins mfgr	PA
Glidden Panama	Paint & resin mfgr	PA
Schering-Plough Corp	193	
Industrias Arco		CR
Schering Corp de Centroamerica	Pharm	CR
Plough Export	Cosmetics & pharm mfgr	GU
Schering Corp de Centroamerica	Pharm	PA
Scott Paper Co	137	
Scott Paper de Costa Rica	Paper mill & toilet paper mfgr	CR
Scovill Inc	345	
Comercial Isotex (Costa Rica)	Hydraulic valves	CR
Sea-Land	T14	PA
Colina		CR
Sea-Land Service		CR
Transoceanicas	Containerized ocean carrier	ES
A Villafranca	Containership service	HO
India Transport	Containership service	NI
Ocean Trucking	Containerized ocean carrier	PA
Sears Roebuck & Co	R1	
Sears Roebuck	Retail Store	GU
Sears Roebuck	Retail store	HO
Banco de Credito Intl	Consumer products	PA
Sears Roebuck	Retail store	PA
Security Pacific	B7	
Security Pacific Natl Bank (Panama)	Banking	PA
Shell Oil Co [7]	13	
Shell Belize		BE
Quimica Costarricense	Ag chem	CR
Refineria Petrolera Acajutla	Oil refinery	ES
Shell El Salvador	Petro	ES
Shell Quimica de El Salvador	Ag chem mfgr	ES
Compania Distribuidora Guatemala Shell	Petro & petro products	GU
Refineria Petrolera de Guate-Calif	Oil refinery	GU
Shell Quimica de Guatemala	Ag chem	GU
Shell Honduras	Oil exploration	HO
Shell Company Limited Panama	Petro & petro products	PA
Sherwin-Williams Co	177	
Sherwin-Williams de Costa Rica	Paint mfgr	CR

Parent Corporation
   Subsidiary Company
	Corporate Rank
	   Kind of Business
		Location *

Sherwin-Williams de Centroamerica	Paint mfgr	ES
Sherwin-Williams Centroamericana, Guat	Paints	GU
Sherwin-Williams de Panama	Paint mfgr	PA
Signal Companies	54	
Garrett y Asociados	Insurance	CR
Signal Oil & Gas	Oil exploration	HO
Singer Co	148	
Singer Commercial Sula	Sewing machines	HO
SmithKline/Beckman Corp	136	
SmithKline & French	Pharm	CR
Square D Co	247	
Square D Centroamericana	Electrical equip mfgr	CR
Squibb Corp	191	
Laboratorio Farmaceutico Squibb	Pharm mfgr	GU
Standard Oil of Indiana	10	
Amoco Guatemala Petroleum	Oil exploration	GU
Standard Oil of Ohio (SOHIO)	24	
Kennecott Costa Rica	Metals & minerals	CR
Pfaudler Development	Lab products	PA
Stanley Works	280	
Herrmientas Collins	Hand tools	GU
Luis Aroldo Garcia	Hand tools	GU
Stanley Centroamericana	Hand tools	HO
Stanley Centroamericana	Hand tools	PA
Stauffer Chemical Co	235	
Compania Panamena de Industrias Quimicas	Pesticides	PA
Sterling Drug Inc	196	
Sterling Products Intl	Cosmetics & pharm mfgr	CR
Sterling Products Intl	Cosmetics & pharm	GU
Sterling Products Intl	Pharm mfgr	HO
Sterling Products Intl	Pharm mfgr	PA
Sun Chemical Co	335	
Sun Chemical de Centro Amer	Printing ink mfgr	ES
Sun Chemical de Panama	Printing ink mfgr	PA

Parent Corporation Subsidiary Company	Corporate Rank Kind of Business	Location *
Texaco Inc	5	
Texaco Belize	Petro products	BE
Texaco Caribbean	Petro products	CR
Texaco Caribbean	Petro products	ES
Getty Oil (Guatemala)	Oil exploration	GU
Texaco Exploration Guatemala	Oil exploration	GU
Texaco Guatemala	Petro	GU
Texas Petroleum	Oil refinery	GU
Refineria Texaco de Honduras	Oil refinery	HO
Texaco Caribbean	Petro & petro products	HO
Texaco Caribbean	Petro & petro products	NI
Panama Exploration	Oil exploration	PA
Refineria Panama	Oil refinery	PA
Texaco Antilles	Petro	PA
Texaco Panama	Petro & petro products	PA
Touche Ross & Co	A7	
Touche Ross	Accounting	GU
Touche Ross	Accounting	PA
Trans World Airlines Inc	T11	
Trans World Airlines	Airline ticket sales	CR
Trans World Corp	R39	
Plas-Tikal		GU
Hilton of Panama	Hotel	PA
Transamerica Corp	F17	
Budget Rent-A-Car	Car rental	CR
Budget Rent-A-Car	Car rental	GU
Budget Rent-A-Car	Car rental	HO
Budget Rent-A-Car	Car rental	NI
Budget Rent-A-Car	Car rental	PA
Transway Intl	S67	
Coordinated Caribbean Transport (CCT)	Ocean Transportation	CR
Tropigas de Costa Rica	Liquid Gas	CR
Coordinated Caribbean Transport (CCT)	Ocean transportation	ES
Tropigas de El Salvador	Liquid gas	ES
Coordinated Caribbean Transport (CCT)	Ocean transportation	GU
Terminales de Gas	Petro	GU
Tropical Gas de Guatemala (Tropigas)	Liquid gas	GU
Coordinated Caribbean Transport (CCT)	Ocean transportation	HO
Tropigal Gas (TROPIGAS)	Liquid gas	HO

Parent Corporation Subsidiary Company	Corporate Rank Kind of Business	Location *
Coordinated Caribbean Transport (CCT)	Ocean transportation	NI
Tropigas de Nicaragua	Liquid gas	NI
Antroca	Liquid gas refinery	PA
Constabilidad y Servicios	Accounting	PA
Gases de Petroleo	Liquid gas refinery	PA
Transporte Tropigas	Liquid gas refinery	PA
Tropigas	Liquid gas	PA
Tropigas de Chiriqui	Liquid gas refinery	PA
Tropigas de Panama	Liquid gas refinery	PA
UAL Inc	T4	
Hotel Camino Real	Hotel	ES
Hoteles Camino Real de Guatemala	Hotel	GU
UNOCAL	27	
Union Oil Co de Honduras	Oil exploration	HO
US Steel Corp	15	
Marathon Petroleum Belize	Oil exploration	BE
Indus de Tubos y Perfiles (INTUPERSA)	Piping & tubing mfgr	GU
Union Carbide Corp	35	
Union Carbide Centro-Americana	Cell batteries, pesticides	CR
UNICAR	Pesticides	GU
Union Carbide Interamerica	Chemical products	PA
Uniroyal	164	CR
Uniroyal Chemical	Pesticides	CR
United Brands Co	117	
Riversdale Services		BE
Compania Bananera Atlantica (COBAL)	Banana production	CR

Compania Bananera de Costa
    Rica
	Banana & palm oil
	    production
		CR

Numar de Costa Rica	Palm oil mfgr	CR
Polymer de Costa Rica	Plastics mfgr	CR
Polymer United	Plastics mfgr	CR
Unimar	Palm oil mfgr	CR
Compania Agricola de Rio Tinto	Banana puree mfgr	HO
Compania Numar de Honduras	Palm oil mfgr	HO
Empresa Hondurena de Vapores		HO
Polymer	Plastic bag mfgr	HO
Tela Railroad	Banana production	HO
UNIMAR (United Marketing-SA)	Palm oil mfgr	HO
Aceitera Corona	Palm oil mfgr	NI
Polymer Uniteda	Plastics mfgr	NI

Parent Corporation Subsidiary Company	Corporate Rank Kind of Business	Location *
UNIMAR (United Marketing-SA)	Palm oil mfgr	NI
Balboa Shipping	Banana shipping	PA
Chiriqui Lard	Banana production	PA
United Merchants & Manufacturers Inc	433	
Panameritex de Panama	Textiles	PA
United States Tobacco	485	
Centroamerica Cigars	Cigar mfgr	HO
Fabrica de Molduras y Cajas	Box & molding mfgr	HO
Processadora de Tobacos	Tobacco processing	HO
Tabacos de Honduras	Tobacco plantation	HO
United Technologies Corp	16	
Otis Elevator	Elevators	CR
Otis Elevator	Elevators	ES
Otis Elevator	Elevators	GU
Otis Elevator	Elevators	HO
Otis Elevator	Elevators	PA
Universal Foods Corp	493	
Universal Food Products Intl	Food products	CR
Levaduras Universal	Yeast mfgr	GU
Universal Leaf Tobacco Co	S59	
CASA Export	Tobacco production	GU
CASA Export	Tobacco exporter	HO
Upjohn Co	166	
Farmaceutica Upjohn	Pharm mfgr	GU
Upjohn	Chem & pharm	PA
WR Grace & Co	50	
Productos Darex	Cement products	GU
Wang Laboratories Inc	165	
Wang de Panama (CEPEC)	Computers	PA
Warnaco Inc	434	
Warner's de Costa Rica	Clothes mfgr	CR
Warner's de Honduras	Bra mfgr	HO
Warner Lambert Co	126	
Distribuidora Mercantil de Costa Rica		CR
Compania Farmaceutica Parke-Davis	Pharm mfgr	GU
Lab de Productos Farmaceut (LAPROFA)	Pharm	GU

Parent Corporation Subsidiary Company	Corporate Rank Kind of Business	Location *
Productos Adams	Candy & gum mfgr	GU
Warner-Lambert de Panama	Pharm	PA
Weyerhaeuser Co	66	
Cajas y Empaques de Guatemala	Cardboard box mfgr	GU
Witco Chemical Corp	236	
Agro-Inversiones	Ornamental plant production	GU
Agro-Quimicas de Guatemala	Insecticide mfgr	GU
Xerox Corp	38	
Xerox de Costa Rica	Office equip & supplies mfgr	CR
Xerox de El Salvador	Office equip & supplies mfgr	ES
Xerox de Guatemala	Office equip & supplies mfgr	GU
Xerox de Honduras	Business machines	HO
Xerox de Nicaragua	Business machines	NI
Xerox de Panama	Office equip & supplies mfgr	PA

* Country within which the subsidiary is located

Country abbreviations: BE = Belize; CR = Costa Rica; ES = El Salvador; GU = Guatemala; HO = Honduras; NI = Nicaragua; PA = Panama

Rank based on *Fortune*'s 500 largest industrial corporations and 500 largest US service corporations (B = banks; F = financial; L = life insurance; R = retailing; S = diversified; T = transportation; and U = utilities); the 100 largest US private corporations (P); the top 8 US accounting firms (A); and the top 10 US advertising firms (AD)

Seven listed TNCs (and their subsidiaries) have a foreign based ultimate parent corporation; [1 BOC Group Plc, United Kingdom; [2 Esselte Pendaflex Corp, Sweden; [3 Joseph E Seagram & Sons, Canada; [4 Hong Kong & Shanghai Banking Corp, Hong Kong; [5 Bayer AG, West Germany; [6 Unilever NV, The Netherlands; and [7 Royal Dutch/Shell Group of Companies, United Kingdom and The Netherlands.

Major Sources: Annual Reports, 10-K Reports and correspondence with selected U.S. corporations; *1984/1985 International Directory of Corporate Affiliations: 1984 Directory of American Firms Operating in Foreign Countries; 1985 Directory of Corporate Affiliations; Fortune's 1984 Directory of U.S. Corporations; Fortune,* April 29, 1985; *1984 Ward's Directory of 51,000 Largest U.S. Corporations; 1984 Who Owns Whom; 1984 American's Corporate Families and International Affiliates; 1983/1984 Caribbean/American Directory; 1985 Dun & Bradstreet's Principal International Businesses;* OPIC, *Political Risk Insurance Allocations Through 1984;* El Salvador's Departamento de Control de Cambios Listing (January–May 1984); *1984 American Chamber of Commerce and Industry of Panama Directory; 1984 American Chamber of Commerce of Guatemala Membership Directory; 1984 Costa Rican American Chamber of Commerce Membership Directory;* "1984 American Chamber of Commerce of El Salvador Membership List"; "American Chamber of Commerce of Nicaragua Membership List"; 1985 Honduran-American Chamber of Commerce Membership List.

Minor Sources: "American Firms, Subsidiaries and Affiliates—Honduras", U.S. Embassy, May 1985; *Envio,* January 1984; "Firms Operating in Nicaragua with American Capital, Distributorship or Royalties", U.S. Embassy; FUSADES, "List of U.S. Investors, Local Branches of U.S. Firms, Licenses and Franchises"; 1984 "List of U.S. Investors in Belize", U.S. Embassy; *1985*

Petrochemical Worldwide Directory; 1984 Pipelines and Contractors Worldwide Directory; 1984 Refining and Gas Processing Worldwide Directory; 1980 Top 1500 Private Companies; U.S. Embassy-Belize correspondence, December 1984; "1984 U.S. Embassy Listing of U.S Corporations in Guatemala"; U.S. Embassy-Nicaragua correspondence, May 1985: "1984 U.S. Embassy Listing of U.S. Corporations in Guatemala"; U.S. Embassy-Nicaragua correspondence, May 1985; U.S. Embassy-Panama correspondence, January 1985; "1983 U.S. Investors in El Salvador"; *1984 Who Audits America; 1984–1985 Guia de Exportadores Costa Rica;* and *1984 Guatemala Directorio de Exportadores.*

INDEX